Current Legal Issues in Criminal Justice

Readings

Craig Hemmens
Boise State University

Roxbury Publishing Company
Los Angeles, California

Library of Congress Cataloging-in-Publication Data

Current legal issues in criminal justice: Readings / edited by Craig Hemmens.
p. cm.
Includes bibliographical references and index.
ISBN 1-933220-92-9 (alk. paper)
1. Criminal procedure—United States. 2. Constitutional law—United States. I.
Hemmens, Craig.
KF9619.C87 2007
345.73'05—dc22   2006019798

Publisher: Claude Teweles
Managing Editor: Dawn VanDercreek
Production Editor: Renee Burkhammer Ergazos
Typography: SDS Design, info@sds-design.com
Cover Design: Marnie Kenney

Printed on acid-free paper in the United States of America. This paper meets the standards for recycling of the Environmental Protection Agency.

ISBN 1-933220-92-9

Roxbury Publishing Company
P.O. Box 491044
Los Angeles, California 90049-9044
Voice: (310) 473-3312 • Fax: (310) 473-4490
Email: roxbury@roxbury.net
Website: www.roxbury.net

Contents

Section I: Legal Issues and Police

Police and Thieves:
The Supreme Court Examines the Knock and Announce Rule

Craig Hemmens

Professor Hemmens examines the history of the Knock and Announce Rule and critiques the Supreme Court's recent decisions applying the rule to the Fourth Amendment.

Surveillance Technology and the Law

Kathryn Scarborough, Pam Collins, and Ryan Baggett

The authors review recent advancements in surveillance technology (focusing on closed circuit television) and discuss how such technology may affect privacy laws.

The USA PATRIOT Act:
A Review of the Major Components

Jim Ruiz and Kathleen H. Winters

Key components of the USA PATRIOT Act are discussed along with the implications that the act has on search and seizure law.

Section IV: Legal Issues and Juvenile Justice

Section V: Miscellaneous Legal Issues

Foreword by Rolando V. del Carmen

A Book for a Wider Audience

Law is an integral component of criminal justice. The axiom is indeed true: without law there is no criminal justice, and academic criminal justice would be indistinguishable from other social science disciplines.

Criminal justice curricula on the undergraduate and graduate levels in the United States abound with courses that address the need for students and professionals to know the basics of law. These curricula include such traditional offerings as criminal procedure, criminal law, legal aspects of corrections, and law and society. Beyond these, many colleges and universities also offer courses on the legal aspects of the death penalty, prison law, judicial process, and legal research. Additionally, over the years law offerings in various criminal justice programs have responded to new developments and to student need for updated knowledge on fast-changing law topics. In the last few years colleges and universities have developed and offered courses related to terrorism, the USA PATRIOT Act, the Homeland Security Act, technological surveillance, rights of victims, and hate-related crimes. Times have moved forward with recent events and are indeed changing. This book represents an awareness of that change.

Law books now compete for shelf space in the current market for criminal justice undergraduate and graduate students. Most focus on traditional topics in law and are written by authors who address singular topics using the traditional black letter law (what the law is) approach. A void is evident for law books that are broader in scope but also address specific topics in depth. This text fills that void. It addresses such diverse criminal justice concerns as juvenile waiver laws, inmate litigation, assisted suicides, drug tests, the death penalty, pornography, and hate speech. Given the span and breadth of topics, this book is best suited for a capstone course for undergraduates or a legal issues seminar for graduate students. It does deserve to be read, however, by a much wider audience of students and criminal justice professionals.

The articles are written by current notable scholars, all of whom are recognized names in criminal justice and law. They represent various fields but have in common an expertise in law; all have had experience in teaching criminal justice. This explains why the articles are bereft of unwanted legalese but are not "dumbed down" either. The writers are familiar with their reading audience and have responded with articles that best fit that clientele. The book is a contribution by individuals whose educational backgrounds go beyond law. Many have law and Ph.D. degrees. This is significant because that educational background enables them to discuss their topics from legal and sociological perspectives. That benefits criminal justice students and professionals who are best exposed to both perspectives.

Writing law-related articles for nonlawyers can be treacherous because legal terms sometimes defy accurate translation into nonlegal concepts. That challenge, however, is well met in this book. The articles are original and written solely for this book by scholars who are well aware of the legal/nonlegal terminology divide. The product is not simply a compilation of unrelated legal writings or a collection of previously published articles taken from sources and that merely coincidentally represent diverse opinions.

The editor, writers, and current colleagues should all be commended for putting together a book that responds to an immediate need and that should appeal to both students and field practitioners in law enforcement, national security, courts, and corrections. This book is a notable addition to existing criminal justice literature. It represents a job well done and provides a welcome service to the criminal justice discipline. ✦

—Rolando V. del Carmen
Distinguished Professor of
Criminal Justice and Law
Sam Houston State University

Acknowledgments

I would like to thank my wife, Mary Stohr, and my stepdaughter, Emily Rose Stohr-Gillmore, for putting up with me for the past decade or so. Thanks also to Sera, Amber, and Max, for reminding me what matters most. I am grateful to Claude Teweles and the fine folks at Roxbury Publishing Company. Without their support and enthusiasm for this project, it would never have been completed.

I would also like to thank all the authors who contributed to this volume. This book is theirs more than it is mine. They endured countless emails and requests for changes with a uniform good humor. It is exciting for me to see the increased attention that is being given to legal issues in the criminal justice system. Criminal justice scholars deferred to legal scholars for too many years. As the variety of contributors to this volume indicates, the law and criminal justice system are being more closely examined today than ever before.

The editor and the chapter authors would like to thank the following reviewers for their helpful and insightful suggestions. Their comments helped improve the organization of the book as well as the content of the individual chapters. In particular I would like to thank William P. Bloss, Jack E. Call, Richard De Lung, Ayn Embar-Seddon along with Allan D. Pass, Andrew E. Franz, Robert A. Harvie, W. Richard Janikowski, James L. Jengeleski, David M. Jones, Richard S. Michelson, Darrell L. Ross, Gregory D. Russell, and Christopher E. Smith. ✦

About the Editor

Craig Hemmens holds a juris doctorate from North Carolina Central University School of Law and a Ph.D. in Criminal Justice from Sam Houston State University. He is a professor in the Department of Criminal Justice Administration, and academic director of the Paralegal Studies Program at Boise State University, where he has taught since 1996. Professor Hemmens has published ten books and more than one hundred articles on a variety of criminal justice topics. His primary research interests are criminal law and procedure and corrections. He has served as the editor of the *Journal of Criminal Justice Education.* His publications have appeared in *Justice Quarterly,* the *Journal of Criminal Justice, Crime and Delinquency,* the *Criminal Law Bulletin,* and the *Prison Journal.* ✦

About the Contributors

Janice Ahmad is an assistant professor in the Department of Criminal Justice at the University of Houston–Downtown. She earned a Ph.D. in criminal justice at Sam Houston State University. She is co-author of a police management book and several publications and has presented research at numerous national and regional professional conferences. Her current research and teaching interests include police management issues, women in policing, and crime victims.

Ryan Baggett is the deputy director of technology of the Justice and Safety Center, in the College of Justice and Safety at Eastern Kentucky University. He manages various public safety projects from the Department of Justice and the Department of Homeland Security (DHS). He also serves as an instructor in the Criminal Justice and Police Studies Department and the Loss Prevention and Safety Department within the college. Mr. Baggett holds an M.S. in criminal justice from Eastern Kentucky University.

Jeremy D. Ball is an assistant professor in the Department of Criminal Justice Administration at Boise State University. He holds a J.D. from Indiana University–Indianapolis and a Ph.D. in criminal justice from the University of Nebraska–Omaha. His research interests are in the areas of plea bargaining decisions, prosecutorial discretion, sentencing, court processing decisions, and domestic violence. He has been published in the *Journal of Criminal Justice Studies* and the *Encyclopedia of Criminology*.

Barbara Belbot is an associate professor of criminal justice at the University of Houston–Downtown. She holds a J.D. from the University of Houston Law Center and a Ph.D. in criminal justice from Sam Houston State University. She served as a monitor in the Office of the Special Master in the Texas prison reform class action lawsuit *Ruiz v. Estelle*. She teaches and publishes in the areas of corrections law and policy and criminal law and is currently working on a study of prison reform organizations.

Katherine Bennett is currently the interim director of the Office of Institutional Research at Armstrong Atlantic State University. She earned a Ph.D. in criminal justice at Sam Houston State University. Her teaching areas include research methods, criminology, and corrections, and she has published primarily in the area of legal issues in corrections.

Ashley G. Blackburn is an assistant professor in the Department of Criminal Justice at the University of North Texas. She received her Ph.D. in criminal justice from Sam Houston State University. She has also studied at the University of Lausanne, Switzerland, where she was able to collaborate on its International Violence Against Women Survey. She has conducted research in a number of areas, including same-sex intimate partner violence and media portrayals of rape victims in celebrity cases.

David C. Brody is an associate professor in the Department of Political Science/Criminal Justice Program at Washington State University–Spokane. He holds a J.D. from the University of Arizona College of Law and a Ph.D. in criminal justice from the State University of New York at Albany. He is the author of two textbooks and over twenty scholarly articles that have been published in such journals as the *American Criminal Law Review, Crime and Delinquency, Judicature,* and the *Hastings Women's Law Journal*. He has served as a technical advisor for the Washington State

Jury Commission and on the steering committee of the Washington Judicial Selection Coalition. His research focuses on jury reform, judicial selection and evaluation, and the interaction between law and criminal justice policy.

Jacqueline Buffington-Vollum is a forensic psychology fellow at the University of Virginia's Institute of Law, Psychiatry, and Public Policy. She received her Ph.D. in clinical psychology from Sam Houston State University. Her research has focused on institutional violence, the assessment and predictive validity of psychopathy, and mental health professionals' involvement in providing expert testimony, especially at capital sentencing, as well as death penalty attitudes more generally. Her work has been published in *Justice Quarterly, Criminal Justice and Behavior,* and *Law and Human Behavior.*

Simon A. Cole is an assistant professor in the Department of Criminology, Law and Society at the University of California–Irvine, where he specializes in the historical and sociological study of the interaction between science, technology, law, and criminal justice. Dr. Cole is the author of *Suspect Identities: A History of Fingerprinting and Criminal Identification* (Harvard University Press, 2001), and he is a member of the American Judicature Society Commission on Forensic Science and Public Policy. His current interests are the sociology of forensic science and the development of criminal identification databases and biometric technologies.

Pam Collins is a professor of security studies and the executive director of the Justice and Safety Center at Eastern Kentucky University. She holds an Ed.D. from the University of Kentucky. She has published in the areas of private security, homeland security, and criminal justice technology.

Craig Hemmens is a professor in the Department of Criminal Justice Administration at Boise State University. He holds a J.D. from North Carolina Central University School of Law and a Ph.D. in criminal justice from Sam Houston State University. He has published 10 books and more than

100 articles on a variety of issues in criminal justice.

Michelle E. Heward is a professor in the Criminal Justice Department at Weber State University. She holds a J.D. from the University of Utah College of Law and has worked in both a private law practice and as a prosecutor for the Weber County Attorney's Office in Utah. She presently sits as a justice court judge in a city that has a substance abuse specialty court. She has also served on youth court boards on the local, state, and national levels. Her current areas of interest include constitutional law, diversity issues, and specialty courts.

John Liederbach is an assistant professor in the Department of Criminal Justice at the University of North Texas. He received his Ph.D. degree in criminal justice from the University of Cincinnati. His research interests include the street-level behavior of police officers, white-collar and medical crime, and digital crime. He is a co-author of the text *Digital Crime and Digital Terrorism.* His work has been published in *Justice Quarterly, The American Journal of Criminal Justice,* and *Policing: An International Journal of Police Strategies and Management.*

Jeff Maahs is an assistant professor in the Department of Sociology and Anthropology at the University of Minnesota–Duluth. He has a Ph.D. in criminal justice from the University of Cincinnati. He has authored several publications in criminology-related journals, including *Justice Quarterly, Crime and Delinquency,* and *Corrections Management Quarterly,* and edited books. He co-authored the forthcoming text *Criminology: Theory, Research, and Policy.* His main areas of interest are criminological theory, corrections (private prisons, the roles and attitudes of corrections officers, correctional officer use of force), and legal aspects of criminal justice (search and seizure, prison litigation).

James W. Marquart is the director of the Program in Crime and Justice Studies at the University of Texas at Dallas. He has published five books and over fifty refereed articles. His current research involves the long-term consequences of victimization, sexual victimization in prison, desistance from criminal careers among juvenile offenders, and racial desegregation in prisons.

Janet L. Mullings is an associate professor and associate dean in the College of Criminal Justice at Sam Houston State University. Her research interests include corrections, victimology, and child maltreatment. She has recently published a book, *The Victimization of Children.*

David Murphy is an assistant professor in the Criminal Justice Department at Weber State University. He received his Ph.D. in political science with an emphasis in criminal justice from Washington State University in 2003. His current research agenda is focused on exploring the dynamics of police-probation partnerships. He has published in *Justice Quarterly* and *Policing: An International Journal of Police Strategies and Management.* He recently completed his first book, *Making Police-Probation Partnerships Work* (LFB Scholarly, 2005).

Megan Reynolds is a recent graduate of the criminal justice M.A. program at Pennsylvania State University–Harrisburg and is now a doctoral student in the Ph.D. program in criminal justice at Temple University.

Jim Ruiz is an assistant professor of criminal justice in the School of Public Affairs at Pennsylvania State University–Harrisburg. He received his Ph.D. in criminal justice from Sam Houston State University. He began his career in criminal justice as a police officer with the New Orleans Police Department in 1967, serving in the patrol, communications, and mounted divisions as well as the emergency services section and N.C.I.C. He retired in 1985. He has published in the *American Journal of Police, Journal of Police and Criminal Psychology, Criminal Justice Ethics, International Journal of Public Administration, International Journal of Police Science and Management, The Critical Criminologist,* and *Police Forum.* He is also the author of *The Black Hood of the Ku Klux Klan.* His research interests include police administration and supervision, ethics in policing, police inter-

action with persons with mental illness, use of force, canine deployment, and the Ku Klux Klan.

Claudia San Miguel is an assistant professor of criminal justice at Texas A&M International University. She teaches courses in policing, legal issues, and criminology. She has also taught at the International Law Enforcement Academy in Roswell, New Mexico. She is co-author of *The Death Penalty: Constitutional Issues, Commentaries, and Cases* and is currently working on research involving border violence between the United States and Mexico. She is also working on research involving the trafficking of women and children and school violence.

Kathryn Scarborough is a professor in the College of Criminal Justice at Eastern Kentucky University and the director for research, evaluation, and testing for the Justice and Safety Center. She holds a Ph.D. in criminal justice from Sam Houston State University. Prior to her teaching at Eastern Kentucky University, she was a police officer in Portsmouth, Virginia, a U.S. Navy Hospital corpsman/emergency medical technician, and a chemical dependency technician. Her current teaching and research interests include criminal investigation, law enforcement technology, cyber crime and security, police administration, and women in law enforcement. Her publications include textbooks on workplace violence, women in law enforcement, and police administration. Dr. Scarborough has also had articles in *Police Quarterly, American Journal of Police,* and *Crime Prevention and Community Safety: An International Journey.*

Barbara Sims is an associate professor of criminal justice in the School of Public Affairs at Pennsylvania State–Harrisburg. She received her Ph.D. in criminal justice from Sam Houston State University. She currently serves as program coordinator for the criminal justice undergraduate program and for the master's program in criminal justice. She has authored numerous articles in such refereed journals as *Crime and Delinquency, Criminal Justice Review, Criminal Justice Policy Review, Journal of*

Research in Crime and Delinquency, Corrections Management Quarterly, The Justice Professional, The Police Quarterly, Corrections Compendium, Journal of Contemporary Criminal Justice, Policing: An International Journal of Police Strategies and Management, and the *Prison Journal.*

Benjamin Steiner is a doctoral candidate in criminal justice at the University of Cincinnati. His research interests are in the areas of juvenile justice and institutional corrections. Mr. Steiner holds an M.A. from Boise State University and a B.S. from North Dakota State University, and he has worked as a juvenile probation officer. He is the co-author of *Significant Case in Juvenile Justice* (2004) and has published a number of articles on juvenile justice in journals such as *Justice Quarterly, Juvenile and Family Court Journal,* and *Criminal Justice Studies.*

William C. Thompson, J.D., Ph.D., is professor and chair of the Department of Criminology, Law and Society at the University of California–Irvine, and he is a member of the California Bar. He writes about the use (and misuse) of scientific evidence, particularly DNA tests, and about jury decision-making. He also occasionally represents criminal defendants who are challenging novel or controversial applications of scientific and statistical evidence and assists news organizations in investigating error and corruption in forensic laboratories. He has consulted with police departments, coroners, and lawyers on a variety of cases involving scientific evidence in the United States, the United Kingdom, and Australia.

Peggy M. Tobolowsky is professor and associate chair of criminal justice at the University of North Texas. She received her J.D. from George Washington University in 1977. Her research interests include criminal law and procedure, capital punishment, and crime victim issues. Her articles on these subjects have appeared in journals such as the *American Journal of Criminal Law, Journal of Legislation,* and *Judicature.*

Chad R. Trulson is an assistant professor in the Department of Criminal Justice at the University of North Texas. He has

published in numerous professional journals and recently co-authored *Juvenile Justice: The System, Process, and Law* with Rolando V. del Carmen (Wadsworth, 2005). His current research interests involve recidivism among institutionalized delinquents, and racial desegregation and violence in prisons.

Kathleen H. Winters is a graduate of the Pennsylvania State University at Harrisburg and is currently a graduate student at Ohio State University, where she is pursuing her Ph.D. in Political Science. Her research interests include judicial politics, the U.S. Constitution, and legal decision-making.

John L. Worrall is an associate professor in the Crime and Justice Studies Program at the University of Texas–Dallas. He received his Ph.D. in political science from Washington State University in 1999. His research interests are crime control policy, prosecution, and legal issues in policing. He is the author of six books, the most recent of which is *Crime Control in America: An Assessment of the Evidence* (Allyn and Bacon, 2006). His work has also appeared in *Justice Quarterly, Evaluation Review,* and *Social Science Research* among other journals.

Marvin Zalman is professor of criminal justice at Wayne State University. He has a J.D. from Brooklyn Law School and a Ph.D. in criminal justice from the State University of New York at Albany. He began his teaching career at Ahmadu Bello University in northern Nigeria while a Peace Corps volunteer from 1967 to 1969. He teaches classes on criminal procedure, criminal justice policy, and wrongful convictions. He has authored *Criminal Procedure: Constitution and Society* (Fourth Edition) and *Essentials of Criminal Procedure.* Recent publications include examinations of Fifth Amendment doctrine and the post-*Miranda* cases. Current research projects include a survey of police departments regarding interrogation practices and views of confessions law and a survey of state criminal justice officials concerning wrongful conviction. He has published articles on assisted suicide, drug asset forfeiture and Republican values, venue, law and domestic violence, jail crowding lawsuits, and the relation of criminal justice and civil liberties. ✦

Introduction

This book is intended to serve as a reader devoted to the coverage of legal issues in criminal justice. This topic encompasses a number of areas, including search and seizure law, confessions and interrogations law, corrections law, constitutional law as it relates to activities within the criminal justice system, the death penalty, *habeas corpus*, and civil liability. The purpose of the reader is to facilitate and encourage discussion on legal issues in criminal justice.

There is a tremendous amount of interest in legal issues in criminal justice. Legal issues are constantly in the news. The USA PATRIOT Act, recent Supreme Court decisions on issues such as the death penalty and the Fourth Amendment, and high-profile controversial cases (such as the Kobe Bryant rape case) all create interest in legal issues related to criminal justice. Students and faculty are also tremendously interested in the subject. Legal issues in criminal justice comprise a significant portion of the typical undergraduate criminal justice curriculum. Courses on criminal law, criminal procedure, evidence law, and corrections law are commonplace, and many other courses include sections dealing with legal issues in criminal justice.

Despite this great interest, only a handful of readers are devoted to legal issues in criminal justice. Several of these readers include material beyond the scope of a traditional criminal justice course (such as abortion, affirmative action, and school prayer), and are thus ill-suited to a criminal justice course. Some texts are a compilation of previously published material, a format that often makes the book out of date before it is published and that does not allow for a full discussion of both sides of an issue. Other texts follow a pro/con discussion format, offering a short essay on each side of an issue. These essays typically lack depth.

Each chapter in this text was written especially for this book—there are no reprinted articles. Thus, the material is as timely as the publishing time lag can allow. Additionally, this reader does not follow a pro/con essay format but instead has one chapter devoted to one issue, with the author covering that issue in depth, including material on both sides of the controversy. This format allows for greater currency, depth, and accuracy.

This book can serve as a text for a capstone undergraduate course or a graduate class in law. It is intended to expose students to a variety of legal issues in criminal justice. The chapters are well researched and clearly written. The authors have attempted to write at a level that does not sacrifice accuracy for simplicity. The law is sometimes like a foreign language, and it takes the uninitiated a while to adapt to the different terminology. If they are diligent, however, I am confident that students can fully comprehend the material presented in these pages. ✦

Section I

Legal Issues and Police

Chapter 1
Police and Thieves

The Supreme Court Examines the Knock and Announce Rule

Craig Hemmens

In this chapter, the author reviews the history and current Supreme Court decisions involving the Knock and Announce Rule. The Knock and Announce Rule requires police officers to announce their presence and purpose prior to executing a search or arrest warrant. It serves to reduce violence and destruction of property and to protect a citizen's constitutional right of privacy.

This chapter begins with a description of the history of the Knock and Announce Rule, which can be traced back over 700 years to English common law. The rule was not specifically included in the Fourth Amendment, but many state and federal courts assumed that it was part of the "reasonableness" requirement of the Fourth Amendment. Not until the 1950s did the United States Supreme Court begin to address the issue of unannounced police entry in a string of cases beginning with *Miller v. United States* and leading up to *United States v. Banks* in 2003. Although the court did not clearly incorporate the Knock and Announce Rule into the Fourth Amendment in the early cases, it did begin to recognize that there may be various exceptions (exigent circumstances) in which the failure to knock and announce is justifiable.

Lower courts interpreted each case through the use of either (1) the *blanket approach,* which gives police justification to enter a dwelling unannounced when they have probable cause, such as possession of illegal drugs, or (2) the *particularity approach,* which does not allow police to enter unannounced based on the nature of the evidence; rather, the police must cite justifiable facts supporting such evidence, such as the attempt to destroy evidence. Beginning in 1995, the Court made it clear that the Knock and Announce Rule is a part of the Fourth Amendment. However, subsequent Court decisions made it apparent that cer-

tain specific circumstances did exist that allowed police to enter unannounced. Precisely what these circumstances are remains to be seen. The Knock and Announce Rule illustrates the difficulty in balancing constitutional rights and the work of law enforcement officers and provides a resource in comparison to other issues raised in the other chapters in Section I.

Introduction

The United States is embroiled in a war on drugs. Police are aggressively pursuing drug offenders using technologies (such as chemical drug tests and infrared heat scanners) and new methods (such as pretext stops, knock and talks, and profiling). The Supreme Court has been generally supportive of these new technologies and methods (Hemmens, Worrall, and Thompson 2004).

A primary example of proactive policing methods is the increase in applications for "no-knock" warrants and efforts to circumvent the common law "Knock and Announce" Rule. The *Knock and Announce Rule* requires police officers seeking to enter a home to first notify occupants of their presence and purpose. The rule was intended to provide some protection to homeowners from unwarned police entries. The rule is not absolute, however, as courts recognize several exceptions. While the Knock and Announce Rule has a long history, dating back to the Statute of Westminster (1275), and has been examined by every state and federal court (Hemmens 1997), its applicability to the Fourth Amendment was not expressly determined by the Supreme Court until 1995. Since 1995, however, the Supreme Court has decided four cases involving the Knock and Announce Rule. This chapter discusses the history of the rule and examines the Supreme Court's recent decisions.

The Knock and Announce Rule

The Knock and Announce Rule requires police officers to (1) identify themselves and (2) give notice of their purpose prior to entering a home. Exactly what constitutes identification and notice of purpose has engendered some debate. Generally, what is required is that police officers (1) identify themselves, (2) demand entry, (3) inform the occupants of the legal basis for their authority to enter, and (4) give the occupants an opportunity to admit them before resorting to forcible entry (Note 1970; LaFave 1996). In common practice, this translates to police officers calling out on the doorstep: "Police officers. We have a search warrant." The demand to enter can be as simple and direct as "Open the door," or it may be inferred from statements such as "We have a search warrant." Once notice and announcement are made, the police must provide the occupants a reasonable opportunity to open the door before resorting to forcible entry. Jurisdictions vary widely on what constitutes a "reasonable opportunity," with some requiring mere seconds (Hemmens 1997). Refusal to admit the officer may be inferred from the circumstances, such as the sound of footsteps running away from the door, a window breaking, or the sound of a toilet flushing (LaFave 1996).

The Knock and Announce Rule is not intended to prevent police entry, but merely to ensure that entry is as peaceful and nondestructive as possible under the circumstances. Consequently, entry without notice has been allowed in certain situations since the early common law. These instances, often grouped together under the heading of "exigent circumstances," include danger to innocent occupants of the premises, danger to the police, the possibility of the destruction of evidence, and the possibility that the occupants will escape (Annotation 1976). Announcement is also unnecessary when it would be a "useless gesture" (LaFave 1996)—that is, when the presence and purpose of the police is already known to the occupants. Entry by force is permissible after notice and announcement is given and refused, or if there is no response to the officer's announcement of his or her presence and purpose.

The Knock and Announce Rule serves at least four purposes. First, the rule helps prevent violence by reducing the number of unannounced entries into homes, thereby eliminating the possibility that a homeowner will mistake the police for a burglar or other un-authorized intruder. Second, the rule helps reduce the destruction of property by providing the homeowner with the opportunity to admit the police peacefully, eliminating the need for the police to break into the home. Third, the rule allows the homeowner to redirect police officers who are at the wrong address. Fourth, and perhaps most important, the rule helps protect an individual's right to privacy (LaFave 1996; Mericli 1989).

The Knock and Announce Rule 1604–1958

The Knock and Announce Rule dates from the early common law period. It was mentioned in the Statute of Westminster (1275), which apparently codified existing common law (Blackstone 1978). The first recorded case discussing the Knock and Announce Rule was decided in 1604. In *Semayne's Case* (1604) the court broadly stated that "the sheriff (if the doors be not open) may break the party's house, either to arrest him, or to do other execution of the King's process, if otherwise he cannot enter. *But before he breaks it, he ought to signify the cause of his coming, and to make request to open the doors*" (emphasis added).

While *Semayne's Case* involved a civil writ, later English cases dealt with execution of criminal process. In *Curtis's Case* (1757), the court announced that law enforcement officers were justified in entering by force only if they first demanded admittance and gave notice that the officer was acting under proper authority, and not as a trespasser. Several scholars of the time indicate that notice and announcement were generally required in the execution of all warrants (Blackstone 1978; Hale 1847).

Early American colonial case law followed the English tradition. Writs of assistance were commonly used by colonial officials searching for prohibited goods. Yet even these writs, with their broad language and scope, could be executed only after notice was first given to the suspect (Cuddihy 1990; Lasson 1937). After the American Revolution, at least seven of the original thirteen states codified the Common Law Rule by enacting statutes requiring notice and announcement prior to the execution of warrants (Driscoll 1995).

Such was the state of the common law when the Bill of Rights, including the Fourth Amendment, was adopted in 1791. The framers of the Fourth Amendment were aware of the general dislike of writs of assistance and were also aware that notice and announcement were predicates to execution of a warrant or writ. While studies of the debates surrounding passage of the Bill of Rights indicate that the manner of warrant execution was not discussed (Cuddihy 1990), and neither the Fourth Amendment nor any of the state statutes on search warrants mention the manner of warrant execution, it seems reasonable to conclude that the standard for execution of a warrant under the federal constitution would not be any less than that which was required under the despised writs of assistance.

The earliest known American case mentioning the Knock and Announce Rule is *Read v. Case,* decided in 1822. A number of exceptions to the notice and announcement requirement were developed by courts during the nineteenth century. These exceptions closely tracked the English common law exceptions (Blakey 1964). During the twentieth century a number of states enacted statutes dealing with the manner of warrant service. A majority of the states passed statutes requiring notice and announcement, but these statutes also often codified exceptions to the general rule. Currently, at least 40 states have either case law or statute requiring police to knock and announce (Hemmens 1997; 1998a).

Several states have enacted legislation authorizing the issuance of "no-knock" warrants. No-knock warrants are warrants issued by a magistrate, based on probable cause, which permit police to avoid the knock and announce requirement. Generally, such warrants are issued only when the police can demonstrate to the magistrate that there is some exigent circumstance that justifies ignoring the Knock and Announce Rule (LaFave 1996). The idea behind such warrants is that they will eliminate the problem of police officers deciding on the spot whether it is appropriate to ignore the Knock and Announce Rule—here they have already sought and obtained the approval of a neutral and detached magistrate. The Supreme Court has not, to date, ruled on their constitutionality.

In 1917 Congress enacted 18 U.S.C. 3109, which essentially codified the Knock and Announce Rule for federal law enforcement officers executing search warrants. The statute permitted a federal law enforcement officer to enter a dwelling forcibly if, after giving notice of his presence, authority, and purpose, admittance was denied or there was no response (Note 1970). Courts and commentators have indicated that Section 3109 serves the same purposes as the Knock and Announce Rule: (1) the prevention of violence to both the police and innocent persons, (2) the prevention of unnecessary property damage, and (3) the prevention of unnecessary infringement on the occupant's privacy interests (Note 1970; LaFave 1996).

Significantly, Congress did not include in the statute any exceptions to the knock and announce requirement. Lower court decisions interpreting the statute quickly created exceptions, however. These exceptions closely tracked the common law exceptions to the rule (Blakey 1964). Courts based their adoption of these exceptions on the assumption that since Section 3109 effectively codified the common law Knock and Announce Rule, it must have also codified the exceptions to that principle recognized at common law (LaFave 1996).

The Knock and Announce Rule and the Supreme Court

The United States Supreme Court did not address the issue of unannounced police entry until 1958. Prior to that time, the state and federal courts were forced to act without guidance from the Court. The Supreme Court in 1958 finally accepted a case involving the Knock and Announce Rule: *Miller v. United States* (1958).

Miller v. United States (1958)

The facts in *Miller* were as follows: District of Columbia police officers went to Miller's apartment at 3:35 in the morning, without a warrant, intending to arrest him for selling narcotics. Arriving at the apartment, the officers knocked on the front door but did not announce who they were. Miller opened the still-chained door slightly. When he saw the police, he tried to close the door, but the officers forced their way in. Upon searching the apartment the police found marked money, which was used as evidence at trial, leading to Miller's conviction. On appeal, Miller argued that the search of his apartment had violated the Fourth Amendment because the police broke in without giving notice of their purpose. While 18 U.S.C. 3109 delineated the proper method of entry *with* a search warrant, Miller argued that its rationale should also apply in this case, where there was an entry *without* a search warrant.

Justice Brennan, writing for the Court, noted that 18 U.S.C. 3109 codified the common law requirement of notice and announcement. He determined that the entry and arrest were unlawful because the police failed to announce the purpose of their visit to Miller's apartment prior to their entry. Justice Brennan discussed the common law authorities and concluded that at common law an announcement of both lawful authority and purpose was required before the police could break and enter a home. He also noted that a number of states had enacted knock and announce statutes that adopted the Common Law Rule.

In addition, Brennan noted that exceptions to the Knock and Announce Rule existed, both at common law and in more recent lower-court decisions. These exceptions were not at issue, however, as the police did not claim that any exigent circumstances existed to justify their failure to knock and announce. Justice Brennan acknowledged that there might be situations in which police officers would be "virtually certain" that a statement of purpose would be a "useless gesture," but this was not the situation here, and hence the Court did not resolve this issue.

Ultimately, the decision in *Miller* was based not on Fourth Amendment principles or 18 U.S.C. 3109, but on District of Columbia law. The Court declined to expressly incorporate the Knock and Announce Rule into the Fourth Amendment or to mandate notice and announcement in the execution of warrants in all federal cases, preferring to decide the case on nonconstitutional grounds. Consequently, state courts considering the validity of unannounced police were still free to decide such cases on the basis of state law, and federal courts were left to interpret 18 U.S.C. 3109 with little guidance from the Court.

Wong Sun v. United States (1963)

Just five years after the decision in *Miller,* the Supreme Court revisited the Knock and Announce Rule. In *Wong Sun v. United States* (1963) federal narcotics agents came to the door of a business and entered without notice. Upon seeing the officers enter, the suspect fled from the business into his living quarters at the rear of the building. The police pursued and arrested him. The suspect then made statements incriminating Wong Sun, who was subsequently arrested and convicted. Wong Sun appealed his conviction, claiming the incriminating statements were obtained by the police in violation of the Knock and Announce Rule and the Fourth Amendment.

Wong Sun's conviction was upheld on other grounds, but in discussing the entry without notice, Justice Brennan, again writing for the Court, intimated that exceptions to the Knock and Announce Rule might exist. Among these potential exceptions were the "imminent destruction of vital evidence, or the need to rescue a victim in peril." Lower courts, both state and federal, had already recognized such exceptions to the rule, and Brennan's opinion seemed designed to invite appeals based on these grounds.

Ker v. California (1964)

The year after the decision in *Wong Sun,* the Supreme Court did not expressly hold that the common law knock and announce requirement was included in the Fourth Amendment, but it did hold that failure to knock and announce was acceptable only in certain circumstances and that these circumstances should be judged based on the

Reasonableness Clause of the Fourth Amendment (*Ker v. California* 1964). The Court in *Ker* was badly divided, however. While eight justices agreed that under certain circumstances failure to knock and announce was justified, the justices split 4-to-4 on whether the particular circumstances of this case justified ignoring the Knock and Announce Rule. Justice Harlan concurred only in the result of Justice Clark's plurality opinion, basing his decision on the Fourteenth Amendment and "fundamental fairness" rather than the Fourth Amendment and the Reasonableness Clause. With Harlan's vote and the four votes for the Clark plurality opinion, *Ker*'s conviction was upheld, but lower courts searching for guidance were left to chose from either the Clark or Brennan opinions, both of which commanded four votes.

The facts in *Ker* were as follows: Los Angeles police officers with a warrant went to Ker's apartment to arrest him. Upon arrival at the apartment complex where Ker lived, they obtained a passkey from the manager and used it to enter Ker's apartment without notice or announcement. They seized Ker and searched his apartment, finding narcotics that were subsequently used against him at trial. The police defended their failure to knock and announce prior to entry on the ground that they believed Ker would attempt to destroy evidence if he were made aware that the police were trying to enter the apartment.

Justice Brennan's plurality opinion held that the police in this case *were not* justified in ignoring the Knock and Announce Rule. He argued that unannounced entry into a home violated the Fourth Amendment, except in three limited situations. These exceptions were when "(1) the persons within already know of the officers' authority and purpose, or (2) where the officers are justified in the belief that persons within are in imminent peril of bodily harm, or (3) where those within, made aware of the presence of someone outside (because, for example, there has been a knock on the door), are then engaged in activity which justifies the officers in the belief that an escape or the destruction of evidence is being attempted."

Justice Brennan based his argument that the Knock and Announce Rule is part of the Reasonableness Clause of the Fourth Amendment on his analysis of the common law at the time of the framing of the Bill of Rights. He concluded that the Knock and Announce Rule was firmly established by 1791. The exceptions to the rule, he concluded, were created after passage of the Bill of Rights. Any such exceptions should consequently be narrowly tailored, so as not to frustrate the intent of the framers.

Justice Clark's plurality opinion held that the police in this case *were* justified in ignoring the Knock and Announce Rule. According to Clark, police should be able to evade the rule whenever "exigent circumstances" mandated it. Clark did not specify what sort of activity would constitute exigent circumstances per se, focusing instead on the specific facts in *Ker*. Confusion was created, however, by his apparent endorsement of police officer knowledge of narcotics possession as a justification for ignoring the Knock and Announce Rule. Prior to this, the exceptions were generally limited to situations in which there was danger to the officers or someone inside the home, the possibility of the suspect escaping, or the possibility that evidence would be destroyed.

Did Clark's opinion mean that any time a suspect is in possession of easily destructible evidence (such as narcotics) that the Knock and Announce Rule does not apply? Prior cases suggested police could avoid knocking and announcing only if there was some indication that suspects would in fact destroy evidence, regardless of its form, if police gave notice prior to entry. Clark's language suggested that the very nature of some contraband (such as narcotics) might create an exigency, without any indication that the suspects were in fact prepared to destroy such evidence. Considerable confusion in state and federal courts following this decision indicates lower courts were unsure how far the destruction of evidence exception should be extended.

While the Court in *Ker* failed to provide lower courts with clear guidance as to what constituted an acceptable exception to the Knock and Announce Rule, it appeared that the Court was willing to concede that the Fourth Amendment did apply to the manner in which warrants were executed. While neither the Brennan nor Clark opinions expressly incorporated the Knock and Announce Rule into the Fourth Amendment, both opinions proceeded on the assumption that the circumstances in which entry without notice is permitted are governed by the Reasonableness Clause of the Fourth Amendment.

Sabbath v. United States (1968)

The next case decided by the Court involving the Knock and Announce Rule was *Sabbath v. United States* (1968). In this case federal customs officers apprehended a man named Jones attempting to smuggle cocaine into the country. The customs officers persuaded Jones to deliver the cocaine to its intended recipient, Sabbath. While the officers watched, Jones went to Sabbath's apartment with the drugs and was admitted. Shortly thereafter, the officers knocked on the door and, getting no response, opened the unlocked door and entered without notice and announcement. They arrested Sabbath and searched his apartment, seizing evidence that was used to convict him at trial.

On appeal, Sabbath asserted that the customs officers had violated 18 U.S.C. 3109 by "breaking and entering" his apartment without notice. The Court held that the officers had violated 18 U.S.C. 3109 by failing to knock and announce without having a "substantial basis" for their belief that obeying the Knock and Announce Rule would in some way imperil them. The decision in this case turned on an interpretation of 18 U.S.C. 3109 rather than the Fourth Amendment, however, so it was not clear that state police officers were required to meet the "substantial basis" requirement. The Court did make it clear, however, that as Section 3109 codified the common law knock and announce principle, it was subject to those exceptions to the principle recognized at common law. Interestingly, the Court did hold that no exigent circumstances were present to justify ignoring the Knock and Announce Rule, even though Sabbath was suspected of being a drug dealer.

After these cases, state courts remained divided over whether the presence of illegal drugs alone justified unannounced police entry on the theory that pausing to announce the search will enable the destruction of evidence. Courts tended to interpret the situation in one of two ways: taking a "blanket approach" or a "particularity approach" (Mericli 1989; Garcia 1993).

The *blanket approach* states that when police officers have probable cause to search a dwelling for drugs, the Knock and Announce Rule may be ignored. It is derived from Justice Clark's opinion in *Ker*. This approach operates on the premise that it is not unreasonable for police officers to assume that people who possess illegal drugs in a dwelling with indoor plumbing are likely to attempt to destroy these drugs if apprehension appears imminent. If the police can demonstrate there are drugs within the dwelling, using the blanket approach they are justified in ignoring the Knock and Announce Rule (Garcia 1993). No-knock warrants are essentially a variant of the blanket approach, substituting the judgment of a neutral magistrate prior to execution of the warrant for that of the police at time of execution of the warrant (LaFave 1996; Mericli 1989).

The *particularity approach* is derived in large part from Justice Brennan's opinion in *Ker*. Under this approach, police must follow the Knock and Announce Rule unless they can articulate specific facts to indicate that occupants of a dwelling are engaged in evidence destruction, are fleeing, or are preparing an armed response to the police. Significantly, this approach does not allow for exceptions to the Knock and Announce Rule based on the nature of the evidence sought. Rather, the police must be able to cite facts in a particular case that justify a reasonable belief that evidence is in fact being destroyed. It is not enough to simply show that occupants possess an easily destructible substance; instead, police must show that the occupants are actually attempting to destroy this substance (Garcia 1993).

By the late 1980s, there existed considerable conflict in state courts and lower federal courts regarding the Knock and Announce Rule and its constitutional linkage

(Hemmens 1997). The decisions in *Miller*, *Ker*, and *Sabbath* all avoided an explicit statement that notice was mandated by the Fourth Amendment rather than just required by statute. Several commentators called on the Court to resolve this confusion (Mericli 1989; Garcia 1993; Goddard 1995). In 1995, the Supreme Court finally returned to the Knock and Announce Rule, and in the next decade it issued four decisions involving the rule.

Wilson v. Arkansas (1995)

Police came to Wilson's house, armed with a search warrant for illegal drugs. They found the front door open and the screen door unlatched. Looking inside, they saw a man sitting on the living room sofa. They opened the screen door and entered, only then identifying themselves as police officers and stating that they had a search warrant. The officers then conducted a search, finding a variety of illegal drugs. Based in part on the evidence seized during this search, Wilson was arrested and charged with several drug offenses.

On appeal, Wilson sought to have her conviction overturned and the evidence seized by the police during the search suppressed, on the ground that the police had failed to knock and announce. The Arkansas Supreme Court denied her appeal, baldly asserting, without citation to precedent, that the Fourth Amendment did not require that the police knock and announce before entering a dwelling to execute a search or an arrest warrant.

The U.S. Supreme Court reversed and remanded, Justice Thomas writing for a unanimous Court. In doing so, the Court for the first time squarely held that the common law Knock and Announce Rule was a component of the Fourth Amendment's prohibition of unreasonable searches and seizures. At the same time, Thomas's opinion made it clear that the Knock and Announce Rule is not inflexible and that exigent circumstances might well justify police discountenance of the general rule. The Court left to another day the determination of what constituted a valid exigent circumstance.

To determine whether the Knock and Announce Rule is part of the Fourth Amendment, Justice Thomas looked to "the common law at the time of the framing of the Constitution," and concluded there was "no doubt that the reasonableness of a search and seizure may depend in part on whether the law enforcement officers announced their presence and authority prior to entering."

Justice Thomas did not stop there, however. He went on to say that just as the Knock and Announce Rule was subsumed in the Reasonableness Clause of the Fourth Amendment, so too were possible exceptions to the general rule of notice and announcement. Rather than delineating the circumstances that would make an unannounced entry reasonable, Justice Thomas declined to "attempt a comprehensive catalog" and instead chose to "leave to the lower courts the task of determining the circumstances under which an unannounced entry is reasonable under the Fourth Amendment." Thomas did indicate, however, that some of the more common exceptions to the Knock and Announce Rule already existing in case law might well withstand constitutional scrutiny. Among these were the traditional exceptions of danger to the police and the hot pursuit.

Unfortunately, the Court's decision did not deal with the claim by the police that mere possession of easily disposable contraband, such as narcotics, creates justification for ignoring the requirement to knock and announce. In 1995 the Wisconsin Supreme Court created a blanket rule eliminating the knock and announce requirement for all felony drug search warrants. In 1996, one year after deciding in *Wilson* that the Knock and Announce Rule is a component of the Fourth Amendment, the U.S. Supreme Court granted certiorari in *Richards v. Wisconsin* (1997), to determine whether this blanket exception to the rule of announcement was constitutional.

Richards v. Wisconsin (1997)

At 3:40 in the morning police officers attempted to execute a search warrant to a hotel room occupied by Steiney Richards.

An officer knocked on the door and attempted to gain entry by claiming to be a maintenance man. Richards unlocked and opened the still-chained door slightly, peered through the small opening, and, when the officer attempted to push the door open further, shut and relocked the door. After a wait of "four to five seconds," the officers announced their identity and kicked open the door. As this was happening, Richards fled out the rear window of the hotel room and was immediately apprehended. Police officers searched the hotel room, pursuant to the search warrant, and found cash and cocaine hidden above the ceiling tiles in the bathroom.

Richards was subsequently charged with two drug offenses. Richards sought to have the drugs seized during the search of his hotel room suppressed on the ground that the police failed to knock and announce prior to entering. The trial court denied the suppression motion, holding that the circumstances confronted by the officers at the time of execution of the warrant created a reasonable belief that evidence was about to be destroyed and that this exigency justified abrogation of the Knock and Announce Rule.

Richards then accepted a plea bargain and was sentenced to 13 years' imprisonment. Richards reserved the right to appeal the validity of the search. On appeal, the Wisconsin Supreme Court endorsed a blanket exception to the Knock and Announce Rule for drug possession cases. The basis for creating this blanket exception was (1) the court found that there was a high risk of violence anytime police attempted to execute search warrants involving felony drug possession, and the public interest in officer safety outweighed what the court saw as a minimal intrusion into the privacy rights of citizens; and (2) because drugs are often easily disposed of, they fall under the "destruction of evidence" exception to the knock and announce requirement (Hemmens 1998b).

Richards sought review in the U.S. Supreme Court, and the high court granted certiorari to decide whether the Fourth Amendment permits a blanket exception to the Knock and Announce Rule if drugs are the object of a search warrant. Writing for a unanimous Court, Justice Stevens held that the Fourth Amendment does not permit a blanket exception to the knock and announce requirement for felony drug investigations, and it struck down the Wisconsin Supreme Court's blanket rule as unconstitutional.

The Court did not eliminate no-knock entries, however. Justice Stevens went on to say that a no-knock entry is justified when the police have a "reasonable suspicion" that knocking and announcing their presence, under the particular circumstances (1) would be dangerous or futile, or (2) would inhibit the effective investigation of the crime. Essentially, the high court drew the line at creating a per se rule based on generalizations about suspects and instead left it to the police to determine, on a case-by-case basis, when it is appropriate to enter without knocking and announcing. Additionally, this determination need be based only on reasonable suspicion, not probable cause. Finally, this determination by the police is subject to judicial scrutiny, in light of the Fourth Amendment's mandate that searches be reasonable.

Justice Stevens noted that reasonableness is a flexible requirement, and does not create "a rigid rule of announcement that ignores countervailing law enforcement interests." He acknowledged that while many cases involving drugs pose special risks to officer safety and evidence preservation, not all drug cases would necessarily entail these areas of concern; thus, a blanket rule is inappropriate. Additionally, creation of an exception for one category of criminal behaviors (such as drug possession) leads all too easily to the creation of exceptions for other categories. Basing a per se exception to the Knock and Announce Rule on the hypothetical risk of danger to officers or evidence would render the Fourth Amendment's reasonableness requirement meaningless, as it would remove law enforcement conduct from judicial scrutiny.

While the Court found disfavor with the Wisconsin court's blanket rule, it stopped short of requiring knock and announcement in all instances. Instead, the Court held that a no-knock entry is justified when the police "have a reasonable suspicion that knocking and announcing their presence, under the particular circumstances, would be dangerous or futile, or that it would inhibit the effective investigation of crime." Requiring the police to demonstrate a reasonable suspicion, rather than probable cause, struck an appropriate balance between the interests of law enforcement and individual privacy interests. While this stopped far short of Wisconsin's blanket approach, the reasonable suspicion showing is, by the Court's own admission, not a difficult standard for the police to meet. The crucial element here is that the reasonableness of every no-knock entry is now clearly subject to judicial review, something the Wisconsin approach eliminated (Hemmens 1998b).

United States v. Ramirez (1998)

Lower courts continued to struggle with the particulars of the Knock and Announce Rule. Issues unresolved by the Supreme Court's incorporation of the rule and its common law exceptions into the Fourth Amendment reasonableness requirement included such issues as how long police officers had to wait after announcing their entry and whether police could destroy property while entering without first knocking and announcing. Subsequent to the Supreme Court decision in *Richards,* the Ninth Circuit Court of Appeals held that police officers could not destroy property during a no-knock search unless they had specific evidence justifying the property damage prior to entry.

In *United States v. Ramirez,* law enforcement officers looking for a dangerous escaped prisoner named Shelby obtained a no-knock search warrant for Ramirez's house. Early in the morning, the agents announced their presence over a loudspeaker and simultaneously broke a small window in the garage and pointed a gun through the opening to prevent anyone from obtaining weapons that an informant stated were being kept in the garage. Ramirez awoke to the noise, assumed he was being burglarized, and grabbed a pistol and shot it through the ceiling of the garage. The police returned fire and Ramirez surrendered. The fugitive was never found, but Ramirez was charged with being a felon in possession of a firearm, in violation of federal law.

Ramirez filed a suppression motion, arguing the evidence seized during the search of his home should be excluded because property was destroyed in the course of the police no-knock entry. Ramirez argued that while no-knock warrants were sometimes permissible, in cases where there is property damage the police must have more than reasonable suspicion of the existence of an exigent circumstance to justify an entry that results in property damage. The district court ordered the evidence suppressed. The Ninth Circuit Court of Appeals agreed with Ramirez and held that when a law enforcement officer executes a no-knock warrant by entering a dwelling without knocking and announcing, "more specific inferences of exigency are necessary" to justify the entry if property will be destroyed than if property will not be destroyed.

The Supreme Court, per Chief Justice Rehnquist, unanimously rejected the Ninth Circuit's attempt to hold law enforcement officers to a higher standard of reasonableness when property damage occurs during the execution of a search warrant. The Court, in rejecting the Ninth Circuit's approach, explained that "a no-knock entry is justified if police have a reasonable suspicion that knocking and announcing would be dangerous, futile, or destructive to the purposes of the investigation. Whether such a reasonable suspicion exists depends in no way on whether police must destroy property in order to enter."

In other words, the reasonableness standard is the same regardless how the entry is made. The key is *whether* a forcible entry is justified, not *how* a forcible entry occurs. Once officers have determined that a forcible entry is justified, that ends the reasonableness inquiry (Hemmens and Mathias 2004). The Supreme Court acknowledged that while the manner of execution is a factor in determining the validity of a search warrant, here there was only minor damage. The Court noted, however, that unnecessary, excessive property damage could make an otherwise lawful entry unlawful.

Ramirez means that property damage is not part of the analysis when determining whether the entry itself was reasonable. Rather, the crucial issues in evaluating the reasonableness of an entry are (1) whether admittance has been either actually or constructively refused, and (2) whether some exigent circumstance (such as the possible destruction of evidence) makes immediate entry reasonable. Thus, the proper analysis focuses on how long a reasonable officer would wait before concluding that continued delay would be futile, would risk frustrating the purposes of the warrant, or would expose persons to serious danger. Property destruction is a necessary consequence of the resident's failure to open the door; it is not a factor that requires additional delay (Hemmens and Mathias 2004).

United States v. Banks (2003)

After the decision in *Ramirez*, lower courts continued to struggle with determining what amount of time constitutes a reasonable waiting period when officers knock and announce and do not receive a response. A number of state courts and lower federal courts upheld forcible entries when officers waited approximately 20 to 30 seconds.

In July 1998, a joint federal and state drug task force received information from a confidential informant that a person identified as "Shakes" was selling cocaine from an apartment in Las Vegas. Officers of the Las Vegas Police Department corroborated the accuracy of this tip, and were then able to obtain a search warrant for drugs and drug paraphernalia from a Nevada justice of the peace. Las Vegas police and FBI officers executed the search warrant one week later at the apartment, which was rented by LaShawn Banks.

When the law enforcement officers were positioned in both the front and the rear of the apartment, officers knocked loudly on the front door and shouted "Police, search warrant." After waiting between 15 and 20 seconds without hearing a sound from within the apartment, the officers, clothed in tactical operations gear and carrying automatic weapons, entered the apartment to find Banks standing naked, dripping with soapy water, in front of his shower. Banks claimed that he did not hear the knock and announcement but had heard the officers' forced entry. The officers handcuffed the naked Mr. Banks, escorted him to his kitchen, and then proceeded to search his apartment. The officers discovered several weapons, cash, a scale, and approximately 11 ounces of crack cocaine. Banks was arrested and the items seized.

Banks filed a motion to suppress the items that were seized during the search of his apartment, arguing that the police entry violated the Fourth Amendment as well as 18 U.S.C. 3109. The district court denied Banks's motion, and Banks pled guilty, reserving his right to appeal the denial of his suppression motion. The Ninth Circuit Court of Appeals reversed the trial court, creating a complicated test for what constituted a "reasonable" period of time to wait before entering. The Ninth Circuit created four categories of knock and announce cases. The first category required that exigent circumstances exist and that unforced entry was possible. The second category included entries based on exigent circumstances and accompanied by the destruction of property. The third category included situations in which no exigent circumstances existed, nonforcible entry was possible, and there was either an explicit refusal or the lapse of a "significant" period of time. The fourth category did not require exigent circumstances but did require officers to show that forcible entry was required—again, as a result of an explicit refusal of entry or the "lapse of an even more substantial amount of time." The Ninth Circuit panel placed *Banks* in the fourth category.

After creating the four-category analysis scheme, the Court of Appeals next provided a nonexhaustive list of factors to be considered in assessing the reasonableness of entry once the proper entry category has been ascertained by the police officer on the scene. These factors included the size and location of the residence, the location of the officers in relation to the main living or sleeping areas of the residence, the time of day, the nature of the suspected offense, the suspect's prior convictions, and several other factors.

The Ninth Circuit next asserted that because the officers in *Banks* had not been explicitly denied entrance, they were required to delay their forceful entrance for a "sufficient period of time." The court failed to provide explicit directions as to what would constitute a "sufficient" period of time, however, preferring to resolve that issue on a case-by-case basis. The Ninth Circuit decision was in conflict with decision in several other circuits, all of which had held that a waiting period of approximately 20 seconds was sufficient. In fact, the Ninth Circuit, in a subsequent case, acknowledged that its decision in *Banks* was in conflict with the decisions of others courts of appeal, and with the Ninth Circuit's own cases. Citing this conflict among the circuits, the U.S. Supreme Court granted review.

Writing for another unanimous Court (all four recent knock and announce decisions have been unanimous, a rarity in Supreme Court criminal procedure decisions), Justice Souter held that the law enforcement officers' 15–20 second wait prior to their forcible entry was reasonable under the totality of the circumstances. They reversed the Ninth Circuit and reinstated Banks's conviction. The majority opinion held that the totality of the circumstances can, and must, be assessed to determine whether "the significance of exigency revealed by circumstances" warrants, at that time from the perspective of the officers on scene—"not with the 20/20 vision of hindsight,"—a requirement or dispensing of the knock and announcement.

The Court acknowledged that while "this call is a close one," the police were justified in not waiting any longer or waiting for an explicit refusal before breaking down the door to Banks's apartment. This was because the police had a search warrant for drugs, which are easily and quickly disposed of. The exigent circumstance of the possible destruction of evidence justified not waiting any longer. The case might well be different if the items in the search warrant were different: "Police seeking a stolen piano may be able to spend more time to make sure they really need the battering ram."

The Supreme Court in *Ramirez* rejected the Ninth Circuit's attempt to graft a requirement onto the general reasonableness requirement that when property is destroyed during the execution of a search warrant there must be a showing of heightened exigency. The Supreme Court at oral argument in *Banks* made it clear they perceived the Ninth Circuit's four-part matrix developed in *Banks* as nothing more than an attempt to resurrect an approach the Supreme Court rejected in *Ramirez* (Hemmens and Mathias 2004). The high court noted the Ninth Circuit did not even cite *Ramirez* in its holding in *Banks,* suggesting an unwillingness to deal with the implications of that decision.

Conclusion

After years of being ignored by the Supreme Court, the Knock and Announce Rule has been the subject of intense scrutiny in the past decade. Since 1996, the high court has rendered four decisions regarding it. In these decisions the Court has moved haltingly, taking its familiar case-by-case approach to criminal procedure issues. The Court has declared the Knock and Announce Rule and its common law exceptions part and parcel of the Fourth Amendment. The Court has refused to create a blanket exception to the rule, but has, in *Banks,* made it clear that the rule is relatively easy for law enforcement to follow.

The Court's decision in *Wilson* simply made explicit what many courts already assumed: (1) that the knock and announce principle is a constitutional requirement, not just a common statutory provision or common law principle, and (2) that there are some exceptions to the general rule. This approach was unnecessarily cautious, given that there already existed extensive case law and statutory provisions dealing with exceptions to the Knock and Announce Rule (Hemmens 1997). In addition, the Court's decision in *Ker,* particularly Justice Brennan's plurality opinion, dealt with exceptions to the rule and provided a possible guideline that other courts have used and that the *Wilson* court could have adopted wholesale or in modified form. While emphasizing that the knock and announce principle is not just a Common Law Rule but a constitutional mandate elevates the principle, it does little else.

In *Richards,* the Supreme Court explicated the *Wilson* holding, making it clear that blanket exceptions to the general rule of announcement are not permissible. This was the proper decision, as the blanket rule removes judicial scrutiny from the equation entirely. While it is true that blanket rules involving the Fourth Amendment are not per se unconstitutional, the Court has consistently afforded the home the utmost protection. Unfortunately, the Supreme Court did not go far enough in renouncing the decision of the Wisconsin court. The Supreme Court created a large window of opportunity for the police when it permitted them to disregard the Knock and Announce Rule upon the relatively low threshold of "reasonable suspicion" of danger to the police or destruction of evidence. Normally, reasonableness requires meeting the probable cause standard.

In *Ramirez,* the Supreme Court made it clear that it did not favor complicated rules governing the determination of whether a no-knock entry was reasonable under the Fourth Amendment. The Court struck down the Ninth Circuit's test requiring additional evidence to justify no-knock entries that involve property damage and insisted the police be allowed to determine, on the scene, whether a no-knock entry was reasonable based on the facts known to them at the time of entry. While this decision was reasonable, it is further evidence that the Supreme Court is not going to rigorously apply the Knock and Announce Rule.

In *Banks,* the Supreme Court again struck down the Ninth Circuit's efforts to create a complicated test for the reasonableness of police actions relating to the Knock and Announce Rule. The Court also refused to create a blanket rule for what constitutes a "reasonable" waiting period after announcement and before entry. Instead, the Court insisted such determinations be made on a case-by-case basis, depending on the facts known to the officers at the time of the entry. While the Supreme Court's test is easier to apply, it is also easier for the police to use it to avoid the dictates of the Knock and Announce Rule. This decision is just another step in the continued evisceration of the protections afforded citizens by the common law knock and announce.

From its early adoption at common law to its exercise at LaShawn Banks's Las Vegas apartment, the Knock and Announce Rule has played a significant role in balancing citizen's rights to be left alone and the government's right to engage in effective law enforcement. The war on drugs has brought the police into many homes, leading to a reappraisal and reexamination of the Knock and Announce Rule, once a long-ignored bit of criminal procedure esoterica.

The Fourth Amendment was created largely in response to official invasions of the home, and the Supreme Court has repeatedly upheld the sanctity of an individual's residence. Unannounced entry destroys this privacy interest; consequently, such entries should be limited to the most extraordinary of circumstances. The Knock and Announce Rule is an effort by courts to find a balance between a homeowner's reasonable expectation of privacy and the government's interest in effective law enforcement. Striking this balance is the job of the Supreme Court. Unfortunately, the Supreme Court has not achieved an accurate balance of the privacy rights of individuals and the rights of law enforcement. The Court has given the police tremendous latitude under the Knock and Announce Rule. While the Court has resisted calls to adopt blanket exceptions to the rule, the Court has allowed police to avoid the rule on the lower showing of reasonable suspicion, and the Court has consistently shown a reluctance to second-guess police decisions made on the scene, including decisions to damage property and enter in a short span of time. This deference to law enforcement interests will no doubt encourage police to push the limits of their authority under the Knock and Announce Rule. This situation will in turn no doubt force the Court to revisit the Knock and Announce Rule.

References

Annotation. 1976. "What Constitutes Compliance With Knock and Announce Rule in Search of Premises: State Cases." *American Law Reports (3rd)* 70:217–254.

Blackstone, William. 1978. *Commentaries on the Laws of England* (American edition).

Blakey, Robert. 1964. "The Rule of Announce-ment and Unlawful Entry: *Miller v. United States* and *Ker v. California.*" *University of Pennsylvania Law Review* 112(3):499–561.

Cuddihy, William. 1990. *The Fourth Amendment: Origins and Original Meaning 1602–1791.* Un-published doctoral dissertation, Claremont College, Claremont, California.

Driscoll, Robert J. 1995. "Unannounced Police Entries and Destruction of Evidence After *Wil-son v. Arkansas.*" *Columbia Journal of Law and Social Problems* 29(1):1–38.

Garcia, Charles P. 1993. "Note, The Knock and Announce Rule: A New Approach to the De-struction of Evidence Exception." *Columbia Law Review* 93(4):685–719.

Goddard, Jennifer M. 1995. "Note, The Destruc-tion of Evidence Exception to the Knock and Announce Rule: A Call for Protection of Fourth Amendment Rights." *Boston University Law Review* 75(3):449–476.

Hale, Matthew. 1847. *Pleas of the Crown* (1st American edition).

Hemmens, Craig. 1997. "The Police, The Fourth Amendment, and Unannounced Entry: *Wilson v. Arkansas.*" *Criminal Law Bulletin* 33(1):29–58.

———. 1998a. "Bright Lines, Blanket Rules and the Fourth Amendment: The Supreme Court's Half-hearted Endorsement of the Knock and Announce Rule." *The Justice Professional* 11(4):369–390.

———. 1998b. "I Hear You Knocking: The Su-preme Court Revisits the Knock and An-nounce Rule." *University of Missouri-Kansas City Law Review* 66(3):559–602.

Hemmens, Craig, and Chris Mathias. 2004. "*United States v. Banks:* The Knock and An-nounce Rule Returns to the Supreme Court." *Idaho Law Review* 41(1):1–36.

Hemmens, Craig, John L. Worrall, and Alan Thompson. 2004. *Significant Cases in Criminal Procedure.* Los Angeles: Roxbury.

LaFave, Wayne R. 1996. *Search and Seizure: A Treatise on the Fourth Amendment* (3rd). Min-neapolis: West Publishing.

Lasson, N. 1937. *The History and Development of the Fourth Amendment to the Constitution of the United States.* New York: Johns Hopkins University Press.

Mericli, Kemal A. 1989. "The Apprehension of Peril Exception to the Knock and Announce Rule." *Search and Seizure Law Report* 16(6):129–144.

Note. 1970. "Announcement in Police Entries." *Yale Law Journal* 80(1):139–175.

Cases and Statutes Cited

18 U.S.C. Section 3109 (1917) (originally enacted as the Espionage Act, Chapter 30, title 11, Sec-tion 8, 40 Statute 217, 228-29).

Curtis's Case, Fost. 135, 168 Eng. Rep. 67 (K.B. 1757).

Ker v. California, 374 U.S. 23 (1964).

Miller v. United States, 357 U.S. 301 (1958).

Read v. Case, 4 Conn. 166 (1822).

Richards v. Wisconsin, 520 U.S. 385 (1997).

Sabbath v. United States, 391 U.S. 585 (1968).

Semayne's Case, 77 Eng. Rep. 194, 195 (1604).

Statute of Westminster, 1. Chapter 17, 3 Edward 1 (1275).

United States v. Banks, 540 U.S. 31 (2003).

United States v. Ramirez, 523 U.S. 65 (1998).

Wilson v. Arkansas, 514 U.S. 927 (1995).

Wong Sun v. United States, 371 U.S. 471 (1963).

Related Websites

Knock and Announce: A Fourth Amendment Standard

http://www.fbi.gov/publications/leb/1997/may976.htm

The Knock and Announce Rule (enter search term "Knock and Announce")

http://www.fletc.gov

Fourth Amendment.com

http://www.fourthamendment.com/

Discussion Questions

1. Why did the Supreme Court incorporate the Knock and Announce Rule into the Due Process Clause of the Fourteenth Amendment in *Wilson v. Arkansas*?

2. Why did the Supreme Court incorporate the exceptions to the Knock and An-nounce Rule into the Due Process Clause of the Fourteenth Amendment in *Rich-ards v. Wisconsin*?

3. What interests are served by the Knock and Announce Rule? By its exceptions?

4. What constitutes a "reasonable" waiting time before police enter a dwelling? Ex-plain your answer referencing both *Ramirez* and *Banks.*

5. Explain how a no-knock warrant would be executed under the requirements of the Knock and Announce Rule. ✦

Chapter 2
Surveillance Technology and the Law

Kathryn Scarborough, Pam Collins, and Ryan Baggett

In this chapter, the authors examine the various constitutional issues regarding the use of surveillance technology. In particular, several methods of surveillance are identified, including passenger screening technology, thermal imaging and through-the-wall surveillance, and closed-circuit television (CCTV). Because information gathering through the use of CCTV has been a prevalent technology throughout the years and provides a strong court history for analysis, it is the focus of the discussion.

First, the authors explore the recent shifts in the rates of CCTV usage within the private and public sectors, and in light of recent legislative decisions such as the implementation of the USA PATRIOT Act, which is covered in detail in Chapter 3. The authors also discuss the effect of the Fourth Amendment requirements that a warrant may be issued only when probable cause exists, and that the warrant must describe the place, persons, or things to be searched with particularity. The Supreme Court's interpretation of the Fourth Amendment has evolved since 1791, and as the authors note, the line that constitutes the crossover between private and nonprivate has been muddied by rapidly advancing technology.

Finally, this chapter provides a case-by-case summary of the Court history surrounding electronic surveillance. As noted in Chapter 6, one of the most important Supreme Court decisions was *Katz v. United States* (1967), which stipulated that "the Fourth Amendment protects people, not places" and was to be interpreted as protecting the legitimate personal expectation of privacy and security. Other important Court decisions, such as

Kyllo v. United States (2001), have further clarified the constitutionality of such surveillance techniques as thermal imaging. One must consider the balance of constitutionally guaranteed individual rights with the government's power and responsibility to protect the public.

Introduction

Privacy is a key component of any democratic society. Protecting citizens from the "intrusive activities of others" (Spinello 2002) is of the utmost importance. Brandeis and Warren (1890) summarized the common law roots of privacy while responding to new invasive technologies, such as photography, at that time, indicating that "political, social, and economic changes entail the recognition of new rights, and the common law . . . grows to meet the demands of society" (p. 193). According to Spinello (2002), this article was the impetus for a new cause of action for privacy. Additionally, when we examine privacy legislation, it is apparent that personal protection is "highly reactive and unsystematic" (Spinello 2002, 185) therefore subject to the "flavor of the day."

Can we realistically expect any privacy in today's technological world? This question is asked by Bruce Schneier (2003) in his book, *Beyond Fear: Thinking Sensibly About Security in an Uncertain World.* He discusses the fact that surveillance has become almost inherent in much of our society's infrastructure, such as the Internet, cell phone networks, and the growing network of public and private security cameras. Surveillance can take the form of conventional security camera systems, chemical and biological sensors, electronic surveillance (of phone calls, emails, and web uploads and downloads), computer data mining, rapid DNA-based probes, bomb sniffers, thermal imaging, and radio frequency identification (RFID) (Schneier 2003). All of these are currently being used in varying degrees, with the most prevalent surveillance system being closed-circuit television (CCTV).

According to Schneier (2003) there are numerous advocates for enhanced surveillance, including David Brin, a science fiction author. Brin supports the use of security practices because, in many respects, as a culture, we have become a "transparent society" that allows everyone greater access and visibility, which in turn should require greater reliance on security features.

Schneier argues that "technology has turned the battle for and against privacy into an arms race: the side with the more advanced technology wins and the advantage tends to go toward those who would violate privacy" (Schneier 2003, 249). Schneier's argument is that laws only work if attackers obey the law and that "massive surveillance systems that deprive people of liberty and invade their privacy are never worth it" (p. 249). Schneier's position, like that of some others, is that currently much of the surveillance systems employed in both the United States and the United Kingdom do not prevent terrorist attacks, which is evident from the recent events in London. During the morning rush hour on July 7, 2005, a series of bombings hit London's public transport system. Fifty-six people were killed in the attacks (including the four bombers) and approximately 700 were injured. Investigators in London relied on hundreds of cameras in the underground transit system to help identify the responsible individuals. Within one week of the bombings, police were able to identify the four suspects through the use of CCTV. Due to the large amount of video and the lack of video clarity from some cameras, suspect identification was an arduous task. A manual, police-initiated process was utilized for identification since the sophistication of current surveillance is not advanced enough to automatically recognize known terrorists to alert authorities prior to an attack.

A variety of surveillance technologies are being developed and used within the United States today, including body scans, thermal imaging, through-the-wall surveillance, and CCTV.

One of the more controversial technologies to emerge is the body scan system, which reveals considerable detail regarding the human anatomy. This advanced passenger screening technology was developed to provide front and back body scans of passengers. The scan is estimated to take about the same amount of time as existing metal detectors. The primary difference between the two systems is that metal detectors cannot detect weapons that are ceramic, glass, or wood (Hall 2005). This screening system is a prime example of a situation in which advanced technology would reduce the inconvenience of manual searches and the length of time taken to pass through the airport security screening process, but the public is reluctant to accept it, primarily because it is perceived as being too invasive and violating the reasonable expectation passengers have regarding the viewing of their persons. Interestingly, airport passengers have been much more willing to allow physical patdowns than these types of electronic screenings because of the detailed scan of a person's body shape. Thus privacy concerns for body scans make this technology less likely to be approved by the Federal Aviation Administration (FAA) because it is considered too invasive by the general public (Hall 2005).

Another controversial technology is thermal imaging surveillance systems. Thermal imaging is a type of infrared imaging based on the detection of radiation in the infrared range of the electromagnetic spectrum (Foster 2005). Manufacturers of these technologies often provide a disclaimer that the product is for legal use only, and that it is the sole responsibility of the purchaser to determine local, state, federal, and international regulations prior to use (Collins, Cordner, and Scarborough 2004).

Through-the-wall surveillance (TWS), another controversial surveillance technology, has been the subject of various court cases, to be discussed later in this chapter. A significant amount of work on TWS applications for law enforcement has been conducted by the National Institute of Justice's Office of Science and Technology. TWS technology includes relatively inexpensive handheld devices that alert officers to the presence of an individual behind a wall or door, as well as devices that will enable special weapons and tactics (SWAT) or special operations response team (SORT) commanders to better visualize events during hostage situations (Hunt, Tillery, and Wild 2001).

For purposes of this chapter, we will focus on the issues surrounding observation and information gathering using CCTV surveillance, then follow the discussion with legal cases related to privacy and surveillance, because CCTV is one of the most prevalent and longstanding surveillance technologies in use today. Most of the legal cases to date have involved other types of technology but have set precedent and will undoubtedly be relied on when considering the legality of using CCTV.

Prevalence of CCTV in the United States

While the use of CCTV systems in the United States has been more prevalent in the private sector, law enforcement has been reluctant to embrace this technology. As late as 1997 it was estimated that only 13 city police departments used CCTV video surveillance systems. These systems were used primarily to monitor pedestrian traffic in downtown and residential districts (Nieto, Johnston-Dodds, and Simmons 2002). However, by 2001 the use of CCTV surveillance had increased dramatically and according to the International Association of Chiefs of Police (2001), by 2001 80 percent of law enforcement agencies had used CCTV to some extent. The events of 9/11 have had the greatest single impact on the acceptance and proliferation of CCTV, serving as a force multiplier in the use of CCTV surveillance. A recent survey of nearly 4,000 U.S. companies and a random sample of the American Society for Industrial Security (ASIS) International members who were security managers for various companies indicated an increase in the use of surveillance as well; both law enforcement and security managers had an increase in security spending following 9/11. About 24 percent of the U.S. companies had purchased CCTV surveillance and video cameras, while nearly 83 percent of ASIS security managers had purchased CCTV surveillance systems (Collins, Cordner, and Scarborough 2004).

The reliance on CCTV surveillance will only continue to grow as the United States struggles to develop and maintain greater control of the observation and monitoring of various public transportation and critical infrastructure systems. This growth is as much affected by the fear of terrorism as it is by the low costs associated with technology, which has not always been the case. Schneier suggests that because of the low cost and ease of integration with computer and networked databases, privacy invasions are much cheaper and efficient to conduct than ever before (Schneier 2003). Now that the technology has become more affordable, reliable, and robust, there is an even greater use in public settings, creating a more significant challenge for our society to balance the need for security with that of individual privacy.

A recent example and one of the most noted pieces of legislation regarding surveillance in this country is the Uniting and Strengthening America by Providing Appropriate Tools Required to Intercept and Obstruct Terrorism (USA PATRIOT) Act of 2001. The USA PATRIOT Act expanded the government's authority to monitor its citizens and reduced checks and balances on that authority, such as judicial oversight. Ironically, the government never demonstrated that limited surveillance contributed to the 9/11 attacks, and much of the new legislation had nothing to do with terrorism (Stanley and Steinhardt 2004). Section 206 of the USA PATRIOT Act gives law enforcement the ability to use "roving" wiretaps to investigate terrorism. While the use of CCTV is not a part of the act, reactions to the more liberal use of wiretaps provides an example of the lack of support for the use of technology that may also be seen with CCTV. Critics of the act, and specifically the wiretap section, warn that Congress will "erode the privacy of everyone by authorizing surveillance techniques that are not based on probable cause" (Edgar 2005).

Specific scrutiny of this issue came in 2005 when President Bush gave the National Security Agency (NSA) permission to apply wiretaps on Americans communicating with people overseas. The president defended his actions by stating they were permissible under law. With regard to this issue, Stanley and Steinhardt (2004) indicate that, "privacy and liberty in the United States are at risk. A combination of lightning-fast technological innovation and the erosion of privacy protections threatens to transform Big Brother from an oft-cited but remote threat into a very real part of American life" (p. 1). Currently, there is still a contentious debate regarding whether the president overstepped his boundaries by directing the NSA to conduct the wiretaps.

Conversely, advocates for the increased use of technology argue that the advancements in surveillance technology increase the security of this country by preserving the American way of life. Specifically, advocates of wiretapping argue that this technology has been used for years in drug and organized-crime investigations, so what makes using the same technology in the fight against terrorism any different? This group believes that wiretaps "are essential in an era where terrorists, like other criminals, switch cell-phone providers to evade detection. It permits a federal judge to relieve the burden of returning to court every time a terrorism suspect switches phone service" (Ryan 2005).

To summarize, myriad surveillance technologies currently exist in this country. Additionally, the viewpoints surrounding the application of those technologies are also varied. The next section presents an analysis of the legal issues on this topic.

Legal Issues

Legal issues surrounding surveillance have focused primarily on privacy and have been guided by the Fourth Amendment to the Constitution and significant Supreme Court cases dealing with several types of surveillance.

The Fourth Amendment to the Constitution states:

> The right of the people to be secure in their persons, houses, papers, and effects against unreasonable searches and seizures, shall not be violated, and no Warrants shall issue, but upon probable cause, supported by Oath or affirmation, and particularly describing the place to

be searched, and the persons or things to be seized.

This amendment, adopted in 1791, was an attempt by the framers of the Constitution to strike a balance between the government doing its job of keeping the public secure and safe while simultaneously ensuring that criminal activity is kept to a minimum. At the time the Fourth Amendment was written, a primary concern in this regard was that of physical trespass. It was easily determined whether a violation of the Fourth Amendment had occurred, because there was some sort of physical structure that a representative of the government had to "cross over" without a warrant supporting probable cause for a search.

Almost 100 years later, Brandeis and Warren (1890) expressed concerns about Fourth Amendment violations occurring with the use of photography. With today's technological advancements, society has gone way past the black box photography of the nineteenth century to the world of body scans, thermal imaging, through-the-wall surveillance, and CCTV, as previously indicated. Some of these technologies have the ability to penetrate solid objects using radio waves. While technology has changed, the laws have not necessarily adequately kept pace.

The United States was given a wake-up call on September 11, 2001. As a nation, we had not experienced the devastation that was seen on that day. Many changes have occurred since then—some with support for the changes, and some without. After the attacks on New York City, Washington, D.C., and the skies over Pennsylvania, approximately one-third of U.S. citizens indicated that they supported increased security measures, with the trade-off being more protection for a safer and secure society with less privacy (Basha 2003). Thus, a large segment of the public is willing to sacrifice some of their civil liberties, including privacy, to have the comfort they felt in a pre- 9/11 world.

The Fourth Amendment is one of the cornerstones of privacy, affording us sanctity in our homes and protection from government violations and intrusion. However, as technology has advanced, circumstances have arisen that prevent the once simple interpretation of the Fourth Amendment and have consequently forced the judiciary to reexamine previous decisions in order to accommodate the high-tech world of today.

Surveillance has long been a tactic used by law enforcement to investigate illegal activities and validate suspicions of wrongdoings. The early use of surveillance relied primarily on human beings as sensors, evaluating with the naked eye whatever was in plain sight. These human sensors have been replaced with sophisticated electronic surveillance systems, and while human sensors are still used in some cases, in the majority of cases surveillance is now by CCTV and x-ray vision, or other more advanced technologies.

Whether or not case law designating the analytical requirements necessary to evaluate the Fourth Amendment and privacy with new technologies has evolved consistently still remains to be seen. The following chronicles a series of cases that have given guidance for the analyses of Fourth Amendment challenges in a day much different than the day Brandeis and Warren analyzed the right to privacy of individuals. These are significant cases examining different forms of surveillance and giving rise to the most recent Supreme Court surveillance case using thermal imaging. The cases are *Olmstead v. United States* (1928), *Goldman v. United States* (1942), *Silverman v. United States* (1961), *Katz v. United States* (1967), *Dow Chemical Corporation v. United States* (1986), and *Kyllo v. United States* (2001). *Olmstead, Goldman,* and *Silverman* provide the foundation from which the Court began in deciding cases involving electronic surveillance. More attention is given to *Katz, Dow Chemical Corporation,* and *Kyllo,* as they appear to have had more significant influence upon law enforcement practice and policy.

Supreme Court Cases

Olmstead v. United States (1928) was the first Supreme Court case involving electronic surveillance technology. Here, law enforcement officers obtained incriminating evidence using a microphone outside of the defendant's office. In this case, the Court held that tapping telephones did not violate the Fourth Amendment because no trespassing of the defendant's physical structure occurred. *Olmstead* initiated the doctrine that electronic surveillance did not constitute a search under the Fourth Amendment because there was no physical trespass. This case also foreshadowed the Court's posture in cases to come by illustrating "the speed, or lack thereof, with which Fourth Amendment inquiry was conducted when technological advances began to make evidence-gathering possible without the necessity of physical intrusion" (Aronov 2004, 5).

The Court applied the *Olmstead* doctrine to *Goldman v. United States* (1942). In this case, two federal agents, with the assistance of the building superintendent, obtained access at night to the defendant's office and to an adjoining office and installed a listening device in the partition wall with a wire to be attached to earphones extending into the adjoining office. This setup was for the purpose of overhearing a conference the defendant was to have the following afternoon. But when it was time for the conference, the apparatus did not work. The agents had another, more sensitive device, a detectaphone that they decided to try. With it, the agents overheard and transcribed portions of conversations between the defendant and his partners on several occasions. The agents could also hear what the defendant said when talking on the telephone from his office. In *Goldman,* the Court held that the use of a detectaphone to overhear conversations did not constitute a search under the Fourth Amendment, again because the information was not obtained by trespass or illegal entry and was not in the defendant's homes, thereby supporting *Olmstead.*

While *Olmstead* and *Goldman* followed the electronic surveillance doctrine, *Silverman v. United States* (1961) took a different turn. Officers in this case used a microphone attached to a pole to eavesdrop on defendants. Although the officers themselves did not physically trespass on the defendant's premises, the Court determined that use by the police of a microphone in a ventilating duct in a house to listen to the defendant's conversations was an unreasonable search, violating the Fourth Amendment. Hence, the Court created a new standard for evaluating Fourth Amendment violations, which in turn was countered by *Katz v. United States* (1967).

Katz v. United States (1967) is the standard for Fourth Amendment interpretation and the most significant case linking the concept of privacy to the Fourth Amendment. In this case, Katz was found guilty of violating a federal statute and sought to have evidence that led to his conviction suppressed. Two Federal Bureau of Investigation (FBI) agents used an electronic device, which could record a telephone conversation, outside a telephone booth in which the defendant was conversing. The Supreme Court, in a reversal of lower court decisions, held that a person in a telephone booth could rely on the protections of the Fourth Amendment. More specifically, the Court stated, "The Fourth Amendment protects people, not places" (*Katz v. United States* 1967, 351). The result of the decision, then, was that physical trespass was no longer an essential element for a Fourth Amendment violation. The Court found that "the Fourth Amendment is not to be read only protecting against physical invasion of certain protected areas, but instead was designed to protect legitimate expectations of the people to privacy and security" (Basha 2003, 4).

The *Katz* decision resulted in a two-prong test for analysis of potential Fourth Amendment violations that includes (1) whether there was a subjective expectation of privacy, and (2) whether the expectation of privacy was recognized by the public as reasonable. *Katz* continues to remain the theoretical benchmark for video surveillance cases, and the Court has continued to interpret the case to extend to persons in their homes, where they have a reasonable expectation of privacy and unlawful surveillance is an intrusion into their dwelling.

Dow Chemical Corporation v. United States (1986) is the leading case in implementing the technological approach. In this case, the Supreme Court held that even though the camera being used to photograph the rooftop enhanced human vision, this action did not necessarily violate the Fourth Amendment. Specifically, the Court indicated that "the taking of aerial photographs of an industrial plant complex from navigable airspace is not a search prohibited by the Fourth Amendment" (Basha 2003, n88). What was at issue in this case was the information that was gathered and whether that information provided intimate details that would be protected under the Fourth Amendment. In contrast to other cases, the *Dow* case did not involve the expectation of privacy and protection of the Fourth Amendment in a person's home. In this case, EPA agents were using advanced photography at the defendant's industrial worksite, not his home.

In *Kyllo v. United States* (2001), the defendant was suspected of growing marijuana in his home, which was an apartment building with two other tenants. High-intensity heat must be used to grow marijuana in an environment like that. A U.S. Department of Interior agent and Oregon National Guardsman used thermal imaging to determine whether excess heat was emanating from Kyllo's residence, which could potentially be due to the defendant growing marijuana in his apartment. Without a search warrant, the law enforcement officials used the AGEMA Thermavision 210 to determine whether excessive heat was coming from the defendant's home, in comparison to the other two units in his building. The instrument identified extreme heat on the roof and a sidewall of Kyllo's apartment. No excessive heat was identified in the other two residences. Consequently, the law enforcement officials presented this information to a magistrate and were issued a search warrant for Kyllo's apartment. As suspected by law enforcement, Kyllo was growing marijuana in his apartment and was subsequently indicted by a federal grand jury based on evidence seized in the search of his home.

Kyllo pled not guilty and moved for suppression of evidence, contending that warrantless use of the thermal imager constituted an unreasonable search, violating his Fourth Amendment rights. The district court in Oregon denied Kyllo's motion, indicating that the use of thermal imaging was not an intrusion into Kyllo's home. The circuit court directed the district court to determine whether the AGEMA Thermovision 210 could detect intimate activities of individuals resulting in excessive body heat or simply points where heat was identified escaping from the building. The district court found that the device could not detect any activities of individuals in Kyllo's apartment and that the expectation of privacy in those circumstances would not be deemed reasonable by society. Therefore, the motion to suppress the evidence was denied. Kyllo appealed to the circuit court, which concluded, using the two-prong *Katz* test, that the use of thermal imaging on Kyllo's home did not constitute a Fourth Amendment violation. The Supreme Court granted certiorari to determine whether the warrantless use of thermal imaging of private residences constituted a violation under the Fourth Amendment.

In a 5–4 decision, the Court, using the technological approach, held that "the use of sense enhancing devices does not constitute a search under the Fourth Amendment, as long as the devices do no more than aid law enforcement in gathering information that could otherwise be acquired using their own sensory perceptions" (Basha 2003).

The Court based their decision on two primary points. The first point was the limits of the use of technology by law enforcement and drew on the technological approach analysis to evaluate the thermal imaging device. The second point was the privacy and sanctity of one's home, which the Court contended should be ultimately protected by the Fourth Amendment.

Kyllo v. United States held that the use of thermal imaging devices constitutes an unlawful search and therefore violates the Fourth Amendment. *Kyllo* was a departure from numerous previous lower-court decisions in which the use of thermal imaging had been deemed acceptable, without violating the Fourth Amendment. Previous decisions had relied on three analogous evaluative criteria: (1) the waste heat analogy, (2) the canine sniff analogy, and (3) the technological approach (Basha 2003).

The waste heat analogy likens the excess heat identified using thermal imaging to garbage left on the curbside of one's home. Once garbage is placed on the curbside, citizens have no expectation of privacy or protection from search under the Fourth Amendment. The garbage is viewed as outside the "cartilage of one's home" (*California v. Greenwood* 1988). Even if a citizen had an expectation of privacy for the garbage left on the curbside, "society would not consider that expectation as reasonable" (Basha 2003, 5).

Canines are used by law enforcement to detect illegal drugs, among other things. The canine sniff analogy posits that just like the odors from drugs are identified by canines, the heat that emanates from a given source is detected using thermal imaging, so using this method does not constitute a search under the Fourth Amendment.

The technological approach uses previous Supreme Court cases instead of comparing thermal imaging to other forms of warrantless searches acceptable under the Fourth Amendment. Using this approach, the technological capabilities of a device are examined as well as the information gathered from use of that device (Basha 2003). So, initially the Court determined that a warrantless search of a house is unconstitutional. In the majority of the surveillance cases, a primary consideration is whether visual surveillance constitutes a search under the Fourth Amendment. Modern cases do not advocate that law enforcement officers ignore visible observations of a home from outside on a public street. However, the courts suggest that the key factor in determining whether a visible surveillance constitutes a search a violation of the Fourth Amendment is the two-prong test articulated in *Katz*.

Basha (2003) indicates that *Kyllo* has and will continue to have limited effect on the Fourth Amendment technology challenges because it restricted Fourth Amendment protection to the home and did not apply to other technologies currently in use or having the potential for being used outside the home.

Conclusion

The question of how the courts will treat CCTV in the future remains to be seen. While other types of surveillance technologies have been tested in the courts, CCTV has not been as rigorously evaluated. This situation is perhaps ironic when one considers that in 2003, 26 million survey cameras were installed, with 11 million in the United States. In addition, estimates indicated that an individual in the United Kingdom is filmed by more than 300 cameras in a given day (Farmer and Mann 2003). Spinello (2002) predicts that privacy will be the key, but not to the exclusion of the desires of citizens to be safe and secure in their homes:

> Few of us are really seers of the future, but it does not take much foresight to recognize that the slow evanescence of personal privacy is not likely to abate any time soon. In ten or fifteen years we may wistfully look back to the abundant privacy we enjoyed at the inception of this new millennium. The reason for privacy's gradual demise are complex and varied, ranging from sheer indolence and indifference to our enthusiasm for embracing the huge benefits that the new economy has to offer without reckoning the costs. The surrender of privacy might seem like a small price to pay for more convenient and secure shopping, but many of us may regret those trade-offs when there is little privacy left. Privacy has always been an abstract and almost ineffable value, and this makes it easier to sacrifice for tangible and more immediate benefits. (Spinello 2002, 202).

So, it is up to us to do the cost-benefit analysis and decide what is most important. Some of the decision making will be in our control, and some will not. Important consideration must be undertaken to evaluate just how much of our privacy we are willing to live without.

Stanley and Steinhardt (2004) indicate that in order to save our privacy, which "is not yet dead, (but) is on life support" (p. 73) four things must occur: (1) changing the terms of the debate, (2) enacting comprehensive privacy laws, (3) developing laws that will keep up with technological ad-

vancement, and (4) reviving the Fourth Amendment. Changing the terms of the debate means to consider all the means of surveillance versus capabilities of individual technologies such as CCTV. It is imperative that the "total picture" of surveillance be understood to fully grasp the magnitude of what these technologies used together can provide in terms of information about individuals, irrespective of their privacy. While there are limited laws, such as those dealing with wiretapping, that adequately protect citizen's privacy, the laws are being weakened.

Furthermore, new laws are not being enacted that are strong and protect our total privacy. This is especially apparent in the private sector, oftentimes at the request of the government. The United States lags behind most European countries in developing comprehensive privacy laws that protect citizens against private sector abuse. It is imperative that as technology develops, new laws develop to support the use of these technologies. Historically, technological advancement has been slower, thus giving the Courts and legislators more time to assess the adequacy and protection of the laws. This is not the case today, because of the expediency with which technologies are being created and improved on. Finally, preventing the further erosion of the Fourth Amendment is critical. As with other amendments, the Fourth Amendment must be understood in contemporary terms, not as it was in colonial America, where British authorities used "general warrants" (Stanley and Steinhardt 2004, 76) to thoroughly search suspected rebels, marking some of the first invasions of privacy. Laws must keep pace with technological advancement.

References

Aronov, R. F. 2004. "Privacy in a Public Setting: The Constitutionality of Street Surveillance." *Bridgeport Law Review* 22:769–797.

Basha, R. M. 2003. "*Kyllo v. United States:* The Fourth Amendment Triumphs Over Technology." *Brandeis Law Journal* 41:939–953.

Brandeis, L., and S. Warren. 1890. "The Right to Privacy." *Harvard Law Review* 14(5):193–220.

Collins, P. A., G. Cordner, and K. E. Scarborough. September 2004. *Scope and Trends in Private Security.* Paper presented at the annual meeting of the American Society for Industrial Security-International, Dallas, Texas.

Edgar, T. H. 2005. "Memo to Interested Persons Outlining What Congress Should Do About the Patriot Act Sunsets." http://www.aclu.org/safefree/general/17555leg20050328.html.

Farmer, D., and C. Mann. 2003. "Surveillance Nation." *Technology Review,* Cambridge, MA.

Foster, R. E. 2005. *Police Technology.* Upper Saddle River, NJ: Pearson Prentice Hall.

Hall, W. 2005. *Clear and Present Dangers—Larta Institute.* http://www.larta.org/LAVox/2001/9-24_AviationSecurity.htm.

Hunt, A., C. Tillery, and N. Wild. 2001. *Through the Wall Surveillance.* http://www.ncjrs.org/pdffiles1/nij/07_01.pdf.

International Association of Chiefs of Police (IACP). 2001. *Executive Brief: The Uses of CCTV/Video Cameras in Law Enforcement, Executive Summary.* http://www.theiacp.org/documents/pdfs/Publications/UseofCCTV.pdf.

Nieto, M., K. Johnston-Dodds, and C. Simmons. 2002. *Public and Private Applications of Video Surveillance and Biometric Technologies.* Sacramento: Californian Research Bureau.

Ryan, K. V. 2005. "Patriot Act Has Major Advantages." *Daily Californian,* May: 6.

Schneier, B. 2003. *Beyond Fear: Thinking Sensibly About Security in an Uncertain World.* New York: Copernicus Books.

Spinello, R. A. 2002. *Regulating Cyberspace: The Policies and Technologies of Control.* Westport, CT: Quorum Books.

Stanley, J., and B. Steinhardt. 2004. "Bigger Monster, Weaker Chains: The Growth of American Surveillance Society." In K. B. Darmer, R. M. Baird, and S. E. Rosenbaum (eds.), *Civil Liberties vs. National Security in a Post-9/11 World.* Amherst, NY: Prometheus Books.

Cases Cited

California v. Greenwood, 486 U.S. 35 (1988).

Dow Chemical Company v. United States, 476 U.S. 227 (1986).

Goldman v. United States, 316 U.S. 129 (1942).

Katz v. United States, 389 U.S. 347 (1967).

Kyllo v. United States, 533 U.S. 27 (2001).

Olmstead v. United States, 277 U.S. 438 (1928).

Silverman v. United States, 365 U.S. 505 (1961).

Related Websites

Surveillance and Society
http://www.surveillance-and-society.org
American Civil Liberties Union (Surveillance)
http://www.aclu.org/safefree/spying/index.html
Privacy International—United Kingdom Surveillance Page
http://pi.gn.apc.org/countries/uk/surveillance/
Preserving Life and Liberty
http://www.lifeandliberty.gov
Electronic Privacy Information Center
http://www.epic.org
Center for Democracy and Technology
http://www.cdt.org/security/

Discussion Questions

1. With the surveillance technologies presented in this article as examples, compare and contrast the advantages and disadvantages of the implementation of these technologies in U.S. society.

2. Discuss potential reasons for society's hesitancy in adopting technologies such as the body scan during airport security screenings, but their conformity to invasive physical pat-downs.

3. Why do events such as the attacks against the United States on September 11, 2001, and the bombings in London in 2005 make citizens proponents of surveillance technologies they may not have been in favor of the day before the event?

4. Do you agree with the decision in the *Kyllo* case? Discuss potential advantages and disadvantages to the decision and the potential implications for U.S. society.

5. Discuss the *Katz* two-prong test for analysis of potential Fourth Amendment violations and why physical trespass was no longer an essential element for a Fourth Amendment violation under this ruling. ✦

Chapter 3
The USA PATRIOT Act

A Review of the Major Components

Jim Ruiz and Kathleen H. Winters

In this chapter, the authors present a section-by-section analysis of the major components of the USA PATRIOT Act. The PATRIOT Act was put into place after the September 11, 2001, terrorist attacks, in an effort to address inter- and intra-agency communication regarding the sharing of vital counter-terrorism measures and intelligence and to grant certain government agencies more investigatory power. In particular, the act had a large impact on surveillance and privacy laws. The authors expound on key considerations in light of First Amendment freedom of speech rights, Fourth Amendment expectations of privacy, and due process issues in regards to criminal investigations and search warrants.

The authors summarize the key provisions and limitations of each section of the PATRIOT Act, which covers enhanced domestic security against terrorism, enhanced surveillance procedures, international money laundering, protection of the international borders, removal of investigative obstacles, and the strengthening of criminal laws against terrorism. In an analysis of the PATRIOT Act, one must consider the balance of constitutionally guaranteed individual rights with the government's power and responsibility to protect the citizenry. While reading the following, it is important to keep this question in mind: In facilitating the war on terrorism, does the PATRIOT Act truly protect the innocent by integrating resources in the pursuit of justice, or does it do so at the expense of people's constitutional rights?

An Act

To deter and punish terrorist acts in the United States and around the world, to enhance law enforcement investigatory tools, and for other purposes.

These words constitute the opening line of H.R. 3162, or *the USA PATRIOT Act*. The original title, *Uniting and Strengthening America by Providing Appropriate Tools Required to Intercept and Obstruct Terrorism (USA PATRIOT) Act of 2001,* was considered too cumbersome. The act was responsible for an abundance of legislative changes, chiefly a major increase in the surveillance and investigative authority given to U.S. law enforcement and intelligence agencies.

One of the main objectives of the act was to remedy a lack of communication between federal law enforcement and intelligence agencies that were all individually trying to fight terrorism. According to *The 9/11 Commission Report* (2004), "coping with terrorism was not (and is not) the sole province of any component of the U.S. government" and thus "some coordinating mechanism is necessary" (p. 98). The terrorist attacks on September 11, 2001, demonstrated how critical inter- and intra-agency communications are in order to prevent and respond to such attacks. The act was created, in part, to establish a "coordinating mechanism" to combat terrorism by employing the combined efforts of all U.S. law enforcement and intelligence agencies, rather than rely on several independent agencies within the United States. In the new transnational arena of terrorism, it has become obvious that all these agencies must share resources and information if the United States is to effectively wage a "war on terror."

The two agencies vital in this effort are the Federal Bureau of Investigation (FBI) and the Central Intelligence Agency (CIA). The lack of interagency communication was one of the major issues that both Democrats and Republicans wanted to address with the passage of the act. Senator John Edwards (D-NC) stated, "We simply cannot prevail in the battle against terrorism if the right hand of our government has no idea what the left hand is doing" (Ball 2004, 48). Additionally, Speaker of the House, Dennis Hastert (R-IL) stated,

> I am most pleased that this bipartisan compromise knocks down current legal barriers that prevent the FBI, the CIA, and other law enforcement officials from sharing information with one another. . . . Our goal must be stopping terror- ists . . . rather than wasting time, energy, and resources fighting bureaucratic legal hurdles. (Ball 2004, 48)

The lack of interagency communication was a by-product of multiple federal law en- forcement and intelligence agencies gather- ing information on terrorism but failing to share that intelligence with other depart- ments, much less with other agencies. For example, citing security concerns, the CIA often compartmentalized its information to lessen the likelihood of interception (*9/11 Commission Report* 2004). Likewise, the Na- tional Security Agency (NSA) exhibited an "almost obsessive protection of sources and methods" (*9/11 Commission Report* 2004, 88), thus forcing other agencies to possibly duplicate investigations to obtain informa- tion that had already been collected by the NSA or other federal agencies. Additionally, "pressure from the Office of Intelligence Pol- icy Review, FBI leadership, and the FISA Court built barriers between agents—even agents serving on the same squads" (*9/11 Commission Report* 2004, 79). Furthermore, the distinction between intelligence gather- ing and criminal prosecution "regulated the manner in which such information could be shared from the intelligence side of the house to the criminal side" (*9/11 Commis- sion Report* 2004, 79). All of these factors combined to inhibit the investigation and prosecution of suspected terrorists, espe- cially those involved in domestic terrorism. Historically, the NSA has been forbidden to perform domestic investigations. Federal law forbade the NSA to "deliberately collect data on U.S. citizens or on persons in the United States without a warrant based on foreign intelligence requirements" (*9/11 Commission Report* 2004, 87). Thus the FBI was left with collecting data regarding U.S. citizens living both abroad and domestically.

This responsibility included monitoring communications between U.S. citizens and foreign nationals (*9/11 Commission Report* 2004). It is believed that a lack of communi- cation between the NSA and the FBI enabled U.S. citizens and foreign nationals to com- municate unmonitored when some could have been legally monitored.

A second major purpose of the act was to allow government agencies more freedom and power when investigating terrorism within the borders of the United States. The national security strategy upon which the United States had been operating was cre- ated in the late 1940s. Needless to say, the na- tional and international scene has changed dramatically since the end of the Cold War. Hence, the United States was in need of a new national security policy, mostly because of the new climate of terrorism. Prior to Sep- tember 11, 2001, the United States was fo- cused on combating international terrorism. However, the focus has shifted and is now heavily concentrated on both domestic and international terrorism. Domestic terrorism has a tendency to be more difficult to expose, let alone prosecute. That may be why Sena- tor Joe Bidden (D-DE) stated, "The FBI could get a wiretap to investigate the Mafia, but they could not get one to investigate ter- rorists. To put it bluntly, that was crazy! What's good for the mob should be good for terrorists" (Ball 2004, 48). The fact that do- mestic terrorism was rarely used in the crim- inal statutes made policy and procedure re- garding the investigation of such terrorism scarce.

The act brought about broad modifica- tions to United States law consisting of amendments to many existing statutes. The 342-page act contains 10 main headings to- taling 196 separate sections. Clearly, it is be- yond the scope of this article to provide an in-depth analysis of the entire act. With that in mind, we have addressed what we con- sider to be the most salient sections that ap- pear to have a direct effect on the rights and privileges of most U.S. citizens. Titles VI and VII will not be addressed because they per- tain to victim compensation and informa- tion sharing between federal, state, and local law enforcement agencies.

The Act's Effect on Surveillance and Privacy Laws

The act greatly increased the federal government's power to closely monitor and capture communications. In that regard, three key laws establish the basis for the government's acquisition of communications: Title III, the Electronic Communications Privacy Act (ECPA), and the Foreign Intelligence Surveillance Act (FISA).

Title III

Title III controls the contents of communications and requires probable cause, a lofty legal criterion to meet, in order for a judge to issue an order for real-time capture of voice and data communication content. The Supreme Court ruled that the contents of a communication are allowed complete Fourth Amendment protection. As such, the government's right to access content is restricted by constitutional search and seizure requisites. In doing so, Title III places strict boundaries on the government's ability to acquire communication content. Thus, a law enforcement agency may intercept content only upon issuance of a court order after a showing of probable cause that (a) a person is perpetrating a specific crime; (b) communications regarding the enumerated offense will be accessed; and (c) the location specified is usually used by the person or used in relation with the alleged crime.

Title III also stipulates that (a) only certain officials can sanction such interception; (b) the seizure is approved for a restricted period of time; and (c) such interception is subject to a statutory exclusionary rule in that all information acquired in contravention of the wiretap statute cannot be admitted into evidence in any judicial or administrative proceeding. On the other hand, the Supreme Court ruled that no constitutionally established privacy interest exists in the telephone numbers intercepted by a pen register or trap and trace device.

Electronic Communications Privacy Act (ECPA)

The ECPA restricts government admittance to stored email and other electronic communications. The pen register statute within the ECPA regulates real-time seizure of telephone numbers dialed or transmitted via landline. Installation of the device necessitates a court order, but probable cause is not needed to obtain the required court order. This occurs absent judicial discretion, and the court must validate the surveillance upon government certification. Counsel for the government is required only to declare to the court that the intelligence expected to be acquired will be germane to an ongoing criminal investigation. As such, the pen register and trap and trace statute is without several of the privacy protections contained in the wiretap statute.

Foreign Intelligence Surveillance Act (FISA)

The FISA empowers the government to conduct electronic surveillance on any individual including, American citizens. This surveillance may be conducted within the United States simply by acquiring an order from a judge by a showing of probable cause that the target is a foreign power or an agent of a foreign power. Because FISA pertains principally to the government's power in foreign intelligence and counterintelligence cases, it does not provide many of the safeguards necessary under the federal wiretap statute.

Enhanced Domestic Security Against Terrorism

As with most legislation, one of the first orders of business is funding. Section 101 of the act established a "Counterterrorism Fund" to reimburse any Department of Justice office for costs encountered in connection with reestablishing locations damaged or destroyed as the result of any domestic or international terrorism incident. This section also provides support for the prosecution of "domestic or international terrorism" as well as establishing the payment of rewards "without limitation" to achieve these goals. It amended Section 203 of the International Emergency Powers Act (50 U.S.C. 1702) by permitting the president to "confiscate any property, subject to the jurisdiction of the United States, of any foreign person, foreign organization, or foreign country that he determines has planned, authorized, aided, or engaged in terrorism" when the United States "is engaged in armed hostilities or has been attacked by a foreign country or foreign nationals." The president may exercise these powers through the courts privately absent "any right to judicial review." This section also includes a statement condemning discrimination against Arab and Muslim Americans.

Enhanced Surveillance Procedures

Terrorism and Computer Crimes as Predicate Offenses Allowing Seizure of Communications Under the Wiretap Act

Section 201 grants "Authority to Intercept Oral, Wire, or Electronic Communications Relating to Terrorism." With this authority, federal agencies are given more latitude in procuring search warrants to seize communications thought to be relevant to terrorism. In such cases, the burden of probable cause, which is typically necessary for a search warrant, is skirted. Instead, the burden is mere relevancy to a terrorism or intelligence investigation. If a person is suspected of these crimes, suspicion alone provides sufficient grounds for the government to obtain a wiretap of that individual's communications. Under FISA, the government had considerable power to get a wiretap of a suspected terrorist. This revision allows wiretapping of a United States citizen suspected of domestic terrorism.

Section 202 takes this concept even further, as it explicitly includes other computer-related offenses as sufficient grounds to obtain a warrant based on a relation to domestic terrorism. This, in turn, affects the standard used to determine the suitability of a warrant. However, with the addition of certain computer offenses, these warrants are possible to obtain for criminal investigations, rather than be limited to intelligence investigations. Section 202 added "a felony violation of section 1030 (relating to computer fraud and abuse)" as a crime supplying grounds for a wiretap application. Included under Section 1030 are intentional, unauthorized access to a protected government computer to obtain and communicate classified information for a clandestine foreign power "with reason to believe that such information so obtained could be used to the injury of the United States or to the advantage of any foreign nation"; access to a protected computer causing more than $5,000 damage; access to a protected computer with the intent to extort; or any second offense. Sections 201 and 202 did not alter the definition of communications subject to intercept or the benchmark that the government must attain in order to get an intercept. Domestic terrorism-based warrants are discussed in more depth in the following sections.

Greater Distribution of Information Acquired During Criminal Investigations

Since one of the goals of the PATRIOT Act was to enable greater communication among federal agencies, Section 203 could be considered most geared toward that particular goal. Section 203 permits the sharing of criminal investigation information among agencies as long as it is pertinent to an intelligence or counterintelligence investigation. This information includes testimony given during a grand jury indictment, which is characteristically barred to outside sources.

Section 203 revised the Federal Rules of Criminal Procedure to allow revelation of "matters occurring before the grand jury" when they "involve foreign intelligence or counterintelligence" to "any federal law enforcement, intelligence, protective, immigration, national defense, or national security official in order to assist the official receiving that information in the performance of his official duties." Prior to the act, disclosure was allowed only (1) when directed by a court in association with a judicial proceeding; (2) when allowed by a court by application of the defendant, or upon a demonstration that the information reveals a violation of a state criminal law; or (3) when revealed by the prosecutor to another grand jury.

The act now compels that disclosure be made under the new exception, under seal, to the court. Once again, the standard is simple relevancy to an intelligence investigation, rather than suspicion of terrorist involvement. Although this section opens doors of communication between federal agencies, the question remains as to how closed the doors of a grand jury indictment really are.

Section 203 also changed 18 U.S.C. 2517, which regulated the permissible revelation and utilization of intercepted communications. Now, intercepted information linked to "foreign intelligence or counterintelligence" may be revealed to "any federal law enforcement, intelligence, protective, immigration, national defense, or national security official" and that "such disclosure is appropriate to the proper performance of the official duties of the officer making or receiving the disclosure," and it can be made use of by any law enforcement officer duly in custody of the information to aid "in the performance of his official duties."

Voice-Mail Messages

Section 204 of the act revised Title III and the Stored Communications Access Act in that stored-up voice-mail communications can be acquired by the government through a search warrant rather than the more rigorous wiretap orders. Section 204 also places voice mail under Section 209, which allows nationwide search warrants. Yet, voice communications collected on an answering machine tape remain beyond the reach of either statute.

Additional Government Authority to Combat Terrorism

Section 205 of the act allows for greater employment of translators by the FBI and designated five more judges to be seated on the FISA Court, increasing the number from 7 to 11 seats. These conditions are proposed to amplify the FBI's human intelligence powers and to supply supplementary judicial management of enhanced FISA authority. Both revisions assist the government in thwarting terrorist acts and in sustaining a system scrutinizing infringement on citizens' civil liberties.

Roving Wiretaps

The government's ability to obtain roving wiretaps was expanded by Section 206 of the act. This section permits the interception of any communications placed to or by an intelligence target with no identification of the specific telephone line, computer, or other facility to be monitored. Previous statutes compelled third parties designated in court-ordered surveillance to supply any support essential to carry out the surveillance. The amendment broadens that responsibility to unidentified and unstipulated third parties.

This new, broad power to issue such orders may well have a major influence on those who gain access to the Internet by way of open services, such as libraries, university computer labs, and cyber cafés. Requiring only suspicion that an intelligence target could use such a service, the FBI can now scrutinize all communications broadcast at the facility. The situation is complicated in that the receiver of the assistance order (library, university computer lab, or cyber café) would be forbidden from divulging the fact that monitoring is taking place. The revised roving wiretap orders appear to circumvent the Fourth Amendment's requisite that any search warrant, above all, describes the place to be searched.

Roving wiretaps have been in place for criminal cases since 1986. However, Section 206 does not require law enforcement agencies to identify the actual target, while previously the target was required to be specified. Nor does the act require that knowledge be gained as to whether the target is actually using a specific telephone line.

Expanded Scope of Subpoenas for Electronic Communications Records

Prior to the act, law enforcement used a subpoena to gain access to the name, address, local and long distance telephone toll billing records, telephone number or other subscriber number or identity, the length of service, and the type of services the subscriber or customer utilized from an Internet service provider (ISP). Section 210 of the act increases the kind of information that a provider must divulge to law enforcement to include time and duration of sessions, any allotted network address, and method or origin of payment. This enhanced power to use subpoenas instead of court orders to gain a wider and more revealing grade of information is not restricted to investigations of suspected terrorist activity.

Cable Companies and Electronic Surveillance

Section 211 revised Title III such that when a cable company supplies telephone or Internet services, it must abide by the laws concerning interception and disclosure of communications by other telephone companies or ISPs. The new law overrides the initial specifications of the Cable Act regarding mandatory and intentional release of subscriber information, but the revision does provide an exemption for "customer cable television viewing activity."

'Sneak and Peek': The Authority to Conduct Secret Searches

Section 213 of the act abolishes the obligation that law enforcement supply an individual who is subject to a search warrant with simultaneous announcement of the search. This new secret search proviso is valid where the court "finds reasonable cause to believe that providing immediate notification of the execution of the warrant may have an adverse effect." The new power is principally intended to sanction deferred announcement of a search. It also allows confiscation of any tangible property or communications where the court finds "reasonable necessity" for this seizure. The law calls for notice to be given within a "reasonable period." However, the court may lengthen that period for what the section terms as "good cause."

This modification pertains to all government searches for anything that "constitutes evidence of a criminal offense in violation of the laws of the United States" and is not restricted to investigations of terrorist endeavors. Prior to this amendment, the law sanctioned deferred notice of a search only in a small number of circumstances, such as clandestine electronic surveillance.

Section 213 has no "sunset"; it does not expire. Since the section is already law, the only way it can be repealed is if the Supreme Court rules it unconstitutional. However, this may be fairly difficult, since if a person has no knowledge a search occurred, how can that person challenge the constitutionality of that search?

Liberalized Use of Pen Register/Trap and Trace Devices Under FISA

Section 214 of the act does away with the statutory obligation that prior to securing a pen register/trap and trace order under the FISA, the government demonstrate that the surveillance target is an agent of a foreign power. Consequently, the government acquired a pen register/trap and trace device only for an investigation to collect foreign intelligence information, without a demonstration that the device has, is, or will be made use of by a foreign agent or by a person committing international terrorism or clandestine intelligence operations.

The amendment eliminates the constitutional grounds for the requirements that were relevant to foreign intelligence surveillance. However, the act does incorporate a proviso barring use of FISA pen register surveillance in any situation against an American citizen when the investigation is performed "solely on the basis of activities protected by the First Amendment."

Section 214 is almost parallel to Section 206, which refers to the use of roving wiretaps. The majority of the provisions governing Section 206 also apply to Section 214. The main difference is that Section 214 pertains to specific rather than roving wiretaps. The most substantial addition is Section 214's elimination of the necessity to present evidence that the person to be wiretapped is actually in the service of a foreign country. With this elimination, probable cause is no longer necessary to obtain a warrant for the use of a pen register or tap and trace device. Instead, mere relevancy is again used as the standard necessary to obtain a warrant.

Tangible Things, aka 'The Library Provision'

Under Section 215 of the act, the FBI is given the power to apply for an order "requiring the production of any tangible things" that would be pertinent to an investigation of international terrorism or clandestine intelligence activities. These things would include books, records, papers, documents, and other matters. While the amendment is entitled "Access to Certain Business Records for Foreign Intelligence and International Terrorism Investigations," this power is much wider and is relevant to any records pertinent to the individual. This amendment takes precedence over state library confidentiality laws and allows the FBI to force delivery of business, medical, educational, and library records devoid of showing "probable cause." The government is only required to declare that the records might be connected to a current investigation linked to terrorism or intelligence activities. Persons served with a search warrant originating under FISA rules cannot reveal, under penalty of law, the knowledge of the warrant or the information that records were turned over to the government. This rider includes a significant passage constraining the possible exploitation of the law. Even though the act removed the condition that any records asked for be relevant to an agent of a foreign power or to a foreign power, the act bans the investigation of an American citizen exclusively on the premise of activities protected by the First Amendment. The act preserves the constraint of preexisting law, allowing access to records only upon court order.

The extent to which secrecy is maintained may be demonstrated by the procedure used to obtain the order. First, a law enforcement agent approaches a federal judge to obtain a court order permitting a seizure of records. The judge is then required to permit the seizure of records if the standard is met. The standard set forth by the act is that the information be necessary "to protect against international terrorism or clandestine intelligence activities." The judge has no discretion in the matter as long as the information is relevant for a terrorism or intelligence investigation purpose. Additionally, once the records are seized, the person (or persons) is under an obligation not to tell anyone about the seizure. This gag order also restricts communication with an attorney regarding such a seizure. However, this provision does

protect against a person warning associates about an investigation or pending seizure of records. If a person is unaware that his or her associates have had records seized, he or she is less likely to destroy records prior to their seizure.

The Act and Online Privacy: Pen Registers, the Internet, and Carnivore

The act's impact on online privacy is substantial. It enhances the capability of law enforcement agencies to set up pen registers and trap and trace devices,[1] as well as the installation of such instruments to document all computer routing, addressing, and signaling information. Before the act was signed into law, the statute permitting the use of pen registers and trap and trace devices regulated real-time capturing of telephone numbers dialed or otherwise sent out on a landline to which such a device was attached. The act broadens the government's capability to acquire access to personal financial and student information devoid of any trace of unlawful activity. Although a court order is required to install such a device, a showing of probable cause is not required. Judicial discretion is absent because the statute that permits monitoring merely requires certification by a government attorney that the information expected to be acquired by the device is pertinent to an ongoing criminal investigation.

Section 216 appreciably extends the power of law enforcement to use trap and trace and pen register devices. Preceding law regarding their use was drawn up to be relevant to the telephone business; consequently, the writing in the statute speaks only to the gathering of numbers dialed on a telephone line as well as the telephone number from which the call originated.

Under the new legislation, a *pen register* is identified as a mechanism or method that records or decodes dialing, routing, addressing, or signaling information sent by any device or service from which a wire or electronic communication is transmitted. A *trap and trace device* is identified as a mechanism or method that acquires incoming electronic or other impulses that identify the originating number or other dialing, routing, addressing, and signaling information expected to recognize the source of a wire or electronic communication. The new law expands the information characteristics that can be obtained, thereby extending pen register functions to the Internet, electronic mail, and web surfing, as well as all other types of electronic communications.

Assessment of this expansion of power is not easy to measure because the legal clarity is lacking regarding the kinds of information allowed to be intercepted, and the language is subject to wide-ranging interpretations. Although the provision proscribes the capture of content, it fails to satisfactorily account for the singular character of information captured electronically, which includes data far more enlightening than phone numbers. For example, URLs created while surfing the web frequently possess much more information and could not possibly be considered the equal of a telephone number.

When the FBI first gave details of their use of the Carnivore[2] online-detection software, congressional members expressed great concern as well as a desire to explore the questions surrounding its use and their desire to draft suitable legislation governing its use. To assist in that course of action, former Attorney General Janet Reno declared that a Justice Department review panel would address concerns relative to Carnivore and that its suggestions would be shared with the public. By the time Reno left office, her promise had not been fulfilled.

When John Ashcroft took over, he did not honor that promise. Instead, he delegated completion of the review process to a top department official. Unfortunately, September 11, 2001, occurred before the end of the review. Consequently, Congress lacked the assistance of the promised findings and suggestions before passing the act. Because Carnivore supplies the FBI with access to the communications of all subscribers of a supervised ISP and not simply the target authorized by the court, it brings up significant privacy issues.

The act includes a condition compelling law enforcement officers to file, under seal, with the court documentation of installations of pen register/trap and trace devices.

This amendment offers some degree of judicial oversight on the use of this greater surveillance power.

Interception of Computer Trespasser Communications

Prior to the act, purposely intercepting or revealing the contents of any communications unless such intercept conformed to the requirements of the wiretap statute was illegal except if the capture and revelation rested within one of a number of statutory exceptions. Section 217 of the act created a new exception by allowing government interception of the "communications of a computer trespasser" as long as the owner or operator of a "protected computer" sanctions the interception. A "protected computer" consists of any "which is used in interstate or foreign commerce or communication." As written and because of the Internet, this would seem to encompass virtually any computer. This provision allows wiretapping of the intruder's communications devoid of judicial oversight, and, unlike most federal communication intercepts, no impartial supervision is required from a source external to the investigation.

The act leaves the determination squarely at the feet of law enforcement and the system's owner or operator. When an intercept does not end in prosecution, the intercept's targets will not receive an occasion to contest the action by way of a suppression proceeding, because they will never have been aware that their communications were subject to warrantless interception. Then again, the act does incorporate an exception barring surveillance of a person known by the owner of the protected computer "to have an existing contractual relationship with the owner or operator of the protected computer for access to all or part of the protected computer."

Lowering the Standard for Foreign Intelligence Surveillance

Section 218 of the act increases the purpose of FISA to those circumstances in which foreign intelligence collection is simply "a significant" objective of an investigation, instead of the only or central purpose of an investigation, as written in the earlier FISA statute. No definition is provided for the term "significant." These more permissive standards are claimed appropriate because FISA's provisions assist in the gathering of foreign intelligence information, instead of criminal evidence that revises the constitutional balance mirrored in the previous legal procedure controlling electronic surveillance. This section allows information to be gathered without probable cause that a crime has been or will be committed and to be used in a criminal trial.

Single Jurisdiction Search Warrants

Section 219 institutes the use of single jurisdiction search warrants. Previously, whenever a law enforcement agency wanted to conduct a search, it had to procure a search warrant from a judge in the jurisdiction in which the search was to be conducted. However, the act requires that a law enforcement agency need only obtain a single warrant in order to conduct a search in multiple jurisdictions. This revision alleviates much red tape in procuring multiple search warrants for a single investigation occurring in multiple jurisdictions. A person wishing to challenge the validity of such a search warrant must go to the judge and jurisdiction where the warrant was authorized.

Nationwide Application of Surveillance Orders and Search Warrants

Before the act, laws concerning wiretaps and pen register/trap and trace devices approved implementation of a court order only within the geographic jurisdiction of the court issuing the order. Sections 216 and 220 increase the court's jurisdictional power to sanction installation of a surveillance device anywhere in the United States. Should a distant service provider wish to challenge a court order, he or she must come before the issuing court and object to legal or procedural defects.

Section 220 of the act amends the Federal Rules of Criminal Procedure and expands the jurisdictional power of a court to permit search warrants outside of a judicial district when investigating domestic or interna-

tional terrorism. Allowing nationwide application of search warrants increases the range of surveillance orders, thus making it difficult for those served with such warrants to object to legal or procedural defects.

Civil Liability

Section 223 attempts to balance the government's power with civil sanctions if misuse or abuse of granted authority occurs. It is expected that the use of "sneak and peek" and single jurisdiction search warrants will make such allegations infrequent. If a target is unaware that information has been seized, it is unlikely that he or she will bring forth a challenge of abuse. Additionally, as mentioned previously, single-jurisdiction warrants inhibit a person's ability to challenge them.

Section 223 limits utilization of the information to an appropriate investigation, and legal sanctions may be imposed for wrongful use or unauthorized disclosure of the information. It makes available civil liability for unlawful revelation of information acquired through surveillance, which helps limit exploitation of communications captured by means of lawful surveillance.

Sunset Provision

Section 224 of the act included a sunset provision, ending a number of the amendments boosting electronic surveillance power on December 31, 2005. Since the law provides the government with surveillance capability much greater than before, a sunset was believed vital to ascertain how properly the tools work, how successful they have been, and how correctly they have been used. Of those listed above, the sunset provision did not pertain to the extension of pen register/trap and trace power to the Internet; authority to share grand jury information; expansion of law enforcement authority over cable providers; expanded scope of subpoenas for electronic evidence; authority for delaying notice of the execution of a warrant; and expansion of jurisdictional authority of search warrants for terrorism investigations. The reauthorization of the sunset provision will be discussed later.

International Money Laundering Abatement and Antiterrorist Financing Act of 2001

As Section III of the act bears more on United States banking transactions with foreign persons, foreign organizations, or foreign countries suspected of direct or indirect support of terrorist organizations, we will highlight only the major areas. Though this section outlines measures and provisions for financial institutions with regard to international transactions, particular emphasis is placed on money laundering as well as prohibitions on transactions with foreign "shell banks."

Section 316 of the act provides the forfeiture procedure for assets held in U.S. banks by foreign nationals, organizations, and countries, as well as providing the procedure for contesting such forfeitures. Amendments relating to reporting suspicious banking activities carry the same restrictions of non-notification of the suspected individual regarding the report. This section also outlines provisions and penalties for counterfeiting domestic and foreign currency and also applies to any person outside of the United States who engages in any prohibited acts contained in this section.

Protecting the Border

Waiver of Hiring Caps

Section 401 of the act authorizes the U.S. attorney general to waive any hiring caps on personnel assigned to the Immigration and Naturalization Service on the Northern Border. Section 402 provided $50 million to accomplish that task, and Section 403 granted the Immigration and Naturalization Service (INS) and the State Department access to criminal history records of persons applying for visas and for admission into the United States.

Indefinite Detention of Noncitizens

Section 412 deserves special attention in that it pertains to mandatory detention of suspected terrorists. This section states that the U.S. attorney general shall take into custody any alien whom he or she has reason to believe is engaged in any activity that is a danger to the national security of the United States. The attorney general must either charge or release the suspect within seven days. However, if the attorney general determines that charges will not be forthcoming within the seven-day period but deems that releasing the person will present a danger to the national security of the United States, that person may be detained an additional six months. At the end of six months, the attorney general is required to review the detention, and if he or she deems that the person remains a threat to the national security of the United States, the attorney general has the power to enforce an additional six-month detention. This process appears to be one that could continue indefinitely, requiring only that the attorney general, after review at the end of the six-month period, deems that the person remains a threat to national security.

Judicial review of this action is available only by habeas corpus petition. Application of such petition may only be filed with any justice of the Supreme Court; any circuit judge of the United States Court of Appeals for the District of Columbia Circuit; or any district court otherwise having jurisdiction to entertain it. The Supreme Court and the United States Court of Appeals for the District of Columbia Circuit shall be regarded as the rule of decision in such habeas corpus proceedings.

Aside from the obvious due process divergence of Section 218, Section 412 may contain the strongest dichotomy between the U.S. Supreme Court and the PATRIOT Act. The Supreme Court ruled in *Zadvydas v. Davis* (2001) that indefinite detention of noncitizens who are unable to be deported is unconstitutional. However, this case did not include indefinite detention on the grounds of domestic terrorism. Therefore, even though the Supreme Court explicitly ruled that indefinite detention is unconstitutional, such detention can still take place if a noncitizen is waiting to be deported because of possible involvement in terrorism or a threat to national security.

Removing Obstacles to Investigating Terrorism

Sections 501 and 502 authorize rewards to be paid by both the attorney general and secretary of state, respectively. Section 503 is small but possesses a significant impact with regard to setting a national DNA registry, because it allows DNA samples to be collected for a number of offenses. The element that widens the net immensely is that "Any crime of violence (as defined in Section 16^3 of Title 18, United States Code)" makes the person eligible for DNA collection, so virtually anyone arrested under the code is a candidate for DNA collection.

Section 507 of the act also empowers the attorney general to submit, in secret, an application to a court to obtain educational records "relevant to an authorized investigation or prosecution" of an act of domestic or international terrorism or "for official purposes related to the investigation or prosecution of an offense." This section also requires the educational institution to refrain from notifying the student that the attorney general has acquired these records.

National Security Letters

National Security Letters, or letters from the Justice Department that can order the seizure of various kinds of records, were in use prior to the act. However, Section 505 lowered the standard to determine whether these letters could be used. Such letters are based completely on the judgment of the Justice Department, and not even the Supreme Court can review their use in individual cases. A National Security Letter also issues a gag order on the recipient of the letter, much like that in Section 215.

Educational Records Disclosure

Both Sections 507 and 508 are similar in policy and procedure to Section 215 in that they require a judge to sign a warrant authorizing the seizure of records—in this case, educational records—if a minimum standard of relevancy to a domestic terrorism investigation is met. Section 507 includes any and all records kept by the educational institution in question, and are not limited to aca-demic records. Medical, social, and financial records are also included. Furthermore, Section 508 specifies that any data collected for statistical purposes by an educational institution can also be collected with a warrant obtained under the minimum standard outlined above. Much of the data collected for statistical purposes by educational institutions is not even relevant to education. This data can include family income, race, religion, marital status, and drug or alcohol use, to name a few. These two sections also serve to circumvent the criminal standard of probable cause for a search or seizure, as discussed in Section 218.

Strengthening Criminal Laws Against Terrorism

Domestic Terrorism Defined

Of particular note in this portion of the act is Section 802, which defines domestic terrorism. The new definition and amplification of three prior definitions greatly increased the range of permitted investigative activities. In Section 802, the original definition of "domestic terrorism" contained in 18 U.S.C. §2331 was amended. The language now increases the possibility of lawful protesters being charged and prosecuted as terrorists, especially in cases where violence occurs.

Prior to the terrorist attacks on September 11, 2001, domestic terrorism was all but ignored. Few measures were taken to ensure that future episodes of domestic terrorism, such as the Oklahoma City bombing in April 1995, would not occur. Since 2001, a shift has focused priority on domestic terrorism. Hence, the act includes a section to more broadly define domestic terrorism. As defined in Section 802, domestic terrorism must "involve acts dangerous to human life;" "appear to be intended to intimidate or coerce a civilian population, to influence the policy of a government by intimidation or coercion, or to affect the conduct of a government by mass destruction, assassination or kidnapping;" and, of course, take place predominantly in the jurisdiction of the United States or its territories. Prior to the act, domestic terrorism was included in the criminal statutes. However, Section 802 broadens the scope of what is considered to be domestic terrorism. Additionally, measures that can be taken to investigate domestic terrorism have been expanded and enhanced.

Seizure of Assets

Civil asset forfeiture has long been used by law enforcement agencies when pursuing criminal activities. If, for example, a car is involved in drug trafficking, it may be seized under criminal asset forfeiture laws. Section 806 expands asset forfeiture to include charges of suspected active or passive involvement in domestic terrorism. All of the previous procedures relating to asset forfeiture apply to terrorism asset forfeiture as well. This includes seizure before trial, no notice of a pending seizure, and a suit to regain items forfeited. Because this suit takes place in a civil court, a mere preponderance of the evidence is needed to show that an individual was engaged actively or passively in the furtherance of domestic terrorism, rather than the standard of beyond a reasonable doubt as used by criminal courts.

Provisions Originally Due to Expire December 31, 2005

The following provisions contained were due to expire on December 31, 2005, but were renewed in modified form:

- §201. Authority to Intercept Wire, Oral, and Electronic Communications Relating to Terrorism.
- §202. Authority to Intercept Wire, Oral, and Electronic Communications Relating to Computer Fraud and Abuse Offenses.
- §203(b), (d). Authority to Share Criminal Investigative Information.
- §206. Roving Surveillance Authority Under the Foreign Intelligence Surveillance Act of 1978.
- §207. Duration of FISA Surveillance of Non-United States Persons Who Are Agents of a Foreign Power.

- §209. Seizure of Voice-Mail Messages Pursuant to Warrants.
- §212. Emergency Disclosure of Electronic Communications to Protect Life and Limb.
- §214. Pen Register and Trap and Trace Authority Under FISA.
- §215. Access to Records and Other Items Under FISA.
- §217. Interception of Computer Trespasser Communications.
- §218. Foreign Intelligence Information.
- §220. Nationwide Service of Search Warrants for Electronic Evidence.
- §223. Civil Liability for Certain Unauthorized Disclosures (EEF).

Provisions That Do Not Expire

- §203(a), (c). Authority to Share Criminal Investigative Information.
- §208. Designation of Judges.
- §210. Scope of Subpoenas for Records of Electronic Communications.
- §211. Clarification of Scope.
- §213. Authority for Delaying Notice of the Execution of a Warrant.
- §216. Modification of Authorities Relating to Use of Pen Registers and Trap and Trace Devices.
- §219. Single-Jurisdiction Search Warrants for Terrorism.
- §222. Assistance to Law Enforcement Agencies.
- §225. Immunity for Compliance With FISA Wiretap (EEF).

H.R. 3199 USA PATRIOT Improvement and Reauthorization Act of 2005

On March 9, 2006, President George W. Bush signed the USA PATRIOT Improvement and Reauthorization Act of 2005, and in doing so repealed the Sunset Provision of the 2001 Act. The 2005 Reauthorization Act makes all sections of the 2001 act permanent, including the section on National Security Letters. Although some sections were amended slightly, none were deleted (Congressional Research Service—Library of Congress 2006).

The 2005 Reauthorization Act makes 14 of the 16 sections of the 2001 act permanent that were due to expire on December 31, 2005. At the same time, it mandated four-year expirations on the authority to conduct roving surveillance under FISA and the authority to require production of business records under FISA (Sections 206 and 215 of the 2001 act, respectively) (U.S. Department of Justice 2006).

The 2005 Reauthorization Act also allows the U.S. attorney general to restructure the Department of Justice by appointing a new assistant attorney general for national security. This redeployment would unify the attorneys from the Criminal Division's Counterterrorism and Counterespionage sections as well as the attorneys from the Office of Intelligence Policy and Review (OIPR), with their specialized expertise in the Foreign Intelligence Surveillance Act and other intelligence matters (U.S. Department of Justice 2006).

Noteworthy is the Combat Methamphetamine Epidemic Act of 2005, which was included in this bill. This section makes it more difficult for persons to obtain the necessary ingredients used in the manufacture of methamphetamine.

Discussion

Unnecessary Powers

Opponents of the USA PATRIOT Act argue that while measures should be taken to facilitate the war on terrorism, the act went too far by granting certain resources for combating terrorism at the expense of constitutional rights. In 1759, Benjamin Franklin said, "Those who would give up essential liberties to purchase a little temporary safety, deserve neither liberty nor safety" (Ball 2004, 65). Would Franklin have considered this statement to apply to the act? Some would agree that the act is no more than a facade of security covering an uncertain future. Critics have also called the act a type of preventive justice that undermines the basic rights granted by the Constitution and the Bill of Rights, and that especially diminishes the right of due process under the law, as well as the concept of "innocent until proven guilty."

The Balance of Justice

One of the main issues underlying the act is balancing individual rights with governmental power. Proponents assert that the act is necessary to combat terrorism and that certain rights may be conceded to the government during a time of war. In 1944, the Supreme Court ruled that in times of war Congress has the authority to compromise certain rights if the circumstances warrant it (*Korematsu v. United States* 1944). Conversely, opponents claim that the act gives too much weight to the government's side of the balance. Furthermore, the act is not limited solely to times of war. In fact, the "war on terrorism" is an ongoing war; whether or not it will ever end remains to be seen. A balance must be struck between the pursuit of justice and protection of the innocent.

Summary

The act contains many causes for concern that we will attempt to summarize:

1. Amplified surveillance with lesser checks and balances. The act greatly enhances the long-established surveillance equipment of law enforcement such as wiretaps, search warrants, pen/trap orders, and subpoenas. All online activity by U.S. citizens can now be monitored and tracked by the government. The threshold to gain such access has been dramatically lowered by simply advising a judge or magistrate anywhere in the United States that such intelligence work may lead to information germane to a current criminal investigation. The person monitored need not be the focus of the investigation. A proper application presented before a judge or magistrate must be granted without the usual return to the court, and the individual being monitored is denied the right to know of the government's action.

2. The Central Intelligence Agency (CIA) enjoys a similar expansion of its previous powers granted under the Foreign Intelligence Surveillance Act (FISA).

3. Government investigators may now use "roving wiretaps," which allows the FBI and CIA to monitor any phone or computer that a suspect may use or communicate with. With a single Title III wiretap, FISA wiretap, or pen/trap order, the government may monitor the communications made, irrespective of whether they are to or from the person named in the original order. This surveillance can be done without a return to the court where served or information acquired.

4. Internet service providers (ISPs) may now provide more information to the government without a court order. The act allows them to turn over all noncontent information to the government (Section 212) and expands the records that the government may seek with a nonreviewable court subpoena. These records would include session times and durations, network addresses, and method and source of payment, which would include any bank account or credit card numbers (Sections 210, 211).

5. The new definition of terrorism and amplification of three prior definitions greatly increases the range of permitted investigative activities. In Section 802 of the act, the original definition of "domestic terrorism" contained in 18 USC §2331 was amended. The language now increases the possibility of lawful protesters being charged and prosecuted as terrorists, especially in cases where violence occurs.

6. The act appears to have overextended itself and gone beyond a narrow scope of terrorism. For example:

   a. It permits government monitoring of computer trespassers without a court order (Section 218).

   b. It allows DNA samples to be collected from terrorists and persons convicted of "any crime of violence" to be placed in a database (Section 503).

   c. It permits wiretaps for suspected violations of the Computer Fraud and Abuse Act (Section 202) as well as markedly amplifying the range and penalties for that violation (Section 814).

   d. It makes it easier for U.S. Foreign Intelligence Services to spy on American citizens and non-U.S. citizens.

7. The act in some measure rescinded the barrier on information sharing between national law enforcement and intelligence agencies. Congress erected this firewall in the 1970s as a result of revelations of the misconduct of the FBI and CIA during the McCarthy investigations and the illegal surveillance of Dr. Martin Luther King.

8. The U.S. attorney general can now avoid domestic surveillance restrictions on wiretaps against any U.S. citizen by claiming that the individual is suspected of being a foreign government agent.

Costs and Benefits: Balancing the Scales

Because the act has been in effect for over four years, it would seem that by now there would be some measure of success in the war on terror. However, we have very little information to analyze regarding the act's success or failure. It could be said that announcing success or failure would provide information to terrorists. On the other hand, this could be a strategy to avoid the issue entirely.

What standard can be used to measure the success or failure of the act? Is a lack of terrorist acts on U.S. soil sufficient justification to proclaim the act a success? Or, is a lack of substantive charges or convictions of terrorist or terrorist plots construed as failure? Theoretically, the act has served to open the corridors of communication between federal agencies. This provision alone enables the United States to fight, defend, and learn more about nationwide crime, including domestic terrorism. If such is the purpose, one could assert that the act has successfully met its goal.

We must also consider the possibility of abuse of the broad powers granted by the act. Coincidentally, on the day President Bush signed the 2005 Reauthorization Act into law, the Department of Justice reported that the FBI had "found apparent violations of its own wiretapping and other intelligence-gathering procedures more than 100 times in the last two years, and problems appear to have grown more frequent" (Lichtblau 2006). Although some problems were considered "technical glitches," the department's inspector general reported others as "significant." For example, certain wiretaps were "much broader in scope than approved by a court and others were allowed to continue for weeks or sometimes months longer than authorized" (Lichtblau 2006). It is entirely possible that the reason other such abuses have not come to light is that much of the act relies on secrecy and would be rather difficult to expose.

Conclusion

On October 21, 2001, President Bush signed the USA PATRIOT Act into law with the hope that diminishing our freedoms would provide safety and security. Since then, terrorist attacks have continued around the world, with some of the most significant occurring in Bali, Indonesia, Madrid, and two attacks in London. The act bestowed broad new powers upon United States intelligence and law enforcement services, both at home and abroad. Most notable was the absence of the constitutional checks and balances contained in past legislation, which provided the courts with the occasion to make certain that such powers were not misused. To say that the act was rushed though Congress would be an understatement. The 342-page bill made varied changes in over 15 separate statutes, greatly expanding the federal government's powers. In 2001, disclosure of the surveillance abuse powers by the FBI and foreign intelligence services who had spied on over 10,000 U.S. citizens, including Dr. Martin Luther King, were still fresh in the memories of many.

Now on March 9, 2006, President Bush signed the USA PATRIOT Reauthorization Act of 2005 surrounded by supporters declaring the absolute necessity of such stringent measures. Little evidence has been forthcoming to demonstrate the need for these measures, and evidence has begun to bubble up of abuses of these wide-ranging powers. We can only hope that our state and federal law enforcement agencies will use these powers judiciously on legitimate investigations involving terrorism and that the courts will realize their responsibility to punish those found misusing these powers.

Notes

1. A pen register gathers the outgoing phone numbers made from a particular telephone line. A trap and trace device acquires incoming numbers made to a certain phone line. A caller-ID box is a trap and trace device.

2. Project Carnivore is part of a third generation of online-detection software programs used by the FBI and is a part of a larger, more comprehensive system, the Dragonware Suite, which allows the Bureau to reconstruct email messages, and to downloaded files or even webpages. Although the FBI has provided minimal information to the public about the Dragonware Suite, and little detailed information regarding Carnivore, the system is basically referred to in computer terms as a "packet sniffer." A relatively common technology that has been available since early 2000, a packet sniffer is a program that can see all of the information on a specific network, examining or "sniffing" packets of data streams. The software is capable of reconstructing any webpages, web-based text documents, and the contents of email messages. Thus, as a mechanism of social control, Project Carnivore operates primarily as a means of offender and offense identification.

3. Section 16. The term *crime of violence* means:

> (a) an offense that has as an element of the use, attempted use, or threatened use of physical force against the person or property of another, or
>
> (b) any other offense that is a felony and that, by its nature, involves a substantial risk that physical force against the person or property of another may be used in the course of committing the offense. (Retrieved August 17, 2005, from http://caselaw.lp.findlaw.com/ scripts/ts_search.pl?title=18&sec=16.)

References

Ball, H. 2004. *The USA PATRIOT Act of 2001: Balancing Civil Liberties and National Security.* Santa Barbara, CA: ABC-CLIO, Inc.

Congressional Research Service—Library of Congress. 2006. "USA PATRIOT ACT Improvement and Reauthorization Act of 2005 (H.R. 3199): A Legal Analysis of the Conference Bill." http://www.fas.org/sgp/crs/intel/RL33239.pdf.

Lichtblau, E. 2006. "Justice Dept. Report Cites F.B.I. Violations." *New York Times,* March 9: A21.

9/11 Commission Report. 2004. New York: W. W. Norton.

USA PATRIOT Act of 2001 (U.S. H.R. 3162, S. 1510, Public Law 107-56). http://www.epic.org/privacy/terrorism/hr3162.html.

U.S. Department of Justice. 2006. "Preserving Life & Liberty." http:///www.lifeandliberty.gov/.

Cases Cited

Korematsu v. United States, 323 U.S. 214 (1944).

United States v. New York Telephone Co., 434 U.S. 159 (1977).

Zadvydas v. Davis, 533 U.S. 678 (2001).

Related Websites

Debating the PATRIOT Act

http://www.npr.org/templates/story/story.php?storyId=4759727&sourceCode=gaw

The USA PATRIOT Act/The Electronic Privacy Information Center

http://www.epic.org/privacy/terrorism/hr3162.html

The American Civil Liberties Union Review of the USA PATRIOT Act

http://www.aclu.org/safefree/resources/17343res20031114.html

Discussion Questions

1. In what ways does Section 213 alter traditional service of a search warrant, and how does this section represent a drastic departure from the Fourth Amendment principle?

2. Explain the restrictions on pen register/trap and trace devices under FISA and how the act enhanced this method of surveillance.

3. Section 215 of the act, commonly known as "The Library Provision," has had a dramatic effect on privacy rights of ordinary citizens. Describe the implications of Section 215 in detail.

4. Describe in detail how Section 412 of the act impacts the detention of noncitizens and the method of judicial review for this section.

5. How does Section 802 of the act define domestic terrorism? Be certain to explain all of the elements necessary to meet the definition and how this section might impact the First Amendment right to freedom of speech. ✦

Chapter 4
The Meaning of *Miranda* Rights and the Privilege Against Self-Incrimination

Marvin Zalman

In this chapter, the author examines the history surrounding coerced confessions and the use of such confessions in criminal proceedings. This chapter presents valuable information pertaining to our constitutional right against self-incrimination, its roots in historical and recent case law, and the significance of the Fifth Amendment Self-Incrimination Clause and the Fourteenth Amendment Due Process Clause. Additionally, this analysis views the interpretive changes of the Self-Incrimination Clause through the scope of the legendary case *Miranda v. Arizona* (1966).

In the twentieth century, the Supreme Court ruled on over 30 cases involving due process violations under the coerced confession rule, which began with *Brown v. Mississippi* in 1936. Around the time of the *Miranda* decision, the Court found a need to develop an overarching rule that would guide police in interrogation and practice. As you shall see in this chapter, they did so by incorporating provisions of the Fourth and Fifth Amendments into the Due Process Clause of the Fourteenth Amendment. As the author notes, the Supreme Court thus opened the door to the *Miranda* decision. In 1966, the Court set the precedent for police custodial interrogation and outlined what we now refer to as a *Miranda* warning, which must be read to a suspect in any setting where the police have control over that person.

Again, the question of balance between individual rights and the ability of law enforcement officers to effectively carry out their jobs is raised. Some believed that the introduction of these warnings would weaken and reduce the frequency of confessions, a situation that did not come to pass. Supreme Court decisions that have taken place after *Miranda* continue to shape how we deal with and interpret criminal procedure. The last portion of this chapter opens the discussion to the sociopolitical tug-of-war surrounding *Miranda*, such as the introduction of nonvoluntary confessions into the trial by the collateral use of statements, which are described here as derivative evidence, impeachment, cured statement, and the public safety exception. Additionally, the author illustrates the conflict between the Court's interpretation of the constitutionality of *Miranda* warnings and that of the Congress, as demonstrated in *Dickerson v. United States* (2000).

Most important, this chapter provides a resource for exploring the many facets of the decision-making processes within the Supreme Court, along with how these decisions affect our everyday lives.

Confessions

The practice by police investigators of asking questions—interviewing witnesses and interrogating suspects—is the most important technique of criminal investigation. Suspects are interrogated for the purpose of gaining confessions and solving crimes. In situations where circumstantial evidence points to a suspect, obtaining a confession makes the solution of the crime more efficient. There are dangers, however, with interrogating suspects. Suspects may be coerced into giving confessions that may be false. And even if accurate, confessions may corrupt the integrity of an investigation if police fail to sufficiently develop the evidence in a case. Thus, some controls on the process of interrogation are necessary. These risks were recognized hundreds of years ago, when court rulings in England and the United States outlawed coerced confessions by making their products inadmissible in court.

This common law exclusionary rule of not allowing the introduction into a trial of involuntary "extrajudicial" confessions applied to confessions obtained by promises, threats, or force. Although the point is subject to historical controversy, the common law rule against coerced confessions developed separately from the privilege against self-incrimination, which allows a defendant to remain silent at trial. Nevertheless, in the twentieth century, the United States Supreme Court brought confessions obtained by the police under the Self-Incrimination Clause of the Fifth Amendment of the United States Constitution. The historical issue became a point of contention in the famous *Miranda v. Arizona* (1966) decision, which created a new chapter in federal confessions law, which in turn generated substantial controversy about the precise meaning of the Self-Incrimination Clause that has not been entirely settled. Before getting to *Miranda* it is necessary to review the development of the federal coerced confessions cases.

The Due Process Clause Coerced Confessions Rule

The United States is a federation. Laws are made and enforced by state governments and by the national (or federal) government. State governments are organized under state constitutions. To create a unified nation, however, the United States Constitution applies to both state and local governments in certain areas. Shortly after the Civil War in 1868, the United States adopted the Fourteenth Amendment to the Constitution, which declares that "No State shall . . . deprive any person of life, liberty, or property, without due process of law." This Due Process Clause means that if a local or state police officer violates the due process rights of a person, whether a citizen or an alien, while enforcing state law, that is also a violation of the person's federal due process rights. In practice, this allows a state defendant to bring a complaint to a federal court, usually through a federal habeas corpus suit, against the state or local police. Of course, a criminal defendant can also complain in a state court that local police coerced a confession and thereby violated a state common law rule, a state statute, or the state constitution's Due

Process Clause that prohibits the introduction of coerced confessions as evidence in a criminal trial. But if a state court finds no violation of state law, a defendant can still turn to federal courts, which are obliged to enforce the rights of persons coming under the protection of the nation's Constitution and laws, for recourse from violations by government officers.

The Supreme Court decided its first case concerning a confession obtained by local officers in 1936. In that era, the Supreme Court ruled that the Bill of Rights in the U.S. Constitution, which includes the Self-Incrimination Clause, did not protect individuals from acts by state or local government or its officers.[1] The United States Supreme Court, therefore, had no jurisdiction under the Fifth Amendment to decide a case that arose in *Brown v. Mississippi* (1936). In this case a confession to murder was obtained by torture at the hands of sheriff's deputies against three African-American farm hands, who were sentenced to death. They were hung by the neck during their interrogation and threatened with death if they did not talk; they were also whipped with a metal-studded belt that tore into their flesh. None of this behavior was denied, and one deputy who was questioned at the trial about whether the whipping was too severe replied, "Not too much for a negro; not as much as I would have done if it were left to me." The Mississippi Supreme Court ruled, in a split decision, that the confessions were not coerced and were properly introduced into evidence. The U.S. Supreme Court took this case, ruling that it had jurisdiction under the Fourteenth Amendment and, differing with the judges in the majority opinion in the Mississippi Supreme Court, that the introduction of a confession obtained by such methods violated suspects' Fourteenth Amendment due process rights and that their compelled confessions were coerced and inadmissible in state criminal trials.

Between 1936 and 1966 the Supreme Court decided more than 30 cases under the due process voluntariness test, ruling that a variety of practices less brutal than those used in *Brown* had violated the Fourteenth Amendment. These cases held that undue psychological pressure to gain a confession constituted the level of coercion that violated federal due process. An early case ruled that a confession made after a suspect was questioned continuously for 36 hours without sleep violated due process (*Ashcraft v. Tennessee* 1944). In such a case the conviction is reversed by the federal courts and the state either has to try the defendant without the confession or release him or her.

Another example of interrogation that violated the Due Process Clause under the coerced confession rule was moving defendants to secret places so that family, lawyers, or friends could not contact them and make them feel as if their situations were hopeless (*Chambers v. Florida* 1940; *Ward v. Texas* 1942). A defendant kept naked for several hours before interrogation had his conviction overturned (*Malinski v. New York* 1945). Coercion existed when a suspect who needed ordinary medical attention was treated by a state-employed psychiatrist who insisted that he was there to help the suspect and would provide medical assistance only upon getting incriminating information (*Leyra v. Denno* 1954). A sheriff who told an African-American teen that if he did not confess he would be handed over to a lynch mob violated the suspect's due process rights (*Payne v. Arkansas* 1958). A police officer and childhood friend of a defendant coerced a confession by telling the defendant in his cell, over a period of days, that the officer would lose his job if he did not get a statement (*Spano v. New York* 1959). Other methods that ran afoul of the Due Process Clause included vigorously interrogating mentally defective or insane suspects (*Blackburn v. Alabama* 1960; *Culombe v. Connecticut* 1961), using "truth serum" on a suspect (*Townsend v. Sain* 1963), and telling a suspect that her children would be taken from her if she failed to cooperate with the police (*Lynumn v. Illinois* 1963).

The continuous stream of confessions cases convinced many Supreme Court justices that the police were evading their constitutional duty by devising more clever ways to pressure suspects into confessing. During the 1960s the Supreme Court made a major change in constitutional doctrine by ruling, in a number of cases, that provisions of the Bill of Rights that had to do with the criminal process applied to local and state law enforcement officers and prosecutors. The Court did so by ruling that provisions like the protection against unreasonable search and seizure in the Fourth Amendment or the privilege against self-incrimination in the Fifth Amendment were components of due process. This was known as the "incorporation doctrine" because the Court ruled that the provisions of the Bill of Rights were incorporated into the Fourteenth Amendment Due Process Clause. It had the effect of extending federal court jurisdiction over state criminal justice in cases where state officers may have violated a suspect's rights under incorporated provisions of the Bill of Rights. In 1964 the Supreme Court "incorporated" the Fifth Amendment privilege against self-incrimination, paving the way to *Miranda v. Arizona* in 1966 (*Malloy v. Hogan* 1964).

The Constitution's text does not use the term "self-incrimination." This phrase is shorthand for the words of the Fifth Amendment: "No person . . . shall be compelled in any criminal case to be a witness against himself. . . ." Despite these plain words of the Fifth Amendment, the Supreme Court has held on numerous occasions that a person can invoke the privilege in a variety of settings (e.g., as a witness in a civil trial or in a Congressional hearing). If a witness in a civil trial made an admission to a crime while in the witness box, that admission could later be used against him or her in a criminal trial. The witness could therefore refuse to answer a question in the civil trial, even though he or she had sworn to tell the truth, by claiming the privilege against self-incrimination if, in the witness' judgment, the answer to the question would tend to incriminate him or her.

The *Miranda* Decision

The Supreme Court in *Miranda v. Arizona* (1966) ruled that whenever a suspect is interrogated while in police custody, the situation is inherently compelling. This "compulsion" brings the Self-Incrimination Clause into play. As quoted above, its actual wording is that "No person . . . shall be *compelled* in any criminal case to be a witness against himself" (emphasis added).

> We are satisfied that all the principles embodied in the privilege apply to informal compulsion exerted by law-enforcement officers during in-custody questioning. An individual swept from familiar surroundings into police custody, surrounded by antagonistic forces, and subjected to the techniques of persuasion described above cannot be otherwise than under compulsion to speak. As a practical matter, the compulsion to speak in the isolated setting of the police station may well be greater than in courts or other official investigations, where there are often impartial observers to guard against intimidation or trickery. (*Miranda v. Arizona* 1966)

This compulsion brings police custodial interrogation within the purview of the privilege against self-incrimination and within the jurisdiction of federal courts. The Court defined "custody" as being deprived of freedom of action in any significant way. It relied on police manuals that instructed interrogators to place a suspect in a psychological setting designed to undermine his or her will to remain silent to conclude that custodial interrogation is inherently compelling.

Because of its compelling atmosphere, custodial interrogation triggers a special responsibility on the part of the police: they must inform suspects that they have a right to remain silent. This right is conferred by the U.S. Constitution. In addition to informing suspects of their basic and absolute right to silence, the *Miranda* warnings spell out the consequences of talking: anything said to the police can be used by them to incriminate a suspect. His or her statements can be put into evidence, and a jury can rely on the statements to find the suspect guilty of a crime. To ensure that a suspect caught up in the toils of interrogation would be able to protect his or her right to silence, the Court fashioned a new protection. Before being questioned, suspects had to be informed of their right to counsel, not under the Sixth Amendment right to the assistance of counsel during a prosecution, but under the Fifth

Amendment. This Fifth Amendment right to counsel was defined as the suspect's "right to consult with a lawyer and to have the lawyer with him during interrogation" (*Miranda v. Arizona* 1966). Suspects must also be told that if they cannot afford an attorney one will be provided at state expense.

After these four warnings are "administered," the suspects are asked whether they understand their rights and if they wish to talk. Under the law, a suspect who has a Fifth Amendment right to remain silent in an official proceeding or while in police custody, but who decides to answer questions, has "waived" his or her rights. The law allows the waiver of certain rights as long as the waiver is voluntary and made with knowledge of the rights that the suspect is giving up. Because *Miranda* requires an affirmative waiver of rights before any admission or confession is admissible in a trial, it is standard practice to have a suspect who waives his or her rights sign a waiver form, although the Supreme Court has allowed oral waivers to stand when placed on the record (*North Carolina v. Butler* 1979).

Miranda included several other rules: (1) the warnings are mandatory and cannot be skipped because the suspect purportedly knows their rights; (2) the *Miranda* exclusionary rule applies both to full confessions and to admissions—statements from which guilt can be inferred; (3) the rule applies to inculpatory (incriminating) as well as to exculpatory statements—statements that a suspect thinks will clear him or her; (4) the burden of proving a voluntary waiver is on the state; (5) the simple fact that a suspect answers questions after being warned is not itself a waiver of rights—the waiver must be explicit; (6) interrogation must cease after a waiver if the suspect indicates in any manner that he wishes to remain silent or consult with an attorney; (7) a person is in custody for *Miranda* purposes if the person is "deprived of his freedom of action in any significant way," and so the warnings have to be given not only in the station house but in other settings where the police have control over a suspect. Each of these points were litigated in the years following *Miranda*, creating a complex body of "*Miranda* law."

The five-justice majority joining in Chief Justice Earl Warren's majority opinion in *Miranda* (1966) saw the ruling as a constitutional rule: "The warnings required and the waiver necessary in accordance with our opinion today are, in the absence of a fully effective equivalent, prerequisites to the admissibility of any statement made by a defendant." The Court went on to say that constitutional safeguards other than the warnings prescribed in *Miranda* could be created by legislative action. "However, unless we are shown other procedures which are at least as effective in apprising accused persons of their right of silence and in assuring a continuous opportunity to exercise it, the following safeguards [i.e., the four warnings] must be observed" (*Miranda v. Arizona* 1966). The majority also saw the decision to be essential to justice as well as constitutionally mandated: "The cases before us raise questions which go to the roots of our concepts of American criminal jurisprudence: the restraints society must observe consistent with the Federal Constitution in prosecuting individuals for crime." The majority, however, was not bent on destroying the police ability to interrogate suspects. Its opinion stated clearly that interrogation was an appropriate police investigation technique and that purely volunteered statements (i.e., statements made before police question a suspect) were admissible although no warnings were given or waiver obtained.

The four dissenting justices in *Miranda* did not see it that way. They correctly noted that there was no clear precedent for the Court's decision and did not view the Court's logic as a natural extension of earlier legal developments, a point about which lawyers can reasonably disagree. Indeed, Justice White noted that the Court had in the past appropriately made "new law and new public policy" but thought that the preconditions for judicial change were not present in regard to confessions. To the dissenters, inferring compulsion from police training manuals belied the fact that in the four cases actually before the Court in *Miranda* the confessions would have been admissible under the Due Process Clause voluntariness rule. The dissenters also interpreted legal history

to sharply distinguish the common law rule excluding involuntary "extrajudicial" confessions from the privilege against self-incrimination, to conclude that the Court had no warrant to apply the privilege to interrogation and confessions. The dissent also argued that the majority's ruling was not aimed at police brutality, as had been the case with the Due Process Clause totality-of-the-circumstances voluntariness test, but rather was aimed at eliminating all pressure. (This has not been borne out by post-*Miranda* interrogation practice, for psychological pressure continues to exist and makes it feasible for the police to obtain a high rate of confessions.) Justice White noted the incoherence of ruling that on the one hand assumes that a suspect is under such compulsion that he or she cannot constitutionally answer questions without being warned but that also assumes the suspect has the capacity to waive his or her rights.

Finally, turning from legal to policy points, some dissents cautioned that the warnings of silence and an ability to consult with counsel would destroy the ability of police to obtain confessions and solve crimes, a somewhat hysterical overreaction that did not come to pass. If the Court wished to take a truly radical step, it could have held that the atmosphere of police interrogation is so coercive that no statement taken during such questioning could ever be admitted into evidence, virtually eliminating confessions.

Four decades have elapsed since *Miranda*, and more than 60 Supreme Court decisions have shaped *Miranda* doctrine, about twice as many as the pre-1966 voluntariness cases that motivated the Warren Court to decide *Miranda* with the hope of providing clarity and uniformity to police interrogation practices. Empirical studies of interrogation show that police, for the most part, routinely read *Miranda* warnings before obtaining inculpatory (guilty) statements. Physical beatings have largely disappeared from the interrogation room, but police sometimes seek to get around the spirit, and often the letter, of *Miranda*.

Cases following *Miranda* addressed a number of issues, including the precise definition of custody and of interrogation, whether a suspect can be reinterrogated after invoking the right of silence or an attorney, whether warnings actually given are constitutionally adequate, and a number of other points. The remainder of this chapter will not address these issues but will instead focus on the most contentious confession issues currently before the courts. But first it is worth commenting that the questions that arise in constitutional law cases typically are not simply technical matters of legal interpretation but rather involve major political and social issues. In criminal procedure that usually involves perspectives that tend to favor the prosecution or the defense side. There is, of course, wide agreement by all that the effective investigation and prosecution of crimes is vital to social stability and also that unchecked government power is profoundly dangerous to the liberty of citizens. Within the parameters of agreement, however, prosecutors, defense attorneys, and citizens who tend to support the "crime control" or the "due process" models of criminal justice differ over the scope of many police procedures, especially concerning search and seizure and interrogation (Packer 1968). Such differences are often reflected in Supreme Court decisions. In fact, justices who tend to regularly, but not slavishly, vote in a consistent direction on such issues, are labeled "conservative" or "liberal." The labels at times oversimplify the extent to which some decisions are based on the facts of cases and typically overlook the reasoning that justices employ. Nevertheless, the labels do capture the important reality that ideological splits develop between the justices. As a result, in some areas of constitutional law the justices battle to achieve goals. The *Miranda* case and the cases that followed it are a prime example of a constitutional contest that has been going on for four decades.

Undermining *Miranda*

President Richard Nixon, four of whose appointees to the Supreme Court were confirmed by the Senate (two were not), ran in 1968 on a platform that included overturn-

ing the *Miranda* decision. In fact, *Miranda* was so unpopular that in 1968, just two years after the ruling, Congress passed a law (18 U.S.C. §3501) mandating that in any federal prosecution a confession "shall be admissible in evidence if it is voluntarily given." Under the statute, being advised of one's right to remain silent is not required for a confession to be admissible, but is only one factor to be taken into account to determine whether the confession is voluntary. The law sought, in effect, to overrule *Miranda*, but it remained unenforced for three decades before it emerged to play a bizarre role in the *Miranda* saga.

Miranda was decided by a 5–4 vote, but the Supreme Court was unable or unwilling later to overrule the decision. By 1972 the Supreme Court's composition, thanks to President Nixon's appointees, had shifted from a slim liberal majority to a conservative majority. In the years since, through the Burger Court (1969–1986), the Rehnquist Court (1986–2005), and now the Roberts Court, the Supreme Court has had a more or less conservative cast. For much of this period the Court has had both liberal and conservative justices and a few "swing" justices whose decisions were not so predictable, in part because they would decide cases more in accord with the facts of the case. While the Court has tended to make decisions supporting the prosecution and has strengthened *Miranda* in some ways, for the most part it has chipped away at the ruling.

One of the ways in which the Supreme Court undermined *Miranda* was by allowing "collateral uses" of statements taken in violation of *Miranda* and by creating one clear exception to the *Miranda* rule. In so doing, the Court exposed a deeply divided understanding of the privilege against self-incrimination itself. To begin, think of *Miranda* as an exclusionary rule—any statement taken during custodial interrogation when *Miranda* warnings were not administered or were improperly or incompletely administered is not admissible in a trial to prove guilt. In several cases the prosecution, blocked from introducing *Miranda*-violated statements, sought to gain collateral advantage. The Supreme Court has ruled that although the "tainted" statements could not be used in a trial to prove guilt, they could be used for collateral purposes. To get to this conclusion the Court had to separate the warnings from the privilege against self-incrimination.

What are collateral uses? The post-*Miranda* cases involve three examples: derivative use, impeachment, and "cured" statements.

Derivative Evidence

In *Michigan v. Tucker* (1974), *Miranda*-deficient warnings (Tucker was not informed of the right to appointed counsel) were given to Tucker before an interrogation about a suspected rape. Tucker gave police the name of an acquaintance whom he thought would exonerate him; instead the witness told the police that Tucker had talked about the rape. Nothing that Tucker said was used against him in trial, but derivative evidence—i.e., the witness's statement—was used against him to prove his guilt of a rape. The Court upheld its admissibility.

Impeachment

In *Harris v. New York* (1971), deficient warnings were given to Harris, a suspected drug seller, during custodial interrogation at which he made incriminating statements. Harris took the witness stand at his trial and testified that he sold baking powder in order to defraud a known undercover agent. Asked if he made statements shortly after the arrest that contradicted this story, Harris said he could not recall. The state then introduced evidence of his contradictory statement. The jury, which convicted him, was instructed that the statement could be used only to consider Harris' credibility, and not as evidence of guilt. The Supreme Court held that this use of the statement to impeach Harris' credibility was constitutional.

The Court confirmed the use of a defective statement for purposes of impeachment in *Oregon v. Hass* (1975), in which a suspect, who was read *Miranda* warnings, asked for a lawyer while being driven to the police station. The officer replied that Hass could telephone his attorney when they "got to the office." Hass thereafter made incriminating statements and pointed out the location of a

stolen bicycle. At trial, Hass took the stand and minimized his involvement in the crime. The officer then testified to Hass' postinvocation statements that pointed to his guilt. The judge cautioned the jury to use the statement only to impeach Hass' credibility. This was held proper by the Supreme Court.

Cured Statement

A cured statement occurs subsequent to an incriminating statement that was taken either without *Miranda* warnings or after defective warnings. At a later time, the suspect is properly Mirandized and makes an admission or confession. The argument against allowing the second, or "cured" statement into evidence is that the suspect has been psychologically "softened up" by having already admitted to a crime. Having done so, the suspect may feel that there is no use in remaining silent at the second interrogation. This tactic could be used by police officers to get a "proper" statement from a suspect on the rebound after an improper interrogation. The Supreme Court upheld the introduction of a "cured" statement into evidence in *Oregon v. Elstad* (1985). In that case the police suspected a teenager of having burglarized property from the home of a friend. Police were let into Elstad's house by his mother, and in the living room they asked Elstad whether he knew the friend. Elstad volunteered that he heard about a burglary, and when an officer told Elstad that they suspected him, he replied, "Yes, I was there." No *Miranda* warnings were given. A "cured" statement was obtained a few hours later in the afternoon at a police station after *Miranda* warnings were properly administered before Elstad was again interrogated. It seemed clear that the police did not deliberately decide in advance to ignore Elstad's *Miranda* rights when he was questioned in his home, but they did interrogate him while in police custody without giving the proper warnings.

To fully appreciate the impact of the Court's "collateral use" cases, one must know that the prosecution cannot in *any* way use involuntary statements or statements obtained in direct violation of the privilege against self-incrimination. In *Mincey v. Arizona* (1978) the Supreme Court held that a confession was made involuntarily—i.e., in violation of the due process rule in effect since 1936 (*Brown v. Mississippi* 1936). Mincey had been wounded in a shootout during which a police officer was killed. In the hospital "Tubes were inserted into [Mincey's] throat to help him breathe, and through his nose into his stomach to keep him from vomiting; a catheter was inserted into his bladder. He received various drugs, and a device was attached to his arm so that he could be fed intravenously. He was then taken to the intensive care unit." When Detective Hust went to the ICU to interrogate him "Mincey was unable to talk because of the tube in his mouth, and so he responded to Detective Hust's questions by writing answers on pieces of paper provided by the hospital." Hust told Mincey he was under arrest for the murder of an officer and read him his *Miranda* rights. "Although Mincey asked repeatedly that the interrogation stop until he could get a lawyer, Hust continued to question him until almost midnight." Evidence indicated that Mincey was in extreme pain, was "depressed almost to the point of coma," was confused and unable to think clearly, and was "encumbered by tubes, needles, and breathing apparatus," and his written answers were not coherent.

Mincey took the stand at trial, and the state sought to use statements made to Detective Hust to impeach his testimony. The Supreme Court reversed the trial court's conclusion that Mincey's statements were voluntary: "Mincey was weakened by pain and shock, isolated from family, friends, and legal counsel, and barely conscious, and his will was simply overborne." The Court then flatly stated the rule: "Due process of law requires that statements obtained as these were cannot be used *in any way* against a defendant at his trial" (*Mincey v. Arizona* 1978, emphasis added). Likewise, *New Jersey v. Portash* (1979) held that grand jury testimony that was compelled by a grant of immunity could not be used to impeach the witness at a later trial because such use was a violation of the Self-Incrimination Clause.

If statements taken in direct violation of the Due Process Clause or the Self-Incrimination Clause cannot be used in *any* way, why has the Supreme Court allowed derivative use of statements taken in violation of *Miranda*? The answer is that in those cases the Supreme Court separated the *Miranda* warnings from the privilege and said that the warnings are not in themselves constitutional rights but only protective or prophylactic devices designed to protect the underlying privilege. The reasoning was spelled out in Justice Rehnquist's opinion in *Michigan v. Tucker* (1974). If *Miranda* warnings are prophylactic rules developed to protect the underlying right of silence in the Self-Incrimination Clause, and not constitutional rules in their own right, then police failure to give warnings did not violate Tucker's privilege against self-incrimination but only the protective rules of *Miranda*. Thus, although the statement could not be introduced at trial, evidence derived from the statement was admissible.

This interpretation of *Miranda* was arrived at by selectively reading the case. Justice Rehnquist quoted the following passage from *Miranda*: "We cannot say that the Constitution necessarily requires adherence to any particular solution for the inherent compulsions of the interrogation process as it is presently conducted," suggesting that the warnings specified in *Miranda* are not essential parts of the privilege against self-incrimination. But in his opinion in *Tucker*, this highly proficient justice failed to quote the following passage from *Miranda*, appearing three sentences later: "However, unless we are shown other procedures which are at least as effective in apprising accused persons of their right of silence and in assuring a continuous opportunity to exercise it, the [*Miranda*] safeguards must be observed." The *mandatory* nature of the warnings' requirement, plus the statement that the Constitution requires the protections, makes it clear that the Warren Court majority viewed *Miranda* warnings as integral to and inseparable from the Fifth Amendment privilege. The decision in *Tucker* is an example of how the common law process works: A "later" Court (i.e., the *Tucker* Court) can interpret (or reinterpret) the meaning of a previously decided case without clearly overruling it.

The *Tucker* majority interpreted these words in *Miranda* as dictum—that is, not as language in the earlier opinion that was essential to its ruling but as words that were not essential to the decision of the case. The majority in *Tucker* concluded that the police did not violate Tucker's right against compulsory self-incrimination "but rather failed to make available to him the full measure of procedural safeguards associated with that right since *Miranda*." Because a violation of the *Miranda* warnings was not deemed a violation of the right against self-incrimination, it did not require the exclusion of derivative evidence. The majority added that no additional deterrence to police misconduct could be expected by the use of evidence derived from a good-faith failure to follow the *Miranda* rules.

Public Safety Exception

One other use was made of the reasoning employed in *Tucker* and later collateral-use cases. Based on the reasoning that downgraded the *Miranda* rule to a mere protective device, the Supreme Court in *New York v. Quarles* (1984) carved out a clear-cut exception that allowed the introduction of a *Miranda*-violated statement into evidence when it was obtained under conditions of a threat to public safety. In *Quarles* a rape suspect was cornered in a supermarket by a police officer with a drawn gun. The officer noticed an empty holster and asked Quarles where the gun was. Quarles replied, "The gun is over there." The statement and the gun itself were held to be properly introduced into evidence under the public safety exception. Were the *Miranda* rule found to be an element of the privilege against self-incrimination (as the *Miranda* case itself intended), Quarles' statement and evidence derived from it could not have been introduced, because the Fifth Amendment is an absolute exclusionary rule unless it is voluntarily waived by a person testifying or subject to custodial interrogation by the police.

Confessions law remained in uneasy tension for a decade and a half after these exceptions to *Miranda* were established by the Su-

preme Court. Conservative critics felt that if *Miranda* was not a constitutional rule, the Supreme Court had no jurisdiction to impose it on the states. Liberal scholars believed that the Supreme Court had undermined *Miranda*'s constitutional doctrine as a prelude to finally overruling the decision entirely.

Saving *Miranda*

To the astonishment of most observers, the Supreme Court upheld *Miranda* as a constitutional rule in *Dickerson v. United States* (2000). For decades the Justice Department avoided relying on 18 U.S.C. §3501 (the statute passed in 1968 that attempted to "overrule" *Miranda*) in order to prevent a clash between the Court and Congress. Dickerson was indicted by a federal grand jury for bank robbery. He moved to suppress a statement he made to FBI agents during an interrogation on the ground that he had not received *Miranda* warnings. The district court granted the motion and specifically ruled that the confession was otherwise voluntary. On appeal by federal prosecutors, the Court of Appeals found that although the *Miranda* warnings were defective, the confession was admissible under 18 U.S.C. §3501, which says that in any federal prosecution a confession "shall be admissible in evidence if it is voluntarily given." The Court of Appeals, taking the U.S. Supreme Court at its word, ruled that *Miranda* is not a constitutional rule, meaning that Congress could override *Miranda*. The stage was thus set for a showdown between the Supreme Court and Congress over *Miranda*. It is fundamental to American constitutionalism that Congress can by legislation modify or void a court-made rule *except* for a court-made doctrine of constitutional law, which is deemed to be an authoritative interpretation of the Constitution.

Chief Justice Rehnquist's majority opinion rebuffed the Congress: "We hold that *Miranda*, being a constitutional decision of this Court, may not be in effect overruled by an act of Congress, and we decline to overrule *Miranda* ourselves. We therefore hold that *Miranda* and its progeny in this Court govern the admissibility of statements made during custodial interrogation in both state and federal courts" (*Dickerson v. United States* 2000). His opinion simply brushed aside decades of calling *Miranda* a prophylactic rule: "We concede that there is language in some of our opinions that supports the view" that *Miranda* is not a constitutional rule. Some of the reasons provided in the *Dickerson* opinion to support its decision were simply circular—for example, saying that *Miranda* is not based on the Court's supervisory power because the Court had applied the *Miranda* rule to the states from the very beginning; or saying that all the justices in the *Miranda* case understood its ruling as a constitutional rule. Another rationale offered by the *Dickerson* opinion was that *Miranda* warnings have not been superseded by other methods of securing a suspect's right to remain silent in the coercive atmosphere of a police station.

These are unsatisfactory reasons for the decision. The stronger reason was the doctrine of *stare decisis,* or precedent: "Whether or not we would agree with *Miranda*'s reasoning and its resulting rule, were we addressing the issue in the first instance, the principles of *stare decisis* weigh heavily against overruling it now. . . . While *stare decisis* is not an inexorable command, particularly when we are interpreting the Constitution, even in constitutional cases, the doctrine carries such persuasive force that we have always required a departure from precedent to be supported by some special justification" (*Dickerson v. United States* 2000).

The Court candidly discussed the social and policy backdrop to its decision. First, it was well established that police lose few cases because of *Miranda* warning errors, so there was no great "cost" to retaining *Miranda*. Further, the Chief Justice expressed a concern that overruling *Miranda* would create popular misunderstanding: "We do not think there is such justification for overruling *Miranda*. *Miranda* has become embedded in routine police practice to the point where the warnings have become part of our national culture" (*Dickerson v. United States* 2000). Another practical reason was

that the due process voluntariness test "is more difficult than *Miranda* for law enforcement officers to conform to, and for courts to apply in a consistent manner."

Despite the Court's declaration that *Miranda* was a constitutional ruling, it indicated that its ruling did not undermine the collateral use cases by asserting that a constitutional rule can have exceptions. The tension between *Miranda* law and the *Mincey* and *Portash* doctrines of the Fifth Amendment privilege therefore remained unresolved. This glaring contradiction was highlighted by ultraconservative Justices Scalia and Thomas, who dissented from the Court's about-face. Justice Scalia's dissent suggested that the majority did not fully establish the constitutionality of *Miranda* warnings. The Court used phrases like "*Miranda* is a constitutional decision," "*Miranda* is constitutionally based," and *Miranda* has "constitutional underpinnings," without saying "that custodial interrogation that is not preceded by *Miranda* warnings or their equivalent violates the Constitution of the United States" (*Dickerson v. United States* 2000, Justice Scalia dissenting). The dissent saw a fundamental violation of constitutional principle. Chief Justice Rehnquist's adroit opinion, on the other hand, can be seen as a mature reflection of the fact that constitutional government can be based on constitutional understandings that develop over time.

After *Dickerson*: Confusion

Three cases decided after *Dickerson* (2000) expose the unsettled understanding not only of *Miranda* but of the privilege against self-incrimination as well. *Chavez v. Martinez* (2003) was a civil lawsuit brought by a person who, after being shot and severely wounded and on the brink of death, was interrogated by a police sergeant in the EMS ambulance. Although Martinez might have made an incriminating statement, he was never charged with a crime. He brought a federal civil rights suit against the police, claiming that his due process and self-incrimination rights were violated by the abusive questioning. The Supreme Court remanded on the due process issue but ruled that abusive interrogation does not violate the Self-Incrimination Clause. The basis for the Court's general decision is the notion that when closely analyzed, the privilege against self-incrimination does not forbid the government from compelling persons to speak. It is well established that a person can lawfully be compelled to speak by a governmental grant of immunity from prosecution (as was the case in *Portash*). In such a case the government gets the testimony it needs and the witness is guaranteed not to be prosecuted on the basis of the testimony given. A witness who refuses to talk after granted immunity can be held in contempt of court and jailed until he or she talks, and this is lawful and constitutional "compulsion."

In *Chavez* (2003), all nine justices agreed that a simple failure to read *Miranda* warnings to a suspect during custodial interrogation does not violate the suspect's self-incrimination rights. A three-justice dissent written by Justice Kennedy argued that Martinez, however, was subjected to the "use of torture or its equivalent in an attempt to induce a statement" when Sgt. Chavez gave Martinez, who was blinded and paralyzed and was screaming for medical attention, the impression that he would be treated only if he answered the questions. This was the equivalent of the police creating the injuries to Martinez in order to get him to talk. In reply, a four-justice plurality opinion written by Justice Thomas held that even torture during interrogation is not a violation of the Fifth Amendment because the privilege against self-incrimination can be violated only by the *introduction* of tainted evidence into a criminal trial. That is, the plurality saw the privilege against self-incrimination as nothing more than an exclusionary rule. Two justices (Souter and Breyer) concurred in the decision that there was no self-incrimination violation in this case, agreeing with the plurality in viewing the core right of the privilege as a right to not be a witness against oneself—i.e., to exclude compelled testimony. Thus, the Supreme Court is closely divided on the question of whether the privilege against self-incrimination is violated when government officers torture a suspect.

Chavez raises the possibility that clear-cut refusals by the police to honor *Miranda*'s rules will result only in the exclusion of admissions and confessions from testimony and preserve the collateral use exceptions. Prior to *Dickerson*, some police departments, on the advice of their legal advisors, were deliberately violating *Miranda* in order to get the collateral use benefits allowed under the pre-*Dickerson* cases. One federal Court of Appeals held that such abuse gave rise to civil liability. Now that the threat of civil liability was removed by *Chavez*, and the privilege against self-incrimination is deemed only an exclusionary rule, are the collateral uses allowed prior to *Dickerson* still available to the police?

A pair of recent cases have split on the question of whether the derivative use of statements obtained in violation of *Miranda* is allowable. In *United States v. Patane* (2004) the Supreme Court held that physical evidence (a gun) obtained from questions asked after giving incomplete *Miranda* warnings is admissable. The plurality opinion reasoned that testimonial evidence (i.e., not physical evidence) is the central concern of the privilege and insisted that there be a "close fit" between the privilege and any protective rule. Thus, a conservative plurality of the Court continues to view *Miranda* as a prophylactic rule that happens to be a constitutional rule as well. Calling it a constitutional rule, however, gives it no greater effect in protecting suspects against government agents than was the case before *Dickerson* (2000). Four dissenters in *Patane* argued that the fruit of the poisonous tree (derivative evidence) doctrine used in Fourth Amendment cases should be applied to *Miranda* situations. Failure to do so gives police added incentive to ignore or violate *Miranda*.

Missouri v. Seibert (2004) was concerned with the cured statement category. In this case a police officer deliberately interviewed murder suspect Patrice Seibert for 40 minutes in the early morning hours without administering *Miranda* warnings. After the initial interview resulted in Ms. Seibert making a criminal admission that had been suggested by the interrogating officer himself, she was given a 20-minute coffee break.

When the interrogation resumed, the officer began by reading *Miranda* warnings to Ms. Seibert. The Supreme Court ruled the post-*Miranda* confession, as well as admissions made during the first interrogation session, inadmissible.

It is worth noting that *Seibert* does not overrule *Oregon v. Elstad* (1985) and does not completely eliminate the cured statement ruling of *Elstad*. Indeed, Justice Kennedy's concurring opinion specifically supported the ruling in *Elstad* and the decision in *Seibert*. Given the close proximity of the questioning sessions in *Seibert*, the plurality in *Seibert* ruled that there was essentially one interrogation session in which a "question-first" strategy was used; that is, the police first question the suspect without administering warnings, but once an admission is given, they read warnings, obtain a waiver, and then obtain a "Mirandized" statement. The plurality concluded that such a strategy undermines the purpose of *Miranda* warnings—to give a suspect the knowledge and ability to personally decide whether to answer questions posed by the police. Warnings given *after* interrogation make a mockery of the *Miranda* rule.

Seibert is a fact-sensitive decision. In its aftermath a number of lower-court decisions have determined whether its rule does or does not fit a variety of factual situations. Dicta in *Seibert* make it clear that the Court will uphold the collateral use of statements that violate *Miranda* for impeachment purposes (i.e., the *Harris v. New York* 1971, rule), because that collateral use upholds the truth-seeking function of the trial. The ruling in the *Chavez* civil rights law decision may impede court inquiry into whether *Miranda*-violated statements, which the state wishes to use to impeach the testimony of a defendant, were gained by a deliberate ploy. In short, the *Miranda* rule that exists today, although deemed a constitutional rule, is a far weaker protection against the psychological manipulation of suspects by police during custodial interrogation than was contemplated by its authors four decades ago.

Conclusion

Miranda v. Arizona (1966) is arguably the most famous Supreme Court decision. Millions of Americans can recite the four *Miranda* warnings. Yet few are aware of the specific rulings by which the protections intended by *Miranda*'s majority have been whittled away by a conservative majority on the Supreme Court in subsequent years. Scholars agree, on the basis of a few empirical studies and indirect evidence, that in practice police routinely read *Miranda* warnings and do not beat suspects. Hundreds of police departments videotape confessions and some videotape entire interrogation sessions (Sullivan 2004). Despite this, a substantial majority of suspects make incriminating statements (Cassell and Hayman 1996; Leo 1996; Thomas 2004). A recent study identified 125 cases in which persons were wrongly convicted on the basis of false confessions (Drizin and Leo 2004). It appears that the psychological tactics identified in *Miranda* as overbearing continue to be used and sometimes produce miscarriages of justice.

Police investigators rely on the interrogation of suspects as a necessary tool in an ambiguous legal atmosphere. Instead of creating clear-cut rules of procedure, the Supreme Court has issued many rulings that give the police substantial discretion. Police can adhere to a legalistic or due process model of interrogation that closely follows the letter and spirit of *Miranda*, or they can follow the more relaxed interpretation of *Miranda* and the privilege against self-incrimination allowed under the Supreme Court's "crime control model" majority (Packer 1968). By creating the prophylactic rule understanding of *Miranda*, an interpretation that at least four justices continue to adhere to, the Court has invited the police to push the envelope of constitutional confessions law and interrogation practice to determine how far they can interrogate without operating within the original *Miranda* model.

Why doesn't the Supreme Court make up its mind and provide clear-cut rules for the guidance of the police? As a court, it is bound by the separation of powers doctrine and cannot directly administer federal, state, or local law enforcement agencies. Its function and its jurisdiction are limited to interpreting the law. As a constitutional court it interprets a document that in many respects is inherently ambiguous, reflecting the competing goals that are part of the tensions of republican government, which must impose an orderly society for the people while ensuring the liberty of the people. As a political institution, the Court consists of nine persons appointed by different presidents, with different experiences and different views about how to resolve the tensions within our constitutional system. The result can be frustrating for police officers seeking unambiguous guidance. For a student exploring the twists and turns of confessions law, the exercise can provide a deeper appreciation of our Constitution, the Supreme Court, and the nature of law.

Note

1. References to "state officers" in this chapter mean local or state law enforcement officers, in contrast to federal agents.

References

Cassell, Paul G., and Bret S. Hayman. 1996. "Police Interrogation in the 1990s: An Empirical Study of the Effects of Miranda." *U.C.L.A. Law Review* 43:839–922.

Drizin, Steven A., and Richard A. Leo. 2004. "The Problem of False Confessions in the Post-DNA World." *North Carolina Law Review* 82:891–1007.

Leo, Richard. 1996. "Inside the Interrogation Room." *Journal of Criminal Law & Criminology* 86:266.

Packer, Herbert. 1968. *The Limits of the Criminal Sanction.* Stanford, CA: Stanford University Press.

Sullivan, Thomas P. 2004. "Police Experiences With Recording Custodial Interrogations." Northwestern University School of Law, Center on Wrongful Conviction, Special Report.

Thomas, George C., III. 2004. "Stories About Miranda." *Michigan Law Review* 102:1959–2000.

Cases Cited

Ashcraft v. Tennessee, 322 U.S. 143 (1944).

Blackburn v. Alabama, 361 U.S. 199 (1960).
Brown v. Mississippi, 297 U.S. 278 (1936).
Chambers v. Florida, 309 U.S. 227 (1940).
Chavez v. Martinez, 538 U.S. 760 (2003).
Culombe v. Connecticut, 367 U.S. 568 (1961).
Dickerson v. United States, 530 U.S. 428 (2000).
Harris v. New York, 401 U.S. 222 (1971).
Leyra v. Denno, 347 U.S. 556 (1954).
Lynumn v. Illinois, 372 U.S. 528 (1963).
Malinski v. New York, 324 U.S. 401 (1945).
Malloy v. Hogan, 378 U.S. 1 (1964).
Michigan v. Tucker, 417 U.S. 433 (1974).
Mincey v. Arizona, 437 U.S. 385 (1978).
Miranda v. Arizona, 384 U.S. 436 (1966).
Missouri v. Seibert, 542 U.S. 600 (2004).
New Jersey v. Portash, 440 U.S. 450 (1979).
New York v. Quarles, 467 U.S. 649 (1984).
North Carolina v. Butler, 441 U.S. 369 (1979).
Oregon v. Elstad, 470 U.S. 298 (1985).
Oregon v. Hass, 420 U.S. 714 (1975).
Payne v. Arkansas, 356 U.S. 560 (1958).
Spano v. New York, 360 U.S. 315 (1959).
Townsend v. Sain, 372 U.S. 293 (1963).
United States v. Patane, 542 U.S. 630 (2004).
Ward v. Texas, 316 U.S. 547 (1942).

Related Websites

The Supreme Court of the United States
http://www.supremecourtus.gov/
National District Attorneys Association
http://www.ndaa.org/
National Association of Criminal Defense Lawyers
http://nacdl.org/public.nsf/freeform/
publicwelcome?opendocument
The Innocence Project
http://www.innocenceproject.org/

Discussion Questions

1. How were the rules established in *Miranda* designed to protect the rights of a suspect who is being interrogated by the police while in custody?

2. Explain the conflicting views of the majority and dissenting justices in *Miranda* as to whether the rules in *Miranda* were constitutional rules.

3. Describe the ways in which the Supreme Court chipped away at *Miranda*

in the collateral use cases. Do you believe that the decisions in these cases were proper?

4. Was the ruling in *Dickerson v. United States* (2000), upholding *Miranda,* a logical ruling? Did it really change the status of confessions law as it stood before 2000?

5. Do the justices of the Supreme Court agree on the nature and basic meaning of the privilege against self-incrimination? Explain. ✦

Chapter 5
Probation/Parole Searches and the Fourth Amendment

John L. Worrall and David Murphy

In this chapter, the authors examine the legal issues surrounding the searching of offenders who are on probation or parole. In particular, they examine how state and federal courts differ in their treatment of such searches.

At issue in the beginning, as illustrated in *Martin v. United States* (1950), was the consideration of the probationer's status in comparison to an ordinary citizen and whether that status affected the constitutionality of a search. The Fourth Circuit Court of Appeals found that it did. Subsequent Supreme Court decisions have furthered the understanding of the permissibility of evidence seized through a warrantless search under what is called a "special needs" search. Briefly, under the special needs test, a probation officer may search a probationer's home without a warrant to determine whether the probationer is adhering to the probationary conditions. However, the probation officer cannot use the search to begin a new criminal investigation, which is referred to as the "mere subterfuge test."

As demonstrated in this chapter, there are some apparent contradictions in regards to special needs and mere subterfuge. Additionally, some argue that probationers hold a diminished expectation of privacy in regard to the Fourth Amendment. Moreover, the confusion within the court decisions creates additional concerns in relation to the penological and societal goals of rehabilitation as part of community corrections. Finally, these considerations are compounded by the increased caseloads of community corrections officers.

Introduction

Probation is among the most common criminal sanction in the United States (Petersilia 1997). It is a community-based sanction that spares certain criminals from a prison sentence and instead grants them release into the community coupled with supervision by a probation officer (Camp and Camp 1999). *Parole,* like probation, is also a form of corrections in the community. It differs from probation insofar as it applies after someone has already served time in prison. Probation and parole are essential features of the American criminal justice system, as there are not enough prison cells to handle all offenders (Clear and Dammer 2000). And without these means of avoiding additional prison crowding, the costs of dealing with crime would rise to an exorbitant level.

Estimates place the number of probationers and parolees in America at around 5 million (Hughes, Beck, and Wilson 2001). This represents roughly 70 percent of all adult criminals under sentence (Hughes, Beck, and Wilson 2001). Add to this estimate the number of juveniles placed on probation, and the figure approaches 6 million (Snyder and Sickmund 1999). More than half of juveniles who receive a juvenile court sanction are placed on probation (Snyder and Sickmund 1999). One researcher has noted that "2.2 percent of *all* adult residents in the United States are serving criminal justice sentences in the community—about 1 in 27 men, 1 in 160 women" (Petersilia 2002). In light of these numbers, it has been argued that the U.S. criminal justice system is mostly a system of community-based sanctioning (Petersilia 2002; see also Zvekic 1996). Prison and other stringent sanctions are very much the exception.

The fact that there are so many probationers and parolees in the community poses interesting problems for criminal justice officials. For example, officers charged with supervising the offenders must deal with growing caseloads. The average probation caseload now sits at roughly 175 probationers per probation officer, in contrast to the 35 or so probationers per officer during the 1960s (Camp and Camp 1999).[1] Parole does not fare much better, with officers supervising an average of 75 offenders (Camp and Camp 1999). At the same time caseloads are increasing, probation and parole agencies must work within a perplexing and contradictory legal environment. For example, there is little agreement in the courts as to the proper level of justification—if any—needed to search probationers and parolees. This concern served as motivation for us to write this chapter.

The surge in probation and parole caseloads and a confusing legal environment pose at least two problems. First, more probationers and parolees means more offenders coming into contact with those responsible for supervising them. Admittedly, there could be *more* contact between individual probation/parole officers and their clients if caseloads were low, but the very fact that so many offenders are placed in or released into the community means that plenty of contact is taking place. Second, when caseloads are high, service invariably takes a backseat to supervision. And since supervision of probationers and parolees is a law enforcement function, legal issues are all the more relevant. For these reasons it is important to give some attention to an environment surrounding probation and parole, an environment that has become complex and befuddling at the same time that more offenders than ever are being sentenced to community-based sanctions.

This chapter begins with some attention to the legal issues surrounding probation and parole. Then it narrows the focus to searches of probationers and parolees. This means the discussion will take on a Fourth Amendment tone, with the intent of describing the circumstances under which probation and parole officers can search their clients. Most of the attention, however, is on probation because that is where the Supreme Court has had the most to say; there are comparatively few search cases dealing with parole. While discussing searches of probationers and parolees, this chapter also gives attention to the conflicting standards found in Supreme Court, federal appellate, and state supreme court decisions. It will become apparent that there is disagreement and confusion with respect to what justification is required to search probationers *and* parolees.

The Legal Environment

One cannot appreciate the legal environment of probation and parole without first considering the goals of these sanctions. Generally, there are three of them: (1) rehabilitation of the offender; (2) deterrence of misconduct; and (3) the protection of public safety (Lewis 2004). Incorporated into this set of goals is the ultimate objective of successfully reintegrating offenders into free society. There is, however, a measure of debate as to which of these goals is more important. For example, the Sentencing Reform Act of 1984 suggests rehabilitation has long since died and been buried, as it explicitly rejects this goal of sentencing (18 U.S.C.S., app. Ch. 5, pt. b). One could also argue that deterrence of misconduct has suffered as a probation/parole goal in light of the growing caseload problems already discussed. That leaves preservation of public safety, which may or may not be possible because of high caseloads (Worrall et al. 2004). At least on paper, though, rehabilitation remains an ideal goal of community-based sanctions. With respect to probation, the Supreme Court has observed that "rehabilitation and protecting society from future criminal violations" are "the two primary goals" (*United States v. Knights* 2001).

Rehabilitation is important for our purposes because it has helped inform court decisions dealing with searches of offenders. As we will see shortly, some courts have relied—at least in part—on the rehabilitative purposes of probation to permit officers to effectively dispense with the Fourth Amendment's search warrant requirement. Yet at the same time that rehabilitation appears to factor prominently into the goals of community-based sanctions, punishment has also become an increasingly prominent goal, as evidenced by a number of bizarre and arcane probation conditions, such as shaming penalties, agreements to surrender profits from criminal activities, and the like (see Worrall 2006). Indeed, the Sentencing Reform Act allows judges to impose any "court-created condition that is reasonably related to the nature and circumstances of the offense, the history and characteristics of the defendant, and the goals of sentencing" (18 U.S.C. §3563[b][22] [Supp. II 1996]).

These issues have resulted in two general streams of court cases that constitute the bulk of the probation/parole legal environment. First, a number of recent cases have dealt with the appropriateness—in particular, the constitutionality—of various probation conditions. As these cases make clear, the courts have been hesitant to declare specific probation (and, by extension, parole) conditions unconstitutional. For example, in *United States v. Terrigno* (1988), the Ninth Circuit upheld a condition that restricted a probationer's First Amendment rights by refusing to allow her to profit from her crime story. Second, and most relevant in the present context, the courts have grappled with what, if any, constitutional requirements need to be satisfied before probation and parole officers can search their clients. In contrast to the conditions-of-supervision cases, though, little consensus exists in this area. In fact, there is outright contradiction between the decisions of the federal and state courts.

Probation Searches

Criminal defendants who are placed on probation often sign so-called "consent-to-search" agreements. These agreements generally contain a clause to the effect that the probationer can, for the duration of his or her period of supervision, be subject to search by a probation or other peace officer at any time and without justification. Consent-to-search agreements can be regarded in two ways. One view is that probation is a privilege and, as such, probationers should expect some level of inconvenience as a part of being granted that privilege. As we will see, this is the approach taken by the California courts. The other view is that consent-to-search agreements can run counter to the

Fourth Amendment or that their validity is at least questionable. With a few exceptions, the federal courts have taken this perspective. As the Supreme Court put it in *United States v. Knights* (2001), "even when a probationer has consented to searches of his home as a condition of his probation, those searches must be conducted for probation purposes and not as a mere subterfuge for the pursuit of criminal investigations" (p. 1145).

To bring additional clarification to these conflicting perspectives, we will present probation case law in six sections. We begin with an important early probation decision, then we discuss the two key decisions handed down by the U.S. Supreme Court. Next, we look at significant probation search cases decided in the Ninth Circuit Court of Appeals and the California Supreme Court. While Supreme Court decisions are obviously far-reaching, the same cannot be said of decisions handed down by the Ninth Circuit and the California Supreme Court. Ninth Circuit decisions are limited to a fairly specific area, and California decisions are even more limited. Even so, the Ninth Circuit has handed down some controversial decisions that help shed light on probation search case law. Indeed, one of its decisions was cited extensively in a recent Supreme Court case. And inasmuch as California is the most populous state, it is also worth focusing on in some depth (and no where else is the confusion and contradiction in probation search decisions more apparent than in the Golden State). We will wrap up the probation search section with a short summary.

An Early Probation Decision

Well before consent-to-search agreements emerged on the probation scene, the Fourth Circuit Court of appeals addressed the role of the Fourth Amendment in the probation search context. In *Martin v. United States* (1950), the court held that a probationer's "status [was] a circumstance to be taken into consideration" when deciding what Fourth Amendment rights he or she enjoyed. The case is interesting for two reasons. First, the court decided that a probation officer's warrantless entry into and search of a probationer's property, which was then followed by the probationer's arrest, was constitutional. In support of its decision, the court reasoned "that there was no certainty that the illicit merchandise which had just been concealed in the garage might not be removed therefrom before a judicial officer could be found and a warrant issued" (p. 440).

At the same time, though, there was some confusion in the court's decision as to what role a probationer's status plays when it comes to deciding on the constitutionality of a search. This was especially true when the court reflected on the arguments presented by both parties to the case: "On the one hand, it is pointed out that Martin was a probationer under sentence of the court, undergoing a 'mode of mild and ambulatory punishment.' . . . On the other hand, it is shown that Fansler [the probation officer] had no warrant for the arrest of Martin or the search of the premises" (p. 439). The court grappled with whether probationers enjoy different constitutional rights than ordinary citizens or simply whether their probationary status should factor into a totality of circumstances analysis aimed at determining the legality of a search. The tension between both views becomes more apparent in subsequent cases, to which we now turn.

The Supreme Court: *Griffin v. Wisconsin*

The first significant Supreme Court decision concerning probation searches was *Griffin v. Wisconsin* (1987). At issue in that case was a Wisconsin statute that lowered the requisite level of suspicion necessary to support a search of a probationer. The law placed probationers under legal custody of the state, "subject . . . to . . . conditions set by the court and rules and regulations established by" the State Department of Health and Social Services (*Griffin v. Wisconsin* 1987). One of the regulations of concern to the Supreme Court was one allowing "any probation officer to search a probationer's home without a warrant as long as his supervisor approved and as long as there [were]

reasonable grounds to believe the presence of contraband—including any item that the probationer cannot possess under the probation conditions" (*Griffin v. Wisconsin* 1987).

The facts of the case were fairly straightforward. A detective informed the probation department that there might be guns in Griffin's possession. Griffin's probation officer was unavailable, however, so the officer's supervisor, another probation officer, and three uniformed police officers went to Griffin's apartment. The probation officers then conducted a warrantless search of the premises while the police officers stood by. They found a gun. Griffin was charged with possession of a weapon by a convicted felon, itself a felony. He sought suppression of the weapon in his trial. The trial court denied his motion, and he was convicted and sentenced to two years' imprisonment. He appealed first to the Wisconsin Court of Appeals and then to the Wisconsin Supreme Court. Both courts affirmed the trial court's decision to deny Griffin's request that the gun be excluded from trial.

The Wisconsin Supreme Court cited a provision in the probation regulations to the effect that a search of a probationer is constitutional as long as the probation officer has "reasonable grounds" to believe contraband was present. While the U.S. Supreme Court agreed with the lower courts' decisions to admit the gun into evidence, it disagreed with the "reasonable grounds" standard. It found that such a standard, which is lower than probable cause, has no constitutional basis. According to the Supreme Court:

> We think the Wisconsin Supreme Court correctly concluded that this warrantless search did not violate the Fourth Amendment. To reach that result, however, we find it unnecessary to embrace a new principle of law, as the Wisconsin court evidently did, that any search of a probationer's home by a probation officer satisfies the Fourth Amendment as long as the information possessed by the officer satisfies a federal "reasonable grounds" standard. . . . The search of Griffin's home satisfied the demands of the Fourth Amendment because it was carried out pursuant to a regulation that itself satis-

fies the Fourth Amendment's reasonableness requirement under well-established principles. (pp. 872–873)

The Supreme Court went on to apply a "special needs" test to uphold that Wisconsin statute. It felt that the government had "special needs" in the supervision of probationers—namely, rehabilitation and the preservation of public safety. The Court argued that a "warrant requirement would interfere to an appreciable degree with the probation system" (p. 876). It further argued that the usual Fourth Amendment probable cause and warrant requirements would set up "a magistrate rather than the probation officer as the judge of how close a supervision the probationer requires. Moreover, the delay inherent in obtaining a warrant would make it more difficult for probation officials to respond quickly to evidence of misconduct and would reduce the deterrent effect that the possibility of expeditious searches would otherwise create" (p. 876).

Griffin is a widely misinterpreted case. It has been interpreted by some to mean that reasonable grounds are necessary to uphold a search of a probationer, but that is not what the Court said. It basically rejected the "reasonable grounds" standard and upheld the search by noting: "The search of Griffin's home satisfied the demands of the Fourth Amendment because it was carried out pursuant to a regulation that itself satisfies the Fourth Amendment's reasonableness requirement under well-established principles" (p. 873). In other words, the Court upheld the search of Griffin because it was reasonable from a Fourth Amendment standpoint.

The Supreme Court: *United States v. Knights*

In 1996, Pacific Gas and Electric (PG&E) filed a theft-of-services complaint against Mark Knights. Shortly after the complaint was filed, PG&E began to complain of various acts of vandalism to their property. A sheriff's deputy noted that "the acts of vandalism coincided with Knights PG&E-related court appearances" (Skrmetti 2002, 1202). Shortly thereafter, Knights became a suspect, but he was not immediately arrested. He did, however, manage to get in trouble through other means. He was arrested, charged, and convicted of various drug crimes and, in 1998, was placed on probation. As part of his probation, Knights agreed to submit his "person, property, place of residence, vehicle, personal effects, to search at anytime, with or without a search warrant, warrant of arrest or reasonable cause by any probation officer or law enforcement officer" (*United States v. Knights* 2001). He also signed the agreement, noting that "I have received a copy, read and understand the above terms and conditions of probation and agree to abide by same" (p. 114).

Three days after Knights was put on probation, PG&E experienced additional vandalism. As before, a sheriff's deputy suspected that Knights was the perpetrator. Accordingly, he set up surveillance of Knights' residence and observed an individual thought to be Knights' accomplice carrying cylindrical items that resembled pipe bombs. Later, the officer—being aware of Knights' probation condition—conducted a warrantless search of Knights' residence and found "a detonation cord, ammunition, liquid chemicals, instruction manuals on chemistry and electrical circuitry, bolt cutters, telephone pole-climbing spurs, drug paraphernalia, and a brass padlock stamped PG&E" (p. 115). When Knights was arrested and charged with various crimes, he sought suppression of the evidence seized from his apartment. The district court found that the deputy had reasonable suspicion to conduct the search of Knights' apartment, but it nevertheless granted Knights' motion to suppress because the search was not conducted for probation-related purposes but rather as part of a new criminal investigation. The Ninth Circuit Court of appeals affirmed.

When the case came before the Supreme Court, however, a different decision was reached. The Court disagreed with Knights' argument that warrantless searches of probationers should be permissible only if they amount to "a 'special needs' search conducted by a probation officer monitoring whether the probationer is complying with probation restrictions" (p. 117). Knights borrowed the "special needs" language from the *Griffin* case discussed earlier, but since the search at issue in *Griffin* was upheld, Knights' argument was unpersuasive. In the Court's words, "[t]his dubious logic—that an opinion upholding the constitutionality of a particular search implicitly holds unconstitutional any search that is not like it—runs contrary to *Griffin*'s express statement that its 'special needs' holding made it 'unnecessary to consider whether' warrantless searches of probationers were otherwise reasonable within the meaning of the Fourth Amendment" (pp. 117–118).

The *Knights* case is also important because, in it, the Supreme Court basically rejected the "mere subterfuge" test articulated in the lower federal courts, such as in the 1985 case of *United States v. Merchant* (see also *United States v. Ooley* 1997). In *Merchant*, for example, the Ninth Circuit held that a search of a probationer could not be upheld if it was a subterfuge for performing a criminal investigation—in contrast to a search related to one's probation conditions. In *Knights*, though, the Court used more of an administrative justification in its decision to uphold the search of Knights' apartment. It argued that Knights enjoyed a diminished expectation of privacy as part of his probation condition and held that "reasonable suspicion" can justify searches of probationers who sign consent-to-search agreements. Moreover, the Court felt that the government's interest in adequately supervising probationers outweighed individual privacy concerns. Reflecting on the Ninth Circuits decision concerning the search, the Court had this to say:

> The State has a dual concern with a probationer. On the one hand is the hope that he will successfully complete probation and be integrated back into the community. On the other is the concern, quite justified, that he will be more likely to engage in criminal conduct than an ordinary member of the community. The view of the Court of Appeals in this case would require the State to shut its eyes to the latter concern and concentrate only on the former. But we hold that the Fourth Amendment does not put the State to such a choice. Its interest in apprehend-
> ing violators of the criminal law, thereby protecting potential victims of criminal enterprise, may therefore justifiably focus on probationers in a way that it does not on the ordinary citizen. (pp. 120–121)

In short, the Supreme Court stated that "reasonable suspicion" is a sufficient standard for searches of probationers and that warrants are not necessary in such an instance. Importantly, whether reasonable suspicion was in place when Knights' apartment was searched was not at issue; the lower courts and Knights conceded that reasonable suspicion was in place. All the Supreme Court did, then, was conclude that reasonable suspicion justified the search. It did *not* expressly require reasonable suspicion for all searches of probationers, and it did not say anything about the constitutionality of consent-to-search agreements. This ambiguity has not helped shed light on what level of justification, if any, is required for searches of probationers to pass constitutional muster. This will become especially apparent once we consider some pertinent probation search cases arising from the Ninth Circuit and the California Supreme Court.

The Ninth Circuit Court of Appeals

The Ninth Circuit Court of Appeals has taken a much stricter stance with respect to probation searches. It has continually rejected warrantless search conditions specified in probationers' consent-to-search agreements. For example, in *United States v. Consuelo-Gonzales* (1975), a probationer agreed to a search clause that was somewhat more ambiguous than those in use today. She agreed to "submit to search of her person or property at any time when requested by a law enforcement officer" (p. 261, n1). Federal and local law enforcement officers searched her home without a warrant and found narcotics. The Ninth Circuit rejected the search, holding that it did not meet "with the purposes intended to be served by the Federal Probation Act" (p. 262). The author of a concurring opinion reasoned that a probationer's "expectations of privacy may be somewhat greater than a parolee's, because the rehabilitative goals of probation are perhaps more pronounced than those of parole, and the societal threat posed by granting a person probation may be less than that posed by paroling a prisoner" (p. 268).

In *United States v. Merchant* (1985), mentioned in passing in the previous section, the Ninth Circuit created the now-familiar "mere subterfuge" test. In that case, the defendant was placed on a three-year probation term. One of his probation conditions was to spend 18 months in jail, with 12 months suspended. He was also required to submit to warrantless searches by probation and parole officers, as well as discontinue criminal activity. Merchant opposed the jail sentence and announced his intention to appeal. Accordingly, no probation officer was assigned to the case until Merchant's planned appeal was to be heard. In effect, Merchant was granted a "stay" of probation.

About three months later, the assistant district attorney who prosecuted Merchant moved for clarification or modification of the stay. The judge granted the motion and probation was reinstated. Importantly, Merchant was not present at the time of the hearing. Thus, he was placed on probation without his knowledge. His attorney was present, but the attorney did not object to the motion. Four days later, the assistant D.A. and four police officers arrived at Merchant's residence to conduct a search. He protested, arguing that he was not on probation. Merchant was allowed to call his attorney before the search began, at which point the attorney informed the assistant D.A. that Merchant had not yet been advised of the judge's order. Despite his and Merchant's protest, a search commenced, and over 80 firearms and additional contraband were found. He was charged with various offenses, was convicted, and was sentenced to ten years in prison and ordered to pay a fine of $25,000.

As in *Consuelo-Gonzales*, the Ninth Circuit rejected the search. It held: "We conclude that Merchant was not on probation on March 3 when the state officers came to search his house because he was not given notice of the February 27 hearing at which his probation ostensibly was 'reinstated.' Additionally, we conclude that the officers' conduct was not objectively reasonable. Therefore, the evidence seized in the search must be suppressed" (pp. 969–970). While this decision may seem agreeable, some important language from *Merchant* has carried forward into additional probation search cases, most notable the U.S. Supreme Court's decision in *Knights*. The Ninth Circuit criticized the search of Merchant's residence, pointing out that "[t]hese facts strongly suggest that the search was a subterfuge for conducting a criminal investigation" (p. 969). In other words, the Ninth Circuit has been of the mindset that searches of probationers are generally unconstitutional when their sole intent is to detect evidence of criminal activity, rather than being probation related. The court cited several other cases that it had decided similarly in the past (e.g., *United States v. Johnson* 1983; *Latta v. Fitzharris* 1975; *United States v. Jarrad* 1985).

The California Supreme Court

California's Supreme Court has taken perhaps the most conservative stance with respect to probation searches. In stark contrast to the Ninth Circuit's decisions, the California Supreme Court has consistently treated consent-to-search as amounting to full waivers of probationers' privacy rights. The first case of note was *People v. Mason* (1971). There, a probationer agreed to "submit his person, place of residence, [or] vehicle, to search and seizure at any time of the day or night, with or without a search warrant, whenever requested to do so by the Probation Officer or any law enforcement officer" (p. 762). Officers later searched the probationer's residence and vehicle without his permission. The court upheld the search, finding that "the probation condition authorized the search of defendant's residence or car" (p. 631). The court *did* reflect on the balance that needs to be achieved between supervising probationers and respecting their privacy rights, but it of course leaned in favor of the government: "A probationer who has been granted the privilege of probation on condition that he submit at any time to a warrantless search may have no reasonable expectation of traditional Fourth Amendment protection (p. 633).

People v. Bravo (1987) is perhaps the most significant California probation search case. The facts of the case were similar to those in *Mason:* a defendant agreed to a probation condition that required he be subjected to warrantless search at any time. Bravo was searched and contraband was found. He was arrested and charged, and he sought exclusion of the evidence. The *Bravo* court decided that "a probationer who has agreed to submit at any time to a warrantless search may have no reasonable expectation of traditional Fourth Amendment protection" (p. 338). The court also noted that consent-to-search agreements should be viewed from the standpoint of a reasonable person, without regard to individual probationers' subjective expectations of privacy. The court did note, however, that it is possible for probation officers and other law enforcement officials to go too far: "A waiver of Fourth Amendment rights as a condition of probation does not permit searches undertaken for harassment or searches for arbitrary and capricious reasons" (p. 342).

In re Tyrell J. (1994) is one of the more recent probation search cases decided by the California Supreme Court, although it is concerned largely with juveniles. In that case, a minor was released from detention and, pursuant to a state law, was required to submit to warrantless searches as a condition of his release. The minor knew of this probation condition, as he was informed of it by his probation officer, and he was later searched and arrested for possession of marijuana. The minor argued that he enjoyed an expectation of privacy to be free from unreasonable searches, but the court disagreed: "Under these circumstances, even if the minor subjectively expected that he would be able to conceal his illegal possession of marijuana from the outside world, we conclude his expectation was unreasonable, being an expectation that society is unwilling to recognize as legitimate" (p. 89).

Tyrell effectively affirmed an earlier case from the California Court of Appeal in which a minor was also required, as part of a probation condition, to submit to warrantless searches (*In re Binh L.*, 1992). In that case, a police officer who had neither probable cause to search nor knowledge of the probation condition detained and searched a juvenile. He found a loaded pistol, and the search was upheld. The *Binh L.* court concluded that the search condition "was rational both to assure that the minor would correct his behavior and in this sense be rehabilitated, and to protect the public against the possibility he would not" (p. 204). So, not only did *Tyrell* and *Binh L.* result in sanctioning of probation conditions permitting warrantless searches, they also did not require knowledge on the part of the searching officer as to whether the probation condition was in place.

Goldilocks and the Three Courts

The point was made early in this chapter that there is confusion in the courts as to the proper justification necessary for conducting warrantless searches of probationers. California has taken the most conservative stance, sanctioning consent-to-search agreements and granting police and probation officers authority to search probationers at any time and without consent (or even knowledge of the probation condition). To borrow from Goldilocks and the Three Bears, one could easily argue that this perspective is "too cold," in the sense that it takes a tough-line stance against probationers. In contrast, it could be argued that the Ninth Circuit approach is "too hot," as it represents the opposite extreme. That court has consistently struck down consent-to-search agreements. The Supreme Court's view, most clearly articulated in the *Knights* decision, could thus be construed as "just right." On the one hand, it deferred to law enforcement officials by allowing them to conduct warrantless searches of probationers with less than probable cause. On the other hand, it did not expressly state that such searches with *no* justification are acceptable.

Parole Searches

In contrast to probation, there are significantly fewer parole cases. In 2003 there were only about 775,000 persons in the United States on parole compared to approximately 4 million persons on probation (Glaze and Palla 2004). Indeed, the U.S. Supreme Court appears to have considered the relationship between the Fourth Amendment and parole only once. In *Pennsylvania Board of Probation and Parole v. Scott* (1998), the Court decided that the exclusionary rule does not bar at parole revocation hearings the introduction of evidence obtained in violation of a parolee's Fourth Amendment rights. In that case, a defendant pleaded nolo contendere to a charge of third-degree murder and was sentenced to prison. He was released on parole shortly thereafter and signed an agreement providing the following: "I expressly consent to the search of my person, property and residence, without a warrant by agents of the Pennsylvania Board of Probation and Parole. Any items, in [*sic*] the possession of which constitutes a violation of parole/reparole shall be subject to seizure, and may be used as evidence in the parole revocation process" (p. 360).

About five months later the parolee was arrested, pursuant to an arrest warrant, for alleged violations of his parole conditions. Before he was transferred to a correctional facility, the parolee gave the arresting officers the keys to his residence. The officers entered the residence, searched it, and found various weapons. At his revocation hearing, the parolee objected to the introduction of the evidence, but the Supreme Court disagreed with his argument: "We have long been averse to imposing federal requirements upon the parole systems of the States. A federal requirement that parole boards apply the exclusionary rule, which is itself a 'grudgingly taken medicant' . . . would severely disrupt the traditionally informal, administrative process of parole revocation. . . . We therefore hold that parole boards are not required by federal law to exclude evidence obtained in violation of the Fourth Amendment" (p. 369).

Scott was an interesting case, for two reasons. First, it was a bright line decision, subject to little interpretation. This stands in contrast to certain probation cases, such as *Knights*, where the Court was ambiguous in

some of its language. Second, Scott signed a consent-to-search agreement, but the Court opted not to focus on it. Rather, it focused on the possible deterrent benefits associated with requiring that the exclusionary rule operate the same way in parole revocation hearings as it does in criminal trials. This refusal to address the constitutionality of consent-to-search agreements may not seem problematic at a glance, but in moving to decisions of the lower federal courts, the omission is somewhat troubling. Just as there is confusion in the lower courts about the relationship between consent-to-search agreements and the Fourth Amendment, so too is there confusion with respect to parole searches. In the remainder of this section we consider two cases that illustrate the confusion.

The Tenth Circuit has given parole agents some latitude in terms of conducting searches. At issue in *United States v. Trujillo* (2005) was an agreement that placed significant restrictions on a parolee's liberties. Part of the agreement required Trujillo to "permit agents of Adult Probation and Parole to search my person, residence, vehicle or any other property under my control, without a warrant, at any time, day or night, upon reasonable suspicion to ensure compliance with the conditions of my parole" (p. 1238). After Trujillo was on parole for about a year, it became apparent that he was not complying with certain parole conditions. In November 2001, Trujillo submitted a urine sample that tested positive for drugs. Trujillo also started to violate other parole conditions. Officers secured an arrest warrant, arrested Trujillo, then searched his residence. The warrantless search turned up weapons and narcotics paraphernalia. Trujillo was charged with various crimes and sought exclusion of the evidence. He raised two arguments, first that the arrest terminated the search provision of his parole agreement (see, e.g., *United States v. Jones* 1998; *United States v. Martin* 1994; *United States v. Hill* 1992), and, second, that the searching officers did not have the reasonable suspicion necessary to engage in the search. With respect to Trujillo's first argument, the court interpreted it in this way:

Mr. Trujillo next argues that the parole agreement was intended to place conditions on his liberty only so long as he remained free on parole. Once police took him into custody, the argument continues, he lost the liberty of parole and the agreement ceased to operate. While this may be Mr. Trujillo's understanding of the agreement, there is nothing in the text of the agreement to suggest that it terminates at the moment a law enforcement officer takes Mr. Trujillo into custody. (p. 1244)

As for Trujillo's second argument, the court was unconvinced that the officers did not have reasonable suspicion to conduct the search: "Once there was reason to believe that Mr. Trujillo violated his parole agreement [by, for example, testing positive for drugs], there is, by definition, reasonable suspicion to support a search of his residence to 'ensure compliance' with the conditions of parole" (p. 1245). In short, the Tenth Circuit has sanctioned parole searches based on consent-to-search agreements. Interestingly, though, the agreement at issue in that case mandated a specific degree of suspicion that must be in place before the search can be conducted. There is no uniformity across the states, however, as to whether this is required. Our earlier discussion of probation also illustrates this point.

The Ninth Circuit has, not surprisingly, taken a very different position on parole search agreements. An illustrative case is *United States v. Crawford* (2003). There an FBI agent conducted a warrantless search of a parolee's residence. The search was conducted pursuant to an agreement in Crawford's parole conditions to the effect that he agreed to "search or seizure by a parole officer or other peace officer at any time of the day or night," but the agent did not expect (as he testified) to find any evidence linking Crawford to a robbery that was committed some two years earlier. The agent merely wanted to use the time to "talk" with Crawford about an old bank robbery case. Crawford was asked whether he would mind accompanying the agent to the local FBI field office. He did so. Once at the office, the agent began to advise Crawford of his *Miranda* rights, but he did not finish. Subse-

quently, Crawford confessed. He was later indicted and sought suppression of the statements he made while at the FBI office. The government argued, in part, that Crawford consented to the search by virtue of signing his parole agreement, which contained the consent-to-search provision. The Ninth Circuit disagreed:

> As the record reveals, before a prisoner becomes a parolee, and while still in custody, he is given a sheet of conditions that his prospective parole agent "has" him sign. The purported blanket waiver is among these conditions. If Crawford did not sign the conditions sheet, he would have been denied parole and returned immediately to prison custody. To call this choice—either waiver or certain incarceration—"free and voluntary" would be to misconceive the concept of meaningful consent. (p. 718)

The court did not focus solely on the consent agreement, however. It argued that Crawford enjoyed a measure of privacy in his home and that the lack of individualized suspicion preceding the FBI's search failed to meet Fourth Amendment requirements. The government also argued that, to the extent the initial search was unconstitutional, the taint of that search was purged when Crawford confessed at a later point in time. As suggested in *Wong Sun v. United States* (1963), the court looked at the temporal proximity of the search to the confession, the presence of intervening events, and the "flagrancy" of the constitutional violation. It found that the confession came shortly after a 20-minute drive from Crawford's home to the FBI office, hardly a long period of time. Likewise, the court found no intervening events and concluded that the FBI agent flagrantly violated previous Ninth Circuit decisions specifying that probation/parole searches cannot be conducted without a measure of individualized suspicion. In sum, the court concluded that "in both design and effect, Crawford's statements at the FBI offices were 'come at by exploitation of' the illegal parole search" (p. 722).

Conclusion

At the beginning of this chapter, we pointed out that probation and parole caseloads have increased over time. More probationers and parolees means, quite simply, more searches. This situation has resulted in a lot of work for community corrections officers. We also pointed out that the legal environment surrounding probation and parole, particularly that concerned with searches of offenders, is confusing, contradictory, and continually changing. As we noted, the courts have acknowledged that a balance must be struck between the state's interests in respect to supervising probationers and the privacy rights of probationers. To date, however, the specific circumstances under which the privacy rights of probationers outweigh the state's interests are unclear at best. Moreover, the court has indicated that consent to search agreements does not authorize probation officers to, for instance, conduct searches for purposes of harassing probationers. Nevertheless, the courts have not provided sufficient guidance for distinguishing between the legitimate and illegitimate grounds for searches.

When high caseloads are put together with the legal environment as we have discussed it, constitutional questions concerning probation and parole officers' conduct have emerged, and they will continue to come into focus. Also, since many of the searches in the cases we discussed were performed by police and other law enforcement officers, their actions are also relevant.

Most of our discussion centered on the inconsistencies in court decisions from the Supreme Court, the Ninth Circuit Court of Appeals, and the California Supreme Court. At issue in most of the cases we discussed was the constitutionality of a probation or parole search, usually conducted pursuant to a consent-to-search agreement. The California Supreme Court has decided in favor of criminal justice officials, whereas the Ninth Circuit has decided in the opposite fashion. The Supreme Court, most notably in *Knights*, has staked its claim on the middle ground. What is absent from any of the decisions we discussed, however, was specific attention to the constitutionality of consent-to-search agreements. The Supreme Court has carefully avoided the issue, and the result is confusion in the lower courts.

Note

1. Increases in caseload sizes can, in part, be attributed to the dramatic increase in the number of individuals convicted and sentenced for drug offenses. Drug offenders typically require a lower level of supervision compared to more dangerous violent offenders. As a result, increases in average caseload size do not necessarily require a proportional increase in the actual average probation officer workload.

References

Camp, C., and G. Camp. 1999. *The Corrections Yearbook, 1998.* Middletown, CT: Criminal Justice Institute.

Clear, T. R., and H. R. Dammer. 2000. *The Offender in the Community.* Belmont, CA: Wadsworth.

Glaze, L., and S. Palla. 2004. *Probation and Parole in the United States.* Washington, DC: Bureau of Justice Statistics.

Hughes, T., A. Beck, and D. Wilson. 2001. *Trends in State Parole, 1990–2000.* Washington, DC: U.S. Department of Justice, Office of Justice Programs, Bureau of Justice Statistics.

Lewis, M. R. 2004. "Lost in Probation: Contrasting the Treatment of Probationary Search Agreements in California and Federal Courts." *UCLA Law Review* 51:1703–1750.

Petersilia, J. 1997. "Probation in the United States." In M. Tonry (ed.), *Crime and Justice: A Review of Research* (Vol. 22). Chicago: University of Chicago Press.

———. 2002. "Community Corrections." In J. Q. Wilson and J. Petersilia (eds.), *Crime: Public Policies for Crime Control.* Oakland, CA: Institute for Contemporary Studies.

Skrmetti, J. T. 2002. "The Keys to the Castle: A New Standard for Warrantless Home Searches in *United States v. Knights*." *Harvard Journal of Law and Public Policy* 25:1201–1255.

Snyder, H., and M. Sickmund. 1999. *Juvenile Offenders and Victims: 1999 National Report.* Washington, DC: Office of Juvenile Justice and Delinquency Prevention.

Worrall, J. L. 2006. *Crime Control in America: An Assessment of the Evidence.* Boston, MA: Allyn and Bacon.

Worrall, J. L., P. Schram, E. Hayes, and M. Newman. 2004. "An Analysis of the Relationship Between Probation Caseloads and Property Crime Rates in California Counties." *Journal of Criminal Justice* 32:231–241.

Zvekic, U. 1996. "Probation in International Perspective." *Overcrowded Times* 7(2):1–2.

Cases Cited

Griffin v. Wisconsin, 483 U.S. 868 (1987).

In re Binh L., 6 Cal. Rptr. 2d 678 (Ct. App. 1992).

In re Tyrell J., 876 P.2d 519 (Cal. 1994).

Latta v. Fitzharris, 521 F.2d 246 (9th Cir.), cert. denied, 423 U.S. 897 (1975).

Martin v. United States, 183 F.2d 436 (4th Cir. 1950).

Pennsylvania Board of Probation and Parole v. Scott, 524 U.S. 357 (1998).

People v. Bravo, 738 P.2d 336 (Cal. 1987).

People v. Mason, 488 P.2d 630 (Cal. 1971).

United States v. Consuelo-Gonzales, 521 F.2d 259 (9th Cir. 1975).

United States v. Crawford, 323 F.3d 700 (2003).

United States v. Hill, 967 F.2d 902 (3rd Cir. 1992).

United States v. Jarrad, 754 F.2d 1451 (9th Cir. 1985).

United States v. Johnson, 722 F.2d 525 (9th Cir. 1983).

United States v. Jones, 152 F.3d 680 (7th Cir. 1998).

United States v. Knights, 534 U.S. 112 (2001).

United States v. Martin, 25 F.3d 293 (6th Cir. 1994).

United States v. Merchant, 760 F.2d 963 (9th Cir. 1985).

United States v. Ooley, 116 F.3d 370, 372 (9th. Cir. 1997).

United States v. Terrigno, 838 F.2d 371 (9th Cir. 1988).

United States v. Trujillo, 404 F.3d 1238 (10th Cir. 2005).

Wong Sun v. United States, 371 U.S. 471 (1963).

Related Websites

Police-Probation Partnerships: Boston's Operation Night Light

http://www.sas.upenn.edu/jerrylee/programs/fjc/paper_mar02.pdf

Police-Corrections Partnerships

http://www.ncjrs.gov/pdffiles1/175047.pdf

Surveillance of Probationers

http://ojjdp.ncjrs.org/pubs/gun_violence/sect05-b.html

"Broken Windows" Probation: The Next Step in Fighting Crime

http://www.manhattan-institute.org/html/press_briefing__broken_windows.htm

Discussion Questions

1. Summarize the courts' views on Fourth Amendment waivers.

2. Which court's view on Fourth Amendment waivers is most sensible: the California Supreme Court's, the Ninth Circuit's, or the U.S. Supreme Court's?

3. Should probation/parole officers be given the latitude they currently have to conduct searches of probationers/parolees? Why or why not?

4. What is likely to happen with current standards governing probation/parolee searches as time goes on? Why do you feel this way?

5. Though it was not mentioned in this chapter, many probation agencies are forming partnerships with police agencies (and vice versa). Is this advisable? Why or why not? ✦

Chapter 6
Drug Tests, the Fourth Amendment, and the Supreme Court's Rationale for Warrantless and Suspicionless Searches

Claudia San Miguel

In this chapter, the author examines the key constitutional considerations regarding drug testing. The analysis covers germane Supreme Court cases and historical decisions regarding the formation of drug-testing policy and Fourth Amendment protections; the contentious balancing test; and the implications for private and public employees, students/athletes, and political candidates that have arisen in light of these rulings.

First, the author outlines the history and origin of drug-testing policies though the landmark Supreme Court case *Schmerber v. California* (1966) and adds a brief description of the social and political atmosphere in the 1970s and 1980s that gave birth to "war on drugs" policies. Next, the chapter examines other constitutional issues, such as the Fourth Amendment expectation of privacy and the Fifth Amendment right against self-incrimination.

The author notes that the core principle on which the Supreme Court rests its decisions regarding the constitutionality of drug tests is reasonableness. Generally, the Supreme Court uses a two-pronged analysis to determine such constitu-

tionality: (1) whether the collection of urine, blood, or other samples constitutes a search under the Fourth Amendment, and (2) whether that search is reasonable. It is here that a balance between individual privacy rights and the compelling interests of employers, school officials, governing agencies, and so on, must be made. Moreover, this chapter also illustrates the importance of understanding the various ways in which the constitution may be interpreted, such as the differences between a literal or original interpretation versus a subjective interpretation of the Fourth Amendment.

Introduction

Drug and alcohol abuse remains a serious problem in American society. Although it is difficult to obtain accurate statistics on the problem, the National Survey on Drug Use and Health estimates that more than 20 million Americans use illicit substances (Walker 2006). No doubt the problem of drug and alcohol abuse deserves special consideration as there may be a significant direct and indirect association between these substances and crime. This possible association makes laws and public policy a necessary and a justifiable reaction. However, much controversy exists over what some regard as far-reaching policies that subject individuals, such as employees and even students with perhaps no history of drug or alcohol abuse, to drug tests. Thus, debate ensues over the *necessity and justifiability* as well as the legality of policies that compel such individuals to take such tests.

Drug tests have been and continue to be a contentious issue in American society. Indeed, testing an individual's blood, breath, or urine to detect the presence of alcohol or illegal substances has created a considerable amount of controversy, especially with respect to the constitutionality of the *procedures* used to obtain samples for chemical analysis (Befort 1997; Brewer 1997; Dorancy-Williams 1998). In particular, debates over drug tests have focused mainly on whether the physical intrusion into one's body (the penetration of a needle beneath the skin), the production of a breath (breathalyzer test), or the excretion of bodily waste (urine analysis), constitutes a search and therefore invokes the protections of the Fourth Amendment. Contentions also exist regarding the Supreme Court's interpretation of the warrant and probable cause requirements of the Fourth Amendment (Dorancy-Williams 1998) with respect to drug tests.

Since the 1960s, the Court has gradually recognized circumstances under which it is necessary to relax the warrant requirement of the Fourth Amendment in order to obtain the needed specimen to conduct a drug test. Since the 1980s, the Court has also recognized circumstances in which the probable cause requirement of the Fourth Amendment may be lessened. In fact, in the late 1980s and early 1990s, the Court recognized instances when warrantless and suspicionless drug tests may be allowed. In spite of the implications such rulings have had and continue to have on criminal suspects, much of the debate over drug tests has focused on the rights of employees, working in either the public or private domain. Accordingly, much controversy exists over whether employees can be subjected to drug tests as a condition of employment, for promotion to a sensitive position, a part of return-to-duty policy, or after the occurrence of an accident without the need to abide by the warrant and probable cause requirements of the Fourth Amendment (Dorancy-Williams 1998). Controversy has also ensued over the constitutionality of policies that require students/athletes to be tested for illegal substances and most recently over statutory law that requires political candidates to be tested for substance abuse (Lee 2001; Miller 1996; Wilkinson 1997).

This chapter reviews the legal parameters of drug testing including an analysis of the various constitutional issues that have been raised as a result of such tests. In particular, because the protections of the Fourth Amendment are most often invoked by those subjected to drug tests, this amendment is more thoroughly examined. Also, the Court's rulings with respect to drug tests, which include a contentious balancing test, are evaluated, together with the implications such rulings have on public and private employ-

ees as well as students/athletes and political candidates. Finally, other ramifications of drug tests are explored, including the disclosure of medical information beyond the original purpose of the tests, legal liabilities, and the seeming diminution of the requirements of the Fourth Amendment.

Legal Parameters of Drug Testing

The legal framework for drug-testing policies began to take form in the late 1960s. In the landmark case of *Schmerber v. California*, the Supreme Court reasoned that blood tests were searches within the meaning of the Fourth Amendment. The Court also explained that even the compulsory taking of a blood sample without a warrant was within the constitutional boundaries of the amendment, as long as the procedure used to obtain the sample was reasonable. *Reasonableness*, according to the Court, meant that the blood sample had to be drawn by a medical professional. The Court's declaration regarding the constitutionality of warrantless drug tests in *Schmerber* marked the beginning of the Court's drug-testing doctrine and signified the Court's willingness to liberally interpret and apply the mandates of the Fourth Amendment in such cases. Although *Schmerber* involved the roadside stop of a drunk driver, the Court's rationale, which also took into consideration the exigency of obtaining samples before the alcohol in the suspect's bloodstream disappeared (del Carmen 2004), was instrumental in formulating drug-testing policies in the workplace almost two decades later.

The applicability of warrantless drug tests in *Schmerber* to employees working in the public and private domain inherently alarmed many individuals who quickly envisioned an infringement of constitutional rights. Nevertheless, these physically intrusive and constitutionally charged tests became almost automatic conditions of federal employment by the late 1980s (Lemons 2004). Their endorsement by public and later private industry was, however, preceded by a tremendous government initiative to stop the use of illicit drugs and the recognition of lost productivity and liability that would result from hiring or retaining illicit drug-using employees. As such, the ease with which drug-testing policies were adopted must be understood within the context of several temporal factors that the nation reluctantly struggled with in the decade of the 1980s (Haberberger 1990).

Beginning in the 1970s and extending well into the 1980s, our nation was believed to be besieged by the widespread use of drugs. Statistics by the National Institute on Drug Abuse estimated that marijuana and cocaine use was rampant (Haberberger 1990). This national organization reported that 20 million Americans used marijuana and another 4 million were addicted to cocaine. Preoccupation with this epidemic problem prompted a national and public campaign to rid our cities and neighborhoods of illicit drug use. The "war on drugs" commenced, and policy to tackle the wave of drug use was launched in several directions—including the workplace. Decisions to include the workplace in the "war on drugs" was most likely affected by additional statistics indicating that employee drug and alcohol use "accounted for $76 billion per year in lost productivity and $4.4 billion in lost employment costs" (Haberberger 1990, 348). Estimated costs for health care and accidents due to drug and alcohol use by employees were also staggering.

Statistics compiled by national organizations regarding drug and alcohol use, combined with findings on the exponentially outstanding monetary loss in industry resulting from work-related accidents and lost productivity from illicit drug-using employees, led President Ronald Reagan, in 1986, to issue an executive order titled "Drug-Free Federal Workplace," authorizing the federal government to perform drug tests on all its employees. This order meant the testing of more than 400,000 federal workers. It also served as the catalyst for the mass drug testing of state and local government employees (Mechanic 1988). By 1987, private companies had begun to implement similar drug-testing policies (Haberberger 1990). For instance, one-third of all Fortune 500 companies began to test both job applicants and employees. In 1988, a report by the U.S. Department of Labor indicated that almost 60 percent of private businesses with 5,000 or more employees were testing for drug and alcohol use.

Although drug testing in the workplace became routine by the late 1980s, no uniformity existed as to when employees were to be subjected to such tests. Potential employees could be tested at the pre-employment stage, thus making employment conditional on the results of the test, as well as tested periodically once hired. Employees could also be subjected to tests if employers had reasonable suspicion of illicit drug use and after the occurrence of a work-related accident. Today, the circumstances under which public and private employees are subjected to drug tests continue to vary, as they may be asked to submit a specimen for analysis at virtually any stage of employment. However, the different stages of employment carry variable degrees of constitutional protections. Thus, prehires do not enjoy the same constitutional protections as current employees. In fact, their degree of protection is minimal at best (Mechanic 1988). Additionally, the degree of constitutional safeguards varies between public and private employees. Generally, the guarantees and rights contained in the U.S. Constitution apply to actions of the federal and state governments; therefore, public and government employees have been afforded the most constitutional protections. Conversely, private employees have had difficulty invoking constitutional protections unless they can demonstrate "a sufficient nexus between the actions of the private employer and a government entity" (Haberberger 1990, 356). Of primary importance for private employees is that this so-called nexus between a private and government entity also means that constitutional guarantees such as the warrant and probable cause requirements of the Fourth Amendment may be suspended.

Constitutional Issues

Several constitutional issues are implicit in drug testing. Those subjected to tests may assert their privilege against self-incrimination under the Fifth Amendment. They may also declare that such tests are in violation of their due process rights under the Fifth and Fourteenth Amendments or the Equal Protection Clause of the Fourteenth Amendment. Challenges to the legality of drug tests based on these constitutional issues have met with little success (Haberberger 1990). For instance, with respect to self-incrimination, the Supreme Court has ruled that even the compulsory testing of an individual does not violate the Fifth Amendment's privilege against self-incrimination, since the amendment only protects testimonial evidence and since the amendment is meant to protect only those facing the possibility of criminal prosecution. Because the "withdrawal of blood and use of the analysis . . . does not involve compulsion [to provide testimonial evidence]" (*Schmerber v. California* 1966), the Court has ruled that blood tests are not protected by the Fifth Amendment.

The Due Process Clauses in both the Fifth and Fourteenth Amendments have also been invoked to challenge the constitutionality of drug tests with limited success (Haberberger 1990). Generally, those who assert the protections of these two amendments claim that their *procedural due process* rights have been violated. Some of the procedural due process claims have been raised when the employee has been subjected to a drug test without adequate notice or when he or she has been terminated without a hearing. In either claim, the Court has explained that providing adequate notice is not a prerequisite for employee drug tests. However, an employee must have recourses available to contest any discrepancy in laboratory results prior to his or her termination. For instance, the employee should be able to resubmit a specimen to a laboratory of his or her choosing, and if the test results indicate drug use, a hearing should be conducted to ascertain whether such drugs are illegal. Thus, an employee is entitled to a hearing prior to being discharged from employment and must be provided an opportunity to explain the reasons for a positive test result (Todd 1987).

Only a few challenges have been based on the Equal Protection Clause of the Fourteenth Amendment. Challenges based on the Equal Protection Clause have focused on se-lective drug-testing policies, such as those that subject only employees in certain positions to provide a specimen (Haberberger 1990). These challenges rarely capture the attention of the Court. Perhaps the most successful challenges to drug-testing polices, although limited in number, have been those that rely on the safeguards of the Fourth Amendment (Betts 1990). The Fourth Amendment of the U.S. Constitution states

> The right of the people to be secure in their persons, houses, papers, and effects, against unreasonable searches and seizures, shall not be violated, and no Warrants shall issue, but upon probable cause, supported by Oath or affirmation, and particularly describing the place to be searched, and the persons or things to be seized.

Unquestionably, the Fourth Amendment provides the most ample protections for employees subjected to drug tests, as the amendment has and continues to serve as a defender against unreasonable searches and seizures (Peltason and Davis 2000). Employees wishing to dispute the legality or, more precisely, the constitutionality of a drug test often claim that such tests constitute an illegal search and seizure. Yet, the Fourth Amendment has been constrained in its ability to protect employees in large part because of the Court's evolving guidelines with respect to searches and seizures, particularly with respect to the warrant and probable cause requirements of the amendment (Betts 1990; Dorancy-Williams 1998). Beginning with *Schmerber v. California,* the Court created a *reasonableness* standard that replaced the need for officers to fully abide by the warrant requirement of the Fourth Amendment. Arguably, the need to supplant the warrant requirement with a reasonableness standard was attributable to the exigency in obtaining samples before they dissipated into the suspect's bloodstream (del Carmen 2004). However, the Court's initial rationale to forgo the warrant requirement in favor of a reasonableness standard due to exigent circumstances in *Schmerber* was abandoned in subsequent drug-related and drug-testing cases. Indeed, exigency to obtain samples became almost irrelevant.

In *New Jersey v. T.L.O.*, for instance, the Court affirmed its decision in *Schmerber* by holding that warrantless searches are not in violation of the Fourth Amendment, as long as they are reasonable. The reasonableness standard used by the Court in *T.L.O.* was not, however, based on urgent or exigent circumstances. Rather, the Court crafted a reasonableness standard based on the legitimacy of the search. *T.L.O.* involved the search of a student's purse by school administrative personnel after they had established reasonable grounds to conclude that the student possessed items in violation of school policy. Challenged on grounds that school personnel conducted an illegal search, the Court explained that the preservation of safety and order in schools, in addition to the maintenance of an environment conducive to learning, necessitates some easing of the Fourth Amendment. Justice Blackmun captured the sentiment of the Court in *T.L.O* when he wrote that when "special needs, beyond the normal need for law enforcement, make the warrant and probable cause requirement impractical, a court is entitled to change the balancing of interests." Accordingly, the Court held that the goals of pubic schools outweighed not only the student's expectation of privacy but also the need to act in accordance with the warrant requirement. The Court further held that probable cause did not have to precede the search. The only requirement needed was reasonable grounds to suspect wrongdoing.

Despite the Court's reasoning that the Fourth Amendment was applicable to the actions of school personnel, thus making the amendment relevant to the activities of civil as well as criminal authorities (Polloway 1989; del Carmen, Ritter, and Witt 2001), of importance in *T.L.O.* was the establishment of a special exception to the Fourth Amendment—one that would be detrimental to employee challenges of drug-testing policies in the workplace. This exception not only eased the warrant and probable cause requirements but created a balancing test based on *reasonableness*. According to the Court, the Constitution does not prohibit reasonable searches, even those conducted without a warrant or probable cause. Rather, the Constitution only prohibits searches that are unreasonable (Dorancy-Williams 1998). Reasonableness, as explained by the Court, must be balanced or weighed in light of the legitimacy or purpose of the search. As noted, at the height of our nation's war on drugs, overwhelming evidence surfaced regarding not only the liability of hiring or retaining illicit drug-using employees but also of the monetary loss that would result from a decline in employee productivity. The subsequent implementation of drug-testing policies was not only justified on these grounds but also on the need to preserve a safe working environment (Dorancy-Williams 1998). The preservation of safe working conditions for workers and ultimately the safety of the public was the crucial element in the creation of a special exception to the Fourth Amendment in employee drug-testing cases—an element that tipped the balance in favor of the employer and seemingly diminished employee constitutional protections.

Two years after *T.L.O.* the Court elaborated on the reasonableness standard and the special exception to the Fourth Amendment in *O'Connor v. Ortega* (1987) by stating that not even an individual's expectation of privacy in the workplace was sufficient to invoke the full protections of the Fourth Amendment. Although the Court's landmark decision in *Katz v. United States* established that the Fourth Amendment protects "people, not places," meaning that the safeguards of the amendment are applicable to wherever an individual has a reasonable expectation of privacy, the Court in *Ortega* reasoned that public employees whose "work environment constantly permits supervisors and co-workers to frequent one another's office" did not have a legitimate expectation of privacy (Polloway 1989, 153). The Court further stated that even when employees have an expectation of privacy, such privacy may be infringed upon when the government has a legitimate interest in preserving an efficient and safe working environment. As such, the Court in *Ortega* reiterated what is now known as the *special needs* exception to the Fourth Amendment—an exception which discards the warrant and probable cause requirement of the amendment. This exception also creates a two-pronged analysis for determining the constitutionality of drug-testing policies where the Court first determines if a search was in fact conducted and then determines whether the search was reasonable.

Significant Drug-Testing Cases

The *Skinner* Decision. The Court's drug-testing doctrine prior to 1989 established a *bounded* legal criterion to determine the constitutionality of the many policies that mandated employees to submit blood, breath, or urine specimens for chemical analysis. This bounded legal criterion not only balanced the needs of the employer against the privacy rights of the employee but also delineated a specific two-pronged analysis to assess the constitutionality of drug-testing policies (Haberberger 1990; Polloway 1989). Because the analysis compels courts to first consider whether the test constitutes a search followed by an assessment of reasonableness, the two-pronged analysis may be construed as a means to ensure that courts give utmost importance to safeguarding the Fourth Amendment. By 1989 however, the legal parameters of drug-testing policies were expanded once again and the requirements of the Fourth Amendment were again eased. In *Skinner v. Railway Labor Executives Association*, the Court upheld a drug-testing policy devoid of any need for employers to first establish suspicion of drug or alcohol use. Unlike the circumstances in *T.L.O.* and *Ortega* where some degree of suspicion preceded the search or drug test respectively, this precedent-setting ruling purged the need to establish even the smallest amount or degree of suspicion prior to subjecting employees to drug tests.

In *Skinner,* the Court was asked to determine the constitutionality of regulations, promulgated by the Federal Railroad Administration (FRA), which mandated certain employees to submit blood and urine specimens after the occurrence of major train accidents or incidents (FRA Regulations Subpart C) and the constitutionality of a specific regulation that authorized the railroad to administer either breath or urine tests to employees who violated safety rules (FRA Regulations Subpart D). Specifically, the Court was asked to determine whether these regulations, which did not require the employer to first establish any degree of suspicion, violated the Fourth Amendment. To do so, the Court examined whether the Fourth Amendment could provide any protections to employees working in the private sector and conversely whether the amendment could limit the actions of a private party. Generally, the Fourth Amendment does not apply to the actions of the private sector (Haberberger 1990). However, since the 1960s, the Court has endorsed extending the protections of the Fourth Amendment and conversely limiting the actions of the private sector, if the activity of a private actor and the government "are so intertwined for their mutual benefit that the private actor should be subjected to constitutional limitations" (*Burton v. Wilmington Parking Authority* 1961). In a series of cases, the Court created what is known as the *sufficient nexus standard*, which broadens the applicability of the Fourth Amendment to the private sector if it can be demonstrated that the actions of the private employer are interrelated with the actions of the government and if it can be demonstrated that such actions mutually benefit both parties. Accordingly, the Court in *Skinner* explained that the regulations, promulgated by the FRA after collecting evidence of rampant alcohol and drug use in the railroad industry and after numerous attempts to deter employees from indulging in such substances, were a concerted effort to maintain a safe working environment and preserve the safety of the public. Because it is the desire of the government "to share the fruits" of such efforts, the Court declared that the Fourth Amendment was applicable to the railroad industry (Haberberger 1990).

Once the applicability of the Fourth Amendment was established, the Court turned its attention to whether subjecting employees to drug tests after the occurrence of an accident or after the violation of safety rules was an unreasonable search under the Fourth Amendment. In conducting its prescribed two-pronged deliberation, the Court confirmed that the taking of blood and breath for analysis were indeed intrusions into the body, although in varying degrees, and thus must be deemed Fourth Amendment searches. With respect to urine samples, the Court found that because the collection and testing of such specimens "intrude upon the expectations of privacy that society has long recognized as reasonable . . . these intrusions must be deemed searches under the Fourth Amendment" (*Skinner v. Railway Labor Executives Association* 1989).

The Court's most decisive conclusion pertained to the reasonableness of the search. Taking into consideration the constitutional rights of the employee versus the interest in promoting public safety, the Court invoked the special needs exception to the Fourth Amendment and held that the warrant and probable cause requirements were impractical for the railroad and the government's mutual interest in promoting public safety. Particularly, the Court stressed that obtaining a warrant (1) would add little to assure employees that such tests were not arbitrary, since the regulations apply only to employees working in certain positions, such as operating and maintenance crews, and (2) would burden and frustrate the purpose behind the search, since alcohol and drugs dissolve into the bloodstream at a steady pace. More important, the Court stated that searches conducted without probable cause, or even a degree of suspicion, are within the permissible bounds of the Fourth Amendment, since "the privacy interests implicated by the search are minimal." The Court further stated that "where an important government interest furthered by the intrusion would be placed in jeopardy by a requirement of individualized suspicion" (*Skinner v. Railway Labor Executives Association* 1989), the probable cause requirement of the Fourth Amendment may be suspended.

The *Von Raab* Decision. The Court's affirmative stance on the constitutionality of suspicionless and warrantless drug tests in *Skinner* was restated in *National Treasury Employees Union v. Von Raab*. At issue in *Von Raab* was the constitutionality of a drug-testing program that required U.S. Customs Service employees applying for promotion to positions involving the interdiction of drugs,

the carrying of firearms, and the handling of classified materials to submit urine specimens prior to being assigned to these sensitive positions. The Court confirmed that although the collection of urine specimens does not entail a physical intrusion into one's body, it is nonetheless intrusive, since the collection of such samples often requires visual or auditory monitoring of the act of urination, which intrudes on one's expectation of privacy. The Court thus declared the collection of urine specimens a search under the Fourth Amendment (Betts 1990).

The Court also confirmed that the need to formulate probable cause is not required prior to such searches. In particular, the Court clarified that although the probable cause requirement is an essential ingredient to the constitutionality and reasonableness of searches *related to criminal investigations*, it is not necessarily essential in determining the reasonableness of searches conducted as the result of routine administrative functions or policies and procedures such as those promulgated by the Customs Service. In addition, the Court held that no warrant was needed for such searches. Primarily, the Court explained that requiring the Customs Service to obtain a warrant would (1) serve only to divert valuable agency resources away from its primary mission, (2) provide little or nothing in the way of additional protection of personal privacy, and (3) add little to assure that the drug-testing program was not arbitrarily imposed, since only certain employees were subjected to drug tests. In essence, the Court reasoned that because the drug-testing program was narrowly tailored and not designed to gather information that would result in criminal prosecution, the search could be performed without a warrant, probable cause, or degree of suspicion.

The Court's rationale in *Von Raab* was again contingent on the two-pronged analysis of reasonableness. Without hesitation, the Court deemed the Customs Service's policy requiring urine specimens prior to promotion a search under the Fourth Amendment. With more deliberation, however, the Court explained that such searches were reasonable primarily because employees seeking promotion to these sensitive positions had a diminished expectation of privacy that was ultimately outweighed by several compelling interests. Particularly, the need to ensure that employees promoted to these sensitive positions, such as those involved with the interdiction of drugs and the carrying of firearms, be of exemplary moral and ethical character was a factor that the Court found substantially important. It reasoned that to ignore these personal attributes could be detrimental to the lives of others, as it was highly probable that an illicit drug-using employee's judgment could be severely impaired. Additionally, the Court was concerned that armed employees involved in drug interdiction could be susceptible to bribery and blackmail and may be "tempted to divert for their own use portions of any drug shipment they interdict" (*National Treasury Employees Union v. Von Raab* 1989). With respect to the testing of those involved in handling classified material, the Court expressed that if such employees were impaired by illicit drug use, they too could be susceptible to bribery and blackmail that may lead to the release of classified material. Because of these compelling factors, the Court held that warrantless and suspicionless drug tests were not unreasonable.

The *Acton* and *Chandler* Decisions. In 1995, the Court was presented with another opportunity to expound on drug testing in *Vernonia School District v. Acton*. Unlike *Skinner* and *Von Raab*, which involved the privacy interests of employees, *Acton* set forth a new legal boundary regarding the privacy interests of students—a legal boundary that, however, reinforced the Court's existing drug-testing rulings. At issue in *Acton* was the school district's drug policy, which authorized random drug tests for any student involved in interscholastic athletics. Similar to the rudimentary issues in *Skinner* and *Von Raab*, *Acton* challenged the constitutionality of warrantless and suspicionless drug testing under the Fourth Amendment (Miller 1996). In an almost technical manner, the Court explained that urinalysis drug tests were searches under the Fourth Amendment even if conducted without a warrant, probable cause, or degree of suspicion. With re-

spect to schools, the Court insisted that an easing of the Fourth Amendment was justified because requiring schools to obtain a warrant and formulate a degree of suspicion would not only "interfere with the maintenance of the swift and informal disciplinary procedures that are needed in schools" (*Vernonia School District v. Acton* 1995) but also undercut the school's interest in maintaining order.

Upon conducting its analysis of reasonableness, the Court acknowledged the privacy rights of students but held that they are in the temporary custody of the school (*in loco parentis*) and therefore have a diminished expectation of privacy. Moreover, student athletes, who already undergo physical examinations prior to any athletic participation, have a lesser expectation of privacy. Thus, the Court reasoned that students' diminished rights were overshadowed by the state's compelling interest not only to deter drug use among schoolchildren but more specifically to ensure that athletes were not psychologically and physically harmed by drug use and to ensure that other students, which whom an illicit drug-using student may compete with during athletic events, do not suffer any injuries.

Several years after *Acton*, the legal scope of suspicionless drug testing were somewhat modified when the Court recognized the need to reinforce legal boundaries. In *Chandler v. Miller* (1997) Libertarian party nominees for state office in Georgia challenged the constitutionality of a state statute requiring candidates to take a urinalysis drug test 30 days prior to being nominated for office or 30 days prior to an election. In conducting its two-pronged analysis, the Court held that the drug test was a search under the Fourth Amendment. However, on examining the reasonableness of the search, the Court found that the statute exceeded the boundaries of what it had previously considered constitutional (Ames 1997; Brewer 1997). Although the Court expressed adulation for the state's interest in attempting to deter drug use, it ultimately found that the state did not have a compelling interest to infringe on the privacy rights of party nominees. Specifically, the Court found no evidence to demonstrate a problem of drug use among candidates or state officials that would legitimately justify the creation and enforcement of the statute. Additionally, the Court expressed apprehension that the statute was poorly crafted because it allowed candidates to schedule a drug test at their convenience, so long as it met the 30-day rule. This poorly crafted rule allowed any illicit drug-using candidates to easily abstain from using drugs during the pre-testing period and thus allowed them to easily escape detection. Because the statute was not enacted in response to any fear or suspicion of drug use among state officials and was critically flawed, the Court ruled that the statute was unconstitutional under the Fourth Amendment (Brewer 1997).

Discussion

In the later decades of the twentieth century, the Court gradually demarcated the constitutionally permissible boundaries of drug testing. At first, the legal parameters were quite indistinct. The only legal directive issued by the Court was that the collection of specimens for analysis, even if obtained without a warrant, be *reasonable*. Yet it is this notion of *reasonableness* that has been the keystone of the Court's drug-testing policy and one that has sparked many legal contentions. Reasonableness, or more precisely, unreasonableness, has origins in the Fourth Amendment. Although legal scholars contend that reasonable searches and seizures should be synonymous with the obtaining of a warrant based on probable cause (Polloway 1989), the Court has acknowledged the impracticality of fully abiding by these Fourth Amendment requirements. This acknowledgment has guided the Court through its deliberation on the constitutionality of drug-testing polices in the workplace, at school, and even in the political arena.

At present, the constitutional boundaries of drug-testing policies are entrenched in the keystone principle of reasonableness, which authorizes the collection of specimens for analysis even if they are obtained without a warrant, probable cause, or any other degree

of suspicion. Although seemingly devoid of a legal framework, the Court has crafted a two-pronged analysis to assess the constitutionality of such tests in which it first determines whether the collection of specimens constitutes a search within the meaning of the Fourth Amendment and then discerns whether the search is reasonable (Haberberger 1990). It is during the latter analysis that the Court balances individual privacy rights with the compelling interest of any party that wishes to subject those under its control to a drug test. It is also this later analysis that has infuriated many legal scholars over what they believe has been a flagrant attempt by the high court to diminish the protections and requirements of the Fourth Amendment (Dorancy-Williams 1998). Those who disagree with the actions of the Court concur that the temporal issues prevalent in the later decades of the twentieth century necessitated the implementation and enforcement of drug polices in the workplace. However, they contest the Court's approval of policies without a warrant. Perhaps most disconcerting to them has been the approval of policies without probable cause or suspicion (Dorancy-Williams 1998; Brewer 1997). Arguably, the Court has opted to interpret the Fourth Amendment quite liberally and some find any deviation from a literal or original interpretation of the Constitution upsetting. Others, including members of the high court, while agreeing that the Constitution should be open to the subjective interpretation of the Court, have also disagreed with the Court's drug-testing jurisprudence. In *Vernonia School District v. Acton*, for instance, Justice O'Connor, together with Justices Stevens and Souter, argued that warrantless searches, while a necessary deviation from a literal interpretation of the Constitution, must be conducted with some degree of suspicion.

Disagreement with the Court over suspicionless drug-testing policies in particular extends beyond arguments regarding a textual interpretation of the Constitution. With the exception of the regulations promulgated by the FRA after a thorough analysis of the existing drug problem among railroad employees in *Skinner*, critics of the

Court argue that there has been no overriding evidence either in the Customs Service or in the Vernonia School District to suggest a problem with illicit drugs (Brewer 1997; Wilkinson 1997; Polloway 1989). In both cases, drug-testing policies were instituted with hypothetical possibilities of the harm that would likely ensue from the promotion of illicit drug-using employees to sensitive positions or the harm that illicit drug use would have on students participating in athletic sporting competitions, respectively. Thus, they argue that the Court either had no basis to rule on the constitutionality of testing policies in these cases or should have ruled as it did in *Acton* and declared the policies unreasonable because there was no credible evidence of drug use. Aside from the belief that the Court erred, critics, as well as legal rights advocates, also worry that drug tests could reveal more personal information about individuals than merely the use of alcohol or illicit drugs. As noted by Justice Marshall, writing for the dissent in *Skinner,* the Court has deemed the collection of specimens for toxicological analysis a minimal invasion of privacy but overlooks that "technological advances have made it possible to uncover . . . not only drug or alcohol use, but also medical disorders such as epilepsy, diabetes, and clinical depression" (*Skinner v. Railway Labor Executives Association* 1989). These are disorders that according to the Americans with Disabilities Act, cannot be used by employers when making hiring or termination decisions.

Regardless of whether the Court will ever be able to temper criticism of its drug-testing doctrine, it is important to underscore that its rulings are not boundless. The Court has crafted its policy based on a special needs exception to the Fourth Amendment—an exception that permits an easing of the amendment only when "special needs, beyond the normal need for law enforcement, make the warrant and probable cause requirement impractical" (*New Jersey v. T.L.O.* 1985). Thus, it has suspended the requirements of the Fourth Amendment when searches are conducted for non-law enforcement or non-prosecutorial purposes. It has also sanctioned polices that do not arbitrarily subject

all individuals to drug tests but rather ensures that polices are narrowly tailored to certain targeted individuals. The Court has also insisted that recourse be made available to individuals whose test results are positive, such as the opportunity to send specimens to an independent laboratory, an opportunity for a hearing, and an opportunity to explain tests results. It further ensures that any infringement of individual liberties is reasonable and superceded by an important and compelling interest, such as public safety.

Indeed, it was *safety* that first compelled the federal government and later the private sector to implement mass drug-testing policies in the 1980s. Although such policies were and remain unpopular with employees, there is no doubt that the federal government and the private sector would rather face the wrath of civil libertarians who claim that drug tests are unconstitutional than risk work-related accidents resulting from the impaired judgment of an illicit drug-using employee. More important, they would rather face the criticism than risk a threat to public safety. Equally true, school districts (state governments) would rather face the wrath of those who feel drug tests are violative of students' privacy rights than risk dangerous long-term harm to students. All in all, the federal government, the state government, and the private sector have engaged in their own balancing of interests and have considered the safety of others to be a compelling interest to implement and enforce drug tests. Arguably, legal liability has also been a compelling interest. After all, employers as well as school districts that have taken an idle approach to drug use in their respective work environments often lose an inordinate amount of money in tort lawsuits for the negligent hiring or retaining of illicit drug-using employees or for the negligent failure to protect students, respectively (Befort 1997).

Conclusion

Although several constitutional issues may be invoked to challenge the constitutionality of drug tests, most often these challenges are based on the Fourth Amendment.

The Fourth Amendment, which has been regarded as one of the most explicit attempts by the Framers to safeguard individual liberties, contains specific requirements to prevent an abridgement of the right of the people to be secure from unreasonable searches and seizures, such as the need for the government to first obtain a warrant substantiated with the legally integral criterion of probable cause (Peltason and Davis 2000). Despite numerous scholarly attempts to unearth whether the Framers intended to hold any search or seizure conducted without a warrant or probable cause unreasonable and therefore unconstitutional (Brewer 1997), the Court has variably recognized instances when the requirements of the amendment need not be present to declare a search or seizure constitutional. The Court's decisive rulings regarding the requirements of the Fourth Amendment have not been devoid of criticism. However, it is important to consider that the Constitution and its amendments remain viable and malleable to contemporary issues, primarily because of the interpretative function of the Court. It is the Court's interpretative role that sparks many contentious debates, and its interpretation of the Fourth Amendment with respect to drug testing is no exception.

References

Ames, J. L. 1997. *"Chandler v. Miller:* Redefining Special Needs for Suspicionless Drug Testing Under the Fourth Amendment." *Akron Law Review* 31:273–295.

Befort, S. F. 1997. "Pre-Employment Screening and Investigation: Navigating Between a Rock and a Hard Place." *Hofstra Labor Law Journal* 14:365–422.

Betts, K. C. 1990. "Fourth Amendment Suspicionless Urinalysis Testing: A Constitutionally Reasonable Weapon in the Nation's War on Drugs?" *Journal of Criminal Law and Criminology* 80:1018–1051.

Brewer, M. E. 1997. *"Chandler v. Miller:* No Turning Back From a Fourth Amendment Reasonableness Analysis." *Denver University Law Review* 75:275–304.

del Carmen, R. 2004. *Criminal Procedure: Law and Practice.* Belmont, CA: Wadsworth.

del Carmen, R., S. E. Ritter, and B. A. Witt. 2001. *Briefs of Leading Cases in Corrections.* Cincinnati: Anderson Publishing Company.

Dorancy-Williams, J. 1998. "The Difference Between Mine and Thine: The Constitutionality of Public Employee Drug Testing." *New Mexico Law Review* 28:451–485.

Haberberger, S. 1990. "Reasonable Searches Absent Individualized Suspicion: Is There a Drug-Testing Exception to the Fourth Amendment Warrant Requirement After *Skinner v. Railway Labor Executives' Association?*" *University of Hawaii Law Review* 12:343–382.

Lee, B. 2001. "Drug Testing and the Confused Athlete: A Look at the Differing Athletic Drug Testing Programs in High School, College and the Olympics." *Florida Coastal Law Journal* 3:91–112.

Lemons, J. P. 2004. "For Any Reason at All: Reconciling Employment-at-Will With the Rights of Texas Workers After *Mission Petroleum Carriers v. Solomon.*" *St. Mary's Law Journal* 35:741–779.

Mechanic, G. 1988. "Legal Challenges to Drug Testing in Public Employment." *LERC Monograph Series* 7:25–51.

Miller, E. N. 1996. "Suspicionless Drug Testing of High School and College Athletes After *Acton:* Similarities and Differences." *University of Kansas Law Review* 45:301–328.

Peltason, J. W., and S. Davis. 2000. *Understanding the Constitution.* Belmont, CA: Wadsworth.

Polloway, M. 1989. "Does the Fourth Amendment Prohibit Suspicionless Searches or Do Individual Rights Succumb to the Government's So-Called Special Needs?" *Seton Hall Constitutional Journal* 10:143–183.

Todd, S. 1987. "Employee Drug Testing: Issues Facing Private Sector Employees." *North Carolina Law Review* 65:832–847.

Walker, S. 2006. *Sense and Nonsense About Crime and Drugs.* Toronto, Ontario: Thomson Wadsworth.

Wilkinson, R. W. 1997. "Special Needs Exception for Suspicionless Searches Does Not Extend to Candidate Drug Testing—*Chandler v. Miller.*" *Suffolk University Law Review* 31:237–247.

Cases Cited

Burton v. Wilmington Parking Authority, 365 U.S. 715 (1961).

Chandler v. Miller, 117 S Ct. 1295 (1997).

Katz v. United States, 389 U.S. 347 (1967).

National Treasury Employees Union v. Von Raab, 109 S. Ct. 1402 (1989).

New Jersey v. T.L.O., 469 U.S. 325 (1985).

O'Connor v. Ortega, 480 U.S. 709 (1987).

Schmerber v. California, 384 U.S. 757 (1966).

Skinner v. Railway Labor Executives Association,
109 S. Ct. 1402 (1989).

Vernonia School District v. Acton, 115 S. Ct. 2386
(1995).

Related Websites

Drug Policy Alliance: Drug Testing

http://www.drugpolicy.org/law/drugtesting/

**Legal Challenges to Testing Hair for Drugs: A
Review**

http://www.criminology.fsu.edu/journal/
legasp3.html

**Do School Children Have Fourth Amendment
Rights?**

http://www.forensic-evidence.com/site/Police/
school_4th.html

Drug Testing in the Workplace

http://www.texasworkforce.org/news/efte/drug_
testing_in_the_workplace.html

Drug Tests in Schools

http://school.familyeducation.com/drugs-and-al-
cohol/education-administration/37514.html

Student Drug Testing

http://www.whitehousedrugpolicy.gov/publica-
tions/student_drug_testing/before_you_be-
gin.pdf

Discussion Questions

1. What amendment has most frequently
    been used to challenge the constitution-
    ality of drug tests?

2. What factors prompted the implemen-
    tation and enforcement of mass drug
    testing?

3. Does the Constitution provide any
    protections to employees working in
    the private sector?

4. When can individuals be subjected to
    drug tests?

5. What is the "special needs" exception to
    the Fourth Amendment, and how does
    the Court use this exception to justify
    warrantless and suspicionless drug
    tests?

6. What is the Court's two-pronged analy-
    sis of reasonableness?

7. What factors have caused some to re-
    gard the Court's actions as unconstitu-
    tional with respect to drug tests?

8. Why did the Court refuse to uphold
    Georgia's statute for candidate drug
    tests? ✦

Section II

Legal Issues and Courts

Chapter 7
Problem-Solving Courts

Changing the Way Courts Conduct Business

Michelle E. Heward

In this chapter, the author summarizes the key issues surrounding problem-solving courts, such as drug courts, domestic violence courts, mental health courts, and several others. As the author points out, although each court addresses a distinct social issue, they all share core principles. This chapter begins by providing a brief summary of some recent historical events that have influenced the progression of problem-solving courts. One considerable influence originated from the shift from a rehabilitative focus in our criminal justice system to a more punitive direction, marked by "tough on crime" and "war on drugs" legislation. Other pressures originated from increased caseloads, overcrowding issues in correctional settings, and the resulting expenses. Problem-solving courts have been created to meet the needs of the criminal justice system, as well as respond to the growing need to develop a collaborative network of key stakeholders, to address the growing needs of an overburdened justice system in an organized manner, while remaining cost-effective.

Next, the author presents an overview of the shared (core) principles that many of the problem-solving courts have in common. First, there is a shift in the traditional roles of the judge and court process from an assembly-line adjudication process to a more individualized method. Second, stakeholders address the problem from a team-orientated approach, which provides a broader base of support and expertise to both the victim and offender. Third, other court personnel contribute to the determination of disciplinary sanctions. Fourth, following the therapeutic justice model, a main goal of problem-solving courts re-

mains focused on offender reintegration into society or giving those in need the tools to stand on their own two feet.

The last two sections of this chapter cover the various types of problem-solving courts, including drug courts, domestic violence courts, mental health courts, youth courts, and several others, along with a brief analysis addressing the question of effectiveness. Research has shown that these courts reflect positive outcomes in many areas, such as lower recidivism rates and cost effectiveness. However, significant concerns remain centering on role changes within the traditional court and the changes in the adversarial process, which some people argue may lead to the overstepping of constitutional rights such as due process.

Introduction

American courts have always been involved in resolving disputes that involve societal problems. In recent years, increased and complex societal issues have produced criticism and a lack of confidence in the traditional handling of some cases by the courts. *Problem-solving courts,* also known as *specialty courts,* have grown rapidly in response to these concerns. They represent an alternative to traditional courts, generally focusing on a particular group of offenses (such as DWIs, drug offenses, domestic violence, and truancy) or population (drug offenders, mental disorders, youth).

Drug courts are the most common type of problem-solving court, but there are a significant number of other courts, including community, domestic violence, DWI, gambling, gun, mental health, livability, teen/youth, and truancy courts. Problem-solving courts are each unique, addressing particular problems of the communities they serve, yet they share principles and a model of approach that distinguish them from conventional courts. This chapter will look at the history and progression of problem-solving courts in the United States, examine their shared principles, introduce several problem-solving courts, review the research aimed at determining their effectiveness, and identify criticisms surrounding the courts.

History and Progression of Problem-Solving Courts

No single event led to the advent of problem-solving courts. A likely contributing factor was the national concern over drug abuse, which reached epidemic proportions in the 1980s. The federal government and law enforcement officials responded with the "war on drugs" and community policing initiatives, focusing on a coordinated response of the community to the problems.

Also cited as contributing to the need for problem-solving courts was a "get tough" response to minor offenses by law enforcement. The "broken windows" theory advanced by Wilson and Kelling (1982) supported getting police out of their squad cars and back on foot patrol. The theory supports increased enforcement of minor or seemingly harmless offenses, such as public drunkenness, prostitution, smoking, low-level drug use, and vagrancy. The effect of such enforcement was not only to increase public perception of safety and order, but by fixing these "broken windows" to make it less likely that more serious crime would be committed.

As a result of increased law enforcement efforts, and without much warning, court caseloads substantially increased. According to Berman and Feinblatt (2002), between 1984 and 1998, criminal filings in the United States increased by 50 percent. During that same period, case filings for domestic violence increased by 75 percent. As many as three out of every four defendants in major cities tested positive for drugs at the time of arrest (Feinblatt, Berman, and Denckla 2000, citing NIJ, ADAM Reports).

Regardless of the factors causing the problems, it is hard to dispute a general frustration with the American criminal justice system. Some of these frustrations include complaints of overcrowded correctional facilities, the expense and burden of increasing court case loads, the "revolving door" phenomenon of repeat offenders, the impersonal and assembly-line quality of "McJustice," job dissatisfaction among lawyers and judges, and the win-at-all-costs mentality of modern trial advocacy (Nolan 2003). Rottman and Casey (1999) argue that the breakdown in societal structures and an inadequate response from social service institutions placed courts on the frontline to deal with substance abuse, family breakdown, and mental illness. Problem-solving courts evolved to meet the needs that were thrust upon them.

New York State Chief Judge Judith S. Kaye reported that courts often saw the same defendants returning for similar offenses. She suggested that

> [i]n many of today's cases, the traditional approach yields unsatisfying results. The addict arrested for drug dealing is adjudicated, does time, then goes right back to dealing on the street. The battered wife obtains a protective order, goes home, and is beaten again. Every legal right of the litigants is protected, all procedures are followed, yet we aren't making a dent in the underlying problem. Not good for the parties involved. Not good for the community. Not good for the courts. (Berman and Feinblatt 2002)

Initially, courts responded with dedicated calendars to handle particular problems. The Center for Court Innovation (2005) reports a number of events in the growth of problem-solving courts. In 1984, Cook County, Illinois, established one of the first criminal domestic violence calendars. Security personnel staffed a waiting room for abused adults and their children so that children would have a safe place to stay while their mothers appeared in court. Courts then moved toward a more coordinated response to the pressing cases on their calendars, consulting with police, prosecution, treatment providers, and defense counsel in their efforts. In 1987 Quincy County, Massachusetts, initiated the Domestic Violence Prevention Program, utilizing the police, prosecution, and court in response to family violence. The program increased monitoring of probation for offenders and services for victims.

In 1989, Dade County, Florida, is credited with starting the first drug court in the United States, sentencing addicted defendants to "long-term, judicially supervised drug treatment instead of incarceration."

Problem-solving courts continued to evolve and in 1993 the Midtown Community Court opened its doors in the Times Square area of Manhattan. Targeted at quality-of-life crimes such as low-level drug possession, subway fare beating, and illegal vending, this court sought to punish offenders through court-ordered participation in community projects, while also providing onsite drug treatment, job training, and counseling.

In 1997, the first court to call itself a mental health court opened in Broward County, Florida. It sought to provide judicially monitored treatment for mentally ill misdemeanor offenders. As court officials and communities around the country looked for effective ways to respond to increased caseloads and subsequent social problems, problem-solving courts continued to increase. The National Drug Court Institute (NDCI) reported that by 2004 there were 1,621 active drug courts of various forms in the United States (Huddleston, Freeman-Wilson, Marlowe, and Roussel 2005). NDCI similarly reported an additional 937 active problem-solving courts. These numbers are likely low because of an underreporting of youth/teen courts and potentially community courts that are sometimes not associated with the traditional court system.

Not only has the number of problem-solving courts grown, but they have also received endorsements and recognition from prestigious national legal organizations. In 2000, the Conference of Chief Justices and the Conference of State Court Administrators unanimously passed a joint resolution to promote the widespread integration of problem-solving courts into the state court systems. Amongst other things, they resolved to

> [t]ake steps to expand and better integrate the principles and methods of well-functioning drug courts into ongoing court operations; [a]dvance the careful study and evaluation of the principles and methods employed in problem-solving courts and their application to other significant issues facing state courts; and [e]ncourage, where appropriate, the broad integration over the next decade of the principles and methods employed in

the problem-solving courts into the administration of justice to improve court processes and outcomes while preserving the rule of law, enhancing judicial effectiveness, and meeting the needs and expectations of litigants, victims and the community.

The American Bar Association (2002) endorsed by resolution the development of problem-solving courts to improve court processes and court outcomes for litigants, victims, and communities. It further endorsed the use of principles and methods employed by problem-solving courts in the daily administration of justice while preserving the rule of law and traditional due process protections and adherence to the Model Code of Judicial Conduct. Finally, the legislative branch of government has also endorsed problem-solving courts. Congress and various state legislatures have, often with bipartisan support, appropriated large amounts of money for the establishment of various problem-solving courts. (Huddleston et al. 2005, Table V).

The rapid growth of problem-solving courts, and endorsement of their new approach by prestigious legal organizations, is evidence that they are more than a trend in the legal landscape of jurisprudence in the United States.

Shared Principles of Problem-Solving Courts

One of the purported strengths of problem-solving courts is the ability to individualize their response and address the needs of the communities they serve. Even with their individual characteristics, however, they share several principles. Judge Judith Kaye (2004) wrote:

> What these courts have in common is an idea we call problem-solving justice. The underlying premise is that courts should do more than just process cases—really people—who we know from experience will be back before us again and again with the very same problem, like drug offenders. Adjudicating these cases is not the same thing as resolving them. In the end, the business of courts is not only get-

ting through a day's calendar, but also dispensing effective justice. That is what problem-solving courts are about.

Problem-solving courts significantly shift the traditional role of judges and the traditional procedure of the court.

> [P]rosecutors and defenders . . . work together to encourage defendants to succeed in drug treatment and judges become actively involved in their communities, meeting with residents and brokering relationships with local service providers. . . . [C]itizens are welcomed into the process, participating in advisory boards, organizing community service projects and meeting face to face with offenders to explain the impact of their crimes on neighborhoods. (ABA 2002)

A team approach of stakeholders provides the court with a broad range of both support and expertise to meet the needs of defendants, victims, and communities.

Defendants are required to make regular court appearances in front of a judge who closely monitors their compliance with the conditions of the court. For example, a drug court defendant could be required to engage in substance abuse treatment, submit to random and frequent testing, and attend Alcoholics Anonymous (AA) meetings. His compliance would be monitored by members of the drug court team and reported to the drug court at frequent court appearances by the defendant. This close monitoring helps provide the court with current information with which it can specifically tailor a plan to meet the needs of the defendant. Frequent monitoring also holds the defendant immediately accountable for his or her actions and helps the system protect the public.

Problem-solving court judges who preside over a defendants' initial appearances, follow that case through the adjudication and postadjudication or probation stages. This continuity is intended to individualize the defendant to the court as well as the program to the defendant. It also promotes the development of expertise by the judge and professional staff in the types of cases handled by the court.

In many problem-solving courts, decisions are made with input by the court members, modifying the traditional roles they play in a conventional court. For example, a drug court may be staffed by several people including the defense counsel, prosecutor, probation officer, treatment providers, and law enforcement. Sanctions, as well as rewards, are often determined with input from these various sources.

The term "therapeutic justice" has been used to describe the philosophy used by many new problem-solving courts. Carns, Hotchkin, and Andrews (2002) discuss the difference between therapeutic, restorative, and retributive justice models:

> Therapeutic justice emphasizes the need to address the root causes of a specific offender's criminality, to treat the offender to remove the problems and to return the offender to the community as a responsible citizen. Restorative justice emphasizes repair of the relationships between the victim, community and offender. Retributive justice, the model on which much of the United States' criminal justice system is based, emphasizes fairness and punishment as more important values than rehabilitation or other interests. Each model seeks to express community condemnation in order to protect public safety and deter or dissuade the specific offender and others from similar behavior in the future. (citations omitted)

Problem-solving courts often follow a therapeutic justice model, using the courts as a vehicle to return the offender to society as a productive member. The concepts of a restorative justice model, taking into account the needs of the community, victims, and offenders in fashioning a response to the unlawful behavior, are also addressed. Less emphasis is placed on the retributive justice model (Nolan 2003).

While "therapeutic justice" is often used when describing what problem-solving courts do, some have raised concern that the label does not adequately describe their origins or methods and aligns them too closely with pure rehabilitation. Greg Berman (2004) points out that in addition to rehabilitative efforts, problem-solving courts act in ways that are not purely rehabilitative. For instance, a court that sentences offenders to community service may do so in an effort to benefit the neighborhood harmed by a crime. A batterer may have to return to court frequently in an effort to protect the victim.

In summary, problem-solving courts attempt to dispense effective justice using a restorative and therapeutic justice response that considers not only the defendant, but the impact on the victim and the community. Collaboration by various private and public stakeholders seeks to improve the effectiveness of the court's response. Close monitoring by a single judge who has developed expertise in a specific area enables frequent and immediate responses to defendants under supervision. Finally, the court does not operate in a vacuum. It is provided with input from various players in the system, some of whom may assume nontraditional roles.

Types of Problem-Solving Courts

Problem-solving courts specialize in a specific problem or with a particular group of defendants. The most well-recognized group of problem-solving courts are drug courts. Other problem-solving courts include community, domestic violence, mental health, prostitution, gambling, gun, truancy, child support, and teen courts. Although not exhaustive, this section provides an overview of a variety of problem-solving courts in the United States.

Drug Courts

Drug courts, and the model they follow, are substantially changing the way the American courts respond to defendants involved with controlled substances. Drug courts can be found in both the juvenile and adult justice systems. They also target groups of individuals, leading to DWI courts, family dependency treatment courts, tribal healing to wellness courts, campus drug courts, and reentry drug courts.

Drug Courts in Action. According to the National Drug Court Institute, drug court goals are typically "to reduce drug use and associated criminal behavior by engaging and retaining drug-involved offenders in treatment services; to concentrate expertise about drug cases in a single courtroom; to address other defendant needs through clinical assessment and effective case management; and to remove drug cases from traditional courtrooms, freeing these courts to adjudicate nondrug cases" (Huddleston and Wosje 2005).

Drug courts are established with "clear and certain" rules, which are measurable and within the defendant's ability to perform. The participant knows when he or she must attend court, attend treatment sessions, and engage in drug testing. These requirements are easily understood and monitored. The person's performance is "immediately and directly communicated to the judge, who rewards progress or penalizes noncompliance. A drug court establishes an environment that the participant can understand—a system in which clear choices are presented and individuals are encouraged to take control of their own recovery" (NADCP 1997, 7).

Generally, drug court defendants appear in front of a single judge who specializes in the operation of a drug court. The judge and the court stakeholders get to know the defendants. It is common for a defendant appearing before the court to be asked how many days he or she has been "clean." When the number of days is given, the members of the court applaud to express their support for the defendant's efforts. When a defendant has tested "dirty" for a banned substance or has otherwise violated a condition of the drug court, he or she is similarly brought before the court and participants to be held accountable. Defendants can expect both substance abuse and mental health treatment, frequent drug testing, probation supervision, and regular court appearances. They may also receive "life skill" services, such as job skill training, financial counseling, and time management training (NDCI 2005).

The Drug Court Standards Committee of the National Association of Drug Court Professionals (1997) constructed a list of ten key components of drug courts. This list provides best practices for drug courts to follow and a good picture of a model drug court:

1. Drug courts integrate alcohol and other drug treatment services with justice system case processing.

2. Using a nonadversarial approach, prosecution and defense counsel promote public safety while protecting participants' due process rights.

3. Eligible participants are identified early and are promptly placed in the drug court program.

4. Drug courts provide access to a continuum of alcohol, drug, and other related treatment and rehabilitation services.

5. Abstinence is monitored by frequent alcohol and other drug testing.

6. A coordinated strategy governs drug court responses to participants' compliance.

7. Ongoing judicial interaction with each drug court participant is essential.

8. Monitoring and evaluation measure the achievement of program goals and gauge effectiveness.

9. Continuing interdisciplinary education promotes effective drug court planning, implementation, and operations.

10. Forging partnerships among drug courts, public agencies, and community-based organizations generates local support and enhances drug court program effectiveness.

The individuals participating in drug courts vary depending on the court and the community in which they are found. An extensive national review of drug court research found the typical drug court participant to be predominately male with poor employment and educational achievements, a fairly extensive criminal history, and prior failed treatments (Belenko 2001).

Defendants may find themselves in drug court as a result of a diversion or other pre-plea procedure from a traditional court. For instance, a driving while impaired (DWI) defendant may plead guilty to the offense but enter into a plea-in-abeyance agreement by which their plea is held pending a number of conditions, one of them being the successful completion of drug court. If the defendant successfully completes drug court, generally a process of 12 to 18 months, and satisfies other conditions of the plea-in-abeyance agreement, the original court does not enter the guilty plea and ultimately dismisses the case upon successful completion.

In some jurisdictions, felony drug offenses for first-time or small-quantity offenders are simply diverted out of the criminal justice system if the defendant successfully completes specified drug treatment. These diversions are not necessarily part of a drug court. Prosecutors may monitor these offenders by simply holding the cases pending the drug treatment. If the treatment is successfully completed, the case is not prosecuted.

A repeat felony drug defendant may be screened for adult felony drug court upon charging or at some point prior to arraignment. Screening conditions may include an unsuccessful drug diversion (discussed above) or another prior drug conviction. Such defendants may have possessed or used a small amount of drugs, as opposed to manufacturing or selling, or been involved in an offense where violence was also alleged. These defendants may enter into an agreement with the court and prosecution to plead guilty to their offense, which is held in abeyance, but engage in drug court as a condition to the ultimate dismissal of the charge. As with the DWI example, the guilty plea would not be entered pending the defendant's successful completion of drug court. The defendant may be required, as a condition of the agreement, to give up a number of constitutional rights. Defendants often agree to waive Fourth Amendment search and seizure protections as well as limited Fifth and Fourteenth Amendment due process protection.

As drug courts have evolved, the conditions of drug court involvement have also changed. Drug courts are frequently being used as a condition of probation. These circumstances suggest that drug courts are being used alongside the traditional courts for more high-risk offenders, recognizing the effectiveness of the drug court model. This process protects society by providing a record of the offense but generally gives the defendants a break in the amount or type of incarceration or other penalty they would otherwise have received had they not completed drug court.

Another evolution of the drug court model for high-risk offenders has come with "reentry" drug courts. These courts are used for offenders who are being released back into society from local or state correctional facilities. While imprisonment may curtail, or at least slow down, the use of illegal substances for the period of incarceration, probation and parole officers commonly deal with drug addicts who return to drugs once they are out of the correctional facility. These people are targeted and are required to engage in a reentry drug court as a condition of their probation or parole. The reentry drug court and its stakeholders assist the probation or parole officer in holding the offender accountable through frequent monitoring, testing, treatment, and court appearances.

Juvenile Drug Courts. Key West, Florida, is credited with starting the first juvenile drug court in 1993. Juvenile drug courts are generally special dockets within a traditional juvenile or family court that target juveniles identified as having alcohol or drug dependency. Juvenile drug court programs tend to be small and involve a small percentage of the target population they could serve (Belenko 2001). Juvenile courts follow the drug court model of frequent court appearances, drug testing, treatment, and supervision, with a single judge leading a team approach. A unique aspect of the juvenile drug court is the involvement of parents or guardians in the process.

Youths participating in juvenile drug courts differ across the country, but some reported characteristics may help to better understand the population participating in the programs nationally. Nearly all have had at least one prior criminal justice contact. The drugs of choice are marijuana and alcohol. Almost all juvenile programs in the research studied by Belenko (2001) listed educational underachievement as a special need of their clients. Reading below grade level and some attention deficit disorder were also listed as problems (Belenko 2001).

DWI Courts. Driving while intoxicated (DWI) courts are set up as drug courts addressing the particular issues raised by drivers who are drug or alcohol impaired. Public safety is a key goal in these courts, addressed through individualized treatment of the offender using the drug court model described above. DWI court defendants are required to abstain from the use of alcohol as well as illegal substances during the course of the program. Like the regular drug court participants, they are required to engage in a substance abuse court program and follow various conditions. These conditions generally require that they receive substance abuse treatment, engage in cognitive restructuring or other mental health treatment, attend Alcoholics Anonymous (AA) meetings, attend frequent court reviews, submit to random alcohol and drug testing, undergo intensive supervision, keep journals/diaries, be employed, engage with DWI victims groups, and pay for their treatment. Compliance is rewarded; noncompliance is swiftly punished through increased sanctions, jail time, ultimately termination from the program, entry of the conviction, and sentencing.

One rather unique feature of DWI courts is transportation difficulties that arise from suspended or revoked driving privileges. Generally, lack of transportation is not an excuse for failing to meet court obligations, and violations for driving on a suspended or revoked license are sternly treated. Participants are encouraged and often assisted in obtaining information about public and private transportation, as well as alternative forms of transportation, such as bicycle rental and loan programs (Huddleston and Wosje 2005).

Huddleston and Wosje, proponents of DWI courts, suggest that in areas where stand-alone DWI courts are not available, drug courts should handle DWI offenders through a hybrid system. They state that treatment with intensive supervision works with this population, and promises better long-term outcomes through decreased recidivism than traditional approaches. Although individual DWI courts have been evaluated, large-scale research of multiple programs by independent sources has not yet been done to evaluate the effectiveness of these courts.

Family Dependency Treatment Court. The first family dependency treatment court opened in Reno, Nevada, in 1994. As with other problem-solving courts, the numbers for these courts have quickly grown. Family dependency treatment courts are generally found in juvenile or family courts where substance abuse is a primary factor in parental neglect. These may be stand-alone courts, or they may refer to a separate docket of a juvenile or family court dedicated to handling these cases with a drug court model (Huddleston, Freeman-Wilson, Marlowe, and Roussel 2005).

Following the drug court model, participants receive intensive supervision, substance abuse, and mental health treatment; submit to random substance abuse testing; participate in frequent court reviews; and undergo parenting education. An interdisciplinary team pools its resources and expertise to devise a plan to address the needs of the children and their parents. The "court team provides children with quick access to permanency and offers parents a viable chance to achieve sobriety, provide a safe and nurturing home, and hold their families together" (NDCI 2004). While jail may be used as a sanction for contempt, the biggest sanction facing participants is the very real likelihood that without substantial changes, parental rights will be terminated.

Time is a major factor because children need permanency. A year for a child can seem much longer than that same year for an adult. Parents do not have the luxury of a lengthy period within which to come to terms with their addiction. The Manhattan Family Treatment Court claims to have reduced the length of time for children in foster care in their program to 11 months, while the citywide average for all children in foster care was four years. They were also able to start termination proceedings against unsuccessful participants within 13 months, which was substantially less than for those who were not in the program (Wolfe 2000).

Evaluations have been done on individual programs, although large-scale research of multiple programs by independent sources have not yet been conducted to evaluate the effectiveness of family dependency courts.

Other Substance Abuse Problem-Solving Courts. Other problem-solving drug courts have developed in lesser numbers to meet the needs of particular communities. Campus drug courts focus on violations of campus rules resulting from substance abuse. Participants in these cases may be facing legal problems as well as administrative processes for school discipline. Campus courts seek to hold students accountable to the university and make positive lifestyle changes, decrease substance abuse and maintain the student in school through a highly structured process.

Huddleston et al. (2005) report a significant number of tribal courts that round out the picture of drug courts in the United States. Tribal Healing to Wellness Courts are a component of the tribal justice system, as opposed to a stand-alone court. As with other drug courts, the healing-to-wellness model seeks to provide more structure and accountability to members of the native community charged with substance abuse offenses. They incorporate traditional native problem-solving methods within this community-based system (Huddleston et al. 2005).

Community Courts

The Midtown Community Court is credited with being the first community court having opened in 1993 and serving 350 blocks of Midtown Manhattan. The neighborhood suffered from many minor quality-of-life offenses such as prostitution, shoplifting, subway turnstile jumping, minor drug possession, assaults, and vending violations, among others (Anderson 1996). The community court was the product of a collaboration of the court, bar, City of New York, business and residential neighborhoods, corporations and foundations, and two dozen social service agencies and civic organizations (Kaye 2004).

This community court is technically a branch of the New York Criminal Court and occupies a refurbished traditional court just a few blocks from Times Square. Efficiency is a main goal of the court, and offenders are quickly arraigned and held accountable. Defendants appearing before the court receive a pretrial assessment, similar to that in traditional criminal courts, but they are also asked questions about housing, employment, financial status, health, and substance abuse (Kaye 2004).

The court works with the police and the Times Square Business Improvement District to coordinate community service projects that directly benefit the community the court serves. Only seven percent of offenders receive jail time. The court also has access to a large number of social services and providers to assist the court in addressing the root causes of the offenses (Anderson 1996).

While the Midtown Community Court is illustrative and may be among the best-known, there are other community courts around the country. Community courts do not have the track record that drug courts have in terms of research to support their efforts. What research has been completed so far appears supportive, however preliminary (e.g., Sviridoff et al. 1997; Feinblatt, Berman, and Sviridoff 1998).

Criticisms have also been raised about community courts. Are courts the best place to address societal problems or are such problems better left to more traditional segments of the society, like families, churches, and social service entities? Other concerns include the strong involvement of the business community that directly benefits from and in some instances finances the courts. There are also concerns over marginalizing segments of communities that would rather address their problems through means other than the coercive force of the criminal justice system (e.g., Hoffman 2002; Kundu 2005; Nolan 2003; and Thompson 2002).

Domestic Violence Courts

Domestic violence courts may be stand-alone courts or a separate docket of a traditional court dedicated to handling domestic violence cases with a problem-solving model. They primarily handle felony domestic violence cases, although a subset of these courts deal with misdemeanor domestic violence. They are a growing model of problem-solving courts and generally focus on the goals of improving defendant accountability and enhancing the safety of victims (Wolfe, Aldrich, and Moore 2004) while fairly judging the merits of each case (Kaye 2004).

Some factors make domestic violence courts unique among problem-solving courts. They involve not only criminal behavior but also complex social relationships that make each step of the case more difficult (Huddleston et al. 2005). Victims may choose not to cooperate because of financial, emotional, and safety concerns not usually present in other court cases. Domestic violence courts monitor defendants closely, requiring frequent in-court reviews "so that the judge can ensure there is no violation of bail conditions, orders of protection, or conditions of probation. Defendants know that they will be held accountable for any errant behavior" (Kaye 2004).

The best practices require immediacy (swift court action); intensive monitoring; coordination between the court, police, prosecutors, defense attorneys, victim advocates, and others so that everyone working with the case has access to necessary information; and specialized staff who have expertise with domestic violence issues (Wolfe et al. 2004).

Mental Health Courts

Another growing group of problem-solving courts are mental health courts. All such courts are currently voluntary, where traditional criminal courts can divert defendants with a mental illness. Defendants who choose to engage in the community-based supervision appear at regular reviews in front of a specialized court, they are subject to conditions, and a team of court staff, social services, and mental health professionals work together to develop treatment plans and supervise participants in the community (Huddleston et al. 2005).

Youth Courts

Youth courts (also called teen and peer courts) are dispositional alternatives to the juvenile justice system in which trained youth volunteers hold youthful offenders accountable for their wrongful actions. Youth courts follow various models. Some courts look much like a juvenile court, with youth filling all of the positions; others have youth juries that advise an adult judge of a recommended disposition; and still others have a panel of youth judges who make a sentencing decision (Heward 1999).

Youth courts may be school based, community based, or a combination of both. Most youth courts are dispositional, handling only those cases in which the youth has admitted the offense. A few are fact-finding courts determining guilt. A strong concept behind youth courts is the use of positive peer pressure and involvement to make a difference in changing delinquent behavior.

According to the National Youth Court Center (2006), at the time of this writing there are 1,109 youth court programs in 49 states and the District Columbia. The most comprehensive, independent research on the effectiveness of youth courts was done by Jeffrey Butts and colleagues (2002) for the Urban Institute. That research found overall positive results regarding recidivism rates for youth court participants and suggests there "may be something" to the use of positive peer pressure, through the youth court model, to combat delinquency.

Research in this area has tended to focus on individual, small programs, but some patterns are emerging, revealing generally favorable results (e.g. Forgays and DeMilio 2005; Dick et al. 2003; 2004; Butts et al. 2002; Harrison, Maupin, and Mays 2001). The research has also revealed concerns about "net-widening" and "labeling" (Rasmussen 2004). Are youth courts attracting youth into their system who, without the youth court, would have been handled informally and released? Are youths being labeled as delinquent through this net-widening process, resulting in further negative impact on them? Are youth courts any more or less effective than other diversion programs from traditional juvenile justice processing (Patrick and Marsh 2005)? Some research has attempted to determine which youths are most likely to benefit from youth court participation (e.g., Dick et al. 2003; Harrison et al. 2001; Rasmussen 2004). While the weight of the research at this point has been positive,

more investigation is necessary to determine just what it is about youth courts that make them effective, or not, so that programs can use this information to engage in best practices (Butts, Buck, and Coggeshall 2002).

Other Problem-Solving Courts

Various other problem-solving courts exist, including gun, homeless, prostitution, and truancy courts. Descriptions, the prevalence of, and research regarding these courts in the United States may be obtained from Huddleston et al. (2005).

Do Problem-Solving Courts Work?

With substantial resources and funding dedicated to problem-solving courts, it is fair to ask, "Do problem-solving courts work?" The research completed thus far has been preliminary, revealing few definitive answers. One of the obstacles to the research is funding, the other is the relatively short period of time that problem-solving courts have been around. Most programs have been in existence for months to a few years. This section will look at the current research to determine the legitimacy of problem-solving courts and finish with a review of some concerns that have been raised about these courts.

What the Research Indicates

The Government Accountability Office (GAO) (2005) conducted a study of adult drug courts to determine their effectiveness at reducing recidivism and costs. Its research found generally positive results regarding recidivism during the period of the program and for some period of time after completion of the program. It further found:

1. Lower percentages of drug court program participants than comparison group members were rearrested or reconvicted.

2. Program participants had fewer recidivism events than comparison group members.

3. Recidivism reductions occurred for participants who had committed different types of offenses.

4. Evidence was inconclusive that specific drug court components, such as the behavior of the judge or the amount of treatment received, affected participants' recidivism while in the program.

Another piece of authoritative research was completed at the National Center on Addiction and Substance Abuse at Columbia University (Belenko 2001). Belenko reviewed independently administered published and unpublished evaluations completed by 37 drug courts between 1999 and 2001. Unlike the GAO study, Belenko's study included seven juvenile drug courts, one DWI court, and one family court. Belenko was also able to compare his findings to similar studies he conducted in 1998 and 1999, concluding that his most recent findings were consistent with the earlier studies.

Belenko concluded that "drug courts have achieved considerable local support and have provided intensive, long-term treatment services to offenders with long histories of drug use and criminal justice contacts, previous treatment failures, and high rates of health and social problems. Program completion rates . . . average 47% of participants graduating." Consistent with the GAO findings, Belenko also found that drug use and criminal activity are relatively reduced while participants are in the program. The GAO (2005) found that self-reported results, however, generally showed no significant reductions in drug use.

Belenko (2001) suggests that future research examine the individual characteristics of the program that affect outcomes, so that drug courts can maximize their impact and cost effectiveness. The GAO appears to echo this concern. As with the GAO research, Belenko also found the long-term postprogram impacts of drug courts on recidivism and other outcomes "less clear," inviting further research in those areas. In the Belenko research, four of the six studies that measured postprogram recidivism found reduced recidivism, although the amount varied.

Individual courts have evaluated their own programs with varying, mostly positive, results. Besides drug courts, the body of independent research for other problem-solving courts is relatively sparse, although growing. Berman and Gulick (2003) argue that society prefers definitive answers over cautious preliminary findings and is likely to mistake uncertainty of results for proof of failure. Yet the research thus far on problem-solving courts does not offer many definitive conclusions. That will take time and money.

Criticisms of Problem-Solving Courts

Numerous concerns about problem-solving courts have arisen in the literature. Three of the more pressing criticisms are that they (1) consume precious court resources; (2) substantially change the roles of judges and defense counsel; and (3) substantially change the adversarial model to that of a therapeutic model of jurisprudence. The latter two concerns can affect the rights of the defendants in favor of more efficient case outcomes. We address each of these concerns below, although this section is not intended as a point-for-point argument in each area but as an opportunity to raise issues for further study.

Court Resources. As compared to traditional courts, problem-solving courts require additional staffing of cases, monitoring and supervision, court reviews, and intensive treatment by social services providers. Critics argue that at a time when court dockets are full and government resources are stretched, and given the sparse empirical data to support the programs, money could be better spent.

Proponents respond that the investment is worth it, pointing to research showing that while drug court programs cost more than traditional programs, in terms of *net* positive benefits, drug courts' benefits exceed the costs (GAO 2005; Belenko 2001). The net benefits take into account reductions in recidivism affecting judicial system costs and the avoided costs to potential victims.

Role Changes. One of the biggest criticisms of problem-solving courts is the substantial change in the roles assumed by the judge and defense counsel. In a traditional adversarial court, lawyers bring a case before the judge, with each side advocating its particular position. The judge, being neutral and detached, hears both sides and makes a fair decision based on all the information brought before him. Critics argue that a problem-solving court becomes less "lawyer driven" and more "judge driven" in a nonadversarial setting where treatment and change of the defendant become the focus rather than protection of rights and a critical analysis of evidence. Formalized procedures to protect defendants' rights give way to informal procedures (see generally Thompson 2002). The traditional neutral judge is replaced with a judge who is an active agent, advocating for social changes with a "team" of other players (Goldkamp 2000).

Concerns also revolve around a judge who becomes personally invested in the success of a defendant. "In the event of failure, the judge may react personally and increase punishment inappropriately. In addition, there are often class and race implications, since many who pass before drug court judges are people of color" (Thompson 2002).

Further concerns over due process protections arise with the changing roles of the players. Hoffman (2002) argues that when the judge, prosecutor, public defender, and a representative of the therapeutic community staff the day's cases, they typically do not involve the defendant or private defense counsel. At these precourt staffings, the judge hears from everyone and then reaches decisions, off the record. "[T]hese staffing sessions symbolize what is wrong with having judges join with prosecutors, defense lawyers, and therapists: substantive decisions are being made about a felony defendant by some interbranch committee acting more like a support group than a court of law" (Hoffman 2002).

These staffing sessions are also used to illustrate the concern over the changed role of the defense attorney, who traditionally acts as an advocate for his or her client, vigorously protecting his constitutional rights. What may be "best" for the defendant in terms of treatment and rehabilitation may be at odds with his or her constitutional rights and keeping him out of jail (Nolan 2003).

In response to claims that defense attorneys have little or no role in problem-solving courts, Berman (2004) acknowledges that the response from the defense bar has ranged from "open hostility to grudging acceptance to growing endorsement." He claims, however, that those who endorse problem-solving courts do so because good drug courts include them in planning and provide them a voice in the process. Drug courts provide their clients with treatment as opposed to incarceration.

> . . . [T]he good drug courts have not, in fact, lost sight of proportionality. The moment that drug courts start trying to send first-time offenders arrested for shoplifting to eighteen months of in-patient treatment is the moment when public defenders will opt for trial instead of encouraging their clients to plead. Defenders vote with their feet; if drug courts didn't offer them (and their clients) a good deal, they wouldn't agree to play. (Berman 2004)

Changes in the Adversarial Process. Related to the change in the traditional roles of the court "players" is a concern that the adversarial system, constitutional due process and procedural protections that have evolved over 200 years in this country are being rashly set aside. In its place is a nonadversarial, relaxed, rehabilitative, and therapeutic process run by judges who are not particularly experienced in the therapeutic process.

The juvenile court is used as an example of one of the first "specialty" courts. In 1899, the first juvenile court was started in Cook County, Illinois, using such a nonadversarial, relaxed, rehabilitative process. As the juvenile court evolved, unchecked power left the system with significant problems resulting ultimately in the U.S. Supreme Court intervention in *In Re Gault*, which mandated significant due process rights for juveniles. Critics argue that problem-solving courts are repeating the same mistakes made by the early juvenile courts, resulting in similar denials of constitutionally protected rights.

Further, to participate in drug courts, defendants must generally admit guilt, giving up the presumption of innocence, and sign forms surrendering various constitutional rights, including the right to trial by jury, the right to a speedy trial, the right to a preliminary hearing, and the requirement of probable cause for a search and seizure (Nolan 2003). Critics complain that forcing participants to give up these rights in order to participate in the court raises various concerns. First, it is a form of coercion, and coercing someone into treatment is not the most productive way to start treatment. Second, it dilutes the role of the defense attorney as an advocate for the client because of his or her inability to effectively challenge the evidence and make the criminal justice system work. Finally, police could become lazy, violating constitutional rights, such as search and seizure rights of the Fourth Amendment, knowing that their actions are not likely to be challenged.

Supporters of problem-solving courts propose that it is necessary for defendants to give up rights in order to become involved in the therapeutic process as quickly as possible. Where the courts are generally preadjudicative, defendants *choose* whether to engage in the program or stay in the traditional courts, where they have full access to traditional court procedures and due process protections. They argue that this voluntary decision is no different than many other instances in which defendants, for a variety of self-motivated reasons, waive constitutional rights. This justification is not, however, applicable to postadjudicative programs in which the defendant is required to complete the program as a condition of probation (Nolan 2003).

Berman (2004, 4) responds that the reality of our current American justice system provides criminal defendants with neither the due process protections of the adversarial model nor the effective sentencing of the problem-solving model. He argues that plea negotiations and the intermediate sanction of probation, both used by problem-solving courts, are the rule in the majority of adversarial cases in American courts today. Plea negotiations arranged by prosecutors and defense attorneys occur in nine out of ten cases in state courts. Probation occurs for close to half of felony offenders and for even more misdemeanant offenders. There-

fore, with or without problem-solving courts, "The American criminal justice system is in the business of linking offenders to community-based services and supervision."

Unfortunately, however, traditional courts are not doing a particularly good job of linking defendants to community-based sanctions. "Probation caseloads in some cities are as high as 1,000 cases per officer. It should come as little surprise that half of all probationers fail to complete their sanctions as ordered, and two-thirds of probationers are rearrested within three years." He concludes that "it is difficult to marshal a persuasive argument in favor of maintaining the status quo in the state courts." Problem-solving courts, Berman (2004) continues, are merely an acknowledgment by courts that change is necessary:

> What problem-solving courts have done is to improve court infrastructure, bringing new tools—technology, accountability mechanisms, research data, links to effective treatment regimens—into the courthouse. In doing so, problem-solving courts have improved the compliance of offenders with intermediate sanctions and encouraged courts to make greater use of alternatives to incarceration where appropriate. They have also changed the life-trajectories of thousands of offenders, helping them move from addiction to sobriety and from crime to law-abiding behavior. (Berman 2004, 5)

Conclusion

Problem-solving courts represent a strong departure from the traditional American court system. They are more than an experiment and cannot be ignored as a powerful alteration in the way cases are handled. Even by cautious assessments, they have proven effective in terms of recidivism and reducing illegal behavior. Critics, however, raise strong concerns. Care should be taken to assure that the lessons learned from over 200 years of American jurisprudence are not lost. Constitutional protections should not give way to courtroom efficiency. Courts should, through critical evaluation, assure that defendants receive a fair and constitutionally sound process. Errant courts that act outside the constitutional boundaries of fairness should be sanctioned.

Is there room, within the traditional structure, to use the problem-solving model? Ideally, society will combine the best of the traditional court and problem-solving models to meet the complex societal issues facing them today. One thing is clear: The landscape of the American court system has changed. Further research, and time, will reveal whether these changes are a positive adaptation by the courts to meet the needs thrust upon them, or a negative alteration of 200 years of American jurisprudence, infringing on constitutional structure and rights.

References

American Bar Association. 2002. *ABA Resolution and Report From the Coalition for Justice Committee on State Justice Initiatives, to the House of Delegates.* http://www.abanet.org/leadership/2001/117.pdf.

Anderson, D. C. 1996. *In New York City, a "Community Court" and a New Legal Culture.* Washington, DC: National Institute of Justice, Office of Justice Programs, U.S. Department of Justice. http://www.ncjrs.org/pdffiles/commcrt.pdf.

Belenko, S. R. 2001. *Research on Drug Courts: A Critical Review.* The National Center on Addiction and Substance Abuse, Columbia University. http://www.casacolumbia.org/absolutenm/articlefiles/researchondrug.pdf.

Berman, G. 2004. "Comment: Redefining Criminal Courts: Problem-Solving and the Meaning of Justice." *American Criminal Law Review* 41 (Summer):1313–1319.

Berman, G., and J. Feinblatt. 2002. "Beyond Process and Precedent: The Rise of Problem-Solving Courts." *The Judges Journal* 41 (Winter):4–5.

Berman, G., and A. Gulick. 2003. "Special Series: Problem-Solving Courts and Therapeutic Jurisprudence: Just the (Unwieldy, Hard to Gather but Nonetheless Essential) Facts, Ma'am: What We Know and Don't Know About Problem-Solving Courts." *Fordham Urban Law Journal* 30 (March):1027–1053.

Butts, J., J. Buck, and M. Coggeshall. 2002. *The Impact of Teen Court on Young Offenders.* (April) Washington DC: Urban Institute, Justice Policy Center. http://www.urban.org/UploadedPDF/410457.pdf.

Carns, T. W., M. G. Hotchkin, and E. M. Andrews. 2002. "Therapeutic Justice in Alaska's Courts." *Alaska Law Review* 19 (June):1–55. http://www.law.duke.edu/journals/19ALRCarns.

Center for Court Innovation. 2005. "Problem-Solving Courts: Chronology." http://www.problemsolvingcourts.org/ps_chronology.html.

Dick, A., R. Geertsen, and R. Jones. 2003. "Self-Reported Delinquency Among Teen Court Participants." *Journal for Juvenile Justice and Detention Services* 18(1) (Spring):33–49.

Dick, A. J., D. J. Pence, R. M. Jones, and H. R. Geertsen. 2004. "The Need for Theory in Assessing Peer Courts." *The American Behavioral Scientist* 47(11) (July):1448–1461.

Feinblatt, J., G. Berman, and D. Denckla. 2000. "Judicial Innovation at the Crossroads: The Future of Problem-Solving Courts." *The Court Manager* 15 (Winter):28–34.

Feinblatt, J., G. Berman, and M. Sviridoff. 1998. *Neighborhood Justice: Lessons From the Midtown Community Court, Think Piece.* New York: Center Court Innovation. Available at http://www.courtinnovation.org/pdf/neigh_just.pdf (Retrieved August 2005).

Forgays, D. K., and L. DeMilio. 2005. "Is Teen Court Effective for Repeat Offenders? A Test of the Restorative Justice Approach." *International Journal of Offender Therapy and Comparative Criminology* 49(1).

Goldkamp, J. S. 2000. "The Drug Court Response: Issues and Implications for Justice Change." *Albany Law Review* 63:923.

Government Accountability Office. 2005. *Adult Drug Courts: Evidence Indicates Recidivism Reductions and Mixed Results for Other Outcomes.* GAO-05-219. Report to congressional committees. Washington, DC: U.S. Government Accountability Office.

Harrison, P., J. Maupin, and G. Mays. 2001. "Teen Court: An Examination of Processes and Outcomes." *Crime & Delinquency* 47(2) (April):243–264.

Heward, M. 1999. "Youth Court: An Alternative to Juvenile Court?" *Update on Law-Related Education/Juvenile Justice,* American Bar Association, Winter 1999/2000.

Hoffman, M. B. 2002. "Therapeutic Jurisprudence, Neo-Rehabilitationism, and Judicial Collectivism: The Least Dangerous Branch Becomes Most Dangerous." *Fordham Urban Law Journal* 29 (June):2063.

Huddleston, C. W., and R. Wosje. 2005. "DWI Courts, A Promising Sentencing Innovation." Available at http://www.ndci.org/dwi_drug_court.htm (retrieved August, 2005).

Huddleston, C. W., K. Freeman-Wilson, D. Marlowe, and A. Roussel. 2005. *Painting the Current Picture: A National Report Card on Drug Courts and Other Problem-Solving Court Programs in the United States* 1(2) May:1–22. Alexandria, VA: National Drug Court Institute.

Kaye, J. 2004. "Policy Essay: Delivering Justice Today: A Problem-Solving Approach." *Yale Law and Policy Review* 22 Winter:125–151.

Kundu, S. 2005. "Privately Funded Courts and the Homeless: A Critical Look at Community Courts." *Journal of Affordable Housing* 14(2) Winter:173–194.

National Association of Drug Court Professionals. 1997. *Defining Drug Courts: The Key Components.* Washington, DC: Drug Courts Program Office, Office of Justice Programs, U.S. Department of Justice.

National Drug Court Institute. 2005. "Drug Courts: A National Phenomenon." Available at: http://www.ndci.org/courtfacts.htm.

National Drug Court Institute and Center for Substance Abuse Treatment. 2004. *Family Dependency Treatment Courts: Addressing Child Neglect and Abuse Cases Using the Drug Court Model, Monograph.* Washington, DC: Bureau of Justice Assistance, Office of Justice Programs, U.S. Department of Justice.

National Youth Court Center. 2005. Youth Court List by State. http://www.youthcourt.net/national_listing/overview.htm.

Nolan, J. L. Jr. 2003. "Community Courts and Community Justice: Commentary: Redefining Criminal Courts: Problem-Solving and the Meaning of Justice." *American Criminal Law Review* 40 (Fall):1541–1565.

Patrick, S., and R. Marsh. 2005. "Juvenile Diversion: Results of a 3-Year Experimental Study." *Criminal Justice Policy Review* 16, 1 (March):59–73.

Rasmussen, A. 2004. "Teen Court Referral, Sentencing, and Subsequent Recidivism: Two Proportional Hazards Models and a Little Speculation." *Crime & Delinquency* (October):615–635.

Rottman, D., and P. Casey. 1999. "Therapeutic Jurisprudence and the Emergence of Problem-Solving Courts." *National Institute of Justice Journal.* http://www. ncsonline.org.

Sviridoff, M., D. Rottman, B. Ostrom, and R. Curtis. 1997. *Dispensing Justice Locally: The Implementation and Effects of the Midtown Community Court.* Alexandria, VA: State Justice Institute.

Thompson, A. C. 2002. "Access to Justice: The Social Responsibility of Lawyers: Courting Disorder: Some Thoughts on Community Courts." *Washington University Journal of Urban and Contemporary Law* 10:63–99.

Wilson, J. Q., and G. L. Kelling. 1982. "Broken Windows: The Police and Neighborhood Safety." *The Atlantic Monthly* (March):29–38.

Wolfe, R. V. 2000. "Fixing Families: The Story of the Manhattan Family Treatment Court." http://www.courtinnovation.org/pdf/fixing_families.pdf.

Wolfe, R., L. Aldrich, and S. Moore. 2004. *Planning a Domestic Violence Court: The New York State Experience.* New York, NY: Center for Court Innovation.

Case Cited

In Re Gault, 387 U.S. 1; 87 S. Ct. 1428; 18 L. Ed. 2d 527 (1967).

Related Websites

Center for Court Innovation

http://www.courtinnovation.org

National Association of Drug Court Professionals and the National Drug Court Institute

http://www.ndci.org or http://www.nadcp.org

National Center for State Courts

http://www.ncsconline.org/D_Research/ProblemSolvingCourts/Problem-SolvingCourts.html

American University, Justice Programs Office, Drug Court Clearinghouse Project

http://spa.american.edu/justice/drugcourts.php

National Youth Court Center

http://www.youthcourt.net/

Discussion Questions

1. What lessons can be learned from juvenile court history that may be beneficial to problem-solving courts?

2. What impact might community courts have on the homeless and other marginalized segments of the population of an inner city?

3. Do problem-solving courts have an inappropriate "net-widening" effect, pulling those into the court "net" who would not have been traditionally sanctioned?

4. Several strengths and criticisms of problem-solving and traditional courts

are found in this chapter. Do the advantages outweigh the concerns?

5. How effectively are problem-solving courts addressing the needs of your community? ✦

Chapter 8
Sentencing Reforms and the Supreme Court

The Implications of *Apprendi,* *Blakely,* and *Booker*

Jeremy D. Ball

In this chapter the author presents a synopsis of the history of the sentencing reform movement. The sentencing reform movement began in the late 1970s with the creation of sentencing commissions, sentencing guidelines, and mandatory minimum penalties. Over the last 35 years these reforms have been subject to both criticism and support and recently the U.S. Supreme Court rulings in *Apprendi* (2000), *Blakely* (2004), and *Booker* (2005) have had a marked impact on the discretionary power of judges.

The author begins by summarizing the purposes of sentencing reforms, which were implemented to address issues of discrimination (race/ethnicity, sex, and age) by the limiting of judicial discretion. A by-product of such policy change has been the shift from—or reduction in—indeterminate sentencing to an increase in the implementation of more-structured determinate sentencing practices. Moreover, the application of sentencing guidelines and mandatory penalties has forced some to question whether discretionary power has simply transferred from judges to prosecutors and legislators.

Next, the chapter addresses the Supreme Court rulings in *Apprendi* (2000), *Blakely* (2004), and *Booker* (2005). The key question in these cases is whether a sentencing enhancement must be submitted to a jury for consideration and determination. This issue really has to do with whether facts are considered as either elements of the crime (elements rule) or sentencing factors. If ele-

ments, the Supreme Court has held, then increased penalties or upward departures from sentencing guidelines over the statutory maximum sentence must be subject to a jury trial. Both the real and practical impact of these decisions are outlined and discussed within the author's analysis.

Introduction

Up until about 30 years ago, judges made sentencing decisions on a case-by-case basis, and parole boards usually decided when to release particular offenders (Spohn 2002). However, this discretionary system of punishment had the potential for discrimination. "The single most important achievement for criminal justice in the last thirty years has been the recognition of the problem of discretion" (Walker 1993, 146). Sentencing reforms were developed to reduce discretion that, arguably, led to unwarranted disparity. The most notable of these sentencing reforms was the creation of sentencing guidelines (see Spohn 2000).

It has been well documented that sentencing reforms have created a system that is more determinate and more punitive (Spohn 2000; Spohn 2002; Tonry 1996). In other words, judges have been required to follow specific guidelines to make their sentencing decisions. In the last 35 years, the U.S. Supreme Court has left this system relatively untouched, maintaining the sentencing authority with the legislative members and individual judges—that is, until now. In a landmark decision in *Apprendi v. New Jersey* (2000), the Supreme Court changed the face of sentencing law forever.

The objective behind sentencing reforms has been to limit (not eliminate) judicial discretion and to provide uniformity in sentencing decisions to avoid potential discrimination. However, this objective has been challenged by the defendant's right to jury trial under the Sixth Amendment of the U.S. Constitution. This chapter synthesizes the research and commentaries on these potentially conflicting principles. The first part of this chapter summarizes the purpose of sentencing reforms and the empirical research regarding their effectiveness to this end. The second part addresses the recent case law on sentencing and the Sixth Amendment right to jury trial. Lengthier discussions are made on the following cases that have had a major impact on sentencing reform: *Apprendi v. New Jersey* (2000), *Blakely v. Washington* (2004), and *United States v. Booker* (2005). Finally, the chapter discusses the impact of these decisions on sentencing and other court processing decisions.

Sentencing Reforms

Prior to about 30 years ago, the system of sentencing was indeterminate and left much room for judicial discretion. However, there were voices of discontent with the practice of giving the judiciary (and parole boards) so much discretionary power in their sentencing decisions. As Spohn (2002) noted, many scholars feared unwarranted disparity leading to potential discriminatory decisions at sentencing. Therefore, in the late 1970s and early 1980s, state and federal legislatures attempted to correct this wrong by developing determinate sentencing policies—telling the judges how to make their decisions.

One of the major goals of these reforms was to limit discretion. By requiring judges to follow structured sentencing procedures, reformers intended to restrict the discretion of judicial decision-making power (Spohn 2000). By restraining judicial discretionary decision-making, reformers hoped to limit unwarranted disparity—especially with regards to race and ethnicity. By formalizing judicial sentencing decisions, they hoped that similar defendants would be treated similarly regardless of their race or ethnicity. The creation of sentencing guidelines and mandatory minimum penalties introduced a more uniform and, thereby, less individualized system of justice to combat the problems of unwarranted disparity plaguing sentencing decisions of this time period.

Sentencing Guidelines

One of the most notable changes during the reform movement was the creation of sentencing commissions and sentencing guidelines. To provide a fairer system of justice, Judge Marvin E. Frankel, a U.S. District Court Judge, called for more control over discretionary decisions of judges (Stith and Cabranes 1998). In the mid-1970s, Judge Frankel suggested that a separate administrative agency be created to develop new sentencing rules and procedures to realize this goal. Minnesota answered the call by developing the first sentencing commission in 1978, followed by the first set of sentencing guidelines in 1980 (Moore and Miethe 1986). Judges Frankel's suggestion was realized at the federal level with the advent of the Sentencing Reform Act of 1984. "Sentencing guidelines . . . reflect a fundamental dilemma of formal social control—the balance between uniformity . . . and individualization" (Ulmer and Kramer 1996, 383). States such as Pennsylvania and Washington[1] soon followed with their own form of sentencing guidelines. Sentencing guidelines offer a matrix of different ranges of sentences given two factors: prior criminal history and severity of the current offense.

One of the main purposes—arguably, *the* main purpose—of establishing sentencing guidelines was to reduce judicial discretion and thereby reduce unwarranted disparity (Spohn 2000). Has this goal been met? Some studies found unwarranted disparities in sentencing outcomes not to be limited or simply to be displaced to other actors within the criminal court system—namely, the prosecutor (Ulmer and Kramer 1996; Steffensmeier and Demuth 2001; Steffensmeier, Ulmer, and Kramer 1998).

Some authors studying judicial sentencing habits in sentencing guideline jurisdictions found that unwarranted disparity existed in the judge's decision to sentence the offender to incarceration—often termed the "in/out decision" (Ulmer and Kramer 1996; Steffensmeier et al. 1998; Steffensmeier and Demuth 2001; 2000). These disparities have tended to be based on offender characteristics such as race/ethnicity, sex, and age.

Some researchers have found an indirect disparate effect. Ulmer (1997) found that the impact of race and sex had more of an effect in cases that went to trial than cases where the defendant pled guilty. Ulmer also found that the race and sex of the defendant had more of an effect in less serious cases than more serious cases. In other words, the race and sex of the defendant were not an overall effect (see Albonetti 1997 for similar results at the federal level). Spohn (2000) stated that the more interesting question was not "'Does race make a difference?' but, rather, '*When* does race make a difference—under what conditions, for what types of offenders, and in interaction with what other factors?'" (Spohn 2000, 480). In other words, disparity can be found in certain contexts and is hidden if one examines only overall effects.

Disparate treatment is less consistently found for the sentence-length decision. Because the guidelines are meant to reduce disparity by reducing discretion, sentence lengths should be similar across offenders. Ulmer (1997) found racial disparities in sentence length under Pennsylvania sentencing guidelines. However, Ulmer also found that some offender characteristics had less of an impact on sentence length in more urban courts where the guidelines were viewed as a ready-made codification of the "going rates" (see also Engen and Gainey 2000). Again, context plays an important part in this research.

Another way to measure whether the sentencing guidelines have been effective in reducing discretion and thereby reducing disparity is to examine potential sources of disparity within guideline departures. A guideline departure allows a judge to increase or decrease above a particular sentencing range given particular circumstances of the defendant or case. Guideline departures offer the most probable opportunity for the exercise of discretion and the existence of disparity, because the restrictions on such decisions are fairly loosely defined. Steffensmeier and Demuth (2000) found that Hispanic and black offenders were disparately treated in cases that received a departure.

At the federal level, Stith and Cabranes (1998) found that no thorough study demonstrated a decrease in the total amount of disparity under the guidelines. Although unwarranted disparity may still exist, legal variables—that is, seriousness of current offense and prior criminal history—were found to be the most influential in sentencing decisions under a guideline system (Albonetti 1997; Engen and Gainey 2000; Ulmer and Kramer 1996; Moore and Miethe 1986; Ulmer 1997; Ulmer and Kramer 1996). Evidence suggesting that unwarranted disparity exists under the Federal Sentencing Guidelines foreshadows the irony of the Supreme Court's decision in *United States v. Booker* (2005) which is discussed later in this chapter.

Mandatory Penalties

Like sentencing guidelines, mandatory penalties are another form of sentencing reform intended to restrain judicial discretion. These reforms often require harsher penalties and offer court officials little opportunity to engage in individualized justice (Spohn 2000). These reforms mandate a particular minimum sentence or simply add to the minimum sentence defined in the criminal statute. Mandatory penalties—that is, mandatory minimum statutes, automatic sentence enhancements, and three-strikes laws— have suffered from problems similar to those that plagued sentencing guidelines.

Mandatory penalties were developed from a push for a more punitive philosophy of justice. Spohn (2002) suggests that mandatory minimum penalties were a direct result of the "war on crime" and "war on drugs" rationale of the late 1970s and 1980s. However, today, mandatory penalties have come under criticism for several reasons. First, they often result in the imposition of unduly harsh sentences (Tonry 1996). Some uniform penalties impose a harsh sanction on offenders who commit a relatively nonserious offense (Spohn 2002; Tonry 1996). A second criticism is the hydraulic displacement hypothesis. That is, through mandatory minimum penalties the discretionary power shifted from the judge to the prosecutor (Spohn 2002; Tonry 1996). At one time, sentencing was in the power of the judge, whereas today this power is in the hands of the prosecutor through his or her charging or plea bargaining authority.

Although the purpose of mandatory penalties was to reduce discretion and unwarranted disparity, empirical evidence indicates that disparities still existed. Crawford,

Chiricos, and Kleck (1998) found that black offenders were more likely to receive habitual offender sentences than white offenders. After controlling for case seriousness and prior record, Crawford (2000) found that male offenders were over three times more likely to receive mandatory minimum penalties than female offenders.

As we have noted, the purpose of sentencing reforms was to limit discretion and reduce disparity. Yet it appears that unwarranted disparities are not limited as much as had been intended. Another potential unforeseen consequence of sentencing reforms is "hydraulic displacement" of discretion from the judge to the prosecutor (see Miethe 1987; Ulmer and Kramer 1996). The Supreme Court imputed its own understanding of restraining judicial discretion in three recent landmark decisions: *Apprendi, Blakely,* and *Booker.*

United States Supreme Court Decisions

To understand the impact of these three cases on sentencing decisions and the administration of the criminal court system, it is important to understand the holding and analysis of each case.

Background Cases

The United States Supreme Court has virtually avoided questions about sentencing, out of a reliance on the power of legislators and trial judges to change sentencing policy (see Bibas 2001). Over the years, the Court has addressed several constitutional issues regarding important rights in the trial court process. The Sixth Amendment right to jury trial has had the greatest impact on judicial sentencing decisions. The Sixth Amendment states:

> In all criminal prosecutions, the accused shall enjoy the right to a speedy and public trial, by an impartial jury of the State and district wherein the crime shall have been committed, which district shall have been previously ascertained by law, and to be informed of the nature and cause of the accusation; to be confronted with the witnesses against him; to have

compulsory process for obtaining witnesses in his favor, and to have the Assistance of Counsel for his defence.

More specific to sentencing decisions, the Court in *In re Winship* (1970) exhorted that the Constitution required proof beyond a reasonable doubt of "every fact necessary to constitute the crime charged" (363). In so articulating this rule, the Court was concerned about the loss of liberty and the stigma that sentencing had on the defendant. The Court in *Mullaney v. Wilbur* (1975) suggested, though, that only those facts that were considered elements of the crime—not sentencing factors—must be found beyond a reasonable doubt. In this case, the criminal statute for homicide required the defendant to prove the presence of "heat of passion" as an affirmative defense to murder. The Court determined that the proof of the *presence* of the "heat of passion" defense was simply a proof of the *absence* of an element of homicide. Therefore, the Court's actions were unconstitutional according to the principles in *Winship.*

Eleven years later, the Court addressed the constitutionality of Pennsylvania's Mandatory Minimum Sentencing Act in *McMillan v. Pennsylvania* (1986). This statute—often termed a "sentence enhancement"—stated that any defendant found to have possessed a firearm during the commission of a crime would face a mandatory minimum penalty of five years. After the defendant was found guilty of the underlying crime, the judge determined the sentence based on facts found during the sentencing hearing by a preponderance of the evidence. The defendant claimed that his Sixth Amendment constitutional rights were violated per *Winship,* but the Court disagreed. They concluded that since the legislature specifically enumerated this provision to be a "sentencing factor," and not an element factor, the level of burden is a preponderance of evidence rather than beyond a reasonable doubt (*McMillan v. Pennsylvania* 1986).

The Supreme Court decided the constitutionality of sentencing guidelines in *Mistretta v. United States* (1989). This case did not address individual liberties; rather it addressed the authority of the different branches to delegate certain powers. More specifically, the issue was whether Congress' delegation of the creation of the Federal Sentencing Guidelines to the U.S. Sentencing Commission violated the separation of powers enumerated within the Constitution. In *Mistretta* the Court dismissed the claim that "Congress, in constituting the Commission as it did, effected an unconstitutional accumulation of power within the Judicial Branch while at the same time undermining the Judiciary's independence and integrity" (*Mistretta v. United States* 1989, 383). This holding served as a lead-in to *Blakely v. Washington* (2004) and *United States v. Booker* (2005).[2]

These earlier Supreme Court rulings provided context for three cases that have had a great impact on recent sentencing reforms. The Court in *Apprendi v. New Jersey* (2000) examined the Sixth Amendment right to jury trial in a case involving a sentencing enhancement. The Court in *Blakely v. Washington* (2004) and *United States v. Booker* (2005) addressed the Sixth Amendment right to a jury trial in cases involving state sentencing guidelines and Federal Sentencing Guidelines, respectively.

Apprendi v. New Jersey (2000)

Charles Apprendi, Jr. fired shots into the home of an African-American family. He pled guilty to second-degree possession of a firearm for an unlawful purpose, which carried a 5- to 10-year prison sentence, and third-degree possession of an antipersonnel bomb, which carried a 3- to 5-year prison sentence. After Apprendi pled guilty, the prosecutor filed a motion to enhance the sentence under the hate crime statute. The judge heard evidence on the hate crime enhancement and found, by a preponderance of the evidence, that the crime was completed with biased purpose. The judge therefore sentenced Apprendi to a prison term of 12 years.

Apprendi appealed his case to the U.S. Supreme Court, claiming that any fact that increased the statutory maximum for which a defendant was charged and convicted violated his Sixth Amendment right to jury trial. The grounds of his claim were based on Fourteenth Amendment rights of due process and Sixth Amendment rights to jury trial. The Supreme Court held that any fact that raises the sentence above the statutory maximum must be submitted to a jury and be proved beyond a reasonable doubt; Bibas (2001) called this the "elements rule." The only exception to this bright-line rule was the judicial consideration of prior convictions during sentencing. That is, after conviction, the judge could raise the sentence after considering prior criminal history, without a determination of a jury.

Although the State argued that the facts supporting the enhancement penalty were merely "sentencing factors," the Court ruled that these facts were more akin to "element factors"—that is, factors attributed to the elements of the underlying crime—to which the Sixth Amendment right to jury trial attached. In this case, the facts given during the sentencing hearing went toward the defendant's biased purpose, which went toward proving the defendant's state of mind—that is, the mental element of the crime.

Blakely v. Washington (2004)

In *Apprendi*, the Supreme Court addressed a mandatory penalty system, raising the declared sentence above the statutory maximum. Four years after *Apprendi*, the Supreme Court addressed the constitutionality of another sentencing reform practice: sentencing guidelines. In this case, Ralph Blakely, Jr. pleaded guilty to kidnapping his estranged wife. The statutory maximum for this offense was 53 months. The state of Washington has a sentencing guideline system in which prior criminal history and severity of the current offense are used as a guide for the judge to calculate the sentence. Under this sentencing guideline scheme, judges were allowed to make an upward departure—that is, increase the sentence above the guideline range—for a compelling reason. This type of sentence was referred to as an "exceptional" sentence. In *Blakely* the trial judge heard facts and imposed an "exceptional" sentence of 90 months because the defendant acted with "deliberate cruelty" (*Blakely v. Washington* 2004, 2531).

The Supreme Court in *Blakely* used the ruling in *Apprendi* as a precedent to address the defendant's right to jury trial in a determination of facts that raised the sentence above the guideline maximum range through upward departure practices. The Court found that upward departures from the prescribed guideline range maximum violated the defendant's right to a jury trial and the right to have facts against him proven beyond a reasonable doubt.

The Court stated in *Apprendi* that "other than the fact of a prior conviction, any fact that increases the penalty for a crime *beyond the prescribed statutory maximum* must be submitted to a jury, and proved beyond a reasonable doubt" (p. 490, emphasis added). Therefore, the most important issue for the Court in *Blakely* was to determine the meaning of "statutory maximum." The Court ruled that the "statutory maximum" that triggered Sixth Amendment rights was "the maximum sentence a judge may impose *solely on the basis of facts reflected in the jury verdict or admitted by the defendant*" (*Blakely v. Washington* 2004, 2537). The Court ruled that because of the presumptive—or mandatory—nature of the guidelines, the maximum that triggered Sixth Amendment rights to jury trial was the maximum allowed by the statutory guidelines and not the broader-reaching statute. In other words, the maximum of the range of sentence, given the defendant's prior criminal history and the current offense severity, was the ceiling beyond which a judge could not sentence without a determination by the jury.

The Court in *Blakely* addressed the purpose of the protection of the defendant's right to jury trial in sentencing decisions. They concluded that the jury acts as a check against the judicial sentencing power. Although determinate sentencing—such as Washington's sentencing guidelines—did limit judicial discretion, the Court claimed that "determinate judicial-factfinding schemes entail less judicial power than indeterminate schemes, but more judicial power than determinate *jury*-factfinding schemes" (*Blakely v. Washington* 2004, 2539).

There was disagreement between the members of the Court regarding the type of remedy allowed. Justice Bryer dissented because he believed the Court was engaged in legislative action rather than judicial action by claiming juries must make a factual determination to support an upward departure from the guidelines. He believed that defining sentencing practices should be left to the State rather than the judiciary. Justice Bryer offered three possible actions the legislature could take, given the majority rule: create a "pure" determinate sentencing scheme, return to an indeterminate sentencing scheme, or retain the structured sentencing scheme with Sixth Amendment protections specifically enumerated within the guidelines. Justice Bryer suggested, though, that a purely determinate sentencing scheme simply displaced the discretion to the prosecutor. He also concluded that indeterminate sentencing schemes undermined the rationale of the holdings in this case and in *Apprendi,* since judges would retain their discretionary power. Therefore, Justice Bryer argued that retaining the guidelines while adding the *Apprendi* rule within the language of the guidelines was the most logical step; however, that step should be taken by the legislature, and not the judiciary.

United States v. Booker (2005)

Justice Bryer's discussion in his dissent in *Blakely* proved to foreshadow the practical implications in *United States v. Booker* (consolidated with *United States v. Fanfan* 2005). Freddie Booker was charged in a federal court with possession to distribute at least 50 grams of crack cocaine and was found guilty in a jury trial. The statutory maximum for this offense at the federal level was life in prison. The Federal Sentencing Guidelines mandated a "base" sentence range of no less than 210 months and no more than 262 months. During sentencing, the judge found, by a preponderance of the evidence, that Booker had possessed an additional 566 grams of crack—information not presented to the jury. Because of a mandatory enhancement, the judge imposed a sentence of no less than 360 months with the maximum of life imprisonment, after considering this relevant conduct. ("Relevant conduct" is conduct not found in the facts at the time of the trial but substantiated by good evidence during sentencing.)

The Supreme Court considered two issues: (1) Did the Federal Sentencing Guidelines' mandatory enhancements, which were based on facts not proven by a jury beyond a reasonable doubt violate the Sixth Amendment right to jury as defined in *Apprendi* and *Booker*? (2) If this provision did violate the right to jury trial, what was the remedy for such violation? The Supreme Court found that these enhancements *did* violate the right to jury trial protected by the Sixth Amendment.

The Court examined Congress' language and the intent of that language. The Federal Sentencing Guidelines are mandatory and binding on all judges and, thereby, operate as a statute because they "have the force and effect of laws" (*United States v. Booker* 2005, 742). The Court also mirrored *Blakely*'s contention by devoting their legal analysis to the *effect* of this enhancement departure rather than its *form*.

The most decisive rule to be ascertained by the Court in *Booker* was its suggestion for remedy. The Court suggested that the remedy for this error was to eliminate the mandatory nature of the Federal Sentencing Guidelines; the Court ruled that the guidelines are now simply advisory. The Supreme Court saw value in retaining a strong connection between the use of "relevant conduct" or "real offense" factors for purposes of increased uniformity of sentencing. To attain this goal and follow the rule laid out in *Apprendi,* the Court decided to make the guidelines advisory—that is, voluntary and not mandatory. "Congress' basic statutory goal—a system that diminishes sentencing disparity—depends for its success upon judicial efforts to determine, and to base punishment, upon, the *real conduct* that underlies the crime of conviction" (*United States v. Booker* 2005, 743). "Real conduct" is often not proved beyond a reasonable doubt and is often inadmissible in the trial court (Spohn 2000). Sentences based on "real conduct" are often decided on a case-by-case basis. This cognitive dissonance between the goal of the Sentencing Commission to reduce judicial discretion and the importance of the inclusion of relevant conduct in sentencing practices will be discussed in the next part of this chapter.

In the first part of the twenty-first century, the Supreme Court drastically changed the face of sentencing reforms. Although the Court in *Mistretta v. United States* ruled that the sentencing guidelines are constitutional, the Court has now ruled that a judge cannot increase the sentence with facts not determined by a jury beyond a reasonable doubt (*Apprendi v. New Jersey*). A judge also cannot depart above the prescribed guideline range under the same principle whether the sentence is increased over the statutory maximum or not (*Blakely v. Washington* and *United States v. Booker*). Several commentators have addressed the impact of these landmark cases on other court processing decisions.

The Impact of *Apprendi, Blakely,* and *Booker*

The rulings in *Apprendi* and other related cases have affected sentencing in the twenty-first century. Many commentators argue that *Apprendi, Blakely,* and *Booker* have had the practical implications of increased caseloads, rising costs, and the disappearance of accepted sentencing reform practices. These cases have also produced indirect effects, in that it can be argued that judicial sentencing power has been displaced from the judge to the prosecutor and the legislature.

Some scholars suggest that more harm than good was created from the "elements rule" in *Apprendi* (Lillquist 2004). They suggest that requiring juries to make factual decisions on sentencing during the guilt phase of court proceedings may mean that defendants are more likely to be convicted (Lillquist 2004).

Finally, the Court in *Booker* ruled in such a way as to bring sentencing back to a more indeterminate system, which encourages *more* discretion to the judge. The purpose of sentencing reforms was to limit judicial discretion and reduce unwarranted sentencing disparity; however, the real consequence of *Booker* has been to broaden judicial discretion.

Practical Implications

The Supreme Court's decisions in *Apprendi, Blakely,* and *Booker* have had some real and practical effects on the reformed system of justice. Some argue that the sentencing reforms of the last 30 years have been all but eliminated. Bensten (2004) suggests that the ruling in *Apprendi* perfected the "death of the sentence enhancement" (p. 659).

Levine (2002), though, suggests that *Apprendi* did *not* signal the death of sentencing guidelines as the Court in *Apprendi* was concerned with statutory maximums and not necessarily with sentencing guidelines.[3] Levine did suggest, though, that judicial discretion is now even more limited under *Apprendi.* At the time, Levine correctly interpreted *Apprendi* to suggest that judicial discretion would be retained within the sentencing guideline ranges and departures from the guidelines. The Court in *Blakely* and *Booker,* however, has changed that. Reitz (2005) suggests that there might be a backlash to these rulings among state legislatures. Some states may avoid reforming their indeterminate sentencing schemes for fear that their reforms will be found unconstitutional given *Blakely* and *Booker.* In fact, Massachusetts was embarking on a major sentencing reform until the decision in *Blakely* discouraged this effort (Reitz 2005).

Not only were sentencing reforms abolished—or, at least modified considerably—but also caseloads and costs could be on the rise. "Placing sentencing authority in the hands of juries clearly makes more evidence admissible at trial because more evidence *is* admissible" (Lillquist 2004, 675, emphasis added). With more evidence available to the jury, caseloads will rise, and, court costs will also rise (Glass 2001/2002; Lillquist 2004). Caseloads may go even higher if states adopt a bifurcated trial system where juries will sit during the guilt phase *and* the sentencing phase. Some argue, though, that caseloads and court costs will not rise because most cases are usually decided by straight guilty plea or plea agreement (see Levine 2002).

Discretion Displacement

Sentencing reforms were intended to limit judicial discretion and to reduce unwarranted disparity. The "elements rule" adopted in *Apprendi* signified more limits placed on judicial discretion. However, some scholars suggest that this discretion has been displaced to other courtroom actors or other branches of the government (see Bensten 2004; Bibas 2001; Olson 2002).

The importance of the legislative branch in defining punishments—in both type and length—is a well-known principle. "Legislative supremacy over the substance of criminal law is a virtually unchallenged proposition" (Bentsen 2004, 645). Bibas (2001), though, argues that the "elements rule" displaced power from the judge to the legislative branch and reduced the democratic power of the jury. The difficulty is situated with the dilemma in defining which facts are "element facts" and which facts are "sentencing facts."

Other scholars accepted the checks and balances between the legislative branch and judicial branch of the government. Olson (2002) suggests that the Court in *Apprendi* acknowledged the importance of placing constitutional limits on legislative action and made their ruling accordingly. Bensten (2004) argues that it is not a question of displacing the power of the judicial branch to the legislative branch but a question of collaboration between the two branches. The legislative branch determines the substantive criminal law and the judicial branch determines whether there is a fact that is "constitutionally required" for the purposes of sentencing (Bensten 2004). A constitutionally significant fact is "any fact (or set of facts) that alters the constitutionality of a substantive criminal statute" (Bensten 2004, 668). These scholars argue, therefore, that although legislatures may take action to increase penalties and author provisions to counteract the elements rule in *Apprendi,* the judiciary is the ultimate authority of interpreting the constitutionality of statutes.

Another area of concern for some scholars is the potential for displaced discretion from judges to prosecutors. After the elements rule was established in *Apprendi,* Bibas

(2001) noted that this potential for displaced discretion lies within the plea bargaining power of the prosecutor. Although the elements rule was intended to give notice to defendants about the facts that are against them, Bibas argues that prosecutors circumvent this rule through charge bargaining. In 2000, nearly 95 percent of all felony convictions were a result of guilty pleas (Bureau of Justice Statistics 2003). The attention toward plea bargaining practices compared with other court processing issues indicates the level of concern in the criminal justice field about plea bargaining and its potential for harm. Bibas found that in the ten years prior to *Apprendi*, 633 law review articles addressed jury trials, whereas only 62 articles addressed guilty pleas or plea bargaining decisions.

Given the frequency of guilty pleas and the weighted evidence against the defendant with the advent of the elements rule, it is no surprise that at least a few commentators have been concerned with the displacement of discretion to the prosecutor—a virtually unrestrained courtroom actor. Although the Supreme Court limited the discretion of the judge, it gave more authority to the prosecutor either through charging or plea bargaining practices.

Some would argue, though, that the elements rule may actually assist defendants in plea bargaining decisions. With the weight of the evidence *against* the prosecutor to prove beyond a reasonable doubt to a set of jury members—an added burden on the prosecutor—the defendant may find that a negotiated plea is easier with the elements rule than without (Bibas 2001). There is evidence to suggest that those who pled guilty were more likely to have their sentence reduced by two or three levels under the Federal Sentencing Guidelines. There is also evidence to suggest that defendants who pled guilty received a sentence at the bottom of the guideline range and avoided receiving sentence enhancements (Bibas 2001).

More Harm Than Good?

Did the Supreme Court decisions in *Apprendi*, *Blakely*, and *Booker* do more harm than good? According to the elements rule, juries are responsible for deciding facts that could increase the statutory maximum (*Apprendi*) or sentencing guideline range maximum (*Blakely* and *Booker*). Although offenders convicted and sentenced are less likely to receive a harsh penalty, jurors are more likely to convict the defendant if facts important for sentencing purposes are considered with facts for conviction purposes (Lillquist 2004).

The conviction status of the offender is masked by the additional facts required for consideration by the jury beyond a reasonable doubt under the elements rule. Such masked effects could lead to jury mistakes or jury nullification. Glass (2001/2002) suggests that juries could make mistakes in favor of both parties. For example, juries could make the mistake of dismissing a case because certain sentencing facts clouded their judgment regarding the guilt of the defendant. In this situation, juries are likely to acquit the defendant if they believe the facts are irrelevant. On the other hand, Glass suggests that juries could also make the mistake of finding a fact for conviction that was intended to be used for sentencing, bolstering even further the conviction status of the defendant. "Placing sentencing authority in the hands of juries clearly makes more evidence admissible at trial because more evidence is relevant" (Lillquist 2004, 675).

Finally, given the holding in *Booker*, the Supreme Court essentially called for a return to an indeterminate sentencing system by suggesting that the Federal Sentencing Guidelines be advisory. At the time of this writing, very little commentary was available. What is important to note, though, is the purpose of the sentencing reforms—including, the Federal Sentencing Guidelines—was to develop to reduce unwarranted disparity by limiting judicial discretion. Ruling that the Guidelines were advisory, the Supreme Court in *Booker* rallied a return to indeterminate sentencing practices, which had caused the very evil for which the guidelines were created to overcome. "The majority's remedial choice is thus wonderfully ironic: In order to reduce from nullification a statutory scheme designed to eliminate discretionary sentencing, it discards the provisions and eliminates discretionary sentencing" (*United States v. Booker* 2005, 790, Scalia dissent).

Another ironic twist in this decision was the Court's support for the use of "relevant conduct" or "real offense" factors in sentencing. In the Federal Sentencing Guidelines, the commission allowed judges to individualize sentences using factors that could not be used in trial because of strict evidentiary rules (see Stith and Cabranes 1998). Again, the goal of the guidelines was to reduce judicial discretion and unwarranted disparity. The Court in *Booker* applauded the effort of using "real offense" factors in sentencing and based their decision to this end.

Yellen (2005) concludes that the advisory nature of the guidelines will produce great interjudge and interregion disparities—a problem the guidelines were created to solve. Yellen theorizes that the Court's remedy in *Booker* was an indirect way to accommodate the backlash against the Federal Sentencing Guidelines. As noted earlier in this chapter, many opponents of the Federal Sentencing Guidelines viewed the guidelines as too rigid and complex (see Stith and Cabranes 1998; Yellen 2005).

Whether the source of the decision in *Booker* is a social critique of the Federal Sentencing Guidelines or simply a ruling consistent with maintained precedence, the thrust of the decision remains the same: a return to indeterminate sentencing. Whether this return will result in more unfettered discretion and unwarranted disparity than existed during the 30 years prior to sentencing reforms remains to be seen.

Conclusion

Sentencing reforms—that is, mandatory penalties and sentencing guidelines—were developed to restrict judicial discretion and, in the end, limit unwarranted disparity. These reforms mandated certain sentencing policies that were binding on judges. Although judges retained some discretionary powers within these reforms, those powers were rather limited. Judges remained the ultimate decision-makers of sentencing outcomes.

Recently, the Supreme Court decided three landmark cases that changed the face of sentencing practices and policies in the United States. In *Apprendi*, the Court held that any facts that raised the sentence above the statutory maximum must be found by a jury beyond a reasonable doubt. The Court expanded this ruling in *Blakely*, requiring juries to decide facts beyond a reasonable doubt that raised the sentence above the "base" guideline range maximum. Although the Court in *Booker* ruled similarly that the Federal Sentencing Guidelines violated the Sixth Amendment right to jury trial, the Court's remedy—removing the mandatory nature of the guidelines—created a cognitive dissonance with the original intention of the guidelines.

Several commentaries on the recent Supreme Court interest in sentencing practices and policies have discussed the implications of these landmark cases. Some scholars have addressed the practical concerns and consequences of the elements rule articulated in *Apprendi*. Some argue that caseloads and the costs associated with this rule will flood the criminal court system. However, others have noted that the majority of today's cases are the result of guilty pleas and plea agreements.

Given that the bulk of cases are handled outside of the courtroom, some scholars address concerns with the displaced discretion resulting from the rulings in these landmark cases. In other words, limiting the judicial discretion even further with the elements rule may displace the sentencing authority even further into the hands of the prosecutor and legislature. With virtually unfettered discretion within the prosecutor's office, some scholars noted the danger in placing even more discretionary power in those hands. More discretion often results in more opportunity for unwarranted disparity. The transfer of sentencing discretion from the judge to the prosecutor lends to the argument that the unwarranted disparity for which the sentencing reforms were to restrict may just be transferred to prosecutors.

Finally, with the ruling in *Booker* in January 2005, the Court proclaimed the Federal Sentencing Guidelines to be advisory, no longer binding federal judges to its rigid, complex recommendations. The Supreme Court, for the sake of limiting discretion, returned to an indeterminate sentencing system. This return may also cause a return to interjudge discretion and unwarranted disparity. As the first part of this chapter notes, disparate treatment in the sentencing of certain groups of defendants—namely, racial/ethnic minorities—remained even after the sentencing reforms were put into place. However, most of this disparity was found in the more discretionary decisions, such as guideline departures or intrarange sentence differentiations. Although likely, it is not definite that sentencing at the federal level will return to a more indeterminate sentencing system. A close eye on sentencing practices in the years to come will discover any important consequences from these landmark decisions.

Notes

1. In 2004, the state of Washington was at the center of the most recent legal debate over state sentencing guideline systems in *Blakely v. Washington* (2004). The federal sentencing guidelines had a similar dilemma in *United States v. Booker* (2005). These two cases are discussed later in the chapter.

2. The Supreme Court also ruled in *Ring v. Arizona* (2002) regarding the right to a jury trial for determining aggravating circumstances for capital cases.

3. We now know, though, that the Court ruled against judicial discretion under the sentencing guidelines as well (see *United States v. Booker*, 2005).

References

Albonetti, C. A. 1997. "Sentencing Under the Federal Guidelines: Effects of Defendant Characteristics, Guilty Pleas, and Departures on Sentence." *Law & Society* 31:789–822.

Bentsen, D. S. 2004. "Beyond Statutory Elements: The Substantive Effects of the Right to a Jury Trial on Constitutionally Significant Effects." *Virginia Law Review* 90:645–692.

Bibas, S. 2001. "Judicial Fact-Finding and Sentence Enhancements in a World of Guilty Pleas." *The Yale Law Journal* 110:1097–1185.

Bureau of Justice Statistics. 2003. *Felony Sentences in State Courts, 2000*. Washington, DC: U.S. Department of Justice.

Crawford, C. 2000. "Gender Race, and Habitual Offender Sentencing in Florida." *Criminology* 38:263–280.

Crawford, C., T. Chiricos, and G. Kleck. 1998. "Race, Racial Threat, and Sentencing of Habitual Offenders." *Criminology* 36:481–511.

Engen, R. L., and R. R. Gainey. 2000. "Modeling the Effects of Legally Relevant and Extralegal Factors Under Sentencing Guidelines: The Rules Have Changed." *Criminology* 38:1207–1230.

Glass, E. 2001/2002. "Whatever Happened to the Trial by Jury? The Unconstitutionality of Upward Departures Under the United States Sentencing Guidelines." *Gonzaga Law Review* 37:343–375.

Levine, A. M. 2002. "The Confounding Boundaries of '*Apprendi*-land': Statutory Minimums and the Federal Sentencing Guidelines." *American Journal of Criminal Law* 29:377–454.

Lillquist, E. 2004. "The Puzzling Return of Jury Sentencing: Misgiving About *Apprendi*." *North Carolina Law Review* 82:621–715.

Miethe, T. D. 1987. "Charging and Plea Bargaining Practices Under Determinate Sentencing: An Investigation of the Hydraulic Displacement of Discretion." *Journal of Criminal Law and Criminology* 78:155–176.

Moore, C. A., and T. D. Miethe. 1986. "Regulated and Unregulated Sentencing Decisions: An Analysis of First-Year Practices Under Minnesota's Felony Sentencing Guidelines." *Law & Society Review* 20:254–277.

Olson, E. A. 2002. "Rethinking Mandatory Minimums After *Apprendi*." *Northwestern University Law Review* 96:811–842.

Reitz, K. R. 2005. "The New Sentencing Conundrum: Policy and Constitutional Law at Cross-Purposes." *Columbia Law Review* 105:1082–1123.

Spohn, C. 2000. "Thirty Years of Sentencing Reform: The Quest for a Racially Neutral Sentencing Process." *National Institute of Justice: Criminal Justice 2000*. Washington, DC.

———. 2002. *How Do Judges Decide? The Quest for Fairness and Justice in Sentencing*. Thousand Oaks, CA: Pine Forge Press.

Steffensmeier, D. and S. Demuth. 2001. "Ethnicity and Judges' Sentencing Decisions: Hispanic-Black-White Comparisons." *Criminology* 39:145–177.

———. 2000. "Ethnicity and Sentencing Out-comes in U.S. Federal Courts." *American Sociological Review* 65:705–729.

Steffensmeier, D., J. Ulmer, and J. Kramer. 1998. "The Interaction of Race, Gender, and Age, in Criminal Sentencing: The Punishment Cost of Being Young, Black, and Male." *Criminology* 36:763–797.

Stith, K., and J. A. Cabranes. 1998. *Fear of Judging: Sentencing Guidelines in the Federal Courts.* Chicago: University of Chicago Press.

Tonry, M. 1996. *Sentencing Matters.* New York: Oxford University Press.

Ulmer, J. T. 1997. *Social Worlds of Sentencing: Court Communities Under Sentencing Guidelines.* Albany: State University of New York Press.

Ulmer, J. T., and J. H. Kramer. 1996. "Court Communities Under Sentencing Guidelines: Dilemmas of Formal Rationality and Sentencing Disparity." *Criminology* 34:383–407.

Walker, S. 1993. *Taming the Systems: The Control of Discretion in Criminal Justice, 1950–1990.* New York: Oxford University Press.

Yellen, D. 2005. "Saving Federal Sentencing Reform After *Apprendi, Blakely* and *Booker.*" *Villanova Law Review* 50:163–187.

Cases Cited

Apprendi v. New Jersey, 530 U.S. 466 (2000).

Blakely v. Washington, 124 S. Ct. 2531 (2004).

In re Winship, 397 U.S. 358 (1970).

McMillan v. Pennsylvania, 477 U.S. 79 (1986).

Mistretta v. United States, 488 U.S. 361 (1989).

Mullaney v. Wilbur, 421 U.S. 684 (1975).

Ring v. Arizona, 536 U.S. 584 (2002).

United States v. Booker, 125 S. Ct. 738 (2005).

United States v. Fanfan, 125 S. Ct. 738 (2005).

Related Websites

United States Supreme Court
http://www.supremecourtus.gov

United States Sentencing Commission
http://www.ussc.gov

Washington State Sentencing Guidelines Commission
http://www.sgc.wa.gov

Professor Douglas A. Berman's Blog Report
http://sentencing.typepad.com

Discussion Questions

1. Are juries truly equipped to find facts that may affect sentences from the merits of the case?

2. Should the discretion of prosecutors be limited similarly to the discretion of judges? If so, how would you limit the discretion of prosecutors? What are the strengths and weaknesses of doing so?

3. Read *Ring v. Arizona* (2002). What are the Supreme Court's rationales in *Ring*? Are the decisions in *Apprendi, Blakely,* and *Booker* consistent or inconsistent with *Ring*?

4. Did the Supreme Court engage in legislative action in *Apprendi*? If so, why? If not, why not?

5. Define "elements factors." Define "sentencing factors." Give some examples of each.

6. Given the rulings of the three landmark cases (*Apprendi, Blakely,* and *Booker*), is it better to have a determinate sentencing system or an indeterminate sentencing system?

7. Was the Supreme Court right about making the Federal Sentencing Guidelines advisory rather than mandatory? Explain. ✦

Chapter 9
Mental Health and the Death Penalty

Matters of Competency and Culpability

Peggy M. Tobolowsky

In this chapter, the author provides an outline and analysis of key legal concepts and court cases that have affected the way the death penalty is applied to offenders with mental health and mental disability issues. There are three similar, yet distinct, points of reference from which to draw insight regarding the constitutional requirement of competency and culpability when dealing with the sentence of death. Each of these points—which encompass or represent offenders by category of mental health, mental retardation, and age—share or draw upon similar legal considerations and reasoning and can be tracked through landmark court cases.

Mental health, mental disability, and age exceptions fall under the scrutiny of the Fifth, Eighth, and Fourteenth Amendments. Competency inquiries ensure the fundamental fairness of the criminal proceedings. Exclusions from criminal responsibility or capital punishment result from the diminished culpability or blameworthiness associated with mental impairments or youth.

This chapter also presents other crucial legal conceptions related to capital punishment, such as the evolving standards of decency, the proportionality precept, and fundamental fairness, along with an analysis of the intrinsic goals (retribution/deterrence) of capital punishment within our criminal justice system.

Introduction

Over 3,400 offenders who have been sentenced to death are awaiting execution in this country (Death Penalty Information Center 2005). Estimates of the percentage of these offenders who are mentally ill range from 5–70 percent (Hensl 2004; White 1993). Estimates of the percentage of these offenders who are mentally retarded range from 4–20 percent (Tobolowsky 2003). Given these estimates of the prevalence of mental illness and retardation among capital offenders, it is not surprising that the U.S. Supreme Court has addressed mental health issues in defining the constitutional requirements of competency and culpability in its death penalty rulings. This chapter reviews how the Court and capital punishment states have addressed offenders' mental health in the imposition and carrying out of the death penalty.

The Relationship Between Mental Health and the Criminal Justice System

To understand the legal significance of mental health issues in the death penalty context, it is first necessary to have an understanding of the underlying medical conditions. *Mental illness* is a broad term that includes a number of specific disorders, such as schizophrenia, bipolar disorders, and anxiety disorders. These specific disorders often have very different manifestations. Schizophrenia, for example, may include symptoms ranging from confused thinking or speech to psychotic delusions to emotional flatness. On the other hand, bipolar disorders are characterized by significant shifts in mood, energy, and functioning, including episodes of both mania and depression. It is estimated that approximately 2–5 percent of the general population has some type of serious mental illness or disorder (National Alliance for the Mentally Ill 2005; National Mental Health Association 2005).

In contrast to the wide variety of specific mental illnesses, *mental retardation* is more universally understood to apply to persons with significant limitations both in intellectual functioning and adaptive behavior or functioning that originated before age 18. Intellectual functioning is most often measured based on performance on general intelligence tests (IQ tests), with scores of 70–75 usually regarded as the upper limit for this aspect of mental retardation. Limitations in adaptive behavior can be measured by a variety of assessment instruments that examine conceptual, social, and practical functioning in skill areas such as communication, self-care, health and safety, functional academics, work, and social skills. It is estimated that 1–3 percent of the general population is mentally retarded (American Association on Mental Retardation 2002; American Psychiatric Association 2000; Tobolowsky 2003).

Consideration of these mental health issues is not limited to the death penalty context. A defendant accused of any crime can assert that his or her impaired mental health renders him or her criminally incompetent to the degree that the criminal proceedings should be temporarily or indefinitely deferred. In addition, any criminal defendant might claim impaired mental health as a bar to culpability, through the assertion of a criminal insanity defense to the underlying crime. In the capital context, however, mental health issues have additional significance. They can potentially be used as mitigating factors to avoid imposition of a death sentence (*Penry v. Lynaugh* 1989). More important, the Supreme Court has established categorical exclusions from the death penalty for mentally retarded offenders and "insane" offenders who lack the competency for execution (*Atkins v. Virginia* 2002; *Ford v. Wainwright* 1986). Although this chapter will briefly discuss the role that impaired mental health can play regarding general criminal competence and the insanity defense, its primary focus will be on the applications of impaired mental health that are unique to the death penalty.

Mental Health and Criminal Competence Generally

The United States Constitution prohibits the deprivation of "life, liberty, or property"

without due process of law (Amendments V, XIV). Consistent with this requirement of fundamental fairness in American criminal proceedings, the Supreme Court has required that defendants be criminally competent for prosecutions against them (*Drope v. Missouri* 1975; *Dusky v. United States* 1960). The Court's definition of *criminal competence* for constitutional purposes is designed to ensure that defendants can meaningfully participate in the criminal proceedings against them: the "test must be whether [the defendant] has sufficient present ability to consult with his lawyer with a reasonable degree of rational understanding—and whether he has a rational as well as factual understanding of the proceedings against him" (*Dusky v. United States* 1960, 402).

As this definition indicates, impaired mental health does not automatically mean that a defendant is criminally incompetent. The issue of criminal competency can generally be raised at any time during the proceedings by either party or the court itself. Once it is raised, most jurisdictions allow the trial court to appoint an expert to examine the defendant and provide an opinion regarding the defendant's mental status and its impact on the aspects of criminal competence. The defendant is often given the burden of proof to establish his or her incompetence by a preponderance of the evidence. Upon a finding of incompetence, the criminal proceedings are generally delayed so that the defendant can receive treatment to restore his or her competency. If a defendant's competency cannot be restored within a reasonable period of time, jurisdictions have procedures to indefinitely suspend or dismiss the criminal proceedings, initiate civil commitment procedures to involuntarily treat the defendant, or both (*Cooper v. Oklahoma* 1996; *Jackson v. Indiana* 1972; Klotter 2004; *Medina v. California* 1992).

Although it is possible for mentally ill and retarded capital defendants to be found criminally incompetent and have the proceedings against them indefinitely suspended or dismissed, the likelihood of this happening is limited for several reasons. At the outset, the legal standard for criminal competence is fairly low. In fact, it is possible to have significant mental impairments and nevertheless be deemed criminally competent (Campbell 2004; *Pate v. Robinson* 1966). Moreover, even if a capital defendant were found to be criminally incompetent, it is likely that every effort would be made to restore the defendant's competency through treatment—even involuntary treatment—to avoid an indefinite suspension or dismissal of the proceedings in such a serious case (*Sell v. United States* 2003).

Mental Health and the Insanity Defense

Criminal insanity has long been recognized as a legal defense that will excuse the defendant's culpability on the underlying crime. Although the specific definitions of legal *insanity* vary somewhat among jurisdictions, they generally share the requirements of a mental disease or defect that has had some impact on the commission of the crime. The prescribed impact on the commission of the crime may be that the defendant was unable to appreciate the wrongfulness of his or her conduct, understand the nature and quality of the conduct, conform his or her conduct to the requirements of the law, or some similar standard. Most jurisdictions place the burden of proof on the defendant to establish this defense. Upon a defendant's acquittal due to insanity, most jurisdictions require a period of treatment or involuntary hospitalization until either the defendant is no longer mentally impaired or is no longer dangerous to himself/herself or others (*Foucha v. Louisiana* 1992; Klotter 2004).

The insanity defense has always been controversial, largely because of the public perception that it is abused by defendants to escape liability for their crimes. The reality, however, is that relatively few offenders assert this defense, the defense is rarely successful when asserted, and the successful assertion of the defense often results in involuntary hospitalization as long as or longer than the maximum period of incarceration permitted on the underlying crime. Nevertheless, the negative public perceptions persist and have led many jurisdictions to make their insanity standards more restrictive or to add an additional verdict of "guilty, but mentally ill" (Walker 2001). As a result of all of the above, not many capital defendants are likely to escape conviction through the successful assertion of an insanity defense.

Mental Illness and Retardation as a Mitigating Circumstance in Capital Sentencing

When the Court upheld the constitutionality of the death penalty in 1976, it indicated that capital punishment states must ensure that their capital procedures permit the sentencer to focus on the characteristics of the individual offender and crime in assessing sentence (*Gregg v. Georgia* 1976). The Court subsequently elaborated on this requirement by prohibiting capital procedures that limit or preclude the sentencer from considering relevant evidence that might mitigate against the imposition of a death sentence (*Eddings v. Oklahoma* 1982; *Lockett v. Ohio* 1978).

In this connection, many capital punishment states have procedures that permit the sentencing jury to find and weigh aggravating and mitigating factors in determining whether to sentence an offender to death. Mental health issues are frequently included among statutory mitigating factors. For example, an offender's impaired capacity to appreciate the wrongfulness of his conduct or conform his conduct to the requirements of the law—even if insufficient to establish an insanity defense to the underlying crime—can establish a mitigating factor to consider in the imposition of a death sentence. An offender's commission of a capital crime under the influence of an extreme or severe mental or emotional disturbance is another frequently used mental health-related statutory mitigating factor (Fla. Stat. Ann. § 921.141, 2001; 18 U.S.C.A. § 3592, 2000, 2005). In addition to such statutory mitigating factors, offenders can introduce relevant mental health evidence to establish nonstatutory mitigating circumstances that weigh against the imposition of a death sentence (*Hitchcock v. Dugger* 1987).

In *Penry v. Lynaugh* (1989), the Court addressed whether the Texas capital procedure impermissibly restricted the consideration of the offender's mitigating evidence of mental retardation and abused background. A five-justice majority concluded that the defendant's mitigating evidence had relevance to his moral culpability beyond the three sentencing "special issues" used in the Texas capital procedure to determine punishment:

> In this case, in the absence of instructions informing the jury that it could consider and *give effect to* [italics added] the mitigating evidence of Penry's mental retardation and abused background by declining to impose the death penalty, we conclude that the jury was not provided with a vehicle for expressing its "reasoned moral response" to the evidence in rendering its sentencing decision. (*Penry v. Lynaugh* 1989, 328)

The Court consequently found the Texas capital sentencing procedure unconstitutional as applied in the Penry case and overturned the defendant's death sentence. The dissenters in this closely divided case found that the Texas procedure adequately allowed consideration of the offender's mitigating evidence and criticized the perceived expansion of the Court's mitigating circumstances rulings (*Penry v. Lynaugh* 1989).

Although the consideration of mental health evidence in capital sentencing is now well-established as a constitutional matter, the effectiveness of its consideration as a practical matter may be limited. Even if evidence of impaired mental health is presented in mitigation of the imposition of a death sentence, this evidence may not overcome the strength of the government's evidence of aggravating circumstances. Moreover, an offender's impaired mental health has the capacity to be treated or perceived as "double-edged" evidence with both a mitigating *and* an aggravating tendency, such as reflecting an inability to learn from mistakes or alter future behavior (*Penry v. Lynaugh* 1989; Slobogin 2003). In fact, the more limited ability of mentally retarded offenders to make a "persuasive showing of mitigation" in opposition to government evidence of aggravating circumstances was one of the factors that led the Court to establish a categorical exclusion from the death penalty for such offenders (*Atkins v. Virginia* 2002, 320). Capital offenders with other mental health impairments can continue to present such evidence at sentencing in the hope that it will overcome the government's aggravating circumstances evidence and result in a sentence other than death.

Mental Retardation as a Categorical Exclusion From the Death Penalty

Although the ineffectiveness of the consideration of mental retardation as a mitigating factor in the imposition of the death penalty was one of the factors that led to its establishment as a categorical exception to capital punishment, other factors were much more fundamental to the culpability requirements incorporated in the Court's death penalty rulings. The Court rejected the establishment of this categorical exclusion from capital punishment the first time it considered the issue in *Penry v. Lynaugh* (1989). However, the Court subsequently barred the imposition of the death penalty on mentally retarded offenders when it revisited the issue in *Atkins v. Virginia* (2002).

In *Penry,* the Court addressed the case of a mentally retarded offender with an IQ between 50 and 63 who had been found criminally competent and *not* criminally insane and who was subsequently sentenced to death. In examining whether the imposition of the death penalty on mentally retarded offenders such as Penry would violate the Eighth Amendment's prohibition of cruel and unusual punishment, a five-justice majority determined that it would not be deemed unconstitutionally "cruel and unusual" either as that term was understood at the time of the adoption of the Bill of Rights or under the concept of the "evolving standards of decency" used by the Court to interpret this provision in its contemporary context (*Penry v. Lynaugh* 1989; *Trop v. Dulles* 1958).

In terms of the concept's common law application, the Court found that the common law exclusion from punishment for "idiots" and "lunatics" referred to individuals with more severe mental impairments than Penry, whose circumstances were addressed by the criminal competency and insanity procedures in contemporary practice (*Penry v. Lynaugh* 1989, 331–332). The Court further found that the evidence that a national consensus against the execution of mentally retarded offenders had emerged in contemporary times was insufficient, including the fact that Congress and two capital punishment states prohibited this punishment (as well as the 14 noncapital punishment states). The dissenting justices, utilizing the proportionality and punishment purposes concepts of the Court's prior capital punishment rulings, concluded that *all* offenders clinically defined as mentally retarded had insufficient intelligence and adaptive behavioral skills to provide a level of culpability proportionate to a death sentence or to foster the punishment goals of retribution or deterrence. Dissenting justices also noted that offenders' mental retardation decreased the reliability of the outcome and increased the risk of error to a level unacceptable in a capital case (*Penry v. Lynaugh* 1989).

When the Court revisited this issue over a decade later in the case of a mentally retarded offender with an IQ of 59, a six-justice majority concluded that the execution of mentally retarded capital offenders *does* violate the Eighth Amendment (*Atkins v. Virginia* 2002). At the outset, the Court reaffirmed its interpretation that the Eighth Amendment prohibits "excessive" as well as cruel and unusual punishments and requires that punishments be "graduated and proportioned" to the offense (*Atkins v. Virginia* 2002, 311, n 7; Tobolowsky 2004). Moreover, the determination of the excessive nature of a punishment is assessed under the evolving standards of decency reflected by contemporary standards rather than those existing at common law. Finally, although objective evidence of contemporary standards such as enacted legislation or jury practice informs the Court's proportionality review, the ultimate assessment of a punishment's constitutionality must be made by the Court itself (*Atkins v. Virginia* 2002).

Although the basic legal issues raised in *Penry* and *Atkins* were largely the same, legislative action by capital punishment states and capital punishment practice in the intervening years convinced two of the justices who had formed part of the *Penry* majority, as well as three post-*Penry* justices, to join the lone remaining *Penry* dissenting justice in determining that a national consensus against the execution of mentally retarded offenders had emerged. As of the *Atkins* decision, Congress and 18 capital punishment states prohibited the execution of mentally retarded offenders (as well as the 12 noncapital punishment states), and few of the remaining 20 capital punishment states had executed a mentally retarded offender since *Penry*. The Court further determined that the national consensus it had found against the execution of mentally retarded offenders reflected a judgment about the diminished personal culpability of these offenders, the limited relationship between mental retardation and the retribution and deterrence punishment purposes served by the death penalty, and the potential for the characteristics of mental retardation to undermine the procedural protections required in capital cases. In agreement with the national consensus it had found, the Court concluded that the execution of mentally retarded offenders is a constitutionally excessive punishment barred by the Eighth Amendment (*Atkins v. Virginia* 2002).

The dissenting justices advocated an Eighth Amendment review standard limited to an assessment of the common law acceptance of a punishment and a contemporary review restricted to an analysis of legislative and sentencing jury practices—and one that did not consider the "excessive" nature of the punishment. Using this analysis, the dissenting justices found that the execution of mentally retarded offenders was not categorically barred at common law and that the evidence of a contemporary national consensus against the practice was insufficient (*Atkins v. Virginia* 2002).

When the *Atkins* Court barred the execution of mentally retarded offenders, it entrusted to capital punishment jurisdictions the responsibility to identify these offenders and enforce the constitutional ban on their execution. Thus, the 20 capital punishment jurisdictions without pre-*Atkins* bans had to develop a definition of mental retardation for these purposes and procedures to exclude such offenders from execution. Currently, more than half of these capital punishment states have either legislative or judicially established procedures to identify mentally retarded offenders and exclude them from execution (Tobolowsky 2003).

Most pre- and post-*Atkins* jurisdictions have adopted some variation of the nationally recognized clinical definitions of mental retardation requiring subaverage intellectual functioning, deficits in adaptive behavior, and manifestation before age 18. All of the jurisdictions with *Atkins* procedures thus far require or authorize the trial court to make the mental retardation determination in specified circumstances. The majority of these jurisdictions require or authorize this determination to be made prior to trial. All of the jurisdictions that have expressly assigned a burden of proof regarding mental retardation have assigned this burden to the defendant. The majority of the jurisdictions have adopted the preponderance of the evidence standard of proof. In addition to trial-related procedures to identify mentally retarded capital offenders required by *Atkins,* the retroactive nature of the Court's decision also requires the development of post-conviction procedures to identify mentally retarded offenders already sentenced to death and exclude them from execution. Most jurisdictions are adopting or adapting their existing postconviction review process to allow the consideration of *Atkins* claims (Tobolowsky 2003).

In addition to the appellate review of the definitions and procedures adopted to carry out the *Atkins* mandate, appellate courts in capital punishment jurisdictions are reviewing the particular factual findings concerning mental retardation made in individual cases, as well as other application errors. In light of the increased importance of a mental retardation finding in a capital case, it is expected that ineffective assistance of counsel claims regarding the investigation and presentation of this evidence will increase (Tobolowsky 2003). Thus, the Court's decision in *Atkins* has established another important issue in the trial and appellate review of the capital cases of mentally retarded offenders.

The Requirement of Competency for Execution

Prior to its rulings regarding mentally retarded capital offenders, the Court examined whether a death sentence could be constitutionally carried out on an "insane" offender (*Ford v. Wainwright* 1986). Execution of the insane was prohibited at common law and by every contemporary capital punishment jurisdiction. Against this backdrop of historical and contemporary condemnation, a five-justice majority concluded that the execution of the insane is prohibited by the Eighth Amendment either to "protect the condemned from fear and pain without comfort of understanding, or to protect the dignity of society itself from the barbarity of exacting mindless vengeance" (*Ford v. Wainwright* 1986, 410). That the Court's ruling addressed an offender's competency for the carrying out of an imposed death sentence rather than any diminished culpability that would avoid the imposition of a death sentence itself (as established in *Atkins* for mentally retarded offenders) was made clear by the definition of "insanity" in this context offered by one justice in his concurring opinion: "those who are unaware of the punishment they are about to suffer and why they are to suffer it" (*Ford v. Wainwright* 1986, 422). The Court also found that Florida's procedures to determine the offender's competency for execution in this case were constitutionally inadequate.

Two justices rejected the necessity of creating this constitutional exclusion from execution in light of the unanimous state prohibitions of the execution of insane offenders. The two remaining justices also dissented from the Court's ruling that the Eighth Amendment prohibits the execution of insane offenders, but these justices did find a due process violation in the state procedures used to determine the offender's competency for execution and therefore concurred in the Court's result (*Ford v. Wainwright* 1986).

In their opinions in *Ford,* the justices varied considerably regarding the procedures they deemed constitutionally adequate to determine a capital offender's competency for execution. None of these approaches received the support of a majority of the justices. Consequently, each capital punishment jurisdiction was left with the "task of developing appropriate ways to enforce the constitutional restriction on [their] execution of sentences" (*Ford v. Wainwright* 1986, 416–417). As a result, the capital punishment states vary both in their definitions of competence for execution and the procedures to determine it (Horstman 2002).

In terms of definitions of competence for execution, some jurisdictions use a definition similar to that stated in the concurring opinion in *Ford;* others also add a component reflecting an ability to assist counsel; and still others do not define the term in any detail (Ackerson, Brodsky, and Zapf 2005; Jones 2004). State procedures also vary regarding how and when the issue can be raised, the number of times it can be raised, the fact-finding procedure and the prescribed fact-finder, the standard of proof, and the ultimate short- and long-term effect of a finding of incompetency for execution (Horstman 2002). The Court has not addressed the adequacy of any specific procedures since its ruling in *Ford.*

One of the most controversial issues that has arisen since *Ford* is whether medication can be involuntarily administered to a capital offender to restore or maintain his competency for execution. Although the Court has not yet addressed this issue, its rulings regarding the involuntary administration of medication in other contexts provide some guidance. The Court has concluded that the due process provision allows a state to involuntarily treat a seriously mentally ill prison inmate with antipsychotic drugs if he is "dangerous to himself or others and the treatment is in the inmate's medical interest" (*Washington v. Harper* 1990, 227). The Court further concluded that the state's administrative procedures to govern the process in this case were constitutionally adequate (*Washington v. Harper* 1990).

The Court has twice addressed the involuntary administration of antipsychotic drugs to a defendant in the context of trial proceedings. In the first case, the Court found that the trial court had unconstitutionally rejected the defendant's request to suspend the administration of antipsychotic medication to him during his trial in the absence of findings concerning the defendant's need for the drug or its medical appropriateness or reasonable alternatives to its administration (*Riggins v. Nevada* 1992). In the second case, the Court found that

> the Constitution permits the Government involuntarily to administer antipsychotic drugs to a mentally ill defendant facing serious criminal charges in order to render that defendant competent to stand trial, but only if the treatment is medically appropriate, is substantially unlikely to have side effects that may undermine the fairness of the trial, and, taking account of less intrusive alternatives, is necessary significantly to further important governmental trial-related interests. (*Sell v. United States* 2003, 179)

Because the lower court had not made findings consistent with this standard, the Court reversed its authorization of involuntary medication to render the defendant competent to stand trial (*Sell v. United States* 2003).

Very few courts have thus far addressed the permissibility of the involuntary administration of drugs to restore or maintain a capital offender's competency for execution. The supreme courts of Louisiana and South Carolina applied state law to prohibit involuntary administration of antipsychotic medication for the sole purpose of rendering an offender competent for execution (*Singleton v. State* 1993; *State v. Perry* 1992).

A divided federal appellate court, however, upheld the involuntary administration of antipsychotic medication that was ordered on dangerousness grounds, but that also rendered the offender competent for execution (*Singleton v. Norris* 2003). The appellate court found that the government's essential interest in carrying out the imposed death sentence outweighed the offender's liberty interest in refusing medication in this case in which the offender had not opposed the medication prior to the setting of his execution date and had not experienced substantial side effects. The appellate court further found that this forced treatment was necessary to alleviate the offender's psychosis and no less-intrusive treatment was available to ensure his competence. The appellate court concluded that the involuntary administration of the medication was "medically appropriate" despite the fact that it was contrary to the offender's long-term health interests in that it maintained his competence for execution. Finally, the court rejected the contention that *Ford* prohibited the execution of one who was merely "artificially competent" through the involuntary administration of medication. The dissenting judges viewed the medication as merely masking the offender's "insanity" rather than curing it and thus considered his execution still barred by *Ford*. They also noted the ethical dilemma the majority's ruling would pose for the medical community (*Singleton v. Norris* 2003). The Court declined to undertake any further review of this case (*Singleton v. Norris* 2003).

A Categorical Exclusion From Capital Punishment Based on Age: An Extension to Mentally Ill Offenders?

In addition to the issue of the constitutionality of medically induced competency for execution, the other major mental health-related issue that the Court has yet to resolve is the constitutionality of capital punishment for mentally ill offenders. Advocates of a constitutional prohibition of capital punishment for mentally ill offenders have drawn encouragement not only from the Court's prohibition of capital punishment for mentally retarded offenders in *Atkins v. Virginia* (2002) but also from its subsequent prohibition of capital punishment for juvenile offenders who were under the age of 18 at the commission of their capital crime (*Roper v. Simmons* 2005).

In *Simmons*, a five-justice majority used an Eighth Amendment analysis similar to that employed in *Atkins* to overturn the

Court's prior *Penry* ruling regarding mentally retarded offenders. Four justices had previously concluded in *Thompson v. Oklahoma* (1988) that the execution of an offender under 16 at the time of the crime was categorically prohibited by the Eighth Amendment. However, a five-justice majority had subsequently rejected a categorical exclusion from the death penalty for offenders who were 16 and 17 at the time of the crime in *Stanford v. Kentucky* (1989). In *Stanford*, the Court concluded that such executions were not prohibited at common law and that no contemporary national consensus had developed against this practice (*Stanford v. Kentucky* 1989).

In *Simmons*, five of the six justices who formed the *Atkins* majority determined that a national consensus against the execution of juvenile offenders had emerged since *Stanford* and concluded that the death penalty is an unconstitutionally disproportionate punishment for offenders under 18 at the time of their crimes. As in *Atkins*, the Court found that 30 states prohibited the juvenile death penalty—including 18 capital punishment states that prohibited it by legislation or judicial ruling and 12 states that prohibited the death penalty entirely. The Court also found an infrequency of use of the juvenile death penalty in the remaining capital punishment states and a slower, but nevertheless consistent trend toward abolition, as it had found in *Atkins* (*Roper v. Simmons* 2005).

The Court's proportionality analysis regarding juvenile offenders was also similar to that used in *Atkins*. The Court identified three key differences between juveniles under 18 and adults that excluded juveniles from the narrow class of the "worst" offenders for whom the death penalty is reserved: their immaturity and underdeveloped sense of responsibility, their vulnerability to negative influences and outside pressures, and their more transitory character traits. These differences resulted in a reduced culpability for juveniles generally and limited the likelihood that capital punishment could achieve the punishment goals of retribution or deterrence regarding juveniles. Thus, the Court rejected its previous ruling in *Stanford* and concluded that the imposition of a death sentence on an offender under 18 at the time of the crime is prohibited by the Eighth Amendment. The dissenting justices disagreed either with the Court's analytical principles, its factual application of these principles, or both (*Roper v. Simmons* 2005).

Despite the Court's recent recognition of categorical exclusions from the death penalty for mentally retarded offenders and juveniles, the recognition of a similar exclusion for mentally ill capital offenders faces several obstacles. At the outset, "mental illness" is a much broader and more varied diagnosis than mental retardation and clearly a less distinct category than juvenile age, making the identification of a specific category for exclusion from capital punishment more difficult. Moreover, there has been little recognition of such an exclusion for mentally ill capital offenders by capital punishment jurisdictions, making the finding of a "national consensus" against the practice unlikely pursuant to the Court's Eighth Amendment analysis (Conn. Gen. Stat. § 53a-46a, 2005; Slobogin 2003).

As a result of these obstacles, advocates of this exclusion are beginning to make more limited proposals regarding certain categories of mentally ill capital offenders. For example, one proposal suggests a categorical exclusion from capital punishment on Eighth Amendment grounds for capital offenders found to be "volitionally incapacitated" because of their serious mental illness at the time of the crime (Blume and Johnson 2003, 93). Another suggests an equal protection claim by capital offenders who were psychotic at the time of the crime and thus have similar diminished culpability and limited punishment purposes served by capital punishment as mentally retarded and juvenile offenders (Slobogin 2003). Although proposals in this area are growing, most acknowledge the challenges ahead in the establishing of a categorical exclusion from capital punishment for mentally ill offenders (Blume and Johnson 2003; Hall 2004).

Conclusion

The relationship between mental health issues and the criminal justice process has long been recognized through the requirement of criminal competency during the prosecution and the availability of the insanity defense. In the last two decades, the Court has made significant rulings that recognize the unique aspects of this interrelationship in the context of capital punishment. The Court has required that mental health issues and other factors that mitigate against the imposition of a death sentence be considered and given effect in capital sentencing (*Penry v. Lynaugh* 1989). The Court has recognized a categorical exclusion from capital punishment for mentally retarded offenders (*Atkins v. Virginia* 2002). Finally, the Court has prohibited the execution of insane offenders who are not competent for execution (*Ford v. Wainwright* 1986). As discussed in this chapter, other mental health issues related to capital punishment remain for resolution as the Court, and capital punishment jurisdictions continue to define matters of competency and culpability in the administration of the death penalty.

References

Ackerson, K. S., S. L. Brodsky, and P. A. Zapf. 2005. "Judges' and Psychologists' Assessments of Legal and Clinical Factors in Competence for Execution." *Psychology, Public Policy and Law* 11:164–193.

American Association on Mental Retardation. 2002. *Mental Retardation: Definitions, Classification, and Systems of Supports* (10th ed.). Washington, DC: American Association on Mental Retardation.

American Psychiatric Association. 2000. *Diagnostic and Statistical Manual of Mental Disorders* (4th ed., text. rev.). Washington, DC: American Psychiatric Association.

Blume, J. H., and S. L. Johnson. 2003. "Killing the Non-Willing: *Atkins,* the Volitionally Incapacitated, and the Death Penalty." *South Carolina Law Review* 55:93–143.

Campbell, M. S. 2004. "*Sell, Singleton,* and Forcible Medication—Running Roughshod Over Liberty." *University of Toledo Law Review* 35:691–722.

Death Penalty Information Center. 2005. *Death Penalty Information Center.* http://www.deathpenaltyinfo.org.

Hall, T. S. 2004. "Is the Death Penalty on Life Support?: Mental Status and Criminal Culpability After *Atkins v. Virginia.*" *Dayton Law Review* 29:355–377.

Hensl, K. B. 2004. "Restored to Health to Be Put to Death: Reconciling the Legal and Ethical Dilemmas of Medicating to Execute in *Singleton v. Norris.*" *Villanova Law Review* 49:291–328.

Horstman, L. A. 2002. "Commuting Death Sentences of the Insane: A Solution for a Better, More Compassionate Society." *University of San Francisco Law Review* 36:823–852.

Jones, C. J. 2004. "Fit to Be Tried: Bypassing Procedural Safeguards to Involuntarily Medicate Incompetent Defendants to Death." *Roger Williams University Law Review* 10:165–209.

Klotter, J. C. 2004. *Criminal Law* (7th ed.). Cincinnati, OH: Anderson.

National Alliance for the Mentally Ill. 2005. *National Alliance for the Mentally Ill.* http://www.nami.org.

National Mental Health Association. 2005. *National Mental Health Association.* http://www.nmha.org.

Slobogin, C. 2003. "What *Atkins* Could Mean for People With Mental Illness." *New Mexico Law Review* 33:293–314.

Tobolowsky, P. M. 2003. "*Atkins* Aftermath: Identifying Mentally Retarded Offenders and Excluding Them From Execution." *Journal of Legislation* 30:77–141.

———. 2004. "Capital Punishment and the Mentally Retarded Offender." *The Prison Journal* 84:340–360.

Walker, S. 2001. *Sense and Nonsense About Crime and Drugs* (5th ed.). Belmont, CA: Wadsworth/Thomson Learning.

White, W. S. 1993. "Effective Assistance of Counsel in Capital Cases: The Evolving Standard of Care." *University of Illinois Law Review*:323–378.

Cases and Statutes Cited

Atkins v. Virginia, 536 U.S. 304 (2002).

Conn. Gen. Stat. § 53a-46a (2005).

Cooper v. Oklahoma, 517 U.S. 348 (1996).

Drope v. Missouri, 420 U.S. 162 (1975).

Dusky v. United States, 362 U.S. 402 (1960).

Eddings v. Oklahoma, 455 U.S. 104 (1982).

Fla. Stat. Ann. § 921.141 (West 2001).

Ford v. Wainwright, 477 U.S. 399 (1986).

Foucha v. Louisiana, 504 U.S. 71 (1992).

Gregg v. Georgia, 428 U.S. 153 (1976).

Hitchcock v. Dugger, 481 U.S. 393 (1987).

Jackson v. Indiana, 406 U.S. 715 (1972).

Lockett v. Ohio, 438 U.S. 586 (1978).

Medina v. California, 505 U.S. 437 (1992).

Pate v. Robinson, 383 U.S. 375 (1966).

Penry v. Lynaugh, 492 U.S. 302 (1989).

Riggins v. Nevada, 504 U.S. 127 (1992).

Roper v. Simmons, 543 U.S. 551 (2005).

Sell v. United States, 539 U.S. 166 (2003).

Singleton v. Norris, 540 U.S. 832 (2003).

Singleton v. Norris, 319 F.3d 1018 (8th Cir. 2003) (en banc).

Singleton v. State, 437 S.E.2d 53 (S.C. 1993).

Stanford v. Kentucky, 492 U.S. 361 (1989).

State v. Perry, 610 So.2d 746 (La. 1992).

Thompson v. Oklahoma, 487 U.S. 815 (1988).

Trop v. Dulles, 356 U.S. 86 (1958).

18 U.S.C.A. § 3592 (West 2000 & Supp. 2005).

United States Constitution, Amendments V, VIII, XIV.

Washington v. Harper, 494 U.S. 210 (1990).

Related Websites

American Association on Mental Retardation
http://www.aamr.org

American Psychiatric Association
http://www.psych.org

American Psychological Association
http://www.apa.org

Cornell Law School Legal Information Institute
http://www.law.cornell.edu/wex/index.php/Death_penalty

Death Penalty Information Center
http://www.deathpenaltyinfo.org

National Alliance on Mental Illness
http://www.nami.org

National Mental Health Association
http://www.nmha.org

Discussion Questions

1. It has been suggested that sentencing juries often treat evidence of an offender's mental illness or retardation as an aggravating rather than a mitigating factor in the decision to impose a death sentence. Do you agree with this? If so, what are your reasons? How would you feel?

2. Do you agree or disagree with the Court's prohibition of capital punishment for mentally retarded offenders? Why? Should capital punishment be prohibited for offenders who are mentally ill (although not legally insane) at the time of the crime? Why?

3. States vary in the procedures they use to make the determination of an offender's mental retardation for purposes of the exclusion from capital punishment. Develop a model procedure for this determination, including the definition of mental retardation you would use, the timing of the determination (pretrial, at sentencing, or after sentencing), the fact-finder (the judge or jury), and the burden and standard of proof for the determination.

4. States vary in their procedures for defining and determining competency for execution. Develop a model definition of competency for execution: identify the fact-finder (a judge, the governor, prison authorities, or a jury), the timing and frequency of the determination, and the burden and standard of proof.

5. Should the government be permitted to involuntarily administer medication to a capital offender for the purpose of restoring or maintaining his competency for execution? Why? ✦

Chapter 10
Addressing the Rights of Victims in Capital Cases

Ashley G. Blackburn, James W. Marquart, Janet L. Mullings, and Chad R. Trulson

In this chapter, the authors outline both the positive and negative effects that the victims' rights movement has had on the criminal justice process. Particularly, the analysis focuses on victims' rights in capital cases, including victim impact statements, participation in the capital trial, and the right to witness the offender's execution. First, the authors provide a brief description of capital punishment, along with a summary of key United States Supreme Court cases (*Furman v. Georgia* and *Gregg v. Georgia*) that have changed how we treat capital offenders.

Historically, the victims' position within the criminal justice process has transformed from a restorative model, which kept the victim in the forefront of the process, to a retributive approach, which marginalized the victim and shifted the prosecutor or state into the center of the legal process. Recently, there has been a return to a victim-centered approach. Victims' rights in capital cases have increased throughout the United States over the last 20 years in the form of state legislation, referred to as the Victims' Bill of Rights. Statutes vary from state to state; however, many states share the same core victims' rights in regard to capital cases.

In light of equal rights for both the offender and the victim, the authors note that a balance must be achieved. Although rights for victims must be recognized, these rights must not come at the expense of the due process rights afforded to the offender, especially concerning the death sentence. To maintain balance, the Supreme Court has observed several cases that raised question of the constitutionality of victim impact statements, particularly whether these statements violate the offender's Eighth Amendment rights (cruel and unusual punishment). In the 1980s, the Supreme Court ruled that such victim impact statements did violate the offender's constitutional rights. However, subsequent Court rulings in the early 1990s overturned earlier decisions, making victim impact statements admissible in light of certain criteria. Additional questions, in regard to the viewing of the execution by indirect victims, center on whether observing the execution provides the victim's family a sense of closure and relief, or whether seeing such an act makes a traumatic event worse. Nevertheless, the determination of many of these policies have been left to various state agencies, and to date, the Supreme Court has not moved in any direction on this issue.

Introduction

The victims' rights movement has led to numerous changes in criminal justice. In general, victims are becoming more active in the administration of justice, and they are supported by laws and constitutional amendments in various states that have given them a "place" in the criminal justice system. Today, victims have a place in every aspect of criminal justice, from arrest to trial and sentencing to parole release decisions. Perhaps more than any other area in criminal justice, their presence may be most significant in capital murder cases.

Over the past 25 years, family members of murder victims, or *indirect victims*, have been at the forefront, leading change in the pursuit of victims' rights. In many states today, surviving family members have the right to give victim impact statements, the right to participate in the capital trial, and if the offender is sentenced to death, the right to witness the offender's execution. The justification is that indirect victims are representatives of the murder victims, and, for all intents and purposes, act in their place and give them a voice.

This chapter examines some of the advantages and disadvantages of the victims' rights movement for both direct and indirect victims, and for crimes in general and capital cases in specific. Although the movement has made great strides toward the general inclusion of victims in the criminal justice process, there is cause for concern that increased victims' rights may be detrimental to the rights of defendants in capital cases. Ultimately, both sides of the victims' rights movement and associated issues must be examined in order to determine the true impact of the victims' rights movement in the United States.

Capital Punishment

As of 2003, 38 states and the federal government have death penalty laws, and a total of 3,562 offenders were on death row (Bonczar and Snell 2004). In 2005, 59 men and one woman were executed in 16 states, all by lethal injection (Death Penalty Information Center 2006). For offenders to become "eligible" for the death penalty, a homicide is not usually enough. Although there are slight variations among death penalty states, for offenders to be "death eligible" they must have committed a murder in the presence of certain aggravating circumstances, such as a homicide in the commission of a robbery or another defined felony offense. In other cases, death eligible offenders are those who commit a particularly heinous homicide, such as one that includes torture or multiple victims. Further, in some cases, a homicide is enough for death eligibility, but only when the victim is a young child or a known law enforcement officer or when a prison inmate kills another in an escape attempt.

Capital punishment has evolved in numerous ways over the past century. The actual method of execution has become arguably less brutal on the body, progressing from the rope, to the chair, to the needle. One of the most significant changes in capital punishment has been through legal protections and safeguards for capital defendants. A number of safeguards are now in place to ensure that defendants receive due process protections throughout their capital trial.

During the 1970s, these legal changes were initiated by the U.S. Supreme Court in *Furman v. Georgia* (1972) and *Gregg v. Georgia* (1976). These decisions changed the landscape of capital punishment by affording defendants increased due process protections, including the introduction of a separate trial and sentencing process and a weighing of aggravating factors (indicating that the death penalty would be a more appropriate sentence than life in prison) and mitigating factors (indicating that life in prison would be a more appropriate sentence than the death penalty) before the determination of sentence.

Despite numerous legal decisions that have given more protections to capital defendants, significant changes have occurred in the role of indirect victims in capital cases. Over the past three decades, indirect victims such as family members and relatives have been granted rights allowing them to play a more prominent role in capital cases. Indirect victims are now able to participate in the capital trial by giving victim impact statements and, in some states, witnessing the execution of the offender if sentenced to death. Although these modifications are criticized by some as detrimental to defendants in capital cases, what they ultimately reflect are changing views on the role of indirect victims in capital cases. Because the role of indirect victims has been influenced by the victims' rights movement in general, it is important to review the history of the victims' rights movement in the United States and how the movement has evolved.

The Evolution of the Victims' Rights Movement

In the beginning, criminal justice systems were primarily operated by a victim-centered approach. The earliest documented codes of crime and punishment, such as the Code of Hammurabi, prescribed a range of punishments meant primarily to "fix the victim" by restoring the loss from an offender's act. The victim-centered approach began to erode around the eleventh century as a result of the "expansion of authority and kingship, the growth and influence of the Church, the evolution of a structured court system, and evolving concepts of punishment"

(Tobolowsky 2001, 4–5). Eventually, the prosecutor took cause for the newly recognized victim: the state, or society as a whole. *State v. Offender* replaced *Victim v. Offender,* and a criminal act was regarded as something more than a private dispute between a victim and an offender. It became instead an offense against the people and an affront to general societal order. According to the state-centered approach, punishments were meant to be a sanction for violating the rules and boundaries of society, not of an offense committed toward a specific victim. This approach left little room for victims in the criminal justice process. Today, however, there is a resurgence of victim-centered approaches in criminal justice.

What happened to cause the criminal justice system to pay more attention to specific victims and, hence, become more victim centered? Perhaps one of the major causes was increasing crime rates in the 1960s, which prompted new and increased interest in crime causation and prevention (Wallace 1998). Because of the increase in crime and victimizations, crime victims became more interested and outspoken about their place within the criminal justice process and began to devote their time to grassroots development of victim services. Throughout the 1960s and 1970s, commissions at both the federal and state levels were created to study crime and its consequences on society, and by 1972, the first three victims' assistance programs had been established. The founding of the Law Enforcement Assistance Administration (LEAA) in 1968 and the National Crime Victimization Survey (NCVS) in 1972 represented the federal government's response to increased societal concerns about crime and victimization. The LEAA provided funds for law enforcement agencies and also included funding for victim-witness programs, which were intended to provide support to victims and witnesses of criminal acts. The NCVS was established by the Bureau of Justice Statistics (BJS) to gain insight into crime victimization and those crimes that go unreported to law enforcement agencies. Today, it remains as one of the best sources of information about victimizations in the United States. In

1975, the LEAA also established the National Organization for Victim Assistance (NOVA), whose mission is to provide rights and services to crime victims everywhere through advocacy, education and direct services to victims. Today NOVA remains one of the leading victims' support organizations worldwide.

Despite much progress, during the late 1970s the victims' movement began to lose momentum because of a lack of funding, questions of professionalism, and lack of training. As a result, specialized groups emerged that focused on more specific and individualized issues such as sexual assault and domestic violence. Soon after, the victims' movement was infused with new life with the creation of two grassroots programs, the National Organization of Parents of Murdered Children (POMC) in 1978 and Mothers Against Drunk Driving (MADD) in 1980. Today, these two organizations remain at the forefront of the victims' rights movement and continue their efforts to provide victims' services, educate citizens, and advocate for increased victims' rights.

During this same time, victims' rights advocates began using the media as an outlet to raise awareness concerning crime victimization. As a result, in 1981 President Ronald Reagan became involved and established the National Crime Victims' Rights Week, which is currently in its 25th year of annual commemoration and observance (Schmalleger 2005). One year later, President Reagan appointed a Task Force on Victims of Crime, and in 1984 Congress passed the Victims of Crime Act (VOCA), which established the Office for Victims of Crime (OVC) within the Department of Justice, as well as the Crime Victims Fund. The OVC was charged with overseeing the implementation of the recommendations made by the Task Force on Victims of Crime as well as providing grants to states for the improvement and establishment of programs serving victims of crime (OVC 2004). The Crime Victims Fund receives money from federal criminal fines and penalties and provides funding to victims' service organizations and state victim compensation programs (OVC 2002). Through the Crime Victims Fund, the federal government has collected more than $4 billion to aid state crime victim compensation programs, victim service providers, and to train individuals entering victim service careers (OVC 2001).

The victims' rights movement was instrumental in giving crime victims a place in the criminal justice process. Within the movement, specific attention has been paid to the establishment of rights for family members of murdered victims in capital cases. Today, many of the rights and services provided to direct victims of crime through federal and state legislation, including the Victims' Bill of Rights, are also afforded to indirect victims in capital cases.

Victims' Rights in Capital Cases

Over the past 20 years legislation related to crime victims has increased significantly, and more than 27,000 statutes have been enacted nationwide (Bohm and Haley 2005; Gillis 2002). Today, all 50 states, as well as the federal government, have laws affording certain rights and services to crime victims (Kilpatrick, Beatty, and Smith-Howley 1998). Many of these rights and services have also been afforded to indirect victims in capital cases.

Defining Victims

Each state has developed statutes defining what constitutes a victim in regard to the eligibility for victims' rights and services. From a policy standpoint, victims' rights and services provisions in the various states were intended to be inclusive. The bottom line, however, is that exclusion is found, which is demonstrated by various state provisions that apply to only some victims. Eligibility for crime victims' rights and services often depends on the crime itself. For example, states such as Alaska, Arkansas, Maryland, Massachusetts, and Oregon provide victims' rights to all crime victims, whereas states such as Louisiana and Mississippi grant rights only to victims of felony criminal activity (National Center for Victims of Crime 1996). Other states have narrower criteria. For example, in Texas, Pennsylvania, New Mexico, Illinois, and Delaware only indirect

victims of homicide and victims of aggravated assault, kidnapping, and sexual assault are afforded victims' rights (NCVC 1996).

Specifically in capital cases, states have defined indirect or co-victims who can benefit from victims' rights and services. As the direct victims are oftentimes deceased in capital cases, certain states have extended victims' rights and protections to family members of homicide victims as well as to parents or guardians of juveniles or incompetent victims (Wallace 1998). Such indirect victims may include the spouse, parents, children, and grandparents of homicide victims. These family members are afforded such rights because they represent the victim who, because of the offender's actions, can no longer be present to represent themselves.

Rights Afforded to Capital Victims

All 50 states have in place a Victims' Bill of Rights as law or as an amendment to their individual state constitutions. Wisconsin was the first state to enact a bill of rights for crime victims in 1980, and as of 1998, 31 states had passed constitutional amendments ensuring specific rights to crime victims (Gillis 2002). Although all states have now passed some kind of legislation involving victims' rights, the scope of these provisions varies from state to state (Doerner and Lab 2002). Generally, indirect victims in capital cases, across most states where the death penalty is carried out, are afforded the following rights:

- The right to notice of victims' rights
- The right to be treated with fairness, dignity, and respect
- The right to notification of the stages/proceedings in the criminal justice process
- The right to be present and/or to participate in important criminal justice proceedings
- The right to confer with the prosecutor
- The right to reasonable protection from intimidation and harassment
- The right to privacy, including confidentiality of records

- The right to speedy trial provisions
- The right to notice of the release or escape of the offender
- The right to prompt return of the victim's property seized as evidence
- The right to restitution from the offender or compensation from the state (NCVC 1996).

An intense debate is occurring over the influence of victims' rights on the criminal justice process, especially as it pertains to a proposed federal victims' rights constitutional amendment. Although many support increased victims' rights legislation at the federal level, others argue that increased implementation of victims' rights and services will stretch an already overburdened criminal justice system. Further, others maintain that victims' rights have already been overly influential in the development of criminal justice policy and procedure to the detriment of defendants. It has been stated that the proposed victims' rights constitutional amendment will erode defendants' rights. For example, that victims' rights are recognized before a defendant is even found guilty may affect the presumption of innocence in our system of justice. Most important, those against such an amendment dispute the need to amend the U.S. Constitution since there are alternatives, such as increased federal and state legislation, to ensure rights to victims. Because all states and the federal government already have legislation granting rights to crime victims, the question becomes, "Why must the Constitution be altered?"

Those who support the constitutional amendment contend that victims should be provided equal rights to inclusion in the justice process as well as fair and equal treatment. An amendment to the Constitution would further put an end to the inconsistency that now exists in victims' rights between the various states.

It is important to strike a balance between the rights of defendants and the rights of victims. It would be unfair to erode the due process rights of defendants, especially in capital cases, where their lives are at stake. However, it is also important that victims in capital cases be recognized and have a place in the justice system because of the damage inflicted by the crime committed. The debate as to whether the proposed victims' rights constitutional amendment should be passed is ongoing, and only time will tell whether such a change to the U.S. Constitution will occur.

The two most important rights that have been afforded to indirect victims in capital cases are the right to submit an impact statement during the sentencing phase of the capital trial and the right to view the execution of the offender. Both rights have placed victims and their family members in the middle of the capital process. While indirect victims have a choice as to whether they would like to participate in the process, the fact that these avenues are now available is a significant change from the criminal justice system of the past.

Victim Impact Statements

One of the most controversial aspects of capital cases is the use of victim impact statements during sentencing phase of a capital trial. A *victim impact statement* is defined as an oral or written statement provided by a victim concerning the impact of a specific crime (NCVC 1999). In many states, indirect victims have been granted the right to submit an impact statement in capital cases. Statutes define who is responsible for providing information about impact statements to indirect victims. Information on the procedures for submission must be explained to family members acting on behalf of the homicide victim so that statements are not excluded due to a technical error. However, a majority of states have still not made the use of victim impact evidence a mandatory part of the capital punishment process.

Victim impact statements were first developed in the 1970s and were given national attention in 1982 when the President's Task Force on Victims of Crime recommended that "judges allow for and give appropriate weight to input at sentencing from victims of violent crime." Following this report, the 1982 Victim and Witness Protection Act mandated that victim impact evidence be included as part of the sentencing process, giving victims, direct and indirect, the right of allocution in federal court (Schmalleger 2005). By 1988, 44 states and the federal government allowed direct and indirect victims in capital cases to testify about how the crime has impacted their lives (Donahoe 1999). Currently, all 50 states and the federal government acknowledge and accept some sort of victim impact evidence, either written or oral, during the sentencing phase in all felony and capital cases (Weir 2003).

The debate over whether verbal victim impact statements are inflammatory and therefore violate a capital defendants' constitutional rights has been reviewed by the U.S. Supreme Court on a number of occasions. Three primary U.S. Supreme Court cases have examined the constitutionality of victim impact evidence given during the capital sentencing process: *Booth v. Maryland, South Carolina v. Gathers,* and *Payne v. Tennessee.* In *Booth v. Maryland* (1987), the Court held in a 5–4 decision that the introduction of a victim impact statement describing personal characteristics of the victim and statements about the emotional impact of the crime on the victim's family violated the defendant's Eighth Amendment rights. Following the *Booth* decision, victim impact evidence was again found unconstitutional in *South Carolina v. Gathers* (1989), where the Court held that a prosecutor reading a prayer found in the victim's possession violated the Eighth Amendment. These two decisions were based on the majority's argument that such victim impact evidence was irrelevant and "creates a constitutionally unacceptable risk that the jury may impose the death penalty in an arbitrary and capricious manner" (*Booth v. Maryland* 1987).

In *Payne v. Tennessee* (1991), the Court in a 6–3 decision overturned its decision in *Gathers* and partly overturned its decision in *Booth.* The Court held that victim impact evidence is admissible at the sentencing phase of a capital trial as long as it does not violate fundamental fairness protected by the Due Process Clause. The Court held that the amount of harm caused by a defendant in a capital case is relevant to the sentencing decision and that victim impact evidence allows the sentencing authority to better understand the bearing a crime has on its victims (*Payne v. Tennessee* 1991).

While the Court decided in *Payne* that victim impact statements could be introduced during the sentencing phase of capital trials, the decision and subsequent majority opinion left many questions unanswered. For example, no guidelines were set by the Court as to who or how many individuals may provide victim impact statements or what types of information and evidence may be included in a victim impact statement (Blume 2003). These details have been left to legislators in creating final sentencing statutes and procedures. As a result, many state statutes are out of compliance with federal guidelines on impact statements in that they allow victims to include information that is not allowed at the federal level. Because capital cases that begin at the state level are often appealed, if the impact statements given at the state level do not comply with federal regulations, the statements could be excluded from federal appeal trials. It is important that states recognize this problem so that victim impact statements are not left out of important appeal trials.

Research conducted concerning the influence of victim impact statements has provided mixed results. Numerous studies have shown that victim impact evidence has had little bearing on sentencing decisions (Davis and Smith 1994). Although victims and indirect victims can now be heard during the sentencing process in capital cases, this does not guarantee that the sentencing authority will be understanding and sympathetic toward the testimony. Other studies have suggested that victim impact statements promote sentencing decisions based on the value of the victim rather than on the crime itself (Logan 1999; Phillips 1997). Ultimately, more research is needed to determine how such impact statements influence the capital punishment process.

Viewing an Execution

Allowing surviving family members to view an execution has created considerable controversy in capital murder cases. Advocates for family members and other indirect victims of capital cases argue that witnessing the offender's execution will allow the family of a murdered victim to gain closure to a time in their life filled with pain and sorrow (Domino and Boccaccini 2000). Others argue that viewing executions will only increase the trauma felt by victims and family members (Goodwin 1997). Where one stands on this issue is most likely influenced by whether one agrees or disagrees with the use of the death penalty. What is not at issue is the controversy surrounding this right given to indirect victims in recent years.

Executions were, for many years, held in private, usually at night behind prison walls with few witnesses—primarily media representatives, criminal justice representatives, and invited guests of the offender. During the 1990s, however, states utilizing capital punishment passed laws to allow family members and other indirect victims to witness executions. Although states such as Georgia, Montana, and New Mexico do not allow victim witnesses, states such as California, Louisiana, Kentucky, Alabama, Texas, Utah, Oklahoma, Delaware, Washington, Nevada, Oregon, Ohio, Mississippi, and Utah have all changed their laws or correctional policies to allow family members and other indirect victims to be present at the time of execution. Such laws and policies vary from state to state as to who may witness the execution. In Oregon, for example, immediate family of the victim, including parents, spouse, siblings, children, or grandparents are allowed to view the execution. In Texas, up to five victim witnesses are allowed to view an execution whereas only three victim witnesses are allowed in South Carolina. In some states, indirect victims have the right to view the execution via closed-circuit television rather than watching the event firsthand. Still, in other states, allowing family members and other indirect victims to witness the execution is discretionary and is determined by the state's Department of Corrections.

As a result of changing laws concerning victims in capital cases, correctional agencies have had to adapt the process of execution to include indirect victims in capital murder cases. In most death penalty states, indirect victims have the right to be notified of important stages and proceedings in the criminal justice process including the circumstances of execution. For example, the Texas Department of Criminal Justice (TDCJ) Victim Services Division is responsible for notifying indirect victims of pertinent information involving the execution. Such information includes the time and date of the execution and the procedures for viewing the execution.

A detailed explanation of the lethal injection process is also given so that victim witnesses will be prepared for what they will view. Further, the TDCJ must make sure to separate victim and inmate witnesses at the time of execution. The death chamber in Texas contains two separate viewing areas, one for victim witnesses and another for inmate witnesses. These two groups are kept totally separate from each other before, during, and after the execution, leaving less chance for verbal or physical attacks. This is no small feat for correctional systems, especially in Texas, which executes the most offenders nationwide. For example, in 2000, 34 of 40 Texas executions had victim witnesses; in 2001, 14 of 17 executions had victim witnesses; in 2002, 25 of 33 executions had victim witnesses; in 2003, 19 of 24 executions had victim witnesses; and in 2004, all 16 executions had victim witnesses. Having to balance the needs of victim witnesses with the presence of the offender's invited witnesses is indeed a difficult task.

The debate concerning whether indirect victims should be allowed to view executions continues. Those who advocate affording families of murder victims the ability to witness the execution of the offender argue that witnessing the execution will provide the victims' families a sense of justice and a sense of closure that is otherwise unfulfilled by the criminal justice process (Barnes 1996). Others dispute indirect victims' right to be present, arguing that witnessing the execution will not provide satisfaction and closure that it could actually compound the trauma felt by the victims' families instead of relieving it (Goodwin 1997).

Conclusion

Innovation and progress come slowly in the administration of justice. Until quite recently, the process of justice was primarily state-centered, which meant that victims of crime had little voice in the outcomes of cases. Numerous forms of legislation and court rulings at both the state and federal level were crafted to ensure that the rights of the accused were protected at every step in the process of criminal justice. Some called these protections onerous and unfair. Fifty years ago, a grassroots movement swept the nation that not only opened the door of the criminal justice system to victims but also led to legislation granting rights to victims and their families as they come in contact with the system. Some now call these protections onerous and unfair. The pendulum constantly swings toward protecting the rights of defendants on the one hand, and allowing victims to have a voice in the process on the other. This is not a debate that will likely end soon.

This discussion brings to light certain issues that concern the tug-of-war between retributive and restorative justice in our society. In retributive justice, where the purpose is to seek revenge and retribution for wrongs committed against society, the death penalty is the ultimate sanction. However, the victims' rights movement and the involvement of victims bring to mind aspects of restorative justice, in which the goal is to restore the victim and the community to their previctimization status. The direction of justice in our society, whether retributive or more restorative, remains to be seen, and only time will tell where victims will end up in the process.

In capital trials where one or more lives have already been taken and another life is threatened by a sentence of execution, it is imperative that we as a society understand what is at stake for both victims and alleged offenders. The doors to execution chambers have now been pried wide open to the presence of direct and indirect victims. Revenge? Retribution? Restoration? Justice? Closure? The reasons family members and others seek to observe executions are varied. Each situation is different, and some do not even want to witness an execution, let alone support it. Yet the fact that family members and others tied to the victimization are allowed to witness such events is an indication of the place of victims in the criminal justice system today.

Perhaps the bottom line is that the justice system cannot be everything to everyone—either offenders or victims. The victims' rights movement began with good intentions, just as the move toward more rights for criminal defendants did. Certainly, some of those intentions have been realized, but there have also been unanticipated consequences that still need to be worked through to find the appropriate balance for both offenders and victims in criminal justice.

References

Barnes, Patricia. 1996. "Final Reckoning: States Allow Victims' Families to Watch Executions." *American Bar Association* 82 (3):17–24.

Blume, John H. 2003. "Ten Years of *Payne:* Victim Impact Evidence in Capital Cases." *Cornell Law Review* 88:257.

Bohm, Robert, and Keith Haley. 2005. *Introduction to Criminal Justice* (4th ed.). New York: McGraw-Hill.

Bonczar, Thomas, and Tracy Snell. 2004. *Capital Punishment, 2003* (NCJ 206627). Washington DC: U.S. Department of Justice, Office of Justice Programs, Bureau of Justice Statistics.

Davis, Robert C., and Barbara Smith E. 1994. "The Effects of Victim Impact Statements of Sentencing Decisions: A Test in an Urban Setting." *Justice Quarterly* 11:453–469.

Death Penalty Information Center. 2006. *Executions in the United States in 2005.* http://www.deathpenaltyinfo.org/article.php?scid=8&did=1264.

Doerner, William, and Steven Lab. 2002. *Victimology* (3rd ed.). Cincinnati, OH: Anderson Publishing Company.

Domino, Marla, and Marcus Boccaccini. 2000. "Doubting Thomas: Should Family Members of Victims Watch Executions?" *Law and Psychology Review* 24:59–70.

Donahoe, Joel. 1999. "The Changing Role of Victim Impact Evidence in Capital Cases." *Western Criminology Review* 2 (1). http://wcr.sonoma.edu/v2n1/donahoe.html.

Gillis, John W. 2002. *Statement Regarding, S.J. Res. 35: The Proposed Victims' Rights Amendment to the United States Constitution.* http://

www.ojp.usdoj.gov/ovc/publications/infores/071702.htm.

Goodwin, Michael L. 1997. "An Eyeful for an Eye: An Argument Against Allowing the Families of Murder Victims to View Executions." *Brandeis Journal of Family Law* 36:585–604.

Kilpatrick, Dean, David Beatty, and Susan Smith-Howley. 1998. *National Institute of Justice, Research in Brief: The Rights of Crime Victims: Does Legal Protection Make a Difference?* (NCJ 173839). Washington, DC: Office of Justice Programs.

Logan, Wayne A. 1999. "Through the Past Darkly: A Survey of the Uses and Abuses of Victim Impact Evidence in Capital Trials." *Arizona Law Review* 41(1):143.

National Center for Victims of Crime. 1996. *1996 Victims' Rights Sourcebook: A Compilation and Comparison of Victims' Rights Laws.* http://www.ncvc.org/resources/reports/sourcebook.

———. 1999. *Victim Impact Statements.* http://www.ncvc.org/ncvc.

Office for Victims of Crime. 2001. *Report to the Nation 2001: Fiscal Years 1999 and 2000.* http://www.ojp.usdoj.gov/ovc/welcovc/reporttonation2001/.

———. 2002. *Victims of Crime Act: Crime Victims Fund.* http://www.ojp.usdoj.gov/ovc/publications/factshts/vocacvf/welcome.html.

———. 2004. *What Is the Office for Victims of Crime?* http://www.ojp.usdoj.gov/ovc/publications/factshts/what_is_ovc/welcome.html.

Phillips, Amy. 1997. "Thou Shall Not Kill Any Nice People: The Problem of Victim Impact Statements in Capital Sentencing." *American Criminal Law Review* 35 (2):93–118.

President's Task Force on Victims of Crime. 1982. *Final Report.* http://www.ojp.usdoj.gov/ovc/publications/presdntstskforcrprt/welcome.html.

Schmalleger, Frank. 2005. *Criminal Justice Today: An Introductory Text for the 21st Century* (8th Ed.). Saddle River, NJ: Pearson/Prentice Hall.

Tobolowsky, Peggy. 2001. *Crime Victim Rights and Remedies.* Durham, NC: Carolina Academic Press.

Wallace, Harvey. 1998. *Victimology: Legal, Psychological, and Social Perspectives.* Boston: Allyn and Bacon.

Weir, Debbie. 2003. *Voice of the Victim—Victim Impact Statements: A Powerful Tool for Healing.* http://www.Madd.org/victims/1,1056,7068,00.html.

Cases Cited

Booth v. Maryland, 482 U.S. 496 (1987).
Furman v. Georgia, 408 U.S. 238 (1972).
Gregg v. Georgia, 428 U.S. 153 (1976).
Payne v. Tennessee, 501 U.S. 808 (1991).
South Carolina v. Gathers, 490 U.S. 805 (1989).

Related Websites

Office for Victims of Crime
http://www.ojp.usdoj.gov/ovc/

National Organization for Victim Assistance
http://www.trynova.org

National Center for Victims of Crime
http://www.ncvc.org/ncvc/Main.aspx

Office of Justice Programs: Help for Crime Victims
http://www.ojp.state.mn.us/mccvs/index.htm

Texas Department of Criminal Justice: Victim Services Division
http://www.tdcj.state.tx.us/victim/victim-home.htm

Discussion Questions

1. How and why was the victims' rights movement successful in garnering attention to the plight of crime victims?

2. Why is the proposed amendment to modify the Constitution to include a Victim Bill of Rights so controversial?

3. Why is the right to view an execution such a debated topic?

4. Should victim impact statements be admissible in the sentencing stage of capital cases? Why or why not?

5. Do you believe that some victims are viewed as more "valuable" than others? Do you believe this may have an impact on victims' rights eligibility? ✦

Chapter 11
Legal Issues Associated With DNA Evidence [1]

Simon A. Cole and William C. Thompson

In this chapter, the authors review the legal issues involving the use of DNA evidence in criminal prosecutions. DNA typing is an incredibly powerful forensic technology. Forensic DNA typing makes it possible to link individuals to evidence recovered from crime scenes with a high degree of accuracy. In addition, rapidly growing databases containing genetic information are proving very useful in investigating crimes. Law enforcement agencies are understandably excited about the possible assistance DNA typing will provide them in their efforts to solve crime.

While forensic DNA technology holds much promise as a crime-fighting tool, its use raises a number of legal issues. One issue concerns evidence law and the admissibility and weight of forensic DNA evidence. Other concerns are for the Fourth Amendment and the intrusiveness of government collection and storage. This chapter leads the reader through both the science and law.

Like fingerprinting, the science of DNA collection and analysis is not entirely perfect; the results must be interpreted by trained investigators, and the tests must be carefully conducted to prevent contamination of the samples. Several high profile cases have revealed that lab errors can lead to mis-identification of DNA evidence. DNA evidence, like other scientific evidence, is subject to exacting evidentiary rules regarding its admissibility at criminal trials. The authors review the relevant evidence law and the related issues of jury comprehension of the scientific evidence and the opportunity for the defense to conduct independent scientific tests of the evidence.

Last, the authors review the legal issues associated with the growing trend to create large DNA databases, for use in future investigations. These databases raise privacy issues, especially for those who have not been convicted of any crime. Is DNA typing a benign development? Or is it one that will lead to a loss of individual privacy? It remains to be seen how the courts and society adapt the technology to the law.

Introduction

Forensic DNA typing may be the most powerful and new forensic technology to be introduced to the criminal justice system in nearly a century, if not ever. Forensic DNA typing can assist in the administration of justice by linking individuals to evidence recovered from crime scenes with a high degree of specificity. In addition, rapidly growing databases containing genetic information are proving very useful in investigating crimes. Thus, forensic DNA technology is poised to

Figure 11.1 *DNA From Blood*

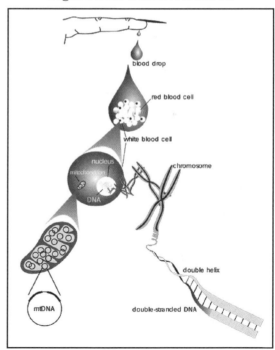

Source: K. Inman and N. Rudin, *An Introduction to Forensic DNA Analysis,* CRC Press, 1997.

have an enormous impact on the criminal justice system.

Forensic DNA technology raises a number of legal issues. Some of these concern evidence law and the admissibility and weight of forensic DNA evidence. Others concern the Fourth Amendment and the inclusiveness and intrusiveness of government collection, storage, and searching of the genetic information of both criminal suspects and nonsuspects (Cole and Lynch 2006).

What Is DNA?

Deoxyribonucleic acid, or *DNA*, is a long, double-stranded molecule configured like a twisted ladder or "double helix." The genetic information of all organisms is encoded in the sequence of four organic compounds (bases) that make up the rungs of the DNA ladder. Most DNA is tightly packed into structures called *chromosomes* in the nuclei of cells. In humans there are 23 pairs of chromosomes, with half of each pair being inherited from the individual's mother and half from the father. The total complement of DNA is called the *genome*.

By some estimates, 99.9 percent of the genetic code is the same in all humans. To identify individuals, DNA tests focus on a few *loci* (plural of *locus*—a specific location on the human genome) where there is variation among individuals. These loci are called *polymorphisms* because the genetic code can take different forms in different individuals. Each possible form is called an *allele*.

Forensic DNA tests have examined two types of polymorphisms. *Sequence polymorphisms* vary in the sequence of the genetic code. *Length polymorphisms* contain repeating sequences of genetic code; the number of repetitions may vary from person to person, making the section longer in some people and shorter in others. Length polymorphisms are more commonly used for practical reasons.

Analysts begin the testing process by extracting DNA from cells and purifying it. They use test tubes, chemical reagents, and other standard procedures of laboratory chemistry.

In sexual assault cases, spermatozoa (containing male DNA) may be mixed with epithelial (skin) cells from the victim. Analysts generally try to separate the male and female components into separate *extracts* (samples) using a process called *differential lysis*, which employs weak detergents to liberate DNA from the epithelial cells followed by stronger detergents to liberate DNA from the tougher spermatozoa.

After the DNA is extracted, it can be "typed" using several methods. We will describe five of these methods here.

RFLP Analysis

When DNA tests were first introduced in the late 1980s, most laboratories used a method called *RFLP analysis* (restriction fragment length polymorphism analysis), which uses enzymes to break the long strands of DNA into shorter fragments (*restriction fragments*) and separates them by length (using a process called *electrophoresis*). A pattern of dark bands on an x-ray or photographic plate reveals the position (and hence the length) of target fragments that contain *length polymorphisms*.

Figure 11.2 shows RFLP analysis of a single *locus* (containing a *length polymorphism*) in a case in which a woman was raped by two men. Each "lane" contains DNA from a different sample. The lanes labeled "size markers" contain DNA fragment of known size from bacteria and are used for calibration. Lanes on the left side show the band patterns produced by reference samples from the victim and two suspects. There are two bands in each lane because each individual has two copies of the relevant locus, one from the paternal half of the chromosome, the other from the maternal half.

Lanes on the right side of Figure 11.2 show the band patterns of evidence samples. The lane labeled "female vaginal extract" contains DNA from the female component (epithelial cells) of a vaginal sample taken from the victim. The DNA in this sample was too degraded to produce a distinct band pattern. The lane labeled "male vaginal extract" shows the band pattern of DNA from the male component (spermatozoa) of the same vaginal sample. This lane contains a band

Figure 11.2
RFLP Autorad in a Rape Case

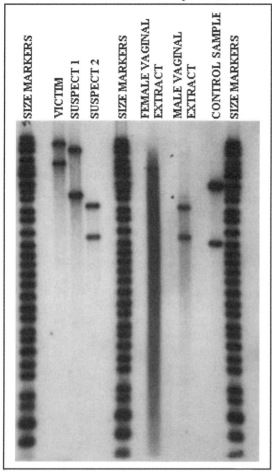

Source: K. Inman and N. Rudin, *An Introduction to Forensic DNA Analysis*, CRC Press, 1997.

pattern similar to that of suspect 2, which indicates that the spermatozoa could have come from suspect 2.

In a typical case, four to six different loci (each containing a different length polymorphism) are examined in this manner. The full set of alleles identified in a sample is called its *DNA profile*. Because the probability of a "matching" pattern at any locus is on the order of one in hundreds to one in thousands, and the probabilities of a match at the various loci are assumed to be statistically independent, the probability of a match at four or more loci is generally put at one in many millions or even billions.

Although RFLP analysis is generally reliable, it sometimes entails subjective judgment. Whether the lane labeled "male vaginal extract" also contains bands corresponding to those of suspect 1 is a matter of judgment on which experts in this case disagreed. Dots to the left of the lane are felt-tip pen marks placed by a forensic analysis to indicate where he thought he saw bands matching those of suspect 1.

RFLP analysis requires samples that are relatively large (blood or semen stains about the size of a quarter) and well preserved. It is also slow. A typical case takes four to six weeks.

DQ-Alpha and Polymarker Tests

In the early 1990s, newer methods of DNA testing were introduced that are faster (producing results in a day or two) and more sensitive (i.e., capable of typing smaller, more degraded samples). The new methods use a procedure called *polymerase chain reaction*

Figure 11.3
Test Strip Showing Polymarker (top) and DQ-Alpha (bottom) Test Results

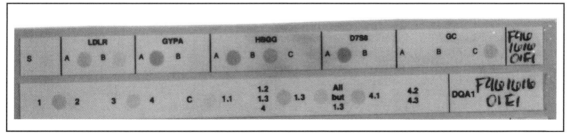

Source: K. Inman and N. Rudin, *An Introduction to Forensic DNA Analysis*, CRC Press, 1997.

(PCR), which can produce billions of copies of target fragments of DNA from one or more loci. These "amplified" DNA fragments (called *amplicons*) can then be typed using several methods.

In 1991, Perkin-Elmer (PE), a biotechnology firm, developed a test kit for amplifying and typing a *sequence polymorphism* known as the *DQ-alpha gene*. Six distinct *alleles* (variants) of this gene can be identified by exposing the amplified DNA to paper test strips containing *allele-specific probes* (see Figure 11.3). The dots on the strip signal the presence of particular alleles. This test has the advantage of great sensitivity (DNA from just a few human cells is sufficient to produce a result) and allows more rapid analysis (1–2 days), but it is not as discriminating as RFLP analysis.

In 1993, PE introduced an improved kit that typed DQ-alpha and five additional genes simultaneously, thereby improving the specificity of this method (see Figure 11.3). With this new kit, known as the polymarker/DQ-alpha test, individual profile frequencies are on the order of one in tens of thousands, however it still is not as discriminating as RFLP analysis. As with

RFLP analysis, interpretation of the test strips may require subjective judgments. For example, experts disagreed on whether the dot labeled 1.3 in the lower strip shown in Figure 11.3 is dark enough to reliably indicate the presence of the allele designated 1.3.

STR Tests

The late 1990s saw the advent of *STR (short tandem repeat)* DNA testing. STR tests combine the sensitivity of a PCR-based test with great specificity (profile frequencies potentially as low as one in trillions) and therefore have quickly supplanted both RFLP analysis and the Polymarker/DQ-alpha test in forensic laboratories.

An *STR* is a DNA locus that contains a length polymorphism. At each STR locus, people have two alleles (one from each parent) that vary in length depending on the number of repetitions of a short core sequence of genetic code. A person with genotype 14, 15 at an STR locus has one allele with 14 repeating units and another with 15 repeating units.

Figure 11.4 shows the results of STR analysis of five samples: blood from a crime scene and reference samples of four sus-

Figure 11.4
STR Test Results

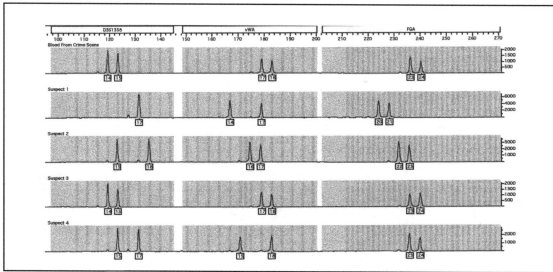

Source: K. Inman and N. Rudin, *An Introduction to Forensic DNA Analysis*, CRC Press, 1997.

pects. This analysis includes three loci, labeled "D3S1358," "vWA," and "FGA." Each person has two alleles (peaks) at each locus, one from the maternal portion and the other from the paternal portion of the chromosome. The position of the "peaks" on each graph (known as an electropherogram) indicates the length (and hence the number of core sequence repeats) of each STR. As can be seen, the profile of suspect 3 corresponds to that of the crime scene sample, indicating he is a possible source. Suspects 1, 2, and 4 are eliminated as possible sources.

In 1997, the FBI identified 13 STR loci that it deemed appropriate for forensic testing. Commercial firms quickly developed test kits and automated equipment for typing these STRs. The leading vendor has been Applied Biosystems International (ABI), a division of Applera Corporation. ABI's most popular STR test kit, known as ProfilerPlus, can simultaneously "amplify" DNA from up to nine STR loci and label the loci with colored dyes. An automated test instrument called a genetic analyzer then separates the resulting amplicons by length (using electrophoresis) and uses a laser to cause fluorescence of the dye-labeled fragments. A computer-controlled electronic camera detects the size and relative position of the fragments, identifies alleles, and displays the results as shown in Figure 11.4. A more recent ABI test kit, called *Identifiler* can simultaneously amplify 16 STR loci.

STR tests have greatly improved the capabilities of forensic laboratories, allowing highly specific DNA profiles to be derived from tiny quantities of cellular material. Test results generally allow a clear-cut determination of whether a particular individual could be the source of an evidentiary sample, although experts have differed over interpretation of results in some cases.

Mitochondrial DNA Tests

The tests described thus far examine DNA from cell nuclei (*nuclear DNA*). DNA is also found in *cell mitochondria,* which are *organelles* (structures) where the process of cellular respiration occurs. Mitochondrial DNA (often designated *mtDNA*) contains *sequence polymorphisms*. In the late 1990s, fo-

rensic scientists began testing *mtDNA* by using a procedure known as *genetic sequencing* to produce a readout of the genetic code from two polymorphic areas of the *mitochondrial genome*. Forensic scientists describe an mtDNA profile by stating how its sequence differs from that of a reference standard called the *Anderson sequence*.

Mitochondrial DNA tests are highly sensitive and can produce results on samples that are not suitable for other DNA tests, such as hair shafts, bone, and teeth. Because mtDNA is present in hundreds or thousands of copies per cell, it often survives much longer than nuclear DNA in old, degraded cellular samples. DNA tests on very old samples, such as the bones of Czar Nicholas II of Russia, have detected and typed mtDNA.

Mitochondrial DNA tests are far less discriminating than STR tests. The frequency of mtDNA profiles is generally put at one in hundreds. Additionally, because mtDNA is inherited maternally, mtDNA tests generally cannot distinguish between individuals in the same maternal line. Hence, sons of the same mother would be expected to have the same mtDNA profile, and this profile would also be found in daughters of the mother's sister and all of their children.

Minor variations are sometimes found in mtDNA profiles of different cells from the same person due to mutations. This phenomenon, known as *heteroplasmy*, complicates the process of determining whether two mtDNA profiles match. The appropriate standards for declaring an mtDNA match, and for estimating the rarity of matching profiles, are issues that have been debated in the courtroom.

Mitochondrial DNA tests are expensive and require special laboratory facilities and techniques. At this time only a few forensic laboratories perform these tests and they are used only where other types of DNA testing fail or cannot work. However, future technical improvements may lead to wider use of mtDNA tests.

Y-STR Tests

Another recent advance has been the development of tests that examine short tandem repeats of the Y chromosome, which is found only in males. *Y-STR* tests have proven useful in sexual assault cases where DNA from the female victim and the male perpetrator is often mixed together. The male component of mixed samples can sometimes be difficult to identify with conventional STR tests because it is overshadowed by larger quantities of female DNA. By detecting only male DNA, Y-STR tests solve this problem.

Like mitochondrial DNA tests, Y-STR tests are far less discriminating than conventional STR tests. Furthermore, Y-STR profiles (sometimes called *haplotypes*) are passed intact from father to son. Because the rate of mutation for Y-STR profiles is low, it is possible to trace the same profile down family trees for ten generations and more. Consequently, male descendants of the same paternal ancestor are likely all to share the same Y-STR type.

The Use of DNA in the Criminal Justice System

English geneticist Alec Jeffreys first described a method for "typing" human DNA in 1985. Since that time, DNA typing technology has advanced rapidly, and the new DNA tests have been embraced eagerly by the criminal justice system. DNA tests are now routinely used to help identify the sources of blood, semen, and hair found at crime scenes and to establish family relationships in cases of disputed parentage. DNA tests have helped prosecutors obtain convictions in thousands of cases and have helped establish the innocence of thousands of individuals who might otherwise have become suspects (Scheck, Neufeld, and Dwyer 2003).

DNA databases have also been expanding rapidly. The United Kingdom's database, the world's first and the largest, held around 2.5 million samples in 2004. The FBI's Combined DNA Index System (CODIS) currently holds 3 million samples and is growing rapidly (Bieber 2006). Despite this growth, DNA typing and DNA databases remain underutilized by police (Pratt et al. 2006). The sensitivity of DNA technology has increased greatly over the past two decades. Laboratories no longer require blood or semen; usable DNA profiles can be gleaned from smaller and less intimate biological materials, such as hair and skin cells. Even with this increased sensitivity, however, a recent U.K. study estimated that searchable DNA profiles were generated by only around 1 percent of recorded crimes (Williams and Johnson 2005). Nonetheless, the use of DNA for criminal investigation can only be expected to increase, and the proactive use of "DNA intelligence databases" for the generation of leads is increasing (Walsh and Buckleton 2005). Thus, the legal issues raised by forensic DNA profiling will only become more salient in the future.

Even as the use of DNA typing has been spreading, the practice continues to be beset by scandals. A number of people have recently been wrongly convicted based on misinterpreted DNA evidence—most famously, Josiah Sutton who was falsely convicted of rape in Houston in 1998 (Thompson 2003). The Sutton case was exposed by an investigation into poor DNA work in the Houston Police Department Crime Laboratory, and other laboratories have also been embroiled in scandals, including the Virginia Crime Laboratory and the FBI Crime Laboratory (Thompson 2006).

One proposed solution to the problem of laboratory error is accreditation. The American Society of Crime Laboratory Directors Laboratory Accreditation Board (ASCLAD-LAB) is a nonprofit organization that reviews the protocols and procedures of forensic DNA laboratories and issues a certificate of accreditation to those meeting its standards. To help assure the competence of laboratory workers, a professional organization called the American Board of Criminology has developed a certification program for DNA analysts. Nonetheless, the regulation of DNA laboratories is still not as strict as some experts think it should be (Thompson 1997, 2006).

Admissibility of DNA Evidence

Judges in the United States have traditionally acted as "gatekeepers" for scientific evidence, excluding evidence that is deemed insufficiently reliable to be heard by a jury. Many state courts apply the *Frye* standard (first articulated in a 1923 appellate case called *Frye v. United States*), which requires that scientific testimony be based on a method or technique that is "generally accepted" by the "relevant scientific community." Since 1993, federal courts (and some state courts) have applied a standard articulated by the U.S. Supreme Court in *Daubert v. Merrell Dow Pharmaceuticals* (1993), which requires the judge to consider whether scientific testimony is "relevant and reliable."

When DNA evidence was first introduced, defense attorneys, baffled by the complexity of the science, made fairly desultory efforts to challenge it, and it was easily found admissible (*Andrews v. State* 1988; *People v. Wesley* 1988). Soon, however, defense attorneys began to recruit their own expert witnesses who challenged not the basic principles of DNA typing, but the practices of the laboratories implementing the typing. One of the best known cases was *People v. Castro* (1989), in which the experts from both sides took the extraordinary step of meeting without attorneys and came to an agreement that the testing in *Castro* was too sloppy to be admitted. In this situation, the court had little choice but to accede and rule the evidence inadmissible (Lander 1992; Mnookin 2006; Aronson 2007).

Castro raised awareness of the importance of rigorous laboratory practices, but a controversy soon erupted among population geneticists over the method used to calculate random match probabilities (the probability that a given DNA profile will match a person chosen at random from a given population). The prevailing method assumed statistical independence of the alleles in a DNA profile. Some geneticists thought this assumption had been inadequately tested and called for additional empirical studies. In 1992, the National Research Council issued a report (NRC I) that acknowledged the controversy and proposed that it be resolved by requiring forensic laboratories to use an extremely conservative method for statistical estimation called *the ceiling principle*. Thereafter, several courts ruled DNA evidence inadmissible under the *Frye* standard in cases where the laboratory failed to apply the ceiling

principle (*Commonwealth v. Curnin* 1991; *People v. Barney* 1992; *State v. Bible* 1993), although many other courts continued to admit DNA evidence with the conventional statistics (*United States v. Bonds* 1993).

Over the next few years, additional research was done to validate the assumption of statistical independence. In 1996, the NRC issued a second report (NRC II), finding that the ceiling principle was unnecessary (National Research Council Commission on DNA Forensic Science 1996). After NRC II, DNA evidence was uniformly found admissible (*People v. Schreck* 2001; *State v. Copeland* 1995). Courts also found mtDNA evidence admissible without much controversy (*State v. Council* 1999; *State v. Underwood* 1999) (Kiely 2001), although some experts continue to question whether adequate databases exist to estimate the random match probabilities for mtDNA (Kaestle et al. 2006).

As each new generation of DNA technology reaches the courtroom, its reliability must be established under the *Frye* or *Daubert* standard. To make this determination, judges sometimes hold pretrial hearings in which the parties can present scientific testimony. Often there is scientific debate about the reliability of new procedures and the adequacy of the underlying validation, so there is a period of uncertainty over whether the "general acceptance" test will be met. The issue has been complicated by the tendency of some forensic laboratories to begin using new tests before the underlying validation research has been published and by the refusal of some commercial vendors to reveal complete scientific details of new methods on grounds that they are trade secrets (Mellon 2001).

Once the admissibility of a particular method is established by appellate ruling, courts in *Frye* jurisdictions generally admit the results of that method automatically. However, under the *Daubert* standard and in a few *Frye* states (California is a prominent example), judges may still rule DNA evidence inadmissible if they find that a laboratory failed to follow reliable scientific procedures in the case at hand.

DNA test results that are admitted into evidence can still be challenged in front of the jury. When lawyers attack DNA evidence, they generally try to show that the results were misinterpreted, that the laboratory may have mixed up or cross-contaminated samples, or that an innocent transfer of DNA could have produced the incriminating results. In the O. J. Simpson trial, for example, defense lawyers argued that the crime laboratory either inadvertently transferred Simpson's blood from a reference vial to samples collected at the crime scene or, alternatively, that Simpson's blood may have been intentionally planted (Thompson 1996).

Issues Concerning the Use of DNA Evidence in Criminal Cases

Jury Understanding

There has been considerable discussion of whether lay juries are competent to deal with complex forms of scientific evidence, such as DNA testing (American Bar Association 1989; Ivkovic and Hans 2003). In an era when forensic science is glorified by television programs like the popular *CSI* series (Podlas 2006), there is little doubt that most jurors understand the importance of DNA evidence and its power for human identification. However, it is less clear whether lay juries can follow the nuances of scientific debate in cases where there is conflicting testimony over the interpretation or meaning of the DNA evidence. The debate over jury competency is unlikely to be resolved soon, because the very concept of "competence" is politically loaded and subject to different interpretations in different contexts (Edmond and Mercer 1997).

Often, what makes DNA evidence impressive is the statistical estimates (usually called random match probabilities) that accompany it. Jurors may be told that the defendant's DNA "matches" the DNA found at the crime scene and that only one person in 100 billion would "match." Jurors may also hear statistical testimony on the probability of an error. Whether jurors can draw appropriate conclusions from such statistics has

been examined in a number of studies (Nance and Morris 2002; Koehler 2001; Schklar and Diamond 1999). These studies suggest that jurors generally understand the significance of the statistics—for example, they give more weight to DNA evidence as the random match probability and the probability of a false positive decrease (Nance and Morris 2005). On the other hand, jurors' evaluations of DNA evidence are often influenced by logically irrelevant factors, such as the language or format in which the statistical estimates are presented (Koehler 2001; Koehler and Macchi 2004). Moreover, people sometimes use fallacious strategies to draw conclusions from statistical evidence, thereby reaching fallacious conclusions (Koehler, Chia, and Lindsey 1995; Thompson and Schumann 1987). These studies suggest that great care is needed when lawyers and expert witnesses present DNA evidence to juries.

Disclosure and Discovery

A lawyer who wants to present DNA evidence in a criminal case must disclose the test results to the other party before trial. This procedure, known as "discovery," avoids a so-called "trial by ambush" in which parties surprise each other with evidence. It allows the opponent to examine the scientific evidence in advance to look for weaknesses and decide how to respond. Although the right to "discovery" of an opponent's scientific evidence is universally recognized, jurisdictions vary greatly in how much must be disclosed about DNA tests. Scholars have argued that liberal discovery rules (requiring more detailed disclosure) promote better-quality scientific work (Murphy Forthcoming; Thompson 2006). They note that most scandals over bad scientific practices have occurred in jurisdictions in which restrictive discovery rules have protected forensic DNA laboratories from outside scrutiny.

Right to Post-Conviction Testing and Preservation of Evidence

As increasing numbers of inmates began using postconviction DNA testing to prove their innocence, reformers began calling for courts or legislatures to establish a right to postconviction DNA testing. Some legislatures, including Illinois, New York, California, and Minnesota, have established such a right.

The U.S. Supreme Court in *Herrera v. Collins* (1993) famously assumed, but did not formally decide, that the execution of an innocent person, absent a violation of the defendant's due process, would be unconstitutional. Postconviction DNA testing would be one compelling way to demonstrate innocence. In *Harvey v. Horan* (2002), the Fourth Circuit Court of Appeals alluded to a "limited" right to post-conviction DNA testing. A bill introduced by Senator Patrick Leahy (D-VT), the Innocence Protection Act, would establish a federal right to postconviction testing, but it has not yet become law. The act would also establish uniform standards concerning the length of time that biological evidence samples must be preserved (Borenstein 2006). In *Lovitt v. True* (2005), a death row inmate in Virginia challenged his conviction and death sentence on grounds that state officials had intentionally destroyed biological samples from his case, thereby preventing postconviction DNA tests that he claimed would have exonerated him. However, the U.S. District Court held that because the state officials had not acted in "bad faith," there had been no violation of the inmate's constitutional rights. In 2005, the U.S. Supreme Court declined to hear an appeal.

In *House v. Bell* (2006), postconviction DNA testing that contradicted blood evidence that had been presented at trial, though not conclusively proving the defendant's innocence, cast doubt on his guilt, along with other evidence. The Court ruled that this evidence, though not meeting the *Herrera* burden of showing actual innocence, was sufficient to trigger a federal habeas proceeding for House, who had been sentenced to death.

Databases and Privacy Issues

The rapid growth of DNA databases has generated a host of legal issues surrounding the state's right to take and retain DNA samples. In general, the taking of DNA samples from convicted felons can be justified with little legal difficulty, either on the basis of a "special need" because of high recidivism or because convicted felons have "diminished expectations" of privacy (Simoncelli and Steinhardt 2005). Similarly, when there is probable cause against a suspect, a warrant can easily be obtained to procure a DNA sample. But a number of other proposed methods of gathering DNA samples pose thornier legal issues.

From a policy perspective, the larger the database, the more useful it is in terms of solving, and even preventing, crimes. Having a DNA database at all allows one to catch some perpetrators who would not have been identified as suspects by other means. If individuals are entered into the database after being convicted of a crime, they may be identified as perpetrators if they commit subsequent crimes. The more perpetrators entered into a database—in other words, the more expansive the criteria used for inclusion in the database—the more perpetrators who will be identified in such fashion. The policy question is where this logic ends. The most useful database of all would be one in which all citizens would be included at birth. Such a database would theoretically identify rapists after the first offense, whereas a felon database would only identify them after their second. But the idea of a universal database is not a popular one, and it is viewed by many as creating "a nation of suspects." If we are not to have a universal database, how expansive should the database be? Should it include violent felons only, all felons, felons and misdemeanants, or everyone even arrested for a crime? What should be the regulations concerning the inclusion of juveniles? Should persons arrested but not convicted be able to have their records expunged from the database?

These are policy questions, but the inclusion of individuals' DNA in state-sponsored databases also has to satisfy legal scrutiny. Virginia, Louisiana, Texas, Minnesota, and California, have expanded DNA collection to include those arrested but not necessarily convicted of a crime, and many other states have such legislation pending. Because arrestees have not been convicted of any crime, inclusion of their DNA in a database probably amounts to a "suspicionless search," and these measures would have to fall under the U.S. Supreme Court's "special needs" doctrine. The Court has also held that the "special need" cannot simply be law enforcement (*Indianapolis v. Edmond* 2000; *Ferguson v. City of Charleston* 2001). Legal scholars have expressed skepticism that arrestee databases will pass constitutional muster under this doctrine, but the Court has yet to rule in such a case (Maclin 2005). Other legal scholars are not convinced that even a universal DNA database, which includes every citizen, poses any insurmountable constitutional problem (Kaye and Smith 2004).

When police have the DNA profile of a perpetrator but cannot establish his or her identity, they sometimes conduct what has become known as a *DNA dragnet,* in which large numbers of individuals in the relevant community are asked to submit samples voluntarily for DNA testing. Police generally collect samples by rubbing the inside of the individual's cheek with a cotton swab. Even if the guilty party does not submit a sample, the DNA dragnet may help police by narrowing the number of possible suspects. The first DNA dragnet, which was chronicled in Joseph Wambaugh's book *The Blooding* (1989), helped police solve two murders in Leicester, England in 1987—the first case in which Jeffreys's new technique of DNA profiling was used. The guilty man was identified when, in an effort to avoid suspicion, he asked a friend to submit a sample in his place. DNA dragnets have since been used repeatedly in Britain and are becoming more common in the United States (Iraola 2005).

Because dragnets generally rely on samples given with the consent of the donors, they typically do not raise the constitutional issues associated with compulsory procedures for obtaining evidence. It has, of course, been argued that the voluntariness of such consent is at least to some extent fictitious, because individuals are well aware that anyone who declines the request to give a sample will be treated as a suspect. In some cases, refusal to consent may even constitute

sufficient grounds to procure a warrant to obtain a sample (Cho and Sankar 2004).

Furthermore, it appears that dragnet samples are typically retained in law enforcement databases beyond the particular investigation for which they were collected, creating what are sometimes known as "usual suspects" databases. Constitutional issues are invoked if individuals are later implicated in other crimes by samples donated as part of a dragnet. Legal scholars suggest that such individuals would probably not succeed in getting the evidence excluded on Fourth or Fifth Amendment grounds. However, individuals might succeed in invoking privacy and due process right to demand the return of genetic material seized in a dragnet (Iraola 2005).

In some instances a database search finds no one whose DNA profile is identical to an offender profile but finds one or more profiles in the database that are "similar" to that of the offender. In such cases, police sometimes seek to test relatives of the "similar" person in the hope that they might match. This strategy occasionally is successful because close relatives are known to have similar profiles (Bieber and Lazer 2004). However, the probability of finding the true perpetrator using this method varies greatly depending on how similar the profiles are and how many possible suspects there are (Paoletti et al. 2006). *Familial searches,* as they are called, raise a host of legal, ethical, and privacy issues. Legal scholars do not see a compelling legal objection to familial searching (Greely et al. 2006), and some scholars have argued that the potential benefits of familial searching clearly outweigh any privacy violations (Bieber, Brenner, and Lazer 2006). However, other scholars contend that familial searching is unacceptable from a policy viewpoint because it would so greatly exacerbate the racial disparities already present in U.S. law enforcement DNA databases (Greely et al. 2006).

A trend in many states has been to indict DNA profiles under "John Doe" warrants when statutes of limitations are about to run out. In such warrants, a DNA profile stands proxy for the anonymous person ("John Doe") who presumably "donated" the evidence to the crime scene. Courts in California and many other states have upheld the legality of such warrants and of any arrests based on them (Imwinkelried 2004). Such warrants typically list a technical description of John Doe's features: the type of profile (e.g., STR), the name of the particular technique, a list of chromosomal loci and alleles found at those loci; and probability figures for three broadly defined "racial" or "ethnic" populations (i.e., Caucasian, African American, and Hispanic).

In addition to suspending statutes of limitations with John Doe warrants, many state officials aim to repeal such statutes altogether. Because so many rape cases (especially "stranger" rapes) rely heavily on eyewitness testimony (often by the victim alone), statutes of limitations for rape prosecutions are used in roughly half of the states to ensure timely prosecution when "memories are still fresh." The advent of DNA evidence has put pressure on legislatures to repeal such statutes.

It also appears that, in some cases, victim samples are retained in databases (Lee 2004; Crouse and Kaye 2000). There is no justification, based on either special needs or diminished privacy expectations for retaining victim samples, but the practice seems to persist simply out of the general utility derived from having more samples in the database. This issue has received little attention and has not yet generated any notable court cases.

In *United States v. Kincade* (2004), the Ninth Circuit Court of Appeals considered a probationer's challenge to the constitutionality of a California statute mandating the taking of DNA samples from individuals on probation. The samples would then be entered into the state and national DNA databases, and future crime-scene samples would be searched against them. These measures constituted a continuous process of "suspicionless" searches lacking individualized suspicion. A plurality of judges joined Judge O'Scannlain's opinion, which upheld the statute, not under "special needs" doctrine, but under a simpler "totality of the circumstances" test. Judge O'Scannlain found that "the overwhelming societal interests so clearly furnished by the collection of DNA information from convicted offenders" outweighed "conditional releasees' substantially diminished expectations of privacy," especially given "the minimal intrusion occasioned by blood sampling."

The deciding vote was cast by Judge Gould, who argued that special needs doctrine *should* be applied; the California statute did not run afoul of the Supreme Court's prohibition against invoking special needs for law enforcement purposes, because its purpose was the deterrence of future crime, rather than the traditional law enforcement function of punishing past crime. Thus, Judge Gould upheld the statute using a different test.

Three dissents were filed. Judge Reinhardt, joined by three other judges, argued that the entering of *anyone's* DNA into state and national databases would meet the requirements of the "totality of the circumstances" test because the entering of *anyone's* DNA into databases would aid in the deterrence and detection of future crimes. The dissenters claimed to have difficulty imaging any circumstances under which the entering of DNA into databases would violate the Fourth Amendment prohibition against suspicionless searches using the test proposed by the plurality.

Judge Kozinski pointed out that, by means of the database, the statute proposed to exploit Kincade's diminished privacy rights while a probationer in order to make it possible to conduct suspicionless searches of his DNA even after he completed probation and regained the full privacy rights of any other citizen. Using the plurality's totality of the circumstances test, this would seem to justify similar exploitation of anyone who made a DNA sample available at some time in their life, which, Judge Kozinski argued, could include a vast proportion of the citizenry.

Judge Hawkins likewise concluded that the plurality's doctrine posed no bar to the eventual inclusion of every citizen's DNA in law enforcement databases. He too argued that the special needs doctrine applied and that the statute failed that test.

Legal restrictions on the collection of DNA samples are further complicated by the phenomenon of "shedding" DNA. Given the sensitivity of current (not to mention future) technology, authorities interested in a particular individual's genetic profile need not necessarily obtain a warrant, because individuals cannot avoid shedding DNA as they go about their daily routine. Collection of "shed" DNA encompasses a range of practices from "tricking" the suspect (such as by offering him or her a soft drink) to surreptitiously following the suspect until he or she discards an object (such as a cigarette butt) likely to contain usable DNA. What limitations, if any, should be placed on the use of shed DNA? The legal status of such DNA is that it is "abandoned," and, therefore, there is little, if any, legal bar to police use of shed DNA. Preventing such use will require the development of legal doctrine that supports the common intuition that DNA is so information-rich and intimate that it must be more than mere "waste" (Joh 2006).

An issue yet to be addressed by appellate courts is the extent to which criminal defense lawyers may have access to government databases for purposes of defending a client incriminated by a DNA database "match." Defense lawyers sometimes want to conduct their own database searches in order, for example, to establish the identity of an unknown person whose DNA was found at a crime scene. Defense lawyers have also been seeking discovery of detailed information about the operation of government databases and the profiles contained within them in order to assess the probative value of a database match. In such cases the defendant's right to fully examine the evidence against him may come into conflict with the government's interest in protecting the privacy of the database.

DNA Typing in the Future

Technical advances will continue to reduce the time and expense of DNA testing. Improvements in test kits should soon allow simultaneous PCR amplification of larger numbers of STRs, affording even greater speed and specificity to STR testing. Gene chip technology is already available that will allow typing of DNA within a few minutes on a custom-designed computer chip. In the near future this technology will make it feasible for police to perform STR typing of suspects and samples in the field using devices small enough to carry by hand (Stevens 2002).

The range of information that can be extracted from biological samples will also improve. New genetic probes are becoming available that can provide information about what a DNA contributor looks like. The British Forensic Science Service has experimented with a probe that detects genes associated with red hair and a ruddy complexion (Lowe et al. 2001).

Genetic tests capable of identifying behavioral propensities have been widely discussed because of their potentially profound ethical and social implications. However, since the association between genes and behavior is complex, the use of DNA tests to predict behavior is unlikely to be feasible in the near future (Allen 2004).

Note

1. Portions of this article are taken from William C. Thompson, "DNA Testing," in David Levinson (ed.), *Encyclopedia of Crime and Punishment* Vol. 2 (Thousand Oaks, CA: Sage, 2002), 536–544. This material is partially based upon work supported by the National Science Foundation under Grant Nos. SES-0115305 and IIS-0527729 and the National Institutes of Health under Grant No. HG-03302. Any opinions, findings, and conclusions or recommendations expressed in this material are those of the authors and do not necessarily reflect the views of the National Science Foundation or the National Institutes of Health.

References

Allen, Garland. 2004. "DNA and Human Behavior Genetics: Implications for the Criminal Justice System." In D. Lazer (ed.), *The Technology of Justice: DNA and the Criminal Justice System.* Cambridge, MA: MIT Press.

American Bar Association. 1989. *Jury Comprehension of Complex Cases.* Chicago: American Bar Association.

Aronson, Jay D. 2007. *DNA Profiling: Science, Law and Controversy in the American Criminal Justice System.* New Brunswick, NJ: Rutgers University Press.

Bieber, Frederick. 2006. "Turning Base Hits into Earned Runs: Improving the Effectiveness of Forensic DNA Data Bank Programs." *Journal of Law, Medicine and Ethics* 34(2):2–13.

Bieber, Frederick, and David Lazer. 2004. "Guilt by Association." *New Scientist* Oct. 23:20.

Bieber, Frederick R., Charles H. Brenner, and David Lazer. 2006. "Finding Criminals Through DNA of Their Relatives." *Science* 312 (5778):1315–1316.

Borenstein, Jason. 2006. "DNA in the Legal System: The Benefits Are Clear, the Problems Aren't Always." *Cardozo Public Law, Policy and Ethics Journal* 3:847–867.

Cho, Mildred K., and Pamela Sankar. 2004. "Forensic Genetics and Ethical, Legal and Social Implications Beyond the Clinic." *Nature Genetics* 36(11):S8–S12.

Cole, Simon A., and Michael Lynch. 2006. "The Social and Legal Construction of Suspects." *Annual Review of Law and Social Science* 2.

Crouse, Cecilia, and David H. Kaye. 2000. "Retention and Subsequent Use of Suspect, Elimination, and Victim DNA Samples or Records: National Commission on the Future of DNA Evidence." Paper presented at the Conference on DNA, Brooklyn Law School, March 2000.

Edmond, Gary, and David Mercer. 1997. "Scientific Literacy and the Jury: Reconsidering Jury 'Competence.'" *Public Understanding of Science* 6:329–357.

Greely, Henry T., Daniel P. Riordan, Nanibaa' A. Garrison, and Joanna L. Mountain. 2006. "Family Ties: The Use of DNA Offender Databases to Catch Offenders' Kin." *Journal of Law, Medicine and Ethics* 34(2):248–262.

Imwinkelried, Edward J. 2004. "The Relative Priority That Should Be Assigned to Trial Stage DNA Issues." In D. Lazer (ed.), *DNA and the Criminal Justice System: The Technology of Justice.* Cambridge, MA: MIT Press.

Iraola, Roberto. 2005. "DNA Dragnets—A Constitutional Catch?" *Drake Law Review* 54:15–51.

Ivkovic, Sanja K., and Valerie P. Hans. 2003. "Jurors' Evaluations of Expert Testimony: Judging the Messenger and the Message." *Law and Social Inquiry* 28:441–482.

Joh, Elizabeth E. 2006. "Reclaiming 'Abandoned' DNA: The Fourth Amendment and Genetic Privacy." *Northwestern Law Review* 100:857–884.

Kaestle, Frederika A., Ricky A. Kittles, Andrea L. Roth, and Edward J. Ungvarsky. 2006. "Database Limitations on the Evidentiary Value of Forensic Mitochondrial DNA Evidence." *American Criminal Law Review* 43:53–88.

Kaye, David H., and Michael E. Smith. 2004. "DNA Databases for Law Enforcement: The Coverage Question and the Case for a Population-Wide Database." In D. Lazer (ed.), *DNA and the Criminal Justice System: The Technology of Justice.* Cambridge, MA: MIT Press.

Kiely, Terrence F. 2001. *Forensic Evidence: Science and the Criminal Law.* Boca Raton, FL: CRC Press.

Koehler, J. J. 2001. "When Are People Persuaded by DNA Match Statistics?" *Law and Human Behavior* 25:493–513.

Koehler, J. J., A. Chia, and S. Lindsey. 1995. "The Random Match Probability in DNA Evidence: Irrelevant and Prejudicial?" *Jurimetrics Journal* 35:201–219.

Koehler, J. J., and L. Macchi. 2004. "Thinking About Low-Probability Events." *Psychological Science* 15:540–546.

Lander, Eric. 1992. "DNA Fingerprinting: Science, Law, and the Ultimate Identifier." In D. J. Kevles and L. Hood (eds.), *The Code of Codes: Scientific and Social Issues in the Human Genome Project.* Cambridge, MA: Harvard University Press.

Lee, Patricia. 2000. "A Gender Critique of Forensic DNA Evidence: Collection, Storage and Applications." In Fiona Miller, Roxanne Mykitiuk, Patricia Lee, Susan Sherwin and Sari Tudiver (eds.), *The Gender of Genetic Futures: The Canadian Biotechnology Strategy, Women and Health.* Proceedings of a National Strategic Workshop held at York University, February 11–12, 2000. Toronto: York University.

———. 2004. "A Gender Critique of Forensic DNA Evidence: Collection Storage and Applications." http://www.cwhn.ca/groups/biotech/availdocs/22-lee.pdf

Lowe, Alex L., Andrew Urquhart, Lindsey A. Foreman, and Ian W. Evett. 2001. "Inferring Ethnic Origin by Means of an STR Profile." *Forensic Science International* 119:17–22.

Maclin, Tracey. 2005. "Is Obtaining an Arrestee's DNA a Valid Special Needs Search Under the Fourth Amendment? What Should (and Will) the Supreme Court Do?" *Journal of Law, Medicine and Ethics* 33:102–118.

Mellon, Jennifer N. 2001. "Manufacturing Convictions: Why Defendants Are Entitled to the Data Underlying Forensic DNA Kits." *Duke Law Journal* 51:1097–1137.

Mnookin, Jennifer L. 2006. "*People v. Castro:* Challenging the Forensic Use of DNA Evidence." In R. Lempert (ed.), *Evidence Stories.* New York: Foundation Press.

Murphy, Erin. Forthcoming. "The New Forensics: Criminal Justice, False Certainty, and the Second Generation of Scientific Evidence." *California Law Review.*

Nance, D. A., and S. B. Morris. 2002. "An Empirical Assessment of Presentation Formats for Trace Evidence With a Relatively Large and Quantifiable Random Match Probability." *Jurimetrics Journal* 42:403–448.

———. 2005. "Jurors Understanding of DNA Evidence: An Empirical Assessment of Presentation Formats for Trace Evidence with Relatively Small Random-Match Probability." *Journal of Legal Studies* 34:395–444.

National Research Council Commission on DNA Forensic Science. 1996. *The Evaluation of Forensic DNA Evidence.* Washington, DC: National Academy Press.

Paoletti, David R., Travis E. Doom, Michael L. Raymer, and Dan E. Krane. 2006. "Assessing the Implications for Close Relatives in the Event of Similar But Nonmatching DNA Profiles." *Jurimetrics* 46(2):161–175.

Podlas, Kimberlianne. 2006. " 'The CSI Effect': Exposing the Media Myth." *Fordham Intellectual Property, Media and Entertainment Law Journal* 16:429–465.

Pratt, Travis C., Michael J. Gaffney, Nicholas P. Lovrich, and Charles L. Johnson. 2006. "This Isn't 'CSI': Estimating the National Backlog of Forensic DNA Cases and the Barriers Associated with Case Processing." *Criminal Justice Policy Review* 17(1):32–47.

Scheck, Barry, Peter Neufeld, and Jim Dwyer. 2003. *Actual Innocence: When Justice Goes Wrong and How to Make It Right.* 2nd ed. New York: New American Library.

Schklar, Jason, and Shari Seidman Diamond. 1999. "Juror Reactions to DNA Evidence: Errors and Expectancies." *Law & Human Behavior* 23(2):159–184.

Simoncelli, Tania, and Barry Steinhardt. 2005. "California's Proposition 69: A Dangerous Precedent for Criminal DNA Databases." *Journal of Law, Medicine and Ethics* 33:279–291.

Stevens, Larry. 2002. "Science on the Case." *Popular Science,* Oct.: 68–69.

Thompson, William C. 1996. "Proving the Case: The Science of DNA: DNA Evidence in the O.J. Simpson Trial." *University of Colorado Law Revew* 67:827–857.

———. 1997. "Accepting Lower Standards: The National Research Council's Second Report on Forensic DNA Evidence." *Jurimetrics* 37 (4):405–424.

———. 2003. "Houston Has a Problem: Bad DNA Evidence Sent the Wrong Man to Prison at Least Once." *Cornerstone* 25(1):16–17.

———. 2006. "Tarnish on the 'Gold Standard': Understanding Recent Problems in Forensic DNA Testing." *The Champion,* Jan./Feb.: 10–16.

Thompson, William C., and Edward L. Schumann. 1987. "Interpretation of Statistical Evidence in Criminal Trials." *Law and Human Behavior* 11:167.

Walsh, Simon, and John Buckleton. 2005. "DNA Intelligence Databases." In J. Buckleton, C. M. Triggs, and S. J. Walsh (eds.), *Forensic DNA Evidence Interpretation.* Boca Raton, FL: CRC Press.

Wambaugh, Joseph. 1989. *The Blooding.* New York: Bantam.

Williams, Robin, and Paul Johnson. 2005. "Inclusiveness, Effectiveness and Intrusiveness: Issues in the Developing Uses of DNA Profiling in Support of Criminal Investigations." *Journal of Law, Medicine and Ethics* 33:545–557.

Cases Cited

Andrews v. State, 533 So.2d 851 (1988).

Commonwealth v. Curnin, 565 N.E.2d 440 (1991).

Daubert v. Merrell Dow Pharmaceuticals, 509 U.S. 579 (1993).

Frye v. United States, 293 F. 1013 (1923).

Ferguson v. City of Charleston, 532 U.S. 67 (2001).

Harvey v. Horan, 285 F.3d 298 (2002).

Herrera v. Collins, 506 U.S. 390 (1993).

House v. Bell, 540 U.S. ___ (2006).

Indianapolis v. Edmond, 531 U.S. 32 (2000).

Lovitt v. True, 403 F.3d 171 (2005).

People v. Barney, 10 Cal. Rptr. 2d 731 (1992).

People v. Castro, 545 N.Y.S.2d (1989).

People v. Shreck, 22 P.3d 68 (2001).

People v. Wesley, 533 N.Y.S.2d 643 (1988).

State v. Bible, 858 P.2d 1152 (1993).

State v. Copeland, 922 P.2d 1304 (1995).

State v. Council, 515 S.E.2d 508 (1999).

State v. Underwood, 518 S.E.2d 231 (1999).

United States v. Bonds, 12 F.3d 540 (1993).

United States v. Kincade, 379 F.3d 813 (2004).

Related Websites

Oak Ridge National Laboratory, "DNA Forensics"

http://www.ornl.gov/sci/techresources/Human_Genome/elsi/forensics.shtml

National Institute of Standards and Technology, Short Tandem Repeat DNA Internet DataBase

http://www.cstl.nist.gov/div831/strbase/

Scientific Testimony: An Online Journal

http://www.scientific.org

Discussion Questions

1. Would you want your DNA profile to be included in a government database? Why or why not? What risks do you think you would face from having your profile included?

2. Should the United States create a universal database including everyone's DNA profile? What would be the benefits and what would be the risks of such a database?

3. Suppose you were a criminal defense lawyer and your client was incriminated by a DNA test. What facts would you need to know and what information would you need to obtain to evaluate the strength of this evidence?

4. Which type of DNA test would be most useful for typing (a) a bloodstain at a crime scene; (b) a human bone found in a shallow unmarked grave; (c) a vaginal sample from a rape victim that contains much more DNA from the victim than the rapist?

5. What is the meaning of the following terms: locus, polymorphism, allele, RFLP, STR, and DNA profile? ✦

Chapter 12
Hate Crimes and Hate Speech

Freedom to Express or License to Harm?

Jacqueline Buffington-Vollum

In this chapter, the author presents a summary of the key issues and cases that have shaped our perceptions concerning hate crimes and hate speech. Historically, the United States began dealing with the issue of discrimination and prejudice in the late nineteenth century, following the Civil War. A century later, the Civil Rights Act of 1968 provided individuals further protection from discriminatory acts based on race, religion, color, sexual orientation, and so forth. From 1981 through the 1990s, virtually all of the states, along with the federal government, enacted some form of anti-hate crime legislation. The author notes that although many hate crime statutes exist, they vary in definition of four main focus areas: motivation (why the offender commited the crime), protected groups (who is protected under the statute), types of crimes (what types of crimes constitute a hate crime), and penalty structure (what the penalty should be).

With these definitional aspects in mind, it is important to analyze and understand the aggregate patterns of such acts through the collection of hate crime data. As the author notes, several sources provide such data, including the FBI Uniform Crime Report and national victimization surveys. It is from these data resources that researchers attempt to explore, describe, and explain the sociocultural, structural, and psychological phenomena that encompass criminal acts of hate. Today, many research perspectives are being used, research centering on the many issues inherent within the hate crime realm is promising, and there is a growing demand to understand and further our knowledge on this topic.

Furthermore, the author notes that hate crimes are fundamentally different from other crimes and that the effects of such crimes are also different. For example, victims are targeted on unchangeable victim characteristics, and the act itself is symbolic and sends a message to a larger group, and the effects on the victims and society are often long term and compounding. At the heart of this matter lies a debate between supporting our civil rights/equal respect (Fourteenth Amendment) and maintaining freedom of speech rights (First Amendment) guaranteed by the U.S. Constitution. The debate has been framed by several famous legal cases, such as *Collin v. Smith* (1978), *R.A.V. v. City of St. Paul* (1992), and *Virginia v. Black* (2003), which have addressed First Amendment issues of free speech. The author also presents valuable information centering on overbreadth and vagueness (due process/equal protection/Fourteenth Amendment), freedom of thought (First Amendment), and cruel and unusual punishment (Eighth Amendment).

Introduction

Prejudice, discrimination, and bias-related crimes have plagued the United States since its founding. History records examples of racial and ethnic tensions fluctuating in response to economic and social changes—the abolition of slavery with the Civil War, the influx of European immigrants in the 1920s, and the desegregation of public schools in the 1950s, to name a few. However, it was not until the 1980s and 1990s that there emerged widespread societal interest and legal action regarding "hate crimes." In fairly rapid succession, the federal Hate Crimes Statistics Act of 1990 was enacted, and the U.S. Supreme Court decided the first two pivotal hate crime cases (*R.A.V. v. City of St. Paul* 1992 and *Wisconsin v. Mitchell* 1993). Since that time, hate crimes have received ever-increasing attention from governing bodies (at the state and federal levels), courts and prosecutors, law enforcement, juvenile justice, victims' rights groups, educators, researchers, and society as a whole. The issue has become a focus of international interest.

Hate Crime Laws

The earliest precursors of hate crime legislation can be traced to the post-Civil War period, when in 1871 members of Congress proposed legislation to recognize as crimes any acts intended to deprive newly freed slaves of the right to equal protection under the Constitution. Although not ultimately enacted, such legislation seemingly foreshadowed events to come. Nearly 100 years later, a provision of the Civil Rights Act of 1968 prohibited interference with federally protected activities if committed because of the victim's race, color, religion, or national origin. This act had a profound impact on the nation as it was known.

The first contemporary state hate crime statutes emerged in 1981 in Washington and Oregon. Since that time, the trend in hate crime legislation has been expansion. The number of states that have adopted hate crime statutes increased from 24 in the 1980s to 41 in the 1990s. Currently, 46 states, plus Washington, D.C., have passed some form of hate crime legislation, with 3 of the remaining 4 states having some sort of statutory provision (either civil remedies or criminalization of institutional vandalism).[1] Interestingly, Wyoming—where one of the most publicized hate crime cases in American history, the murder of Matthew Shepard in 1998, occurred—is the only state without some form of statutory provision regulating hate crimes (Shively 2005).

Hate speech can be considered a subset of hate crimes. Like hate crimes, some forms of hate speech are regulated legally, usually in the form of college/university regulations or city ordinances, rather than as state or federal legislation. These laws generally prohibit expressions "that cause anger, resentment, or violence because of their message of bias against a particular group" (Uhrich 1999, 1474). As decided in several pivotal U.S. Supreme Court cases, "speech" includes not only spoken words but also the use of symbols that communicate a message to another person. Regulating hate speech is a highly controversial area, however, given the First Amendment's guarantee of freedom of speech; therefore, such laws are not as widespread as those found for hate crimes more generally.

Defining Hate Crimes

It seems that it would be easy to define a "hate crime," but a review of the literature and the legal statutes on the topic suggests otherwise. In fact, some have questioned the very use of the term "*hate* crimes," stating that it incorrectly suggests that hatred is always the distinguishing characteristic of the offenses (Levin and McDevitt 1999). To the contrary, while some hate crime offenders experience powerful hatred toward their victim(s), many others are motivated more by peer acceptance and prejudicial attitudes than by intense emotions per se. Moreover, some crimes that involve the intense emotional arousal of hate (e.g., hatred by a scorned lover) would not appropriately be classified as a hate crime. Therefore, some argue that the term "bias crime" is more appropriate. Nevertheless, as "hate crimes" is the term adopted within the general legal nomenclature, this is the term that will be used throughout the rest of this chapter.

Most agree that hate crimes are criminal offenses motivated at least in part by the victim's actual or perceived status in a minority group. State and federal hate crime statutes vary widely in terms of how the motive of hate or bias is determined, which minority groups should be "protected," the exact predicate crimes eligible to be designated as hate crimes if they are found to be motivated by bias or prejudice, and the penalties to be imposed. Each of these aspects is discussed below.

Motivation. The key factor in identifying an offender as having committed a hate crime is the *motivation* for his or her conduct, which relates to *mens rea* in criminal law doctrine. Lawrence (1999) identified three standards of *mens rea* found across all state hate crime statutes: (1) the racial animus model, (2) the discriminatory selection model, and (3) the "because of" standard. According to the racial animus (i.e., animosity) model,[2] bias crimes are defined by the role of the perpetrator's hatred toward the victim's group as the basis for committing the crime. Clearly, this model reflects a literal interpretation of "hate" crimes. Conversely, the discriminatory selection model defines bias crimes in terms of the perpetrator's discriminatory selection of his or her victim. Under this model, the reason for discriminatory selection is irrelevant; the only necessity is that the offender did discriminate in selecting his victim. The difference in these two models clearly reflects Levin and McDevitt's (1999) distinction between crimes motivated by the emotion of hate and crimes in which victim selection is based on bias. Finally, the remaining statutes function under the "because of" standard.[3] These statutes merely indicate that a crime occurred "because of" or "based on" bias or prejudice.

Protected Groups. The groups opined to be worthy of "protection" diverge and have included those groups based on race, ethnicity, national origin, religion, sexual orientation, sex/gender, age, disability, and political affiliation, among others. Most statutes specify race/ethnicity and religion, yet fewer than two-thirds include sexual orientation, and approximately half recognize gender (Shively 2005). The Federal Bureau of Investigation's Uniform Crime Report (UCR) program, which is charged with compiling national data on hate crimes and thereby defines the official parameters of what constitutes hate crimes, recognizes offenses "that are motivated, in whole or in part, by the offender's bias against *a race, religion, sexual orientation, ethnicity/national origin, or disability*" (U.S. Department of Justice 2005, emphasis added). Overall, as with the expansion in the number of states that have adopted hate crime legislation, the trend in most jurisdictions is toward expanding, rather than narrowing, the list of groups protected. This trend is despite some arguments that it would be best to discard the "lists" of designated groups altogether and leave it up to case-by-case interpretation by the courts (Uhrich 1999).

Types of Crimes. Consensus is also lacking about the specific predicate crimes eligible for designation as hate crimes. Some statutes include *any* criminal acts, felony or misdemeanor, committed against persons and property in which the perpetrator is motivated by bias. Others focus solely on bias-motivated *violent* crimes, and still others recognize only crimes of institutional violence toward places of religious worship or schools. The UCR is closest to the first convention, however, as it recognizes three broad classes of offenses as hate crimes if they are motivated by the offender's bias: (1) crimes against persons (murder and non-negligent manslaughter, forcible rape, aggravated assault, simple assault, intimidation); (2) crimes against property (robbery, burglary, larceny-theft, motor vehicle theft, arson, destruction/damage/vandalism); and (3) crimes against society (drug offenses, gambling offenses, prostitution offenses) (U.S. DOJ 2005).

Penalty Structure. Finally, statutes differ in terms of their penalty structure. Most jurisdictions recognize hate crimes as worthy of criminal penalties. In the vast majority of states, the hate motivation element functions as an aggravating circumstance that results in an enhancement of the penalty for the base crime (e.g., a sentence of 5 years, rather than 3 years, for aggravated assault motivated by bias). However, in others a new category of crime is created by the addition of this element (e.g., an individual is convicted of a hate crime rather than vandalism). Two-thirds of states retain some form of provision for civil remedies (e.g., compensatory or punitive damages) for harm inflicted in the commission of the offense.

Hate Crime Statistics

Statistics on hate crimes are provided by a variety of sources. In 1990 Congress enacted the *Hate Crime Statistics Act*, mandating the U.S. attorney general to collect the nation's data, and the UCR has published findings each year since that time. Some states (e.g., Minnesota, California) calculate state-level data. Questions about hate crime victimization have recently been added to the National Crime Victimization Survey. Numerous large, nongovernmental, advocacy groups (such as the Anti-Defamation League and the Southern Poverty Law Center) compile and disseminate their own data. Although each source provides important information, each has strengths and weaknesses, and one will rarely find that the statistics yielded from the various sources reconcile. Thus, at the current time, it is not possible to draw a coherent or consistent picture of the scope and trends of hate crimes in the United States.

Uniform Crime Report

In general, the number of hate crimes reported annually to the FBI's UCR has been fewer than 10,000 per year. The rates have fluctuated between 4,755 incidents in 1991 and 10,706 incidents in 1996, with an average of 8,285 incidents. The most recent survey, *Hate Crime Statistics, 2004*, yielded 7,649 hate crime incidents. Table 12.1 provides a breakdown of the offenses by type of crime and type of bias.

Table 12.1

Hate Crime Incidents by Type of Crime and Type of Bias, 2004

	N	%
Total Number of Incidents	7649	100.0%
Type of Crime		
Crimes against person	4503	58.9
Crimes against property	3333	43.6
Crimes against society	69	0.9
Type of Bias		
Race	4042	52.8
Ethnicity/National origin	972	12.7
Religion	1374	18.0
Sexual orientation	1197	15.6
Disability	57	0.7

Source: U.S. Department of Justice (2005), *Hate Crime Statistics, 2004*. (Washington, DC: Bureau of Justice Statistics.)

It is noteworthy that the rates of hate crime incidents by type of bias have been relatively consistent since 1991. Specifically, the average rate of incidents based on race has remained at around 57 percent, religion at 17 percent, sexual orientation at 14 percent, and ethnicity/national origin at 12 percent. The only noticeable exception to these trends, as many people feared, was a spike in incidents based on ethnicity/national origin (apparently against those of Middle Eastern decent) in 2001, following the September 11

attacks. Indeed, from 2000 to 2001, the number of hate crime incidents perpetrated against persons based on ethnicity more than doubled, and the number of anti-Islamic incidents increased by 17 times (Shively 2005).

By far, the most prevalent form of hate crime is hate speech. In the UCR, the closest proxies to hate speech are "intimidation" crimes and acts of vandalism intended to communicate a message to the victim. These two categories consistently represent the largest numbers of crimes reported in the *Hate Crime Statistics* reports. In 2004 alone, intimidation crimes accounted for 30 percent and vandalism for 37 percent of the total number of hate crime incidents. The types of bias reflected in these incidents generally mirrored those found among hate crimes overall.

Although seemingly informative, the UCR statistics should be approached with caution. For one thing, legal definitions of hate crimes are constantly in flux, so there is no guarantee that the data provided by law enforcement agencies from one year to the next are comparable. Moreover, the federal reporting statute does not require law enforcement agencies to participate, and as a result many opt not to. The Southern Poverty Law Center (2001), in its survey of 50 states and the District of Columbia, identified a variety of obstacles to these data collection efforts. They found that over one-third of police jurisdictions were still not providing data.[4] Even among those jurisdictions that do "officially" participate, opposition (e.g., personal opinions that it is improper to consider hate crimes separate from other types of crimes; belief that the prosecution, not police, should determine motive), indifference (e.g., police officers' tendency to not record the bias aspect of criminal incidents), lack of training, and misunderstanding about what constitutes a hate crime among the personnel responsible for compiling the numbers plague the effort. Furthermore, some agencies fear negative publicity that could damage their communities' reputations if they admit that hate crimes occurred there. Ultimately, some critics have estimated that the real figure is probably closer to 50,000 incidents of hate crime each year (SPLC 2001), rather than the under 10,000 reported by the UCR.

Victimization Surveys

Victimization surveys corroborate that the UCR statistics are huge underestimates of the true incidence of hate crimes, with the majority of incidents not even reported to police. In fact, it is estimated that only 5 percent to 30 percent of hate crime victims actually report their experiences to the officials (Shively 2005), because they do not believe that authorities could or would do anything about it. The fact that law enforcement agencies are frequently lax about complying even with a federal statute to provide their data on hate crimes only adds to the problem. The Justice Department concluded that "when police agencies do not consider hate crime reporting to be a priority—when hate crime victims rightly believe that their complaints will not be considered important—[already reluctant] victims will be discouraged from coming forward" (SPLC 2001). Thus, a promising development toward the accurate compilation of data related to hate crimes is the addition of hate crime victimization to the National Crime Victimization Survey.[5]

Hate Crime Research

Virtually every branch of social science (e.g., psychology, sociology, history, economics, political science) has posited an explanation for hate crimes. Yet, despite the appearance of many descriptive studies and essays over the past 25 years, no single discipline has been able to develop a comprehensive theory that can reliably explain the etiology or predict the perpetration of these crimes. Some experts have focused on the historical and economic factors precipitating increases in hate crimes and the development of hate organizations. For example, sociologists and economists cite the depressed economic conditions in the rural United States in the 1980s for the surge in the development of organized hate groups. Others have examined the cultural (e.g., mass media), social (e.g., family messages, peer pressure), and psychological mechanisms (e.g., learning of stereotypes and prejudice, depersonaliza-

tion of the victim) behind the development of hostility toward minority groups. Yet other scholars turn their attention to institutional and structural forms of discrimination (e.g., employment, criminal justice system). Given the complexity of hate crimes, it is likely a topic best suited to a cross-disciplinary perspective.

Types of Hate Crime Offenders

Among the most noteworthy developments is the typology of hate crime offenders advanced by Levin and McDevitt. Initially developed in 1993 based on 169 hate crime cases in Boston, McDevitt, Levin, and Bennett (2002) expanded their classification to comprise four hate crime offender groups. Each type differs according to the psychological and environmental conditions that motivate him[6] to commit a hate crime. The percentage of hate crime offenders included in each category is provided in parentheses:

1. Thrill-seeking offender (66 percent): This type of hate crime offender commits his crimes based on a desire for excitement and power. More than half the time, offenses of this type are committed by a group of offenders who seek out victims outside their own territory. The vast majority of thrill offenses are unprovoked, often brutal, assaults on strangers. Perpetrators in this category are predominantly white, teenage males, whose reinforcement comes from the social-psychological rewards from their peers.

2. Defensive offender (25 percent): This offender's crimes are motivated by the need to protect his territory or resources from what he perceives to be a threatening outsider. He tends to commit offenses in his own neighborhood, school, or workplace, and he justifies his anger as a defensive response to perceived invasion. Most defensive offenders are white and tend to commit their offenses against strangers.

3. Retaliatory offender (8 percent): This type was not part of the original typology proposed by Levin and McDevitt in 1993. Their follow-up re-

search revealed that a rash of hate crimes often follow a precipitating hate offense. Sometimes even a rumor of such an incident may incite a group to retaliate. Such an offense is motivated by a desire to avenge a real or perceived insult to one's own group.

4. Mission offender (less than 1 percent): Offenders in this category are committed to a moral mission to rid the world of all members of what they perceive to be evil or inferior groups. No precipitating event is necessary. This type of offender may, in some circumstances, suffer from a serious mental illness characterized by delusions of grandeur and impaired ability to reason.

The vast majority of hate crime offenders were not involved in organized hate groups. In fact, the largest group of hate crime offenders, the thrill-seeking offenders, were the least likely to have a firm commitment to bigotry and therefore held the most potential to be prevented from repeating their offense. Thus, what is striking about this typology are the opportunities for intervention.

Current Trends and Future Directions

Despite two decades since hate crimes were officially recognized, research is still by and large in its infancy. Most of the literature up to this time has focused on legal perspectives on hate crime legislation, attitudes about hate crimes, and the effects of victimization. At the governmental level, there has been an explosion of efforts to develop and evaluate the effectiveness of prevention and law enforcement programs; however, most of this research appears as governmental reports with varying levels of scientific rigor.

Currently, as in the general criminological literature, there is a trend toward considering hate crimes from an international or comparative perspective. Likely related to this trend, restorative justice efforts have been receiving more attention. Technologies such as geographic mapping and the Internet are also being increasingly explored as means by which to study hate crimes. Finally, mental health professionals have begun writing about assessing hate crime offenders as a result of speculation that evaluations for the court will become an emerging issue. However, much is yet to be learned about the psychological makeup of this type of offender. Ultimately, longitudinal studies on the development of hate ideology, hate groups, and the effects of hate crime laws are needed.

Hate Crimes: Conflicting Interests

Hate crimes are controversial because they lie at the intersection of two of our intrinsic values as a democracy: (1) civil rights and equal respect, and (2) freedom of speech. On the one hand, the fundamental core of equality protected by the U.S. Constitution assures each citizen equal guarantee of security from harm within society. On the other hand, freedom of speech, which includes freedom of expression and thought, was central to the Founding Fathers' conception of the United States. It is this legal-philosophical dilemma that lies at the crux of the debate surrounding hate crimes and hate crime legislation: When do hate-motivated acts violate others' rights to peace, security, and protection from harm? Are motives of hate worthy of protection from enhanced punishment on grounds of freedom of speech?

Hate Crime Laws: Providing Equal Protection From Harm

The Fourteenth Amendment to the Constitution grants each citizen a legitimate claim to equal access to the goods of society and equal guarantee of security from harm. Eberle (2004) interprets both an internal dimension and an external dimension into these protections. The internal dimension of personal security includes the right "to feel secure, confident, and sure of his or her well-being and safety," ultimately, a right to "live in peace . . . free from fear, terror, abuse or violence" (p. 983). The external dimension comprises the "right to bodily integrity and freedom from unwanted touching and bodily contact" (p. 985). The latter dimension is clearly the focus of most codified criminal law, but the inner realm is also salient in the context of hate crimes. Both dimensions are recognized by hate crime legislation.

Hate Crimes Are Fundamentally Different

The primary argument for the necessity of regulating hate crimes is that hate incidents are inherently different from other types of crime (Levin and McDevitt 1999). First, unlike most conventional offenses, hate crimes are about symbolic (and frequently, explicit) messages directed at large groups of people, rather than being a discrete message addressed to a single individual. In this way, hate crimes have been likened to acts of terrorism. Offenders use a criminal event to warn an entire group of people of impending harm.

Next, since the offense is committed merely as a result of the victim's status within a particular minority group, he or she is essentially interchangeable. Not only would a different member of the victim's group be acceptable, a member of another minority group would usually be sufficient for the perpetrator's purposes. For example, most neo-Nazi groups are just as satisfied to communicate their message of hate to individuals of Islamic faith as to African Americans.

Finally, as found by Levin and McDevitt (1999), most hate offenses are unprovoked by the victim (66 percent) and are perpetrated against a single victim by a group of offenders (73 percent). Moreover, hate crime assaults tend to be especially brutal, with victims requiring hospitalization three times more often than other assault victims. As the victim's characteristic (race, sexual orientation, gender) motivating the crime is usually outside the individual's control and something he or she cannot change, this culmination of factors often leaves the victim helpless to avert the incident or defend him or herself. It also tends to leave the victim feeling vulnerable to future bias-motivated attacks.

The Damage Is Different

Effects on Victims. The psychological literature has provided a wealth of data attesting to the injury and long-term impact of dis-crimination, hate speech, and hate crimes. Although the harms of hate violence are obvious, the damaging effects of hate speech are less readily apparent. It is this subtle, yet penetrating, nature of hate speech that makes it so dangerous. "Psychic injury is no less an injury than being struck in the face, and it often is far more severe" (Lawrence 1990, 431).

Victims of hate speech and hate crimes are more likely to experience stress-related physical disorders (e.g., high blood pressure) and psychological disorders (e.g., alcohol and drug abuse, depression, suicide). Whereas some individuals externalize their response to hate victimization (e.g., anger), many internalize the hate projected onto them. Symptoms of hypervigilance, paranoia, and "impotent despair" (e.g., fear, nightmares, withdrawal from society) (Feagin, Early, and McKinney 2001) are understandable reactions to victims' shattered sense of security. Sometimes victims resort to rejecting their identification with their group. This behavior inevitably leads to isolation, loneliness, and hopelessness, which only exacerbate feelings of depression and paranoia. In turn, these responses can have long-lasting effects on all aspects of an individual's functioning, including lower academic achievement, poor job performance, and, ultimately, economic deprivation. In this way, discrimination and hate can become a self-fulfilling prophesy.

Effects on Society. The effects of hate speech and other hate crimes do not end with the identified victim. Rather, they leave a lasting impression on minority groups, as well as on society as a whole. Hate crimes have been found to possess a "multiplier effect," in which the suffering of the victim is experienced vicariously by the others in the group, who come to brace themselves for their own potential victimization (Feagin and McKinney 2003). In turn, when hate crimes go unpunished, it communicates to society that one of the most important tenets of democracy—that "all men are created equal"— is not being upheld. It leaves the impression that the people in power do not care about the victims. Furthermore, it contributes to the collective belief—among the victims, the perpetrators, and society—that the streets are a dangerous place; and with the introduction of the Internet, the harm extends well beyond the streets. Because of the fundamental seriousness and far-ranging effects of the offenses, from a deterrent perspective, more serious punishment is necessary to communicate to current and potential offenders, as well as to victims and society, that such behavior is taken seriously and will not be tolerated.

Hate Speech Begets Hate Violence

It is widely recognized that hate speech often is a precursor to violence. Hamm (2004), for example, in his description of the development of neo-Nazi hate subcultures discusses how exposure to white power rock music (a form of expression or "speech") serves an initial, powerful indoctrination function. Moreover, history reveals that hate speech usually precedes horrors on a grand scale. Genocidal violence such as the South African apartheid, the Holocaust, and the Hutu extermination of the Tutsi population in Rwanda were paved by campaigns of verbal abuse (Tsesis 2002). Indeed, it was the hate speech preceding the movements that helped to make the later violence possible on such a large scale.

Just Deserts and the Will of the People

Proponents of hate crime legislation argue that conviction for more serious crimes and/or penalty enhancement are just, necessary responses to a more serious and qualitatively different class of offenses (Levin and McDevitt 1999). Moreover, basing punishment on the state of the mind/motivation of the offender has precedent in criminal law (degrees of murder and manslaughter based on mind set and intent). It is also argued that hate crime statutes are a necessary protection for historically victimized groups (Lawrence 1999). Ultimately, it appears that support for hate crime legislation has become the will of the people. This is evident in a February 2000 Gallup Poll, as reported by the Human Rights Campaign, which found that 65 percent of Americans surveyed supported "special laws that provide harsher penalties for crimes motivated

by hate of certain groups." In particular, 81 percent opined that racial minorities, 79 percent that religious and ethnic minorities, 78 percent that women, and 72 percent that homosexuals should be covered by such laws.

Hate Crime Laws: Infringing on Freedom of Speech

Freedom of speech forms the cornerstone of the United States democracy. Its centrality to our Founding Fathers is evident in its inclusion as the very First Amendment in the Constitution's Bill of Rights. It has been described as the "lifeblood of the democracy and the culture," whereby autonomy, human personality, thought process, and motivation, and the purposes of democracy can be expressed (Eberle 2004, 957).

Freedom of Overt Speech and Expressive Conduct

Most critics of hate crime legislation cite the U.S. Constitution in discussing the harms of regulating this particular type of crime. Violations of several amendments have been put forth, but by far the most common is violation of the First Amendment. Obviously, cases of hate speech fall within the province of freedom of speech protections. However, penalty enhancement provisions have also been attacked for imposing additional punishments based on the defendants' motive of hate, which has been construed to be encompassed within "speech."

Hate speech alone is highly powerful. Hate propaganda, such as hate rock, not only attracts potential hatemongers into the fold but also serves to effectively program its group members. Symbolic acts of hate, such as cross burnings, function to bolster the feelings of cohesiveness within the group. Moreover, hate speech is frequently a precursor to hate violence. Yet, no matter how offensive or disagreeable it is to most people, speech, including symbolic speech as expressive conduct (such as cross burnings), generally is constitutionally protected. In fact, in *Texas v. Johnson* (1989), Supreme Court Justice Brennan opined that a principal function of free speech is to invite dispute, to "induce a condition of unrest, create dissatisfaction with conditions as they are, or even stir people to anger" (p. 4).

Nevertheless, there are legally appropriate limitations on speech based on its assault of victims' personal security. These include contexts in which an individual's personal security is threatened, such as incidents of explicit threats and intimidation, both of which are intended to instill fear of impending harm. Persistent hate speech is also grounds for limiting speech when it reaches the point of *harassment* (i.e., unwelcome personal abuse that unreasonably interferes with the target's life or becomes a substantial, intolerable invasion of privacy). Other legally approved limitations on speech that are relevant to a discussion of hate speech and hate crime more generally include libel and defamation, obscenity, incitement, and "fighting words." Specifically, when a close connection can be proven between the speech and "a serious substantive evil that rises far above public inconvenience, annoyance, or unrest" (*Terminiello v. Chicago* 1949), it is permissible to legally squelch speech. For example, fighting words, or "words which by their very utterance inflict injury or tend to incite an immediate breach of the peace," "are of such slight social value . . . that any benefit . . . from them is clearly outweighed by the social interest in order and morality" (*Chaplinsky v. New Hampshire* 1942). However, the focus of the fighting words doctrine is not to ban the *content* of speech, but address inflammatory *modes* of expression (Friedlieb 2005), such that they are "likely to provoke the average person to retaliation" (*Chaplinsky v. New Hampshire* 1942). Subsequent case law clarified that fighting words include only (1) *specific* speech, not generalized profanity (e.g., bumper stickers) or protestations (e.g., burning of the American flag); (2) speech addressing a *particular listener* in face-to-face confrontation, as opposed to being directed at the general public; and (3) speech intended to incite an *immediate* breach of peace or violence.

Several U.S. Supreme Court cases are directly relevant to these matters. First, in 1977, before the adoption of any state hate crime statutes, the National Socialist Party of America (NSPA), a neo-Nazi group, announced its intention to conduct a march in front of the city hall in Skokie, Illinois, a Chicago suburb with a large Jewish population, including numerous Holocaust survivors. In an attempt to prevent the march, the city of Skokie enacted an ordinance that prohibited public demonstrations that would "incite violence, hatred, abuse, or hostility toward a person or group of persons by reason of reference to religious, racial, ethnic, national, or regional affiliation." The Supreme Court stayed a state court injunction, holding that although a Nazi parade could possibly form the basis for a constitutionally permissible civil action for intentional infliction of emotional distress, "it is . . . quite a different matter to criminalize protected First Amendment conduct in anticipation of such results" (*Collin v. Smith* 1978, 1206). The Court noted that marches—a group situation in public—would not fall under the fighting words doctrine and, thus, are constitutionally protected. Even though the march in Skokie never took place, the case marked the point at which "the problem of ethnic intimidation and the associated legal and moral dilemmas flooded the public consciousness" (Gellman 1991, 337).

More than a decade later, on June 21, 1990, a group of white teenagers in St. Paul, Minnesota, assembled a cross, scaled the fence of a neighboring African-American family's home, and set the cross aflame. The cross burning was interpreted as a message of hate toward the victims. Although the defendants' actions could have been punished as a threat or even a property crime, St. Paul chose instead to prosecute them under its bias-motivated crime ordinance, which prohibited any conduct "arousing anger, alarm or resentment in others on the basis of race, color, creed, religion or gender." The Supreme Court, however, struck down the city ordinance as constitutionally invalid because it prohibited speech (*R.A.V. v. City of St. Paul* 1992). The Court held that "the local government's interest in communicating to minority groups that it did not condone such hatred did not justify selectively silencing speech on the basis of its content" (Mueller 1993, 620).

Although seemingly similar, the Court upheld the constitutionality of a Virginia law banning cross burning as a threat *with intent to intimidate* (*Virginia v. Black* 2003). In 1998, two separate incidents involving hate expression transpired in Virginia and were simultaneously brought before the U.S. Supreme Court. The first involved a typical Ku Klux Klan rally (led by defendant Black), held on private property with the permission of the owner, which culminated in the burning of a cross. The other involved two defendants setting afire a cross on the property of a neighbor in order to "get back" at him for having complained about their discharge of firearms in the backyard. Although the three men were convicted under the statute, the Virginia Supreme Court, in perceived keeping with *R.A.V.*, overturned the convictions on the grounds that the statute constituted content discrimination. However, in a surprising decision, the U.S. Supreme Court reversed the decision, reasoning that, while this was true, the convictions were justified because a particular type of threat was singled out in the statute—i.e., cross-burning—and that it was justifiable because it "is a particularly virulent form of intimidation," historically connected with violence (*Virginia v. Black* 2003). Nevertheless, the Court struck down a provision of the statute indicating that cross burning was itself *prima facie* evidence (i.e., evidence that is sufficient, if not rebutted, to prove a particular proposition or fact) of intent to intimidate. Essentially, the symbol could not be banned entirely, thereby demanding a contextualized, individual analysis in future cross-burning cases.

Overbreadth and Vagueness. Due process concerns surrounding limits on free speech relate to overbreadth and vagueness. A chief difficulty in drafting hate crime statutes is making them broad enough to provide adequate protection to victimized groups without reaching the point of constitutionally prohibited overbreadth (Gellman 1991). The primary concern with overbreadth of hate crime statutes is its "chilling effect" on free speech, or limiting expression in situations where it is protected. Moreover to sustain constitutional scrutiny on grounds of vagueness, the language of hate crime statutes must be sufficiently explicit for an individual to know with a reasonable degree of certainty whether their conduct breaks the law. The fighting words doctrine, in particular, has been criticized on grounds of vagueness. No clear list of designated fighting words has been devised, nor would it be possible given the Court's requirement to consider the context of each situation individually. Even *Chaplinsky's* purported "objective" test—i.e., how "men of common intelligence" would respond in the given situation—remains highly subjective and, arguably, unconstitutionally vague (Mannheimer 1993). Furthermore, the standard can change depending on the qualities of the person being verbally attacked (e.g., police officer).

Freedom of Thought

Most hate crime laws focus on the motivation of the offenders, beyond the criminal act or behavior itself. Motivation essentially consists of the emotions and thoughts that propel one toward a goal. As such, critics have argued that punishing an offender based on his motivation is akin to punishing thought, which is protected by the First Amendment (*Abood v. Detroit Board of Education* 1977). This is the very issue that formed the basis of the appeal to the U.S. Supreme Court in the case of *Wisconsin v. Mitchell* (1993). In that case, a group of young African-American males were discussing a scene from the movie *Mississippi Burning,* in which a white man beat a young black boy, who was praying. Shortly thereafter, the group observed a young white boy passing them on the street. The defendant reportedly incited the group to attack the boy, whereby they beat him severely, leaving him in a coma for several days. Because the crime was racially motivated, Wisconsin invoked its hate crime penalty enhancement statute in ascribing punishment for the assault. The case was appealed on grounds that Mitchell's speech, and thus First Amendment protections, were implicated by the role of motive in determining guilt for the hate crime. However, the Supreme Court upheld the hate crime statute as constitutional, opining that since the criminal conduct was proven beyond a reasonable doubt before the bias motive was taken into account, the statute acceptably focused on conduct, and only *incidentally* implicated speech.

It is a classic philosophical debate whether thoughts, unless obviously expressed in speech or other actions, are ever truly knowable. Moreover, the legal question goes, even if one assumes that thoughts can be ascertained, is it possible to determine them (i.e., motive) with legally acceptable levels of certainty (i.e., beyond a reasonable doubt)? Just to complicate the situation further, any given act may have multiple motivations. In such cases, how is hate isolated from other motivations in establishing culpability or punishment?

Equal Protection: The Double-Edged Sword

A Murder(er) Is a Murder(er)

Although the Equal Protection Clause forms the cornerstone of the legal arguments in favor of hate crime statutes, it also has been adopted to oppose them. First, particularly in light of the potential to violate freedom of speech, some have questioned the necessity of considering hate or bias motivation when the core offense (assault, vandalism) is already covered by criminal law. This redundancy implicates equal protection of defendants, questioning whether it is acceptable for certain groups to be punished more severely than those committing equivalent crimes without the hate component. Some have speculated that, in making more work for law enforcement and courts to investigate and prove hate motive, hate crime statutes will be inconsistently implemented. This situation further invokes due process and equal protection questions.

Moreover, some critics have suggested that the differential sentencing inherent to penalty enhancement in hate crime statutes represents excessive punishment, and disproportionate punishment violates the Eighth Amendment prohibition against cruel and unusual punishment. According to this argument, "murder is murder" and all murder should be punished the same.[7] As such, there is no need for legislation, because the underlying act is already criminalized and punishable. Any penalty enhancement for hate crimes, it is argued, excessively punishes the offender.

All Victims Are Created Equal

Similarly, the propriety of protecting certain victimized groups and not others has been questioned on equal protection grounds. How do legislators decide which groups to specify as worthy of protection? Some critics have suggested that codifying hate crimes is actually just an attempt to be politically correct (i.e., identity politics), rather than being based on legitimate legal principles (Jacobs and Potter 1998).

Enactment of hate crime statutes could have a number of deleterious effects on society in general. Analogous to the confirmed impact of affirmative action efforts, imposing governmental safeguards implies to some nonminority group members that protected groups are weak and "are incapable of holding their own without special protection" (Gellman 1991, 385). Resentment may be stirred toward the protected minority group because of the "special treatment" being received. This resentment may be projected by the majority as well as by members of minority groups not so protected (Gerstenfeld 1992), thereby creating further divisions between the protected groups and others. Governmental-sanctioned hate crime statutes could also render us complacent in fighting bigotry on an individual level.

Hate crime statutes discouraging people from expressing and preventing exposure to biased beliefs actually increase the influence of powerful, prejudiced speakers when they arise (Gerstenfeld 1992). Thus, with time it may be found that these statutes actually serve to feed the power of hate groups in our country, propelling perpetrators into positions of heroism in their groups for defying the power of the federal government (Uhrich 1999). On the individual level, from the perspective of the hate crime offender, going to prison tends to reinforce attraction to criminal subcultures (hate groups) and to strengthen racism (Gerstenfeld 1992).

Ironically, hate crime laws might be *most* detrimental to the very groups they were designed to protect. Following the analogy to affirmative action, instead of "leveling the playing field," the implied vulnerability may become internalized by the special classes. In addition, the laws have already been applied to the detriment of the minority members it was intended to protect. In *Wisconsin v. Mitchell* (1993), African-American youths were convicted for assaulting a white boy. It is not incomprehensible that such laws may be used further by the majority to silence minority leaders seeking equitable treatment (Uhrich 1999). Finally, victims may experience further trauma, and revictimization, by having such personal identity issues as one's sexual orientation directly and substantially put at issue. Indeed, the impact of institutionalizing hate crimes—and hate speech, specifically—could be enormous.

Conclusion

The foregoing discussion of hate crimes reveals strong arguments on both sides of the controversy. From a purely legal perspective, this realm of criminal law is fraught with conflict, as freedom of speech and equal protection simultaneously constitute integral bases for our country as a democracy. Yet, from an individual and societal perspective, the harms of hate speech and hate crimes may be too great to neglect their unique nature and society's call for a heightened response.

Careful consideration suggests that although troubled minority-majority group relations clearly deserve attention, formal legislation may not be the magic solution to the problem of prejudice and hate. Nevertheless, state legislatures and politicians continue to champion governmental involvement, apparently without adequate consideration of either the practical difficulties associated with implementation (definitional vagueness) or the unintended consequences (revictimization, heightened divisiveness among groups). Currently, hate

crime law and research remain in their infancy. Although the path they will take is unclear, there is no doubt that this sensitive topic will continue to command attention.

Notes

1. These figures vary depending on the exact definition of what constitutes a hate crime statute. For example, Jenness and Grattet (2001), using a more stringent, narrow standard (i.e., requiring that the statute explicitly create a separate offense category or provide penalty enhancement for existing offenses), identify only 41 states.

2. Lawrence (1999) described this model in relation to hate crimes based on race specifically; however, it could be applied to any minority group subjected to hate crime victimization.

3. Some such statutes require an additional element of maliciousness (Lawrence 1999).

4. Similarly, institutions of higher education, which are by federal statute required to report hate crimes to the U.S. Department of Education or to the FBI UCR Program, have also failed to provide data to the UCR. In 2002, only 400 of nearly 7,000 colleges and universities reported crime data to the UCR (Shively 2005). Although 6,000 did report to the Department of Education, these numbers often do not get forwarded onto the FBI for inclusion in its hate crimes annual reports.

5. This initiative only began in 2001, thus, identifying reliable trends is not yet possible.

6. As the vast majority of hate crime offenders are male, the singular masculine pronoun is used throughout the rest of the chapter.

7. Essentially, any crime could be substituted for "murder" in this statement.

References

Eberle, E. J. 2004. "Cross Burning, Hate Speech, and Free Speech in America." *Arizona State Law Journal* 36:953–1001.

Feagin, J. R., and K. D. McKinney. 2003. *The Many Costs of Racism*. Lanham, MD: Rowman and Littlefield.

Feagin, J. R., K. E. Early, and K. D. McKinney. 2001. "The Many Costs of Discrimination: The Case of Middle-Class African Americans." *Indiana Law Review* 34:1313–1360.

Friedlieb, L. 2005. "The Epitome of an Insult: A Constitutional Approach to Designated Fighting Words." *University of Chicago Law Review* 72:385–415.

Gellman, S. 1991. "Sticks and Stones Can Put You in Jail, but Can Words Increase Your Sentence? Constitutional and Policy Dilemmas of Ethnic Intimidation Laws." *UCLA Law Review* 39:333–396.

Gerstenfeld, P. B. 1992. "Smile When You Call Me That: The Problems With Punishing Hate Motivated Behavior." *Behavioral Sciences and the Law* 10:259–285.

Hamm, M. S. 2004. "Hate Violence." In M. S. Zahn, H. H., Brownstein, and S. L. Jackson (eds.), *Violence: From Theory to Research*. Cincinnati, OH: Anderson Publishing, 227–236.

Human Rights Campaign. n.d. "Public Polling Shows Strong Support for the Local Law Enforcement Enhancement Act." http://www.hrc.org.

Jacobs, J. B., and K. Potter. 1998. *Hate Crimes: Criminal Law and Identity Politics*. New York: Oxford University Press.

Jenness, V., and R. Grattet. 2001. *Making Hate a Crime: From Social Movement to Law Enforcement*. New York: Russell Sage Foundation.

Lawrence, C. R. 1990. "If He Hollers Let Him Go: Regulating Racist Speech on Campus." *Duke Law Journal* 431:458–466.

Lawrence, F. M. 1999. *Punishing Hate: Bias Crimes Under American Law*. Cambridge, MA: Harvard University Press.

Levin, J., and J. McDevitt. 1993. *Hate Crimes: The Rising Tide of Bigotry and Bloodshed*. New York: Plenum Press.

———. 1999. "Hate Crimes." In L. Kurtz (ed.), *Encyclopedia of Violence, Peace, and Conflict*. San Diego, CA: Academic Press.

Mannheimer, M. J. 1993. "The Fighting Words Doctrine." *Columbia Law Review* 93:1543–1545.

McDevitt, J., J. Levin, and S. Bennett. 2002. "Hate Crime Offenders: An Expanded Typology." *Journal of Social Issues* 58:303–317.

Mueller, A. 1993. "Can Motive Matter? A Constitutional and Criminal Law Analysis of Motive in Hate Crime Legislation." *University of Missouri at Kansas City Law Review* 61:619–633.

Shively, M. 2005. *Study of Literature and Legislation on Hate Crime in America* (Award No. OJP-99-C-008). Washington, DC: National Institute of Justice. http://www.ncjrs.org/pdffiles1/nij/grants/210300.pdf.

Southern Poverty Law Center. 2001. "The Hate Crimes Statistics Act: Ten Years Later, the Numbers Don't Add Up." *The Intelligence Report, Issue 104*. http://www.splcenter.org/intel/intelreport/article.jsp?aid=157.

Tsesis, A. 2002. *Destructive Messages: How Hate Speech Paves the Way for Harmful Social Movements*. New York: NYU Press.

Uhrich, C. L. 1999. "Hate Crime Legislation: A Policy Analysis." *Houston Law Review* 36:1467–1529.

U.S. Department of Justice. 2005. *Hate Crime Statistics, 2004*. Washington, DC: Bureau of Justice Statistics.

Cases and Statutes Cited

Abood v. Detroit Board of Education, 431 U.S. 209 (1977).

Chaplinsky v. New Hampshire, 315 U.S. 568 (1942).

Collin v. Smith, 578 F. 2d. 1197 (7th Cir. 1978).

R.A.V. v. City of St. Paul, 505 U.S. 377 (1992).

Terminiello v. Chicago, 337 U.S. 1 (1949).

Texas v. Johnson, 491 U.S. 397 (1989).

Virginia v. Black, 538 U.S. 343 (2003).

Wisconsin v. Mitchell, 508 U.S. 476 (1993).

Related Websites

Uniform Crime Reports
http://www.fbi.gov/ucr/ucr.htm

Hate Crime Legislation
http://www.ncjrs.gov/spotlight/hate_crimes/legislation.html

American Prosecutors Research Institute: Hate Crimes
http://www.ndaa-apri.org/apri/programs/hate_crimes/index.html

Hate Crimes Research Network
http://www.hatecrime.net

The National Center for Victims of Crime: Hate Crimes
http://www.ncvc.org/ncvc/main.aspx?dbName=DocumentViewer&DocumentID=32356

Anti-Defamation League: Hate Crimes Laws
http://www.adl.org/99hatecrime/intro.asp

Tolerance.org
http://www.tolerance.org

Southern Poverty Law Center: Intelligence Project
http://www.splcenter.org/intel/

The Prejudice Institute: Understanding Hate Crimes
http://www.prejudiceinstitute.org/understandinghatecrimes.html

Hate Crimes Information, Resources, and News
http://www.civilrights.org/issues/hate/

ACLU Endorses Federal Hate Crimes Legislation for First Time

http://www.aclu.org/lgbt/gen/12252prs
   20050526.html

Partners Against Hate

http://www.partnersagainsthate.org

Discussion Questions

1. What are the components of a defini-
    tion of hate crimes?

2. What are the challenges to learning the
    true scope of hate crimes?

3. What are the harms of hate crimes?

4. What are the constitutional issues re-
    garding hate crimes? Which is most im-
    portant?

5. Discuss the major U.S. Supreme Court
    cases regarding hate crimes and the
    Court's rulings. How is hate speech im-
    plicated in each of these cases? ✦

Section III

Legal Issues and Corrections

Chapter 13
Inmate Litigation and the Constitution

Barbara Belbot

In this chapter, the author presents a historical case-by-case examination of inmate litigation. Prior to the 1960s, the social and judicial attitudes toward prisoner rights were reflected by the offensive conditions of the prison system. During the 1960s, the United States was experiencing social unrest, fueled by the civil rights movement, war with Vietnam, and an ever-changing sociopolitical climate. This wave of outside protests and reform was also felt within the prison system, which was actively engaged in the prisoners' rights revolution.

Prior to the 1960s, prison officials were largely left alone by courts and the outside world. However, in the landmark case *Cooper v. Pate* (1964), the Supreme Court opened the door to prison lawsuits in federal court. Inmates began flooding the courts with lawsuits raising a variety of constitutional issues. For example, some of the cases cited violations of the First Amendment in regards to access to legal aid, the Fourteenth Amendment's Due Process Clause in regard to the carrying out of punishments within the prison, and the Eighth Amendment's Cruel and Unusual Punishment Clause in regard to living conditions, personal injury, and access to health care.

This torrent of litigation has had a significant impact on the prison system. Decision-making power has been shifted and centralized within state government resulting in uniform policies and standards. Federal court resources have been under significant strain as a result of the large increase in cases filed. An increase in professionalization within the prison workforce has created a hiring vacuum that in some instances has led to increases in inmate violence. To slow the massive influx of inmate lawsuits, Congress enacted the Prison Litigation Reform Act (PLRA) in 1996, to reduce inmate lawsuits by order of an internal grievance system.

Introduction

In *Ruffin v. Commonwealth of Virginia* (1871), the Virginia Court of Appeals described inmates this way: "For the time being, during his term of service in the penitentiary, he is in a state of penal servitude to the state. He has, as a consequence of his crime, not only forfeited his liberty, but all of his personal rights except those which the law in its humanity accords him. He is for the time being the slave of the State. . . ." Although a few court cases held otherwise, it wasn't until the 1960s that prisoners in the United States achieved a legal status beyond what the Virginia appeals court depicted in 1871. There were wide variations among the states in how prisoners were treated and how correctional institutions were managed. Not all prisons were the stereotypical "Big House" where inmates lived under a strict disciplinary regime, eating in silence and working long hours in prison industry. Nor did all prisons fit the Southern plantation stereotype, where prisoners labored in the extreme heat of day, guarded by brutal officers who administered beatings based on trumped-up charges. Nonetheless, prisoners in this country were not protected by the Constitution. Prison administrators had enormous discretion to develop management techniques that often included violence. They were free to maintain discipline through whatever rules and practices they deemed appropriate, including depriving inmates of basic human needs such as health care, nutrition, clothing, and safe and secure institutions. Prisons were closed communities. Officials operated with little outside scrutiny and were held accountable for only the most sensational scandals.

What happened in the 1960s was so significant it is often termed "the prisoners' rights revolution" or the "prisoner litigation revolution." As with every important social movement, however, this "revolution" did not occur in a vacuum. In the 1960s, the civil rights movement took center stage and advocates filed lawsuits and lobbied legislatures challenging race, gender, and ethnic discrimination. The U.S. Supreme Court played an active role in this drama. Until the 1950s and 1960s, business and commerce issues dominated the work conducted in the federal courts. The Warren Court thrust the judiciary into deciding issues involving the constitutional rights of individuals as guaranteed by the Bill of Rights. The prisoners' rights movement drew support and encouragement from this larger civil rights movement (Powers and Rothman 2002). Many of the attorneys who represented inmates in the early prisoners' rights cases had also worked in the civil rights movement (Feeley and Swearingen 2004). The profile of the typical prisoner incarcerated in the United States was in flux. America's prisons were 70 percent white in the 1950s, but minorities were incarcerated in increasingly large numbers beginning in the 1960s so that by the mid 1990s, African Americans and Latinos constituted almost 70 percent of all inmates (Sampson and Lauritsen 1997). Accompanying this change in demographics was a revolution in the political consciousness of inmates. They began to demand greater constitutional protections.

When a prisoner filed a lawsuit prior to 1964, judges were most likely to dismiss the case without extensive review. Following an unofficial hands-off doctrine, judges chose to defer to the expertise of correctional officials when it came to questions about how to operate prisons and jails and manage convicts. Besides, prison management belongs to the executive branch of government, not the judicial branch. Federal judges felt additionally bound by concerns about federalism. Operating correctional institutions is primarily the responsibility of state governments, and federal intervention was considered constitutionally suspect. In *Cooper v. Pate* (1964), the Supreme Court ended the hands-off doctrine and opened the door to prisoner lawsuits in federal courts.

Many inmates have eagerly entered that door during the past 40 years. In *Cooper*, the Court ruled that state prisoners have the right to file lawsuits in federal court alleging that prison officials violated the U.S. Constitution. These lawsuits are filed under a federal statute, 42 U.S.C. section 1983, also known as the Civil Rights Act, passed by Congress in 1871. Until 1964, however, section 1983 was not available to prisoners and their claims of constitutional violations were treated with hands-off. The importance of the *Cooper* decision cannot be overestimated. Cooper complained that his First Amendment right to freedom of religion was violated, but the case's significance goes far beyond his individual complaint. It set the legal precedent that prisoners can file and judges must consider cases alleging that prison officials violated the U.S. Constitution.

Early Prisoner Lawsuits

As prisoners began to flood the federal courts with lawsuits, judges began the difficult and controversial task of considering how and to what extent the Constitution protects them. Although prisoners had the legal right to file claims in state courts alleging violations of state law, they quickly gravitated to federal courts because they perceived federal judges to be more receptive to their claims and more willing to interpret the Constitution in their favor. Unlike many state court judges, federal judges have lifetime appointments and are free to make tough and unpopular decisions without threat of losing their jobs.

Prisoners filed cases that challenged many of the rules and regulations that governed their lives, including their religious practices, access to the courts, correspondence and visiting privileges, disciplinary proceedings, and procedures for assigning security classifications. They also filed lawsuits challenging a range of living conditions, including the quality of health care, overcrowding, sanitation, and excessive use of force. Few areas of prison life went unchallenged. The federal judiciary responded to the wave of inmate litigation with a series of important decisions that dramatically altered the legal status of prisoners in this country. Eventually the Supreme Court decided to hear several cases involving the most important legal issues.

The Fourteenth Amendment's Due Process Clause provided the basis for *Wolff v. McDonnell* (1974), in which the Supreme Court decided that prisoners who face disciplinary charges for serious rule infractions that might lead to solitary confinement or loss of good time must be provided certain due process protections. These protections include written notice of the charges 24 hours before a disciplinary hearing is conducted, a right to provide evidence (including calling witnesses), a right to a neutral decision maker (someone not involved in the incident), a written statement of the evidence relied on and the reasons for deciding on a particular disciplinary action, and assistance in preparing a defense from a counsel substitute (nonattorney) for inmates who are illiterate, or in complex cases. The Court concluded in *Procunier v. Martinez* (1974) that the First Amendment protects individuals who correspond with prisoners from having the letters they receive from prisoners censored by correctional officials. In *Johnson v. Avery* (1969), the Court upheld the right of inmates to obtain assistance from other inmates in preparing legal documents and lawsuits. In *Bounds v. Smith* (1977), the Court decided that in order to provide prisoners the opportunity for meaningful access to the courts, officials must provide prison law libraries or legal assistance programs along with supplies for indigent inmates to engage in legal work—pens, paper, and postage stamps.

Living Conditions Lawsuits

The federal courts were also responsive to inmates' claims that their living conditions were unconstitutional. Conditions were poor in many U.S. prisons in the 1960s and 1970s. There were well-documented instances in which officers used violence to control inmates with the blessing of the administration. In several Southern prison systems, officials hand selected prisoners to guard other inmates. There were too few health care providers working in the institutions. Prisoners worked in harsh, unsafe

conditions. Prison units were old, and housing and food preparation areas were often unsanitary. Although conditions varied widely from state to state and from facility to facility, there was no shortage of serious problems. Inmates claimed those conditions violated the Cruel and Unusual Punishment Clause of the Eighth Amendment. In *Pugh v. Locke* (1976), a federal district court judge in Alabama found a long list of constitutional violations based on evidence about life in the Alabama State Prison System. He concluded that the prisons suffered from severe overcrowding, insect and vermin infestations, inadequate heating and ventilation, decrepit plumbing, unsanitary food service, a classification system that failed to separate violent from nonviolent offenders, inadequate health care, and an inhumane punitive isolation unit called the "dog-house." Judge Frank Johnson ordered Alabama to make significant reforms and appointed a committee of prison experts from outside the state to oversee the changes and report to him on the state's progress. The Alabama case did not stand alone. Federal judges in other jurisdictions tried cases that challenged living conditions in prisons and jails. In Texas, Judge William Wayne Justice declared a host of conditions in the Texas Department of Corrections unconstitutional and appointed a special master under the Federal Rules of Civil Procedure to monitor the Texas system as it implemented reform.

Federal district court judges decided all of the early conditions lawsuits (sometimes called "totality of conditions" cases). The cases were generally filed as class actions and involved claims that numerous conditions in a particular institution or in an entire system violated the Constitution. The claims varied from lawsuit to lawsuit because the allegations were specific to the institutions where the inmates were housed. The judges had to decide which claims the evidence supported and what the appropriate legal remedies should be. The judges would then issue orders requiring certain reforms.

In many cases, the evidence was so overwhelming that prison officials agreed to implement reform before the judge reached a decision or, in some instances, before the case even went to trial. Officials entered into consent decrees with the attorneys for the inmates that spelled out in detail what reforms would be put into place and over what time period. The judge would then review the decree and order its implementation. The lawsuit then moved into a "remedial phase" and the district court judge was responsible for making certain that the reforms happened. The reforms were usually quite extensive and expensive, affecting the entire institution and prison system. They often took years to implement. State legislatures were called upon to appropriate the funds. To monitor the progress, federal judges retained jurisdiction of the cases for years (even decades) after the orders and consent decrees were issued.

Not all Eighth Amendment cases about the Cruel and Unusual Punishment Clause have involved living conditions. One of the most important prisoners' rights cases is *Estelle v. Gamble* (1976), in which the Supreme Court ruled that the Eighth Amendment is violated when officials are deliberately indifferent to an inmate's serious medical needs. Up until this case was decided, prison health care providers could be sued in state court for medical malpractice if they were negligent. But after *Estelle v. Gamble*, if there was evidence that prison officials were deliberately (not negligently) indifferent in caring for a prisoner's serious health issues, they would be found violating that prisoner's civil rights under the Cruel and Unusual Punishment Clause. Not only health care providers were at risk, any correctional official whose actions deliberately contributed to the indifference would be in violation. Administrators who failed to hire the necessary health care workers or to provide needed medical equipment and officers who refused to escort sick inmates to the infirmary risked violating the Eighth Amendment.

The *Estelle* case is significant because it forced correctional agencies to increase the resources dedicated to caring for inmate health. It is also significant because the Court greatly expanded its interpretation of the Cruel and Unusual Punishment Clause.

Nowhere in that clause does it address whether deliberate indifference to prisoner medical needs constitutes cruel and unusual punishment, but the Court's broad reading in 1976 permanently changed the meaning of the amendment.

In corrections, issues surrounding the use of force can also trigger the Eighth Amendment. Prisoners who claim that officials unlawfully used force against them can allege an Eighth Amendment violation as well as a personal injury (tort) action under state law, and in some cases they can file criminal charges under the state penal code. The Supreme Court has never decided on the constitutionality of using corporal punishment to discipline an inmate, however, two lower federal court cases in the 1960s and 1970s found it to be unconstitutional: *Talley v. Stephens* (1965) and *Jackson v. Bishop* (1968). With the decisions in these cases, the official use of corporal punishment, which was still extensive in some prison systems through the 1960s, ended in the United States. The unofficial use of corporal punishment to discipline, of course, is not only illegal, it is grounds for an Eighth Amendment lawsuit. In *Hudson v. McMillian* (1992), the Supreme Court decided that even inmates who suffer nonserious physical injuries as a result of unlawful use of force by officers can allege cruel and unusual punishment.

Judicial Deference

Although it's true that prisoners have won significant constitutional rights and redefined their legal status, federal judges have not been reluctant to rule against inmates' claims. In a series of cases, the Supreme Court has drawn important limits on how much protection the Constitution affords prisoners. In 1979, the Court decided *Bell v. Wolfish* concerning conditions and practices at a federal facility that housed convicted offenders and pretrial detainees. The inmates complained about overcrowding. The Court noted that inmates spent considerable time outside of their cells, which reduced the deleterious effects of a crowded facility. The pretrial detainee plaintiffs complained about being subjected to random strip and body cavity searches that were not based on suspicion of wrongdoing. The Court rejected their arguments because they were not convicted offenders. Instead, the Court announced that officials should be granted substantial discretion to implement practices that are administratively necessary to run an orderly institution. In *Rhodes v. Chapman* (1981), the Supreme Court rejected the claim that housing two prisoners in a cell designed to house one prisoner violates the Cruel and Unusual Punishment Clause. The Court concluded this practice did not amount to a wanton and unnecessary infliction of pain and was not disproportionate to the severity of the prisoners' crimes, and wrote, "[T]he Constitution does not mandate comfortable prisons." In 1996, the Court reduced the protection it gave prisoners to access the courts in *Bounds v. Smith* (1977). In *Lewis v. Casey* (1996), the Court ruled that Bounds did not create an abstract right to a prison law library or legal assistance, as many lower courts had assumed. The *Lewis* Court decided that *Bounds* recognized only a constitutional right of access to the courts. To establish a violation of that right, prisoners must demonstrate that the alleged deficiencies in the library or the legal assistance program had actually hindered their particular efforts to access the courts.

The Court addressed an excessive use-of-force claim in *Whitley v. Albers* (1986), in which an inmate was shot when he got in the way of officers as they attempted to free a hostage. The Court outlined the standard to be applied when a prisoner alleges that excessive force was used while trying to quell a disturbance. The Court ruled that a prisoner must show that the force had been used maliciously and sadistically for the purpose of causing him or her harm. Without malicious intent, there is no constitutional violation even in those circumstances where there is proof the injury was unnecessary or the result of poor procedures or training. The Supreme Court extended the *Whitley* standard to *all* excessive use-of-force claims in *Hudson v. McMillian* (1992).

The decision in *Wilson v. Seiter* (1991) established the standard for courts to use in evaluating claims that prison conditions violate the Eighth Amendment. In that case, inmates complained about overcrowding, excessive noise, poor ventilation, unsanitary conditions, and housing for mentally and physically ill inmates. The Court decided that for conditions to violate the Constitution, there must be evidence that correctional officials were deliberately indifferent to the conditions, either as they developed or continued. Just as the Court determined in *Whitley v. Albers*, prisoners must offer sufficient proof about the officials' intent; it is not enough that conditions fell below acceptable standards or were harmful.

The focus on official intent was further emphasized in *Farmer v. Brennan* (1994), a case involving a transsexual prisoner assigned to a maximum-security facility where other prisoners sexually assaulted him. He alleged that officials were deliberately indifferent to his safety when they transferred him to a high-security institution where violent offenders were housed. He argued that reasonable correctional officials should have known there was a substantial likelihood he would be assaulted. The Supreme Court ruled that prison officials cannot be held liable unless there is evidence they actually knew of the risk and disregarded it. The Court again placed the burden on the inmate to present evidence about the subjective intent of prison authorities. Such evidence, by its very nature, is difficult to discover and argue in court.

One of the Supreme Court's most important prisoner rights decisions is *Turner v. Safely* (1987). In this case, the Court examined several institutional regulations in the Missouri Department of Corrections and created a test to determine when prison rules that limit prisoners' constitutional rights violate the Constitution. The test measures reasonableness and requires a court to decide whether the regulation is reasonably related to a legitimate penological purpose. To that end, a court must examine whether (1) there is a rational connection between the regulation and the purpose it's intended to serve; (2) there are alternative means that prisoners can use to exercise their rights; (3) accommodating the inmates' rights will affect the staff, the allocation of resources, or other inmates; and (4) the regulation being challenged is an exaggerated response to the staffs' concerns.

Obviously, the *Turner* test requires judges to recognize that officials have a great deal of administrative discretion in creating rules and regulations. The Supreme Court used the *Turner* test in *O'Lone v. Shabazz* (1987) to validate a prison rule that was a security measure designed to keep inmates who were working outside the building from returning to the building before a certain time. This rule caused Muslim inmates working outside to miss evening religious services that started in late afternoon. Despite the argument that First Amendment rights are entitled to special protections, the Court applied the *Turner* test and decided that the regulation served a legitimate purpose and was reasonable, even though some prisoners were denied the right to worship.

The Impact of Litigation

Much has been written about the impact of prisoner litigation. Without a doubt, litigation, particularly the conditions lawsuits, has dramatically increased the amount of government resources allocated to institutional corrections. State legislatures were forced to respond by appropriating funds to build new prison units to ease unconstitutional overcrowding, hire additional staff, renovate older institutions, and modernize health care delivery. Court-ordered reform is also credited with forcing corrections to become more professional. Staff must follow rules and regulations and are held accountable for their actions. Accountability requires training. Among other things, training includes learning when and how force can be used legally. Written policies and procedures have to be created. Rules and regulations require a bureaucratic structure. Records must document whether policies and procedures are followed. When correctional employees fail to follow the rules, processes must be in place to discipline them. Bureaucracy rests on the rule of law, not on the whims or charisma of individuals.

With these charges, the administration of correctional institutions became more centralized. Instead of wardens operating their institutions with little oversight from state departments of correction, reform centralized much of the decision making and imposed uniform policies and standards. State correctional agencies introduced internal inmate grievance systems to help channel prisoners' complaints away from litigation by addressing problems quickly in-house. Agency officials kept abreast of what was happening in the courts nationwide and often took preventive steps by introducing reforms before a court ordered them. The courts opened the prison doors to outside scrutiny.

Vincent Nathan (2004), a court-appointed monitor in several large prisoner class action lawsuits over the last 30 years, observes that litigation has gradually affected the mindset of correctional administrators. The new generation of administrators consider the humane and constructive treatment of offenders as a primary responsibility. Feeley and Swearingen (2004, 442) note that "litigation has probably been the single most important source of change in prisons and jails during the past 40 years." In their opinion, litigation has been successful because judges have relied on well-defined standards promoted by corrections experts themselves. Although courts forced change on reluctant correctional officials, at the same time, judges reinforced trends already underway within the field. Litigation encouraged professional associations to promulgate national standards for correctional institutions on a variety of matters (Jacobs 1983).

Prisoner litigation has also had unanticipated and less-positive consequences. Inmates have become more assertive about their rights and have filed lawsuits by the thousands. The number of prisoner lawsuits filed in federal courts increased from 23,230 in 1980 to 68,235 in 1996 (Scalia 2002). The flood of inmate litigation has strained the resources of the federal courts. Because prisoners generally do not have attorneys and represent themselves *pro se*, their legal work is often incomplete and difficult to evaluate.

When Hanson and Daley (1995) studied a random sample of prisoner civil rights lawsuits filed in U.S. District Courts in four different states, they found that courts dismissed 75 percent of the issues raised by prisoners in their lawsuits while another 20 percent were dismissed based on motions to dismiss filed by the defendants. Only 2 percent of the issues resulted in trial verdicts, with fewer than half resulting in a favorable verdict for the prisoner. All in all, 94 percent of the prisoners won nothing. Nonetheless, court staff must spend considerable time reviewing the lawsuits and preparing legal documents associated with the cases.

Critics of the prisoner litigation movement allege that prisoners are more assertive about their legal rights, making it difficult to control correctional facilities. There are also reports of increased prison violence as a result of court-ordered reforms that upset the balance of power within institutions and demoralized the staff (Powers and Rothman 2002). Correctional officers express concern about being sued or subjected to disciplinary measures. In Texas, the court dismantled the building tender system (the administration hand-selecting inmates to guard other inmates), which created a power vacuum before a sufficient number of correctional officers could be hired and trained. That vacuum resulted in a wave of prison violence. In 1984, 404 Texas inmates had been stabbed, 25 of those murdered, a dramatic increase from earlier years (Crouch and Marquart 1989). It took several years for the Texas prison system to regain control of its institutions.

Judicial intervention in prison reform also raises questions about the proper role of the judiciary. Instead of prison administration resting in the hands of the executive branch of government and the legislature, court-imposed reform shifts some of that authority to the courts. Most prisoner rights cases are filed in federal courts so federal judges, who are not popularly elected or accountable to the public, are deciding how prisoners must be treated and how state institutions, which are the responsibility of the executive branch, must implement their decisions. In many conditions cases, where court orders are complex and must be implemented over time, judges retain jurisdiction of cases for years, becoming major players in the administration of public institutions. Critics maintain that judges lack the experience and expertise to act in this capacity—they do not consider the costs of reform or have all the information and understanding needed to enforce it.

Christopher Smith (1986) notes that the primary criticism of judicial intervention is not whether inmates have constitutional rights, but the extent of those rights and the limits of judge-ordered reforms. Critics accuse judges of going beyond their appropriate role of identifying constitutional rights to the role of making public policy, which is the job of democratically elected legislatures and executive branch officers. They counsel for greater judicial restraint. Smith suggests that prisoner lawsuits that raise issues about the constitutionality of specific rules and regulations are not subject to fierce criticism because such cases do not involve large expenditures of funds and substantial reforms. The conflict is primarily over the Eighth Amendment living conditions cases in which courts have interpreted the meaning of the Cruel and Unusual Punishment Clause to find prison conditions unconstitutional and have ordered extensive remedies that affect the day-to-day operation of correctional facilities.

In response to critics, defenders of judicial intervention argue that prisoners are not a politically popular group and are not able to advocate for themselves, and their families are generally members of politically and economically powerless communities. Experience demonstrates that political leaders are not responsive to problems in America's correctional institutions. Judicial activism, they maintain, is the only feasible road to constitutional prisons and jails.

The PLRA

In 1996 the U.S. Congress responded to the explosion of inmate litigation and concerns about judicial intervention by enacting the Prison Litigation Reform Act (PLRA). Supporters of the PLRA point to the burden that inmate lawsuits have imposed on the federal court system and point out that a significant number of these lawsuits are frivolous or without legal basis. A major supporter of the PLRA was the National Association of Attorneys General, the organization of state attorneys who represent the state correctional officers and agencies that inmates sue. Other supporters criticized the role federal judges were playing in prison and jail condition cases.

The PLRA takes two approaches to reducing inmate lawsuits. Several of its provisions try to reduce the number of inmate lawsuits by making it more difficult for inmates to file them. Other provisions place restrictions on how far a federal judge can intervene in a conditions case. One of the PLRA provisions requires inmates to use the internal grievance system available to them before they can file a lawsuit in federal court. This is referred to as "exhausting your administrative remedies" and is a doctrine found in other areas of the law. Although most prison systems have implemented inmate grievance systems, many prisoners do not trust the grievance process. In *Booth v. Churner* (2001), the Supreme Court ruled that prisoners must use the grievance system before filing a lawsuit even in cases where they are asking for money damages and the grievance system is not permitted to award money. A year later, in *Porter v. Nussle* (2002), the Court decided that the PLRA's requirement to exhaust the grievance system before going to court applies to all inmate claims, whether they address general living conditions or incidents involving particular inmates, excessive force, or any other complaint. The Supreme Court has made it clear that the PLRA's exhaustion requirement must be strictly enforced.

Under the PLRA, a prisoner cannot claim money damages for emotional injury he or she may have suffered as a result of an official's unconstitutional conduct unless the prisoner can also show he or she suffered physical injury. The majority of prisoners file their lawsuits *in forma pauperis* (IFP), requesting a waiver so they don't have to pay the costs of filing a lawsuit. The PLRA now requires prisoners who request IFP status to file a certified copy of their inmate trust fund account statement for the six months prior to filing their suit. Federal courts are required to assess a partial filing fee based on a percentage of the average monthly deposits in a prisoner's trust account. Inmates must make monthly partial payments until the full filing fee is paid. In what's referred to as its "three-strikes" provision, the PLRA does not allow a prisoner to file with *in forma pauperis* status if he or she, while incarcerated, has on three or more previous occasions filed a lawsuit that was eventually dismissed because the judge found it to be frivolous or malicious, or to have failed to state a legal claim that a court could recognize. The only exception to the three-strikes provision is if the prisoner can show that he or she faces immediate danger of serious physical injury. Finally, the PLRA has capped the amount of attorneys' fees that can be awarded in those lawsuits where an inmate is represented by a lawyer and is successful.

The PLRA provisions aimed at judicial intervention require that a judge who grants prospective (future) relief in a conditions case must make written findings that the relief he or she ordered is narrowly drawn, extends no further than is necessary to correct the violation, and is the least intrusive means to fix the constitutional problem. The federal judge is also required to consider any adverse impact the order may have on public safety and the operation of the criminal justice system. If a judge fails to make such written findings, a defendant can request the judge to immediately terminate the relief. This is an especially important provision because it applies even to cases decided before the PLRA was enacted and the written findings were required. Prospective relief can be terminated two years after it is granted if one of the parties requests termination or one year after the court denied termination. If a party files a motion for termination, the court must issue an automatic stay of any prospective relief that is to begin within 30 days, or 60 days with good cause.

The PLRA is a comprehensive attempt to reduce inmate litigation and court involvement in correctional agencies. The statute was controversial before it was enacted and remains so today. The inmate lawsuit provisions aim to force inmates to conduct a cost/benefit analysis before deciding to sue. Is a lawsuit worth paying the filing fee? Are there frivolous or malicious claims that could cause a case to be dismissed, creating a count toward a third strike? Is a lawsuit worth an attorney's representation, considering that legal fees will be capped if they're successful? The provisions aimed at federal judges severely restrict a court's ability to remain involved in the remedial phase of a lawsuit—the phase during which court orders and consent decrees are implemented. They also prohibit judges from approving consent decrees that include remedies not obviously required to fix a constitutional violation; in other words, remedies can never go beyond the constitutional minimum.

Studies show the PLRA has reduced the rate at which prisoners are filing civil rights lawsuits (Scalia 2002). Several of those studies warn, however, that unless the PLRA breaks the link between the number of lawsuits and the size of the prisoner population, an increase in the number of people incarcerated will reverse the downward trend in the overall number of lawsuits filed (Chessman, Hanson, and Ostrom 2000).

Conclusion

Prisoner litigation is now a fact of life in corrections. The PLRA may reduce the number of lawsuits filed by inmates, but it will never put the genie back in the bottle. Courts may issue decisions that pay deference to the judgment of correctional officials, but issues will arise that inmates decide to litigate and win. Prison conditions are always in flux. There will be instances where conditions will fall below the constitutional minimum, causing a court to intervene.

Litigation will continue to shape correctional policy and practices. However, it's unlikely to have the same kind of impact on corrections that it had in the 1960s and 1970s—perhaps a sign that the treatment of incarcerated offenders is evolving in a positive direction. What is especially interesting about the prisoners' rights revolution is its link to the larger civil rights movement. Also interesting is how courts have interpreted key provisions of the Constitution within the unique context of correctional institutions. Judges must consider the difference between applying the Constitution to the general public versus applying it to people who are imprisoned. Courts have made unpopular decisions by concluding that the Constitution protects even those who deserve to be punished because they broke the law. The debate now revolves around the extent of those protections and the judiciary's role in correcting constitutional violations.

References

Chessman, F., R. Hanson, and B. J. Ostrom. 2000. "The Tale of Two Laws: The U.S. Congress Confronts Habeas Corpus Petitions and Section 1983 Lawsuits." *Law and Policy* 22(2):89–113.

Crouch, B., and J. Marquart. 1989. *An Appeal to Justice: Litigated Reform of Texas Prisons*. Austin: University of Texas Press.

Feeley, M., and V. Swearingen. 2004. "Taking Stock of the Accomplishments and Failures of Prison Reform Litigation: The Prison Conditions Cases and the Bureaucratization of American Corrections: Influences, Impacts and Implications. *Pace Law Review* 24:433–475.

Hanson, R., and H. Daley. 1995. *Bureau of Justice Statistics Report: Challenging the Conditions of Prisons and Jails: A Report on Section 1983 Litigation*. Washington, DC: Department of Justice.

Jacobs, J. 1983. *New Perspectives on Prisons and Imprisonment*. Ithaca, NY: Cornell University Press.

Nathan, V. 2004. "Taking Stock of the Accomplishments and Failures of Prison Reform Litigation: Have the Courts Made a Difference in the Quality of Prison Conditions? What Have We Accomplished to Date?" *Pace Law Review* 24:419–426.

Powers, S., and S. Rothman. 2002. *The Least Dangerous Branch? Consequences of Judicial Activism*. Westport, CT: Praeger.

Sampson, R., and J. Lauritsen. 1997. "Racial and Ethnic Disparities in Crime and Criminal Justice in the U.S." In M. Tonry (ed.), *Ethnicity, Crime and Immigration: Comparative and Cross-National Perspectives*. Chicago: University of Chicago Press, 311–374.

Scalia, J. 2002. *Bureau of Justice Statistics Special Report: Prisoners' Petitions Filed in U.S.*

District Courts, 2000, With Trends 1980–2000. Washington, DC: Department of Justice.

Smith, C. 1986. "Federal Judges' Role in Prisoner Litigation: What's Necessary? What's Proper?" *Judicature* 70(3):144–150.

———. 2000. *Boundary Changes in Criminal Justice Organizations: The Governance of Corrections: Implications of the Changing Interface of Courts and Corrections.* Washington, DC: National Institute of Justice.

Cases Cited

Bell v. Wolfish, 441 U.S. 520 (1979).

Booth v. Churner, 532 U.S. 731 (2001).

Bounds v. Smith, 430 U.S. 817 (1977).

Cooper v. Pate, 378 U.S. 546 (1964).

Estelle v. Gamble, 429 U.S. 97 (1976).

Farmer v. Brennan, 511 U.S. 825 (1994).

Hudson v. McMillian, 503 U.S. 1 (1992).

Jackson v. Bishop, 404 F.2d 371 (8th Cir. 1968).

Johnson v. Avery, 393 U.S. 483 (1969).

Lewis v. Casey, 518 U.S. 343 (1996).

O'Lone v. Shabazz, 482 U.S. 342 (1987).

Porter v. Nussle, 534 U.S. 516 (2002).

Procunier v. Martinez, 416 U.S. 396 (1974).

Pugh v. Locke, 406 F.Supp.318 (M.D.Ala. 1976).

Rhodes v. Chapman, 452 U.S. 337 (1981).

Ruffin v. Commonwealth of Virginia, 62 Va. 790 (1871).

Talley v. Stephens, 247 F.Supp. 683 (E.D. Ark. 1965).

Turner v. Safely, 482 U.S. 78 (1987).

Whitley v. Albers, 475 U.S. 312 (1986).

Wilson v. Seiter, 501 U.S. 294 (1991).

Wolff v. McDonnell, 418 U.S. 539 (1974).

Related Websites

Commission on Safety and Abuse in America's Prisons

http://www.prisoncommission.org

Habeas and Prison Litigation Case Law Update

http://www.fjc.gov/public/pdf.nsf/lookup/Habeas.pdf/$File/Habeas.pdf

The Prison Litigation Reform Act

http://www.wnylc.net/pb/docs/plra2cir04.pdf

Discussion Questions

1. Discuss the impact prisoner litigation has had on corrections in the United States. Do you think the impact has been good or bad for the criminal justice system?

2. Why are critics of prisoner litigation concerned about the role of the federal courts?

3. Discuss how prisoners could seek to correct inhumane living conditions and constitutional violations if they were never permitted to file lawsuits. How meaningful are these other options?

4. Investigate whether the state prisons where you live have been involved in a living conditions lawsuit. What issues did prisoners raise? Has the court issued any orders?

5. Why did the Supreme Court end the "hands-off" doctrine in 1964? Is the doctrine still alive under the guise of courts paying judicial deference to correctional officials? ✦

Chapter 14
A Failure to Integrate

Equal Protection and Race in American Prisons

Chad R. Trulson, James W. Marquart, and Janet L. Mullings

In this chapter, the authors examine the racial segregation of prison inmates, along with an analysis of the Equal Protection Clause of the Fourteenth Amendment and how it applies to those incarcerated. The main question is whether discriminatory or differential treatment within a prison environment can be considered unconstitutional or a violation of the Equal Protection Clause.

As the authors state, the Equal Protection Clause applies to all United States citizens, both the free and those incarcerated. The clause does not specify that individuals or groups must be treated the same as other individuals or groups. However, the government must treat those individuals or groups who are "similarly situated" equally, as in the case of prisoners compared to free citizens. Nevertheless, prisoners are still provided their constitutional rights, although these rights are often diminished. In cases that raise questions of differential treatment based on subjective factors such as race, the Court has developed standard measures for determining whether differential treatment is found to be unconstitutional. These standards, along with the appropriate classification, are referred to as strict scrutiny (suspect/fundamental rights classification), middle-tier scrutiny (quasi-suspect classification), and the rational basis test (nonsuspect classification). At each of these levels the state prison system must justify the discrimination.

In the prison setting, the topic of race and segregation has been hotly debated. Those in favor of segregation policies cite the safety concerns surrounding race-based violence; those against it refer to the right to be free from racial segregation or blanket segregation policies. The authors provide a history of segregation within the United States prison system, using a variety of states as examples, along with an analysis of key Supreme Court cases, such as *Lee v. Washington* (1968) and *Johnson v. California* (2005), among others.

Introduction

The prison environment is shaped by what occurs outside of the prison walls (Sykes 1958). But at one time, prisons were closed institutions. They were literally closed to the public eye. They were out-of-sight and out-of-mind institutions; their conditions and operation were of little concern among the general public. But prisons were also closed in the sense that they shunned the social and legal progress of the wider society. The sentiment that correctional settings lagged 10 or 20 years behind the advances of the free world was not without merit. This was especially the case concerning the racial desegregation of inmates.

American prisons have been racially segregated to varying degrees for most of their history. Even after the barrage of U.S. Supreme Court rulings in the 1950s and 1960s that struck down segregationist laws and practices in the larger society, prison administrators routinely segregated prisoners well into the 1980s, and beyond in some states. In fact, prisons were one of the final public institutions in American society to be desegregated. And not all of them have done so today; there is much variation in our nation's prisons.

Variations in the level of segregation in U.S. prisons are linked to one's definition of *desegregation*. Almost all prison systems in the country are desegregated to some degree in large areas of the prison environment, such as cellblocks, tiers in a cellblock, dormitories, the yard, and dining halls (Henderson et al. 2000). However, a number of prison systems do not actively desegregate prisoners within the same double cell. Some people believe that if inmates of different races do not share the same double cell, the prison system is still racially segregated to a large degree. Others believe that as long as different-race inmates share other areas of the prison, such as cellblocks and dining halls, they are desegregated. Thus, whether a prison system is segregated or desegregated depends heavily on one's definition of these terms.

Despite these definitional issues, history has shown that little concern existed that prisons did not follow the wider society when it came to racial desegregation. Administrators argued that prisons held the most violent and unstable people in American society—and that they were full of individuals who viewed race as one of the most important influences on their behavior (Irwin 2005; Jacobs 1983). As such, mandates of the wider society to racially integrate did not apply. Prisons were a world unto themselves, and a different set of rules was appropriate, according to prison administrators.

As time passed, however, disfavor fell on the view that prisoners had no rights and could be treated on the whims of prison administrators. In the decade of the 1960s and 1970s, the U.S. Supreme Court carved out guidelines for prison administrators concerning everything from inmate discipline to health care. These rulings conveyed that prison settings were not immune from the progress of the free society, regardless of the views of prison administrators. One litigated issue was the racial desegregation of inmates. On this issue, the Court held that like in the free society, racial discrimination by prison authorities was unconstitutional. It mattered little that those being discriminated against were prison inmates. Racial segregation in prisons and jails, according to the Court, was an invidious discrimination that violated the Equal Protection Clause of the Fourteenth Amendment (Baker 2004, 2).

Equal Protection and Prisons

Equal protection is the constitutional guarantee under the Fourteenth Amendment that persons or classes of persons must be treated equally with respect to governmental laws, regulations, and practices

(*Black's Law Dictionary* 1999, 557). Section 1 of the Fourteenth Amendment reads:

> All persons born or naturalized in the United States, and subject to the jurisdiction thereof, are citizens of the United States and of the State wherein they reside. No State shall make or enforce any law which shall abridge the privileges or immunities of citizens of the United States; nor shall any State deprive any person of life, liberty, or property, without due process of law; *nor deny to any person within its jurisdiction the equal protection of the laws.* (italics added)

The Equal Protection Clause of the Fourteenth Amendment applies to prison inmates in many of the same ways that it applies to free citizens. Although prisoners have diminished constitutional rights when they are incarcerated, the U.S. Supreme Court has held that there is "[n]o iron curtain drawn between the Constitution and the prisons of this country" (*Wolff v. McDonnell* 1974, 556). Thus, like free citizens, prisoners have rights under the Constitution and are protected from differential treatment under the law.

The Fourteenth Amendment's Equal Protection Clause does not specify that the government must treat every person or groups of persons the same as every other individual or group (Baker 2004). What it has been interpreted to mean is that *similarly situated* persons must be treated equally. For example, it is not necessarily an equal protection violation to treat innocent citizens and criminals differently—criminals have broken the law and their status as convicted criminals may justify differential treatment, such as imprisonment (Baker 2004). Innocent citizens and convicted felons are not "similarly situated."

Inmates are not completely barred, however, from claiming that as a group they are treated differently than free citizens and that such differential treatment violates the Constitution. This differential treatment could be an equal protection violation but only under circumstances where the treatment of prisoners is based on a factor not directly related to their status as criminals, such as race (Baker 2004). Using a person's race in devising a governmental policy, for example, is almost never justifiable, regardless of whether the policy is affecting free citizens or prisoners. Additionally, it may be an equal protection violation in some circumstances if a certain group of prisoners is treated differently than another group. For example, giving Catholic inmates certain in-prison privileges but not Muslim prisoners would be an equal protection violation.

Although the equal protection guarantee bars differential treatment, there are occasions in which persons or classes of persons may be legally and constitutionally treated differently from others. In short, not all discrimination or unequal treatment violates the Constitution. This type of legal discrimination may occur when there is some valid governmental reason for doing so. There are, for example, numerous reasons that persons under age 18 may be treated differently than persons over 18. From a governmental standpoint, juveniles are less mature, less experienced, and more vulnerable to harm than adults—thus, their rights are *diminished* in certain areas so that the government may regulate more aspects of their behavior (Peltason and Davis 2000). The rationale is that juveniles' status (being young) indicates that they are not fully ready to handle all life responsibilities and that there is some valid governmental interest in treating them differently from adults to protect them.

Like the treatment of juveniles and adults in the free society, there may be several reasons that treating one group of prisoners differently than another can be justified. For instance, prison administrators may argue that such differential treatment is necessary to operate a secure and controlled prison environment, which could not otherwise be accomplished by giving all inmates or groups of inmates the same degree of "equal protection." Thus, ensuring prison security by treating one group of inmates differently than another group may be a legitimate governmental reason to discriminate in prisons.

Any time governmental legislation impinges on the right to equal protection, however, such impingement must be justified, even in a prison setting. Sometimes the justifications are not enough for the courts; in those cases, discriminatory laws, regulations, and practices are held unconstitutional. Whether or not discriminatory treatment is judged constitutional depends on a number of factors, including the type of differential treatment (such as different treatment by race/gender/age/religion), the arena in which differential treatment occurs (such as in prisons versus outside of prisons), and the rationale or basis for the differential treatment.

Standards for Determining Whether Unequal Treatment Violates Equal Protection

Suspect Classifications and Strict Scrutiny

Four classifications are used, along with three different standards of review, when considering whether differential treatment is justified and hence constitutional. The first classification is *suspect classification*. Race, religion, and alienage (being of noncitizen status) are what the Court considers *suspect classes* (Peltason and Davis 2000). In cases involving suspect classifications, courts evaluate whether differential treatment is of such a *compelling* nature and *narrowly tailored* that it can be justified as valid. This standard is called *strict scrutiny*. In an equal protection analysis, all differential treatment based on suspect classifications is considered inherently invalid and unconstitutional and thus deserves the highest level of scrutiny applied by the courts.

To justify differential treatment of a suspect class under a strict scrutiny analysis, the government (state prison system) must show that there is a compelling governmental interest (such as security in a prison) to discriminate based on a suspect classification (such as race), and that the legislation authorizing the discrimination is the only method that could be used (narrowly tailored) to serve that compelling governmental interest. For example, a prison system with a blanket policy of segregating all inmates by race for generalized fears of racial violence may face an equal protection issue. Under strict scrutiny, the prison system would have to prove that security is a compelling interest of prisons and offer convincing evidence that racially segregating all inmates is the only way that prisons authorities can prevent racial violence (Khoo 2005).

Security is obviously a compelling interest of prison administrators and the state, but it may be difficult to argue that in all instances members of different racial groups must be separated because that is the only way to ensure safety and security in prisons. Such a policy of racial discrimination would not likely be considered "narrowly tailored" by the courts, for there are perhaps other alternatives that could be used to ensure security without having to resort to complete racial segregation of all inmates. Rarely do cases survive strict scrutiny, because it is difficult to justify treating classes of persons differently based on such suspect classifications as race—even in prisons.

Fundamental Rights Classifications and Strict Scrutiny

Outside of suspect classifications, some rights are considered so fundamental that legislation impinging on them is subject to strict scrutiny as with suspect classifications. These so-called *fundamental rights* include the abilities to vote, get married, procreate, access the courts, and others enumerated in the Bill of Rights. Any legislation that infringes on a fundamental right must be justified under strict scrutiny, and thus be supported by a compelling governmental interest. Indeed, the very nature of the right to marry, vote, or procreate is so fundamental to the freedoms of American society that the highest standard of review is used to make sure that diminishing or taking away those rights is absolutely necessary and justified.

Quasi-Suspect Classifications and Middle-Tier Scrutiny

Outside of suspect classifications there are *quasi-suspect classifications,* which include gender and illegitimacy. While suspect classifications and fundamental rights are held to strict scrutiny in an equal protection analysis, quasi-suspect classifications are analyzed under a more lenient test. The *middle-tier scrutiny* (or intermediate scrutiny) standard of review for quasi-suspect classifications means that the government must show that the differential treatment is related to an *important governmental interest* and is *substantially* related to serving that interest (Peltason and Davis 2000).

Nonsuspect Classifications and the Rational Basis Test

In cases involving classifications that are not suspect or quasi-suspect or those involving fundamental rights, the Court uses what is called the *rational basis test* or *minimum scrutiny* to determine whether the legislation authorizing differential treatment is constitutional. Rational basis is the lowest level of scrutiny applied by the courts. Unlike cases involving suspect classifications, fundamental rights, and quasi-suspect classifications, the Court presumes under the rational basis test that governmental actions are valid and constitutional unless it can be otherwise shown that there is no *legitimate governmental interest* for the law, regulation, or practice.

Rational Basis as a Test for Prisons

In 1987 in *Turner v. Safely*, the Court ruled on a case involving a Missouri inmate who sued prison officials over a prison policy that banned correspondence among prisoners at different institutions within the state (Hemmens, Belbot, and Bennett 2004). The Court held that a Missouri correctional system prison regulation that restricted inmates from corresponding with other prison inmates was constitutional. Although sending and receiving correspondence is embodied in the First Amendment, and is thus a fundamental right that would normally be judged under strict scrutiny, the Court held that prison systems must only show that a "legitimate state interest" exists when prison regulations impinge on inmates' constitutional rights. Thus, in Turner, the Court said that the rational basis test was the appropriate standard of review in prison cases where a prisoner's constitutional rights are being violated or diminished; even involving fundamental rights and suspect classifications (Hemmens 2000, 22).

This lower standard of review for prisoners was rationalized by the Court when they recognized the differences between prisons and free world institutions by saying that such "a standard is necessary if prison administrators . . . and not the courts, [are] to make the difficult judgments concerning institutional operations" (*Turner v. Safely* 1987, 89). According to the Court, what rights inmates do retain are those "not inconsistent with his status as a prisoner or the legitimate penological objectives of the corrections system" (*Turner v. Safely* 1987, 790).

Prisons hold some of the most violent and unpredictable individuals in American society. Because of this fact, the Court in *Turner* opted to give prison administrators more leniencies to run their institutions in a safe and secure manner. Thus prisoners' constitutional rights, including fundamental rights and suspect classifications, may be diminished because the safety and secure operation of the prison setting are paramount and override the individual rights of prisoners in some cases (see *O'Lone v. Estate of Shabazz* 1987) for a case involving religious freedom as a suspect classification and the rational basis test in prisons).

The rational basis test has four prongs the Court uses to determine whether a prison regulation that impinges on an inmate's rights is reasonably related to a "legitimate penological interest" (*Turner v. Safely* 1987, 84–91):

1. Whether there is a "valid, rational connection" between the regulation and a legitimate and neutral governmental interest put forward to justify it.

2. Whether there are alternative means of exercising the asserted constitutional right that remain open to inmates.

3. Whether and the extent to which accommodation of the asserted right will have an impact on prison staff, on inmates' liberty, and on the allocation of limited prison resources, which impact, if substantial, will require particular deference to corrections officials.

4. Whether the regulations represent an "exaggerated response" to prison concerns, the existence of a ready alternative that fully accommodates the prisoner's rights at de minimis costs to valid penological interest being evidence of unreasonableness.

These prongs indicate that prison rules that diminish inmates' rights must be reasonable. There must be a valid and rational reason to justify the rules, and the rules must not foreclose all avenues for the inmate to exercise his or her rights, as long as they are consonant to prison security. For example, the Court in *Turner* said that banning inmate-to-inmate correspondence is reasonable because it relates to prison security by preventing hit lists, escape plans, and gang recruitment. But the Missouri prison system regulation did not foreclose all correspondence by inmates, such as correspondence to free citizens.

The rational basis test is obviously a much lower burden to meet for prison officials than strict scrutiny, the test which would normally be required when dealing with suspect classifications and fundamental rights in the free society. As a result, the last several years have been characterized by the Court deferring to correctional administrators in almost all prisoner cases, including those with equal protection issues involving certain suspect classifications and fundamental rights. This is because prison administrators, and not judges, have greater expertise in running a prison (Hemmens 2000). Table 14.1 details levels of scrutiny and appropriate standards.

Despite the fact that prisoners are persons under the Constitution, prisoners' rights are generally diminished when compared to those of free citizens. As mentioned, the Court in the last several years has held that a greater degree of discretion should be given to prison administrators, even in dealing with certain suspect classifications and fundamental rights that would normally require strict scrutiny instead of rational basis (see *O'Lone v. Estate of Shabazz* 1987; *Turner v. Safely* 1987). However, the Court has not subjected race to a lower standard of scrutiny, even involving racial classifications in prisons.

<table>
<tr><td colspan="3" align="center">**Table 14.1**</td></tr>
<tr><td colspan="3" align="center">*Levels of Scrutiny for Violation of Constitutional Rights*</td></tr>
</table>

Level of Scrutiny	Standard	Classifications
Strict scrutiny	Law, regulation, practice is in response to a **compelling governmental interest** and **narrowly tailored** to achieve that interest	Suspect and fundamental rights
		Race, religion, and alienage
		Marriage, voting, and procreation
		Various provisions of the Bill of Rights
Middle-tier scrutiny	Law, regulation, practice is in response to an **important governmental interest** and regulation is **substantially related** to that interest	Quasi-Suspect
		Gender and illegitimacy
Minimum or rational basis	Law, regulation, practice is **rationally related to a legitimate state interest**	All other classifications
		Most prison cases, even those involving fundamental rights and certain suspect classifications

Racial Segregation in Prisons

In terms of equal protection, perhaps no other issue is as divisive and controversial as race. Issues involving equal protection and race in the wider society bring up such controversial topics as racial segregation and affirmative action. The controversy is no less intense in the prison setting, where race has been and continues to have a long and sordid history. In prisons, most of the racial issues have centered on the housing of inmates. The controversy is over whether prison administrators have an affirmative duty to desegregate prisoners in housing areas such as cellblocks and cells, and if so, under what circumstances racial segregation might be permissible to maintain a safe and secure institution.

There are two divergent camps on the issue of desegregation in prisons. Detractors of desegregation policies say that prisons are different places than free world institutions: prisons hold the most violent felons in the country, and race is a salient influence on prison behavior—in fact, it dominates inmates' lives (Irwin 2005; Jacobs 1983). Prisons are not like schools and parks and buses; rather, they are total institutions in and of themselves that require a different set of rules. The world in which prisoners coexist turns the values of most free citizens upside down; prison administrators need deference to run prisons in light of these issues, including the freedom to racially segregate prisoners to prevent race-based violence.

Advocates of desegregation policies in prisons hold that equal protection and the right to be free from racial discrimination apply to prisons just like they do in the free society. While there may be limited and specific instances in which race and racial tensions should be taken into account for security reasons, promoting a blanket segregation policy is divisive for inmates. They hold that segregation promotes stereotyping and exacerbates racial cleavages that lead to race riots and incite the very violence that segregation is supposed to prevent (*Johnson v. California* 2005).

The Court has visited this issue directly only twice in almost 40 years, once in 1968 in *Lee v. Washington* and again in 2005 in *Johnson v. California*. In both cases, the Court held that blanket policies of prisoner segregation are unconstitutional; racial discrimination is "as intolerable within a prison as outside, except as may be essential to prison security and discipline" (*Cruz v. Beto* 1972, 326). Even when prison security may dictate racial separation, however, only under the strictest of scrutiny will such separation be allowed (*Johnson v. California* 2005).

Pre-1968 Prisoner Segregation

Prior to 1968, prison systems around the country were marked by the almost complete segregation of races. For all intents and purposes, the pre-1968 prison was a mirror image of the wider society just 14 years earlier—separation by race was everywhere.

Segregation was most prevalent in Southern prison systems, especially in states like Alabama, Georgia, Mississippi, and Texas. Perhaps linked to the legacy of slavery, no pretense was made about the fact that prisoner segregation by race was based on the belief that white, black, and Hispanic prisoners could not be housed together. Indeed, the infamous Parchman Farm in Mississippi, the Georgia State Prison, the Alabama Cotton Mill, and the Texas prison system's Eastham, Darrington, and Retrieve farms were prime examples of racial segregation in prisons.

In many cases, entire prisons were racially segregated, and this occurred well into the 1960s (Jacobs 1983). A 1963 publication from one Southern prison system makes note of the degree of segregation in their facilities: "[T]he type of prisoners are white, first offenders of all ages . . . habitual criminals and negroes over the age of 25 . . . Latin American first offenders and the best rehabilitative prospects under 25 . . . a prison farm where first offenders, negroes, are confined" (Hammett 1963, 92–93). The above narrative is not much different than the experiences of other state prison systems at the time (see Chilton 1991; Irwin 1980; Jacobs 1983; Oshinsky 1996; Taylor 1993; 1999; Yackle 1989).

Those systems without the facilities or resources to completely segregate entire prisons by race remained as racially segregated as possible in such areas as camps, buildings, cellblocks and dormitories, and in job assignments. Crouch and Marquart (1989) commented on segregation in Texas even after individual prison units were desegregated in 1965. Following unit desegregation, where whites and blacks and Hispanics could live in the same prison, the Texas prison system still maintained segregated work squads such as "white line," "black line," and "Mexican line," where segregated work squads would disperse from "all white tanks," "all black tanks," and "all Hispanic tanks." Likewise, Parchman Farm in Mississippi was "divided into fifteen field camps . . . segregated only by race and sex" until federal district court judge William Keady in *Gates v. Collier* (1972) ordered Parchman officials to "eliminate all racially discriminatory practices at the prison" (Oshinsky 1996, 138, 247).

Inmates prior to the 1960s were viewed as "slaves of the state" with few to no rights, so it is not surprising that prison administrators felt free to carry on the segregation tradition to the prison setting (*Ruffin v. Commonwealth of Virginia* 1871). In 1968, however, the U.S. Supreme Court ruled on a case from the Federal District Court for the Middle District of Alabama that would challenge prisoner segregation policies around the country.

The U.S. Supreme Court and Racial Segregation in Prisons

In 1966, the District Court for the Middle District of Alabama held in *Washington v. Lee* (1966) that an Alabama law allowing prisoner segregation by race was unconstitutional. Two years later on appeal, the U.S. Supreme Court affirmed this ruling in a short *per curiam* decision in *Lee v. Washington* (1968). Concurring with the opinion of the Court, justices Black, Harlan, and Stewart noted:

In joining the opinion of the court, we wish to make explicit something that is left to be gathered only by implication from the Court's opinion. *This is that prison authorities have the right, acting in good faith and in particularized circumstances, to take into account racial tensions in maintaining security, discipline and good order in prisons and jails.* We are unwilling to assume that state and local prison authorities might mistakenly regard such an explicit pronouncement as evincing any dilution of this Court's firm commitment to the Fourteenth Amendment's prohibition of racial discrimination. (italics added, *Lee v. Washington* 1968, 335)

The concurring justices had two major points: (1) in certain circumstances racial tensions may be taken into account to ensure prison security, and (2) such certain circumstances are not to be misinterpreted to mean that broad racial segregation is acceptable in a prison setting. The Fourteenth Amendment's prohibition of racial discrimination applies within as well as outside of prison walls.

Despite the Court's commitment to ending racial segregation in prisons, their short *per curiam* ruling led to several questions regarding the desegregation of inmates. The Court never explained how a prison system should desegregate, such as whether it should be voluntary or forced or whether desegregation should be done in cells, cellblocks, dormitories, or in all of these areas of prisons. Nor did the Court identify and explain which "particularized circumstances" would justify segregation of the races or whether such particularized circumstances implicated a temporary or long-term policy of racial separation. These omissions were important because the Court left many questions for prison officials to figure out as they attempted to desegregate prisoners.

As a result of the ambiguities in the *Lee* case, prison administrators around the country were not quick to desegregate the prison environment. As Jacobs (1983, 84) explained, a "wait-and-see" attitude prevailed among prison administrators. This meant that prison systems around the country would continue to be segregated, especially in the South, where prison administrators

were already building a reputation for balking at orders of the courts when dealing with prison matters. A consequence was that numerous lower federal courts were left to sort out the special circumstances that would justify segregation.

Interpretation of *Lee* by the Lower Courts

Several lower federal court cases have dealt with inmate segregation. The most contentious aspect of these cases was the perspective that desegregation would result in extreme racial violence. Such fears of racial violence, according to prison administrators, satisfied the "particularized circumstances" requirement announced in *Lee* and required the segregation of inmates by race. The lower federal courts were left to decide whether the fears of racial violence proffered by prison administrators were valid, and hence justified racial segregation in prisons.

In one of the earliest post-*Lee* fear-of-violence cases, in *Rentfrow v. Carter* (1968), the District Court for the Northern District of Georgia declined to intervene when a group of white and black prison inmates, fearing racial violence in the face of forced integration, argued for a policy of "voluntary" desegregation. The court remarked that racial tensions do not constitute a "license for 'violent resistance'. . . . Rather, the tensions generate a need for a higher degree of restraint, for those who follow the path of 'violent resistance' will not halt desegregation, but will merely bring their own conduct to a halt by disciplinary action and criminal sanctions" (*Rentfrow v. Carter* 1968, 6).

In *McClelland v. Sigler* (1972) inmate segregation was also found unconstitutional in a maximum security housing unit in the Nebraska Penal and Correctional Complex. In this case, 50 white inmates were housed in "East Cell House" because they refused to be housed with black inmates. The Eighth Circuit Court of Appeals held that Nebraska prison administrators' refusal to integrate based on the fear of racial violence did not justify inmate segregation. The court remarked that "if disruptions would occur as a result of the desegregation of this facility we would expect that administrators would take appropriate action against the offending inmates . . . the image of the entire Nebraska penal system being held at bay by 50 prisoners is unacceptable . . . to reward them for their intransigent racial attitudes, cannot be legally sanctioned" (*McClelland v. Sigler* 1972, 1267).

In *United States v. Wyandotte County, Kansas* (1973), the Tenth Circuit Court of Appeals ruled that the speculative fear of racial violence did not justify a racial segregation policy. The court remarked that desegregation in the Wyandotte County Jail "finally boils down to . . . a vague fear on the part of the authorities that desegregation may result in violence. This is not enough" (*United States v. Wyandotte County, Kansas* 1973, 7).

In *Stewart v. Rhodes* (1979), an Ohio federal district court held that prison officials of the Columbus Correctional Facility were unable to produce evidence to justify a policy of racial segregation based on the mere belief of possible racial violence. The court noted "because integration has not even been attempted. . .within the past ten years, prison officials could not have had any experience with the effects of integration on which to base their apprehensions" (*Stewart v. Rhodes* 1979, 1188).

In 1993, a massive riot broke out in Ohio's Lucasville correctional facility. Although there were many reasons for the riot, a major reason was that prison administrators in Ohio mistakenly believed that integration was to be blind without paying attention to other factors to promote prison security, such as the criminal sophistication of the inmate, prior incarcerations, any racial gang affiliation, and prior prison behavior (Henderson et al. 2000). In response to the violence, the District Court for the Southern District of Ohio in *White v. Morris* (1993) deferred to prison officials' judgment that segregation should take temporary precedence over the integration of offenders in light of the violent uprising. However, this deference was only a short-term measure, not a long-term policy.

One of the most recent desegregation cases in the lower federal courts comes from Louisiana where the Fifth Circuit Court of Appeals held in *Sockwell v. Phelps* (1994) that Angola's prison cells be desegregated. In at-

tempting to show that their policy of segregation was supported by enough "particularized circumstances" to warrant inmate segregation, prison administrators cited several factors: (1) that prison guards were unable to visually monitor cells, (2) prisoners in Angola are the "worst of the worst," (3) two instances of interracial violence occurred involving integrated cell partners, (4) racial supremacy groups existed in the prison ranks, and (5) interracial conflicts may have triggered more generalized racial violence (*Sockwell v. Phelps* 1994, 5–6). The court held that although the "particularized circumstances" exception in *Lee* had not been specifically defined, "The general rule is clear: a generalized or vague fear of racial violence is not a sufficient justification for a broad policy of racial segregation" (*Sockwell v. Phelps* 1994, 7; see also Rideau and Sinclair 1985).

The bottom line is that lower federal courts have had little patience with prison administrators who would cite vague fears of racial violence to justify segregation policies. In almost every instance, the lower federal courts have held that segregation is impermissible unless specific information and experience show that racial segregation is the only way to operate a safe and secure prison environment. Even then, segregation is to be only a temporary solution, not a blanket policy affecting all inmates.

The U.S. Supreme Court and the Last Example of Institutionalized Segregation

With the exception of California, every state correctional system, and the Federal Bureau of Prisons (FBP), officially prohibits the racial segregation of inmates. In California, however, inmates are completely segregated by race in cells in inmate reception centers. Inmates are also racially segregated for a period of time when they are transferred to another prison in the state. After an inmate's initial reception phase (which lasts 60 days), offenders in the California prison system are reportedly desegregated through a voluntary process where they may choose a cell partner of another race, but they are not required to do so. Thus, in California's prisons, it is rare that inmates of different races share the same double cell, although the California prison system is fully desegregated in larger areas such as cellblocks, dormitories, yards, and dining halls.

According to California prison officials, the practice of racial segregation at reception and upon transfer is necessary to prevent violence among rival gangs aligned by race and ethnicity (Taylor 2004). Because administrators lack information about inmates at reception (such as gang affiliation), the claim is that all inmates must be segregated by race so that administrators can have time to observe and evaluate their security needs for proper housing (*Harvard Law Review* 2004).

In 1995, California prison inmate Garrison Johnson filed a complaint in the U.S. District Court for the Central District of California concerning the California prison system's use of race in housing. Johnson said that inmates "are housed in a two-man cell based on their ethnicity, which provokes racial tension and riots among different ethnic groups within California's prison systems" (Khoo 2005, 14). In 2005, the U.S. Supreme Court dealt with Johnson's claims and the CDC's blanket practice of segregating inmates by race.

The Court held in a 5–3 decision that segregation is impermissible unless deemed compelling under a proper strict scrutiny analysis—even in prisons. Delivering the majority opinion for the Court, Justice O'Connor wrote (*Johnson v. California* 2005):

> We have held that all racial classifications . . . must be analyzed by a reviewing court under strict scrutiny. . . .The need for strict scrutiny is no less important here. . . .Indeed, by insisting that inmates be housed only with other inmates of the same race, it is possible that prison officials will breed further hostility among prisoners and reinforce racial and ethnic divisions. By perpetuating that race matters most, racial segregation of inmates may exacerbate the very patterns of violence that it is said to counteract.
>
> The CDC invites us to make an exception to the rule that strict scrutiny applies to all racial classifications. . . .We decline the invitation. . . .Granting the CDC an ex-

emption. . .would undermine our unceasing efforts to eradicate racial prejudice from our criminal justice system.

Justice Thomas, joined by Justice Scalia, dissented to the majority opinion that strict scrutiny must apply to racial classifications within prison walls. Rather than viewing this as a case about race, Thomas felt it was more appropriately viewed as a prison case. Taking this point of view, he maintained that deference should have been given to California prison officials because the practice in California's prisons was not a policy of racism, but rather a way to protect inmates' safety. He remarked:

> The Constitution has always demanded less within the prison walls. Time and again, even when faced with constitutional rights no less fundamental than the right to be free from state-sponsored racial discrimination, we have deferred to the reasonable judgments of officials experienced in running this Nation's prisons. . . . California racially segregates a portion of its inmates, in a part of its prisons, for brief periods of up to 60 days, until the State can arrange permanent housing. The majority is concerned with sparing inmates the indignity and stigma of racial discrimination. California is concerned with their safety and saving their lives.

Although the Supreme Court ruled in *Turner* that prison rules that impinge on inmates' constitutional rights are valid if they are reasonably related to a legitimate penological interest, the Court in *Johnson* did not apply this to policies and practices that would provide for the racial segregation of inmates. Thus, while the rational basis test may apply to other fundamental rights and classifications in prisons, it does not apply to race—race must be evaluated with the strictest of scrutiny.

The Rationale for Desegregation in a Prison Setting

In 1954, the U.S. Supreme Court held in *Brown v. Board of Education* (1954) that "separate but equal" school policies were inherently unequal. According to the Court, segregationist practices, policies, and laws perpetuated a racial caste system that had adverse implications for an individual's opportunities and participation in social and political life (Jacobs 1983). It resulted in a "badge of inferiority" that had significant personal and social consequences (Kluger 1976).

After *Brown*, the Court struck down a number of segregation policies in other public facilities such as beaches (*Mayor and City Council of Baltimore v. Dawson* 1955), golf courses (*Holmes v. City of Atlanta* 1955), public transportation/buses (*Gayle v. Browder* 1956), parks (*Muir v. Louisville Park Theater Association* 1954 and *New Orleans City Park Improvement Association v. Detiege* 1958), athletic events (*State Athletic Commission v. Dorsey* 1959), airport restaurants (*Turner v. City of Memphis* 1962), courtroom seating schemes (*Johnson v. Virginia* 1963), and public auditoriums (*Shiro v. Bynum* 1964). Eventually, the mandate to desegregate was required of prisons with the Court's decision in *Lee v. Washington* (1968).

Although racial segregation in prisons was struck down in *Lee*, the Court never justified why desegregation should apply to prison settings. The Court in *Lee* never explained whether segregation in prisons results in disparate treatment or has other social consequences that were used to justify striking down segregation policies in other aspects of public life, such as in schools or universities. Therefore, it was simply assumed that segregation in prisons was unconstitutional for the same reasons it was in the wider society—namely, that segregation results in a negative label placed on persons or groups of persons simply because they belong to a particular racial group, and such a label can have detrimental personal, social, and political consequences. But in reality, the Court never went so far as to suggest this line of thinking. Rather, by all indications, segregation in prisons was struck down in *Lee* because "racial discrimination by governmental authorities in the use of public facilities cannot be tolerated" (*Washington v. Lee* 1966, 331).

To uncover the justification for desegregation in prisons, one must look to the lower federal courts. A few lower federal court judges justified desegregation in prisons by comparing prison to other social settings, such as schools and parks. Such comparisons created controversy. James Jacobs (1983) argued that prisons are much different places than schools or other public settings in which segregation threatens opportunities and results in other personal, social, and political consequences. He remarked that in prisons "there are few if any benefits at stake. Whereas parents pin their hopes and dreams for their children on educational achievement, the only hope in prison is for survival . . . analysis of prison race relations has, from the beginning, been distorted by the school analogy" (p. 86).

Jacobs's analysis was partly in response to the 1972 Eighth Circuit Court of Appeals case of *McClelland v. Sigler*, in which the court rationalized desegregation in prisons in the same way as desegregation in school settings. In clarifying his position that segregation in schools should be viewed differently than the same concept in prisons, Jacobs (1983, 87) remarked:

> The situation in today's prisons is different. Blacks are frequently the majority, not the minority, and administrative methods for controlling race conflict do not bespeak contempt for either blacks or whites. While the insult to blacks intended by the South's racist system was clear to anyone, black or white, the meaning of certain racially conscious administrative practices in today's prisons is hardly to be understood in the same way. Just as it is the case with affirmative action that there are legitimate reasons for treating people as members of a racial group, so too in prisons there may be good reasons for taking race into account.

While some disagreed with his perspective (see Walker 1985), Jacobs's legal view was that prisons are so inherently different from other free world institutions that "actions appropriate in one context may be wrong in another" (Jacobs 1983, 98). He held that inmates are in a different situation than citizens in the free society, that racially motivated conflict—including extreme violence—is a reality of institutional life, and that the benefits (if any) in prison are equally diminished for all racial groups, whether segregated or not and whether involving minority or majority groups. Thus, Jacobs' suggested that separate is actually equal in a prison—everyone is "equally segregated," and thus any benefits and burdens of segregation are equally applied to all racial groupings.

A few issues have been raised with Jacobs's analysis. First, despite the fact that prisoners have diminished rights and prison authorities have been given due deference to operate their prisons safely and securely, "equal discrimination is still discrimination that violates the individual's constitutional right to be free of. . .segregation and discrimination based on race" (Baker 2004, 3). Second, holding back benefits from one group of prisoners may indicate equal protection violations. For example, rehabilitation programs and work assignments are significant benefits for inmates in prison settings, but there was evidence in some prison systems that members of different racial groups were not treated equally with respect to these programs because of their race (Walker 1985). Differential treatment in these areas by race would mean that one group, simply because of their race, would receive consequences not felt by another group. These perspectives and others fueled the controversy about racial desegregation in prisons.

Despite these relevant concerns, no other factor has sparked more controversy than fear that the free world justification for desegregation would collide with the reality of the prison environment and lead to extreme racial violence.

The Impact of Desegregation on Violence in Prisons

Racial violence was the subject of most federal court cases dealing with prison desegregation, but like many courts have observed, it was supported only by speculative and generalized fears. Such speculative fears of racial violence were not enough, according to the courts, to justify a policy of racial segregation. At the turn of the millennium, evidence began to surface on what happens when inmates are actually desegregated.

In 2000, Henderson and colleagues conducted a national survey of prison wardens on the racial integration of cells. Among other areas, Henderson and colleagues revealed that 70 percent of wardens believed racial desegregation in cells would decrease or have no effect on the level of inmate-on-inmate violence. Moreover, 90 percent of wardens felt that conflict in cells with different race cell partners was much less, less, or about the same as conflict in segregated double-cells (Henderson et al. 2000). Thus, from corrections professionals' perspectives, racial integration would have a negligible if any impact on racial violence in prisons. It should be noted, however, that Henderson and colleagues also revealed that the majority of wardens reported that a large proportion of their inmates were not desegregated within prison cells. Although dining areas and larger housing areas such as cellblocks and dormitories were integrated in general, few inmates nationwide were found to be integrated within prison cells. This reality could certainly have affected wardens' perceptions on the potential for racial violence and conflict.

In 2002, Trulson and Marquart studied the impact of desegregation in the aftermath of *Lamar v. Coffield* (1977), a class action case out of the District Court for the Southern District of Texas that forced desegregation on the entire Texas prison system. The Texas prison system entered into a consent decree to avoid judgment by the court that racial discrimination and equal protection violations existed throughout the system. Despite the consent decree, Texas did not desegregate its prisoners. In fact, Texas prison authorities paid little attention to the desegregation decree for nearly 15 years.

In 1990, and in the face of stiff contempt fines, Texas prison administrators agreed to desegregate their prisoners within cells. Moreover, the court approved an Incident Data Form (IDF) to track inmate-on-inmate assaults following desegregation. This form allowed for the collection of a wealth of information, including the race of the inmates involved in incidents, whether the incident occurred among cell partners, whether it was gang related, and/or whether the incident was racially motivated. The IDF was the first of its kind to track specific levels of violence following the desegregation of prisoners within cells (Trulson and Marquart 2002).

In 1998, Trulson and Marquart were allowed unparalleled access to Texas prison system records dealing with the *Lamar* case and were given full access to ten years of IDF forms (Trulson, Marquart, and Mullings 2004). Trulson and Marquart (2002) analyzed a total of 39,000 inmate-on-inmate incidents in the Texas prison system from 1990 to the end of 1999—an average of about 4,000 inmate-on-inmate incidents per year.

Focusing only on cell partners incidents, Trulson and Marquart (2002) uncovered 6,459 cell partner incidents out of the total 39,000 incidents. Among those cell partner incidents, 52 percent occurred among racially integrated cell partners and 48 percent occurred among same-race cell partners. Overall, however, the *rate* of integrated cell partner violence was less that the rate of violence among cell partners sharing a cell with someone of their own race. At this point, their study revealed that desegregation within cells did not result in any more violence than segregation (Trulson and Marquart 2002).

Just because an incident occurs between two inmates of different races does not necessarily mean that the conflict was motivated by race. Rather, it could be motivated by a number of things, such as choosing a television channel. Taking this into consideration, there were a total of 1,691 racially motivated incidents among all Texas inmates, with only 333 being among racially integrated cell partners. Over the decade of the 1990s, this equaled less than one racially motivated incident per prison unit per year (Trulson and Marquart 2002). Certainly, this is not the level of racial unrest predicted by prison authorities prior to inmate desegregation within cells.

The best evidence on the aftermath of desegregation shows that it has *not* resulted in disproportionate racial violence, in or out of cells. The Henderson study revealed that wardens believed desegregation would have little impact on levels of violence, and some believed it would actually reduce tensions and violence. Moreover, while the 333 racially motivated incidents among integrated cell partners in the Trulson and Marquart study would have been prevented with continued racial segregation, the fact remains that those incidents accounted for less than 1 percent of all incidents in one of the largest and most diverse prison systems in the country. This is not the bloodbath predicted by numerous prison authorities in the aftermath of the *Lee v. Washington* (1968) decision and in other federal court cases since.

What Inmates Think About Desegregation in Prisons

Only one study has tackled the issue of whether inmates believe race is a problem in prisons and specifically whether they prefer segregation to desegregation. Hemmens and Marquart (1999) conducted a survey of recently released "exmates" from the Texas prison system. They asked exmates whether "race is a big problem" and whether they preferred different races to be separated in living areas. In this survey of 775 exmates, white and Hispanic inmates tended to agree or strongly agree that race is a big problem but blacks did not. Specific to desegregation, however, exmates tended to disagree with the statement that inmates should be separated in living areas. Although there was variation in responses, the overall consensus is that the issue of race is a bigger problem for inmates than having to live in desegregated housing areas.

In addition to Hemmens and Marquart's survey of exmates, Trulson and Marquart (2001) placed a general survey in the Texas inmate newspaper, *The Echo* concerning racial desegregation in prisons. Inmates were asked to comment on whether desegregation increased tensions, whether they preferred to be in segregated housing, and what advantages and disadvantages they saw in desegregation. Trulson and Marquart received over 400 responses from inmates. In general, most inmates appeared to be against desegregation, noting that it caused considerable tension and fights. Because this was not a scientific survey and used a convenience sample of inmates, it is likely that Trulson and Marquart received a biased response concerning desegregation. Nonetheless, results from their survey showed that white inmates were most opposed to desegregation, whereas black and Hispanic inmates either supported or were ambivalent toward the policy. Despite their attitudes, however, evidence on assaults from the Texas prison system revealed that integration did not result in disproportionate racial violence. Indeed, sometimes people's actions are much different than what they think or say.

From the best evidence then, the verdict is still out on whether inmates prefer integration to segregation. But in one prison system, it appears that despite preferences for a segregated prison system, desegregating prisoners did not unleash the racial violence and unrest previously predicted.

Discussion: Desegregation Is Not Integration

It is a reality that prisoners of different racial groups will associate with members of their own race and ethnicity to a large part. This is not much different in the wider society, where individuals tend to "stick with their own." Grouping together with similar others for solidarity or other reasons is simply a natural response; it happens on the outside, just as it does in prisons. The bottom line then is that prisons and the wider society are really not *integrated* to a great extent; rather, they are *desegregated*. These two terms, integration and desegregation, imply totally different meanings. Desegregation, in general, means the removal of barriers that force the separation of people of different races. Integration is the incorporation of different races within institutions (*Black's Law Dictionary* 1999, 812). In simpler terms, desegregation is about removing barriers, whereas integration is a state of mind (Steinhorn and Diggs-Brown 1999).

The unfortunate reality of self-segregation and avoidance in prison settings or other batch living environments is that integration is not likely to be accomplished (Carroll 1974/1988; Irwin 1980). But, the Fourteenth Amendment's Equal Protection Clause only pertains to state-sponsored ac-

tions, not those that are the result of voluntary behaviors of prison inmates. Although prison policies and practices that mandate broad and long-term separation of the races are unconstitutional, voluntary actions and freedom of associations are given to prisoners to some degree. Whether desegregated or not, then, chances are prisoners will continue to self-segregate and avoid other racial group members when they have the chance.

To sum up, desegregation may be the best that is hoped for in a prison setting, because integration is a voluntary activity—it is a state of mind that cannot be forced. If integration occurs for some prison inmates because the barriers of segregation have been removed, this is a positive by-product. But integration is not even mandated in prisons, nor is it necessarily the goal. Indeed, if prison administrators can desegregate some of the most violent and problematic individuals in America without extreme violence, perhaps this is as successful as it can get in a place that may breed racial tensions and violence, or at the least, allow those attitudes to strengthen and thrive (Meachum 2000).

Conclusion: In the Most Unlikely of Places

Prisons in the United States had been racially segregated far longer than they have been desegregated. Vestiges of segregation still remain today even following the Court's recent ruling in *Johnson v. California* (2005), just as they did almost four decades ago following the Court's decision in *Lee v. Washington* (1968). Indeed, advances to prison settings usually lag years behind advances in the free society.

What is to be sure is that occurrences in the free world will eventually permeate the prison walls. But the extent of those occurrences is still left at issue in the area prisoner desegregation. Even in the Court's *Johnson* ruling, little guidance was given as to how and to what degree prisons should be desegregated and what specific circumstances justify the continued segregation of inmates by race, with the exception of full-scale race riots. These are only a few of the issues that were left unanswered by the Court. As a result, it will likely be up to lower federal court to carve out the more specific boundaries involving the segregation and desegregation of prison inmates. In the meantime, prison systems that still remain segregated to varying degrees will likely "wait and see" what will happen next, just as they did nearly four decades ago (Jacobs 1983).

What is not at issue, however, is that race remains one of the only classifications in prisons that must survive strict scrutiny to be constitutional—just as it must in the free society. Although prisoners have diminished rights, and the courts have deferred more and more to prison officials in the last several years to keep prisons safe and orderly, the walls of prison are not so thick that the Equal Protection Clause of the Fourteenth Amendment cannot penetrate them. But the fact still remains that desegregation is being done in a number of different ways and degrees in prison systems around the country, and it is still unclear the extent to which the Equal Protection Clause and future court rulings will affect that fact (Henderson et al. 2000). Only time and court rulings will shed more light on this issue and reveal the rules by which prison administrators must operate concerning racial desegregation.

What is interesting is that the prison may have been one of the last institutions in American society to be desegregated—it truly was the last vestige of segregation in American society. However, through court rulings and progressive correctional practices, prisons are fast becoming one of the most desegregated places in America. In some cases, prisons are desegregated to a degree not matched by other institutions in the free world. Despite the fact that they hold the most violent individuals in the country, efforts continue to make sure that prison settings are bound by the same restrictions as institutions in the free world when it comes to racial classifications. Whether this is good or bad, useful or not, makes little difference. The *Johnson* case made clear that only under the strictest of scrutiny may the use of racial classifications be permissible. Significantly then, prisons in the near future may emerge as examples of what might never materialize on the outside with presumably nonviolent and stable citizens.

References

Baker, Thomas. 2004. "Can States Segregate Prisoners by Race—Even Temporarily and for (Arguably) Good Reason?" *Preview* 2:64–68.

Black's Law Dictionary. 1999. 7th edition. St. Paul: West Group.

Carroll, Leo. 1974/1988. *Hacks, Blacks, and Cons: Race Relations in a Maximum Security Prison.* Original edition. Prospect Heights, IL: Waveland. Reprint, Toronto: Lexington Books.

Chilton, Bradley. 1991. *Prisons Under the Gavel: The Federal Court Takeover of Georgia Prisons.* Columbus: Ohio State University Press.

Crouch, Ben, and James Marquart. 1989. *An Appeal to Justice: Litigated Reform of Texas Prisons.* Austin: University of Texas Press.

Hammett, A. 1963. *Miracle Within the Walls.* Corpus Christi: South Texas Publishing Company.

Harvard Law Review. 2004. "Ninth Circuit Holds That Cell Assignments Based on Race Are Permissible." *Harvard Law Review* 117:2448.

Hemmens, Craig. 2000. "No Shades of Grey: The Legal Implications of Voluntary Racial Segregation in Prisons." *Corrections Management Quarterly* 4:20–27.

Hemmens, Craig, Barbara Belbot, and Katherine Bennett. 2004. *Significant Cases in Corrections.* Los Angeles: Roxbury.

Hemmens, Craig, and James Marquart. 1999. "The Impact of Inmate Characteristics on Perceptions of Race Relations in Prison." *International Journal of Offender Therapy and Comparative Criminology* 43:230–247.

Henderson, Martha, Frank Cullen, Leo Carroll, and William Feinberg. 2000. "Race, Rights, and Order in Prison: A National Survey of Wardens on the Racial Integration of Prison Cells." *The Prison Journal* 80:295–308.

Irwin, John. 1980. *Prisons in Turmoil.* Boston: Little, Brown and Company.

———. 2005. *The Warehouse Prison: Disposal of the New Dangerous Class.* Los Angeles: Roxbury.

Jacobs, James. 1977. *Stateville: The Penitentiary in Mass Society.* Chicago: The University of Chicago Press.

———. 1983. *New Perspectives on Prisons and Imprisonment.* Ithaca, New York: Cornell University Press.

Khoo, Adrianna. 2005. "The Defiant Ones: *Johnson v. California." Daily Journal Extra.* March 28, 2005.

Kluger, R. 1976. *Simple Justice.* NY: Alfred A. Knopf.

Meachum, Larry. 2000. "Prisons: Breeding Grounds for Hate?" *Corrections Today:* 130–133.

Oshinsky, David. 1996. *Worse Than Slavery: Parchman Farm and the Ordeal of Jim Crow Justice.* New York: Free Press.

Peltason, J., and Sue Davis. 2000. *Understanding the Constitution.* New York: Harcourt College Publishers.

Rideau, Wilbert, and Billy Sinclair. 1985. "Prisoner Litigation: How It Began in Louisiana." *Louisiana Law Review* 45: 1061.

Steinhorn, L, and B. Diggs-Brown. 1999. *By the Color of Our Skin: The Illusion of Integration and the Reality of Race.* New York: Penguin Group.

Sykes, Gresham. 1958. *The Society of Captives: A Study of a Maximum Security Prison.* Princeton: Princeton University Press.

Taylor, J. 2004. "Racial Segregation in California Prisons." *Loyola of Los Angeles Law Review* 37(1):139–152.

Taylor, William. 1993. *Brokered Justice: Race, Policies, and Mississippi Prisons 1798–1992.* Columbus: Ohio State University Press.

———. 1999. *Down on Parchman Farm: The Great Prison in the Mississippi Delta.* Columbus: Ohio State University Press.

Trulson, Chad, and James Marquart. 2001. Survey of Texas Prison Inmates on the Racial Integration of Prison Cells. Unpublished.

———. 2002. "The Caged Melting Pot: Toward an Understanding of the Consequences of Desegregation in Prisons." *Law and Society Review* 36:743–782.

Trulson, C., J. Marquart, and J. Mullings. 2004. "Breaking In: Gaining Entry to Prisons and Other Hard-to-Access Criminal Justice Organizations." *Journal of Criminal Justice Education* 15(2):451–478.

Walker, Samuel. 1985. "The Limits of Segregation in Prisons: A Reply to Jacobs." *Criminal Law Bulletin* 21:485–494.

Yackle, Larry. 1989. *Reform and Regret: The Story of Federal Judicial Involvement in the Alabama Prison System.* New York: Oxford University Press.

Cases Cited

Brown v. Board of Education, 347 U.S. 483 (1954).

Cruz v. Beto, 405 U.S. 319 (1972).

Gates v. Collier, 349 F. Supp.881 (N.D. Miss. 1972).

Gayle v. Browder, 352 U.S. 903 (1956).

Guthrie v. Evans, 93 F.R.D. 390 (S.D. Ga. 1981).

Holmes v. City of Atlanta, 350 U.S. 879 (1955).

Johnson v. State of California, 207 F.3d 650 (9th Cir. 2000).

Johnson v. California, No. 03-636 U.S. (2005).

Johnson v. Virginia, 373 U.S. 61 (1963).

Lamar v. Coffield, Civil Action No. 72-H-1393 (S.D. Tex. 1977).

Lee v. Washington, 390 U.S. 333 (1968).

Mayor and City Council of Baltimore v. Dawson, 350 U.S. 877 (1955).

McClelland v. Sigler, 456 F.2d 1266 (8th Cir. 1972).

Muir v. Louisville Park Theater Association, 347 U.S. 971 (1954).

New Orleans City Park Improvement Association v. Detiege, 380 U.S. 54 (1958).

O'Lone v. Estate of Shabazz, 482 U.S. 342 (1987).

Rentfrow v. Carter, 296 F. Supp. 301 (N.D. Ga. 1968).

Ruffin v. Commonwealth of Virginia, 62 Va., 21 Gant., 790, Va. (1871).

Shiro v. Bynum, 375 U.S. 395 (1964).

Sockwell v. Phelps, 20 F.3d 187 (5th Cir. 1994).

State Athletic Commission v. Dorsey, 359 U.S. 533 (1959).

Stewart v. Rhodes, 473 F. Supp. 1185 (S.D. Ohio 1979).

Turner v. Safely, 482 U.S. 78 (1987).

Turner v. City of Memphis, 369 U.S. 350 (1962).

United States v. Wyandotte County, Kansas, 480 F. 2d 969 (10th Cir. 1973).

Washington v. Lee, 263 F. Supp.327 (M.D. Ala. 1966).

White v. Morris, 832 F. Supp.1129 (S.D. Ohio 1993).

Wolff v. McDonnell, 418 U.S. 539 (1974).

Related Websites

Supreme Court Debates Use of Segregation in Prisons

http://www.usatoday.com/news/washington/2004-11-02-prison-racial-segration_x.htm?csp=36

Johnson v. California (2005)

http://caselaw.lp.findlaw.com/cgi-bin/getcase.pl?court=US&navby=case&vol=000&invol=03-636

Good Intentions Aside, Separate Still Isn't Equal

http://www.washingtonpost.com/wp-dyn/articles/A18477-2005Feb12.html?sub=AR

End Apartheid in the State Prisons

http://www.prisontalk.com/forums/showthread.php?t=14151

Cornell Law School Legal Information Institute

http://www.law.cornell.edu

Human Rights Watch: No Escape: Male Rape in U.S. Prisons

http://www.hrw.org/reports/2001/prison/

Discussion Questions

1. What are the various classifications and standards of review concerning equal protection issues? What did the Court say in *Turner* about prison rules that impinge on inmates' constitutional rights? What was the Court's rationale for the *Turner* ruling?

2. Discuss the idea that prisoners have "diminished" rights in prisons.

3. What would you say to someone who would advocate racial segregation in prisons?

4. What would you say to someone who would advocate racial desegregation in prisons?

5. Discuss evidence on the aftermath of desegregating prison inmates. Is this what you would have expected to occur? ✦

Chapter 15
Sex Offender Registration, Notification, and Civil Commitment Statutes

Due Process vs. Community Safety

Barbara Sims and Megan Reynolds

In this chapter, the authors examine the highly controversial issue of sex offender legislation. Specifically, it provides an objective look at the constitutional issues surrounding individual rights through key court decisions and sociolegal considerations that arise within both pro and con arguments. From past to present, sex offense crimes have been a hot topic. In some respect, the current political and judicial processes are influenced by public perceptions of violent sex offenders, which are partly fueled by frenzied media responses surrounding brutal but isolated sexual offense cases.

In recent decades, the Supreme Court, researchers, and other stakeholders have attempted to answer the question of whether sex offender registration is a violation of individual privacy rights, and in particular whether it constitutes a violation of the Eighth Amendment's Cruel and Unusual Punishment Clause of the Fourteenth Amendment's Due Process and Equal Protection Clauses. Those who question the constitutionality of sex offender registration and notification statutes cite concerns of extended punishment be-

yond the completed prison or jail sentence, question the efficacy of such policies, and wonder why other violent offenders, such as murderers, are not required to register. Those who support sex offender legislation make reference to public safety issues and say that registration and notification are for continued tracking, not further punishment.

Introduction

Sexual victimization in the United States is a critical social issue that has gained an extraordinary amount of attention in recent years. Rennison (2002a) reports that approximately 248,000 such incidences occurred in 2000. She also reports that over 366,640 attempted or completed rapes and sexual assaults were perpetrated against women over an 8-year period (Rennison 2002b). In 1998, 103,600 substantiated cases of sexual abuse against children were reported (Jones and Finkelhor 2001) in the United States. As noted by Welchans (2005), these numbers are likely to be grossly underestimated because of the vast number of sexual assault victimizations that go unreported each year.

Prison statistics reveal that more and more convicted sex offenders are being incarcerated across the United States and Canada. In one 2-year period (1988–1990) the incarceration of sex offenders increased by 48 percent, and about 33 percent of inmates in 1998 in state correctional facilities were in prison for some type of sexual offense (Becker and Murphy 1998). Motiuk and Belcourt (1996) report that about 24 percent of Canada's federal prison population in 1991 were sexual offenders.

It is not difficult to convince the public of the value and critical importance of sex offender registration and notification laws. The public now fears the worst and expects inappropriate and unacceptable behavior by a sexual offender. The media has contributed to what can best be described as a widespread fear of the sexual offenders living among us. Isolated, but well-publicized, portrayals of young children being snapped up and brutally abused and murdered fuel the current push for even more stringent requirements associated with convicted offenders. In some states, legislation is about to be introduced that would require the lifetime incarceration of repeat sexual offenders, a move that is akin to the three strikes legislation of the 1980s and beyond. In addition, some communities are moving to establish "no sex offender" zones, while others are looking at permanent electronic monitoring for all sex offenders.

Sex Offender Registration and Notification Legislation

Whether any of these measures will come to pass in any sustainable format is yet to be seen. What is certain is that the discourse among policymakers and concerned citizens is at an all-time high. Every state has now implemented registration and notification laws. Thirty states sponsor websites containing information about registered sex offenders (www.klaaskids.org, for example). The purpose of registration is to alert local law enforcement officers as to the whereabouts of sex offenders living within their jurisdictions. In essence, registration is a law enforcement tool, and officers can quickly match the crime scene evidence in a sexual offense against the modus operandi of registered sex offenders.

Notification is viewed as a way to protect citizens from sexual victimizations. Megan Kanka's (more on this case below) parents have argued that registration is not enough and that had they known that a sex offender lived across the street from them, their daughter might still be alive (Terry 2006).

Previous to the well-known case of Megan Kanka (a New Jersey 7-year-old who was sexually abused and murdered), Congress passed the Jacob Wetterling Act in 1994 in reaction to the 1989 kidnapping of an 11-year-old boy who has never been found. In that case, the local community discovered that sex offenders were residing in a local halfway house without notification of citizens. This federal law required states to create a sex offender and child abuse registry. Offenders are to be tracked for 10 years beyond release from incarceration. For chronic, repeat offenders, the legislation re-

quires lifetime registration (Office of the Attorney General 1999).

Megan's Law, passed by Congress in 1995, amended the Jacob Wetterling Act to require communities to implement notification measures when a sex offender is released from prison. This legislation extended the Wetterling Act by requiring state and local law enforcement agencies to release information found in the sex offender registry to local communities in which registered sex offenders have taken up residence. How local law enforcement implements the notification requirements of Megan's Law varies from one state or jurisdiction to another. The guidelines of the federal legislation make it clear, however, that the overall purpose of community notification is to assist both the police and the public in keeping a close and guarded eye on convicted sex offenders. In some communities, notification takes place by more passive measures such as posting information, along with pictures, of sex offenders on a website, while in other communities a more proactive notification system is in place (e.g., posting of placards and other materials in prominent locations throughout the community) (Welchans 2005).

After the sexual assault and near murder of a female real estate agent in Houston, TX, Congress further extended the notion of registration of sex offenders through the Pam Lychner Sexual Offender Tracking and Identification Act of 1996. This legislation requires lifetime registration for repeat offenders and for those whose acts are particularly heinous. In 1998 the Wetterling Act was further amended to include heightened registration requirements for "sexually violent offenders, registration of federal and military offenders, registration of nonresident workers and students, and participation in the National Sex Offender Registry." And in 2000 the Campus Sex Crimes Prevention Act was passed to require registered sex offenders to report their registration requirements to any institution of higher education at which they become employed or enrolled in classes.

The Wetterling Act, Megan's Law, and the Pam Lychner Sexual Offender Tracking and Identification Act were all enabled by a strong sense of outrage among the immediate victims' family members—or in the case of Pam Lychner, family members and herself. These cases provided the public with powerful images that were used by the media to portray the picture of violent sexual predators roaming freely in local neighborhoods. This situation harkens back to an earlier time in U.S. history when newly discovered interest in sexuality and so-called "sex crimes" by the media resulted in an arguably irrational reaction to these types of offenses by both the criminal justice and medical communities (Denno 1998). In 1937, J. Edgar Hoover, then director of the Federal Bureau of Investigation, declared a war on the "sexual criminal" and implored the American people to consider the fact that the "sex fiend, most loathsome of all the vast army of crime, has become a sinister threat to the safety of American childhood and womanhood" (Hoover 1937).

A Violation of Individual Privacy Rights?

Those expressing concerns about the due process of sex offenders in light of punishments added on beyond time served have now taken a seat at the bargaining table, but thus far, those voices have been silenced. Cohen (1995) has noted that registry and notification requirements for sex offenders is a violation of their privacy rights. Further, these requirements can be seen as punishment and thus not allowed under the Eighth Amendment's cruel and unusual punishment prohibition. To date, the courts, however, have failed to recognize such a violation. In *Connecticut Department of Public Safety v. Doe* and *Smith v. Doe* (both 2003) heard by the U.S. Supreme Court did not see a violation of due process rights associated with Megan's Law (the former case) and claimed further that requirements of registry and notification are tracking measures as opposed to means of further punishing sexual offenders (the latter case).

These rulings are not surprising, given an earlier and similar decision by the New Jersey State Supreme Court in *Doe v. Poritz* (1995). The Court ruled that registration and notification statutes do not violate the constitutional rights of sex offenders and refused to accept an argument that, as noted previously, such statutes extend punishment beyond a time when the offender has paid his or her dues to society and is released from incarceration. Nor did the Court see any problem with applying the laws immediately upon passage to all previously convicted sex offenders as opposed to applying them only to those offenders convicted of a sexual offense after the passage of the laws. As the Court so often has done, it created a balancing act, weighing the interest and safety of the public against the constitutional rights of a criminal defendant.

Violations of Equal Protection?

Although legislation ensures that sex offenders must register with local authorities and that local authorities must notify the community of offenders' presence among them, there is a great deal of variation across states when it comes to how notification occurs and for how long offenders must be registered (Terry 2006). In Illinois, for example, sex offenders register for a period of 10 years, while in California, they register for life. Further, in some states, registered sex offenders can petition the court to have their name expunged from the registry after some period of time. Here again, there is a great deal of variation. Whereas sex offenders can request to have their names expunged from the registry after 10 years in Washington, D.C., offenders in Florida cannot do so until after 20 years (Terry 2006).

It should also be pointed out that in most states, notification laws are based on a tier system and level of risk. Typically, no specific charge or charges are associated with a Tier 1, 2, or 3 offender; rather, both type of offense and offender characteristics are considered (Terry 2006). Tier 1 compromises the less serious offenders who are not a high risk for local communities. A Tier 1 sexual offender might be someone who has no prior record of offending, who perpetrated the incident in a nonviolent way, and who perhaps did no touching beyond the outer clothing of the victim (Terry 2006). A Tier 2 sexual offender may not be a violent predator, but touching under the clothing has occurred even though penetration has not. Further, this offender probably has no solid ties in the community and has had inappropriate sexual contact with a victim before. For both Tier 1 and Tier 2 offenders, most have perpetrated their crime against someone they know or even a family member.

Tier 3 sexual offenders pose the greatest threat to local communities. These individuals are often thought of as sexual predators. They usually have many more prior offenses and probably have assaulted a stranger. They may have some type of personality disorder and may have assaulted a young child (Terry 2006).

An argument could be made that because not all sex offenders are treated alike when it comes to registration and notification, a violation of the Equal Protection Clause has occurred. Further, Alexander (2004) has argued that sex offenders' equal protection is violated, since murderers, arsonists, and other felons serve their time and are released from prison with no further incarceration, civil or otherwise, and without having to register with local authorities and have their personal information put up on local law enforcement's website.

The Efficacy of Registration and Notification

In addition to concerns by some about the privacy and due process rights of sexual offenders, other issues are related to the efficacy of registration and notification. To be sure, it makes sense to have mechanisms through which to monitor and supervise people who prey sexually on others, especially the young victim. There is evidence, however, that a type of vigilante justice is occurring in some communities. This type of justice occurs when local citizens take the law into their own hands. As pointed out by Brooks (1996) and Steinbock (1995), *outed* sexual offenders have been violently attacked or faced with hostile demonstrations in front of their homes and while out and about in their local neighborhoods. It is possible that stress serves as a triggering device

for reoffending in the sexual offender (Edwards and Hensley 2001). If that is the case, one could easily argue that threats of violence and embarrassment in one's own immediate home environment could serve as just such a triggering device. Further, and as argued by Steinbock (1995), most child molestation is perpetrated by family members and not the stranger down the street. This means that sex offender laws may not be the best approach toward protecting children from becoming victims of sexual abuse.

Welchans (2005) examined 12 published evaluations in which researchers sought to examine the effectiveness of sexual offender registration and notification laws. Many of these studies concentrated on perceptions of sexual offenders themselves, while others focused on those who treat or monitor this population. In three of the studies, local citizens were queried regarding their views of sex offender legislation and registration and notification requirements. The publication date for these studies range from 1995 to 2003.

Welchans reports that some offenders were not aware of registration requirements. In some areas, however, those who were aware of such requirements did not appear to be overly concerned about them (Zevitz and Farkas 2000a). Very few people cited being violently attacked by community members or some other form of vigilante justice (Zevitz and Farkas 2000a). Some, however, reported that notification had totally disrupted their lives, and a high number reported (72 percent) that community notification regulations acted as a deterrent (Elbogen, Patry, and Scalora 2003). When it comes to surveys of probation/parole officers, most report the difficulties associated with finding housing and work for their clients (Zevitz and Farkas 2000b). One study of treatment providers revealed that about 80 percent of respondents did not believe that registration and notification would protect children from being sexually abused (Malesky and Keim 2001). Malesky and Keim (2001) found that some treatment providers expressed concerns about parents feeling a false sense of security through sex offender registration and notification laws.

Focusing more specifically on outcome-based research, Schram and Darling Milloy (1995) followed 125 sex offenders in Washington State for a period of 54 months who were subjected to community notification. A comparison group of sex offenders who were not subject to notification were also tracked over time. No statistically significant differences were found between the two groups, although those offenders in the notification group were arrested more quickly when a new crime did occur than were those in the no-notification-required group (Schram and Darling Milloy 1995).

Petrosino and Petrosino (1999) conducted a retrospective design looking at 136 diagnosed repeat sexual offenders. By examining the criminal records of these incarcerated individuals, the researchers were able to conclude that only 27 percent had arrests for previous sexual offenses, and of those, only one-third had been perpetrated on a stranger. Further examination of the case files led Petrosino and Petrosino (1999) to conclude that only six offenses among the total committed by the offenders might have been prevented by community notification and registration requirements.

As pointed out by Terry (2006) and others, many sex offenders fail to register with local authorities because of being embarrassed once the community is notified that they will be living among them. Or, if they do register, many do not notify the local authorities if they change addresses. Further, there are reports that the number of sex offenders who are failing to register is higher than once thought. In Massachusetts, for example, there is evidence that over 30,000 high-risk sex offenders cannot be located by local authorities (Mullvihill et al. 2003). There is not always personnel available to track down the whereabouts of sex offenders who have not registered or who have given false addresses and other contact information (Terry 2006). In the meantime, the public feels a sense of being protected and safe from sexual offenders when that may not be the case.

In 2006, Congress passed and the President signed into law H.R. 4472, the Adam Walsh Child Protection and Safety Act (the Act). Within the language of the legislation,

there is a clause recognizing the 25-year anniversary of the kidnap and murder of 6-year-old Adam Walsh. Within the legislation, offenses have been expanded and now include (1) kidnapping or imprisonment of a child; (2) solicitation of a child or actually engaging in a sexual performance with a child; (3) solicitation to engage a child in prostitution; (4) video voyeurism involving a minor; (5) possession, production, or distribution of child pornography; (6) criminal sexual conduct involving a minor or the use of the Internet for same; and (7) any conduct that by its nature is a sex offense against a minor. The act expands the already existing National Sex Offender Registry by linking the various state websites in such a way as to allow for the sharing of information across state lines. This will enhance the ability of child protective agencies to better conduct background checks of individuals seeking to adopt children or to conduct investigations of child abuse allegations.

The act also enhances the penalties associated with crimes against children, including tougher penalties for sex trafficking of children: States will also now find it less difficult to crack down on repeat sex offenders who fixate on children, including civil commitments beyond time spent in state prisons. Federal funds are being allocated to develop and maintain regional Internet Crimes Against Children task forces to deal with those individuals who prey on minors through the Internet.

When it comes to registration and notification, the act enhances penalties associated with sex offenders' failure to register and to keep their address current. Lifetime registration is now required for the more serious sex offender who targets a child, and there are enhanced penalties based on how offenders are classified. For Tier 1 offenders there is a 15-year registration period; for Tier 2 offenders, a 25-year registration period; and for Tier 3 offenders, lifetime registration. Offenders who change addresses will have only three business days to notify local authorities of their new address and risk a year in prison if they do not meet this deadline.

Unintended Consequences of Sexual Offender Registration and Notification Legislation

According to Denno (1998, 1319), "The current sex offender laws reflect yet another attempt toward a legal corrective . . . the same destructive social trends that made possible the original sexual psychopath statutes are also influencing the modern approach to sex offenders." The United States has a history of reacting relatively quickly to concerns about seeming violations of sexual mores and mainstream values. At the beginning of the twentieth century, for example, the introduction to the world of Freudianism and its use in psychiatry provided a backdrop for addressing concerns about the public's fear of a breakdown in the family structure as more knowledge about sexuality was brought to light (Denno 1998). "During the 1920s and 1930s, American psychiatry, the criminal justice system, and the public gradually began to add one more item to what had become the diagnostic wastebasket of psychopathy by viewing the psychopath as also a violent, male, sexual criminal" (Denno 1998, 1332).

As Denno notes, no one argues that sex crimes should go unpunished; rather, many consensual sexual acts between adults during this time period were caught up in the legal system because of a wide casting of the legal net. Efforts to address issues associated with this newly identified cast of deviants aimed to control both the effeminate homosexual and the hypermasculine male who came to be thought of as the violent sexual predator. Denno (1998, 1339) notes:

> Both extremes would eventually characterize the male sexual psychopath who increasingly resembled the Depression era male—an unemployed, nonprocreative, outcast devoid of familial bonds or social controls, defying socially cohesive values.

During this initial heyday associated with the enactment of sex crimes legislation, some states did not distinguish too well between the dangerous sex offender and the less serious offender (exhibitionists, "peeping Toms," people with sexual fetishes) (Denno 1998). As argued by Denno (1998, 1353), "the harmless groups thus constituted a substantial portion of institutionalized sex offenders." Although there was a push within the medical community to allow experts in their field to manage and treat sexual offenders, those efforts were primarily ignored by the lawmakers of the time.

Civil Commitment of Released Sex Offenders: Violations of Due Process?

As early as 1940, the U.S. Supreme Court upheld a state's right to civilly commit a sexual offender. In *Minnesota ex rel. Pearson v. Probate Court of Ramsey County* the Court upheld such action by the state of Minnesota, and for an individual who was assessed to have a psychopathic personality disorder. According to Alexander (2004), the Minnesota law under which Pearson was committed contains an element of eugenics. In other words, it was thought that some individuals, or undesirable classes, are hard wired genetically with a predisposition toward abnormalities and crime. The Pearson case highlighted the fact that the civil commitment statute passed in Minnesota in 1939 was directed toward "persons who were responsible in sexual matters" (Alexander 2004, 364).

Three cases illustrate a continued support by the U.S. Supreme Court of state civil commitment statutes for sexual offenders. It should be noted that all of these cases begin with legislation that has defined *violent predatory sex offenders*. In California, a sexually violent predator is defined as "a person who has been convicted of a sexually violent offense against two or more victims and who has a diagnosed mental disorder that makes the person a danger to the health and safety of others in that it is likely that he or she will engage in sexually violent criminal behavior" (Section 6600-6609.3 of the Welfare and Institutions Code of the state of California). This type of legislation has been passed in all 50 states, according to Doerner and Lab (2002), although far fewer states have moved toward actual civil commitment statutes.

In *Kansas v. Hendricks* (1997), the 1994 Sexually Violent Predator Act of the state of Kansas came under fire. This statute provides for the civil commitment of anyone found to have a mental abnormality or a personality disorder and who is likely to engage in predatory acts of sexual violence (see Kan. Stat. Ann. Section 59-2901 et seq, 1994). Hendricks had a long history of sexually molesting children and was about to be released from prison where he had served 10 years on a conviction of indecent liberties with two 13 year-old boys. By his own admission, treatment that had been administered through the years had not helped Hendricks control his inappropriate sexual attraction, urges, and behavior. The state of Kansas subsequently found Hendricks to be a sexually violent predator, and one who was likely to offend again. He was civilly committed and brought suit against the state for such commitment.

Overruling the finding of the Kansas Supreme Court that the civil commitment of Hendricks violated certain due process rights, the U.S. Supreme Court concluded:

1. there is no absolute right to be free from restraint from the government when there is cause to believe that an individual poses a danger to the larger society;

2. the requirement of some sort of mental disorder prior to restraint is in alignment with previous Court decisions;

3. the fact that the treatment community disagrees with the state of Kansas on the meaning or nomenclature surrounding the term "mental disorder" is not a reasonable defense since the Court has never required states to adopt one common meaning or definition of such terms;

4. since the commitment of Hendricks falls under civil proceedings, the Double Jeopardy Clause of the U.S. Constitution is not in question as that prohibition applies only to criminal proceedings;

5. the purpose of commitment is to monitor Hendricks until such time as he is no longer a perceived threat to society so

the purpose of the statute is not punitive in nature;

6. even if Hendricks is not amenable to treatment, the Court has, in the past, upheld the civil commitment of individuals under the philosophy of incapacitation; thus, Hendrick's argument that the state is further punishing him knowing he cannot get better with treatment, fails; and,

7. similarly, the Ex Post Facto Clause pertains only to criminal proceedings, not civil proceedings.

Four years after *Hendricks*, and in *Selig v. Young* (2001), civil commitment statutes were questioned on constitutional grounds yet again. Young was committed under the Washington State Community Protection Act of 1990, defining a sexually violent predator as "someone who has been convicted of, or charged with, a crime of sexual violence and who suffers from a mental abnormality or personality disorder that makes the person likely to engage in predatory acts of violence if not confined to a secure facility" (as cited in Alexander 2004, 366–367). Similar arguments regarding due process and the fact that commitment is, in fact, a criminal proceeding, failed before the Court. Once again, the Court ruled that such a process was civil in that the constitutional issues typically addressed in criminal proceedings simply do not apply here.

In *Kansas v. Crane* (2002), the Court was asked to reconsider its decision in *Hendricks*. Crane was committed after having exposed himself to two women and ordering one of them to perform oral sex on him. The incident ended, however, without sexual acts committed and with Crane running away from the two women. Yet, the state found that Crane was unable to control his sexual urges and civilly committed him under the Kansas Sexually Violent Predator Act. Crane argued that the state would need to show that he was totally out of control before committing him, but he lost in the higher Court. The U.S. Supreme Court ruled that the state need not show that a defendant is totally out of control; rather, it need only show that an individual is incapable of controlling sexual urges. In essence, the Court upheld its previous holdings when dealing with civil commitments.

Alternatives to Sexual Offender Registration and Notification Laws and Civil Commitment Statutes

It has been suggested (Alexander 2004; Pallone 2003) that other alternatives could be used when it comes to closely managing sex offenders, as opposed to registration and notification and civil commitment. With some expressed firsthand knowledge about the sex offender who murdered Megan Kanka (Jesse Timmendequas), Pallone (2003) argues that a plea bargain should not have been struck for the offense for which he was released just prior to raping and murdering Megan. Rather, and because this was his second and known attack on a child, Timmendequas should have been given a 30-year sentence. Because of plea bargaining, however, the defendant received a sentence of only 10 years.

Because of the Timmendequas case, and perhaps other similar cases, Pallone (2003) declared that plea bargaining should not be an option for pedophiliac rapists and that such a move should be coupled with *enhanced sentencing* in those types of cases. As of 1998, several states had moved to provide enhanced penalties for repeat sex offenders (Boorstein 1998) but it is not clear as to the type of offender being targeted by such legislation. Pallone (2003) is suggesting, as have others, that registration and notification laws were rushed to the floor by policy-makers who refused to pay attention to the social science research on the matter and without considering other possible solutions.

The Future Direction of the Monitoring and Supervising of Sexual Offenders

Despite concerns about due process and the possibility of other mechanisms being available to the justice system when it comes to containing the threats sexual offenders pose to the greater society, it appears that most states will continue to move toward even more punitive measures for managing and supervising this particular population. Approximately 14 states, for example, now require convicted sex offenders to produce a DNA sample, and some states are moving toward the use of more sophisticated electronic monitoring devices for sex offenders in the community. In a number of states, lifetime registration is already in place, and college campuses now contain public information about sex offenders taking classes. In a recent Pennsylvania case, a newborn child was immediately taken from its mother because its father, with whom the mother lived, had been convicted of a sex offense some two decades earlier.

Legislation and instances such as those described here indicate that sex offenders will continue to receive a great deal of attention and "added on" restrictions that go beyond those imposed on other types of offenders. As of now, the U.S. Supreme Court appears set to uphold registration, notification, and civil commitment statutes, so cries by offenders, the treatment community, and some social justice organizations are likely to fall on unhearing ears.

References

Alexander, R., Jr. 2004. "The United States Supreme Court and the Civil Commitment of Sex Offenders." *The Prison Journal* 84(3):361–378.

Becker, J., and Murphy, W. 1998. "What We Know and Do Not Know About Assessing and Treating Sex Offenders." *Psychology, Public Policy and Law* 4(1/2):116–137.

Boorstein, M. 1998. "Three Strikes Laws Being Applied in Few States." *The National Post*, December 11: A17.

Brooks, A. D. 1996. "Megan's Law: Constitutionality and Policy." *Criminal Justice Ethics* 15:56–66.

Cohen, F. 1995. "Sex Offender Registration Laws: Constitutional and Policy Issues." *Criminal Law Bulletin* 31:151–160.

Denno, D. W. 1998. "Life Before the Modern Sex Offender Statutes." *Northwestern University Law Review* 92(4):7–1413.

Doerner, W. G., and S. P. Lab. 2002. *Victimology,* *3rd ed.* Cincinnati, OH: Anderson Press.

Edwards, W., and C. Hensley. 2001. "Contextualizing Sex Offender Management Legislation and Policy: Evaluating the Problem of Latent Consequences in Community Notification Laws." *International Journal of Offender Therapy and Comparative Criminology* 45:83–1901.

Elbogen, E. B., M. Patry, and M. J. Scalora. 2003. "The Impact of Community Notification Laws on Sex Offender Treatment Attitudes." *International Journal of Law & Psychiatry* 26(2):207–219.

Hoover, J. E. 1937. "War on the Sex Criminal." *NY Herald Tribune*, This Week Magazine supplement, September 26: 12.

Jones, L., and D. Finkelhor. 2001. *The Decline in Child Sexual Abuse Cases* (NIJ#184741). Washington, DC: U.S. Department of Justice.

Malesky, A., and J. Keim. 2001. "Mental Health Professionals' Perspectives on Sex Offender Registry Web Sites." *Sexual Abuse: A Journal of Research and Treatment* 13(1):53–63.

Motiuk, L., and Belcourt, R. 1996. "Profiling the Canadian Federal Sex Offender Population." *Forum on Corrections Research* 8:1–8.

Mulvihill, M., J. Meyers, J. Wells, and K. Wisniewski. 2003. "State Losing Track of Sex Offenders." *Boston Herald,* November 5:1.

Office of the Attorney General. 1999. *Megan's Law: Final Guidelines for the Jacob Wetterling Crimes Against Children and Sexually Violent Offender Registration Act* NCJ#98-33377. Washington, DC: U.S. Department of Justice.

Pallone, N. J. 2003. "Without Plea Bargaining, Megan Kanka Would Be Alive Today." *Criminology & Public Policy* 3(1):83–96.

Petrosino, A. J., and C. Petrosino. 1999. "The Public Safety Potential of Megan's Law in Massachusetts: An Assessment From a Sample of Criminal Sexual Psychopaths." *Crime & Delinquency* 45(1):140–158.

Rennison, C. M. 2002a. *Criminal Victimization 2001: Changes 2000–01 With Trends 1993–2001* NCJ#194610. Washington, DC: U.S. Department of Justice.

———. 2002b. *Rape and Sexual Assault: Reporting to Police and Medical Attention, 1992–2000* (NCJ#194530). Washington, DC: U.S. Department of Justice.

Schram, D. D., and C. Darling Milloy. 1995. *Community Notification: A Study of Offender Characteristics and Recidivism.* Olympia: Washington State Institute for Public Policy. http://www.wa.gov/wsipp/crime/cprot.html.

Steinbock, B. 1995. "A Policy Perspective." *Criminal Justice Ethics* 14:4–9.

Terry, K. J. 2006. *Sexual Offenses and Offenders: Theory, Offenses and Offenders.* Belmont, CA: Wadsworth.

Welchans, S. 2005. "Megan's Law: Evaluations of Sexual Offender Registries." *Criminal Justice Policy Review* 16(2):123–140.

Zevitz, R. G., and M. A. Farkas. 2000a. "Sex Offender Community Notification: Managing High-Risk Criminals or Exacting Further Vengeance?" *Behavioral Sciences & the Law* 18(2/3):375–391.

———. 2000b. "The Impact of Sex-Offender Community Notification on Probation/Parole in Wisconsin." *International Journal of Offender Therapy & Comparative Criminology* 44(1):8–21.

Cases Cited

Connecticut Department of Public Safety v. Doe, 271 F.3d 38 (2003).

Doe v. Poritz, 283 N.J. Super. 372, 661A.2d, 1335 (1995).

Kansas v. Crane, 122 S. Ct. 867 (2002).

Kansas v. Hendricks, 521 U.S. 101 (1997).

Minnesota ex rel. Pearson v. Probate Court of Ramsey County, 309 U.S. 270 (1940).

Selig v. Young, 531 U.S. 250 (2001).

Smith v. Doe, 259 F.3d 979 (2003).

Related Websites

Center for Sex Offender Management
http://www.csom.org

National Sex Offender Public Registry
http://www.nsopr.gov

Federal Bureau of Investigation: Investigative Programs Crimes Against Children
http://www.fbi.gov/hq/cid/cac/states.htm

Pennsylvania State Police Megan's Law Website
http://www.pameganslaw.state.pa.us

Discussion Questions

1. What public policy objectives are served by sex offender registration laws and sex offender notification laws? By civil commitment laws?

2. What constitutional rights may be impacted by sex offender registration and notification laws? What reasons have courts given for upholding these laws?

3. What has led legislatures to pass special legislation that treats sex offenders differently from other offenders?

4. According to research, how effective are sex offender registration and notification laws in reducing recidivism?

5. Why does civil commitment of a sex offender after that offender has served a prison term not violate the Due Process Clause of the U.S. Constitution? ✦

Section IV

Legal Issues and Juvenile Justice

Chapter 16
Juvenile Waiver Laws

Benjamin Steiner

In this chapter, the author examines the history of juvenile waiver laws. Juvenile waiver deals with the transfer of a youth from a juvenile court to an adult court. The act of waiving a juvenile to an adult court raises critical questions about the purpose of the juvenile court as an institution. The chapter begins with a description of the history of the juvenile justice system parallel to the development of adjoining legal expectancies. The juvenile justice system developed under the *parens patriae* principle, which was guided by the goals of individualized treatment, rehabilitation, and control, instead of the adult penological goals of punishment and retribution.

In the 1960s, the sociopolitical atmosphere began to change and the individualized system of justice was criticized for being soft on crime. As the author notes, the attention of the system shifted from the offender to the offense—a change that shifted attention onto fairness and Fourteenth Amendment due process issues. Two critical Supreme Court cases during this time, *Kent v. United States* (1966) and *In re Gault* (1967), expanded the constitutional rights afforded to juveniles in regards to due process. With these changes came a formalizing of the juvenile court, which affected the restriction of judiciary and prosecutorial discretionary powers.

After addressesing the history of juvenile waiver decisions, the author reviews the question of deterrence and whether the ability to prosecute youth in adult court serves to deter youth from committing criminal acts. Following the evaluation of the effects of juvenile waiver laws, the author explores the various opinions of public and criminal justice system personnel. The act of juvenile transfer to adult court has elicited questions surrounding the effectiveness of such laws, arbitrary enforcement, and arguments centered on the justification of a separate juvenile justice system and intrinsic goals, which delineate it from the adult system.

Introduction

Juvenile waiver laws are the mechanisms by which youthful defendants who have not reached the age of adulthood (as statutorily defined for a particular jurisdiction) can be transferred out of the juvenile court into adult criminal court, where they are subject to prosecution as an adult. Once waived to criminal court, the juvenile is treated as if he or she is an adult and is afforded all the procedural safeguards provided to other criminal defendants. If convicted, however, the juvenile is also vulnerable to the same range of punishments as other criminal defendants.

Although the practice of waiving juveniles to criminal court is relatively rare when compared to the number of cases processed in either juvenile or criminal court (Puzzanchera 2001), it is one of the most heavily debated legal issues among both scholars and practitioners. While it is generally agreed upon that waiver is appropriate for certain juveniles at certain times (see, e.g., Bilchik 1998; Bishop 2004; Fagan and Zimring 2000), there is much less consensus as to who, when, and for what offenses a waiver is suitable. Critics of juvenile waiver laws argue that waiving a juvenile to criminal court conflicts with the theoretical purposes of a separate and distinct juvenile court (e.g., Steinberg and Cauffman 2000), while proponents of such laws argue that serious or violent juvenile offenders are beyond the scope of what the juvenile justice system can handle (e.g., Sanborn 2003). Thus, the waiver of juvenile offenders to adult criminal court for prosecution represents the nexus between the more deterministic and rehabilitative premises of the juvenile court and the free will and punishment assumptions of the adult criminal justice system (Feld 2000).

This chapter discusses the history of the application of juvenile waiver laws and their various forms within the context of the development of the juvenile justice system.

Within this framework, the justifications for juvenile waiver laws are outlined. Findings from many empirical studies that have evaluated various aspects surrounding the application of these laws are also presented in order to illustrate the effects of juvenile waiver laws in practice. In the end, the question is left open for the reader to decide when, or if, the waiver of juvenile offenders to adult criminal court is appropriate or necessary.

History and Development of Juvenile Waiver Laws

The underpinning fabric of juvenile justice in the United States was borrowed heavily from England. In the late 1700s and through the early 1800s, common law governed. Children under the age of 7 were considered incapable of criminal intent. Juveniles between the ages of 7 and 14 could be found guilty of a crime but were still treated as if they could not distinguish right from wrong. In a few cases, however, this presumption was challenged and these youth were tried as adults. After the age of 14, juveniles were considered fully responsible for their actions and treated as if they were adults (Tanenhaus 2000). Any youth who was sentenced to incarceration was housed with adult inmates until 1825, when New York's House of Refuge was opened. Although juvenile offenders continued to be punished similarly to adults, they were beginning to gain recognition as a separate class; by 1899 there were 65 facilities for juveniles across the United States (Binder, Geis, and Dickson 2001).

Toward a Separate and Distinct System of Justice

In the later part of the nineteenth century, rapid industrialization, economic innovation, urbanization, and immigration overwhelmed traditional solidity, posing problems for conventional means of social control (such as family) (Feld 1987). The breakdown in informal social control coupled with increased poverty led to a growth in what was called the "dangerous class," which represented the faction of young and poor individuals found in urban centers. It was in this period that the progressive movement began. Progressive reformers viewed the young urban poor as misguided children in need of saving. Social policies that emphasized informal and individualized methods in order to rehabilitate the delinquent child were implemented. By the turn of the century, juveniles not only had separate facilities, they had their own probation system as well as separate trials and dockets. In 1899, Illinois passed the first Juvenile Court Act, which established the first juvenile court in Cook County (Chicago). Other states soon followed, and by 1928 all but two states had separate systems for juveniles (Binder et al. 2001).

The primary purpose for creating a separate juvenile justice system was to distinguish between punishment and treatment. At the turn of the century, the criminal justice system emphasized the punishment and deterrence as proper goals. Separating juvenile offenders from adult criminals allowed the juveniles to be treated instead of punished (Feld 1987). Juvenile proceedings were held in their own courtrooms, with judges who heard only juvenile cases. Juvenile court procedure was markedly different from that of the general jurisdiction court. Juvenile court jurisdiction was classified as civil rather than criminal. Hearings were private and informal, and juvenile court judges enjoyed enormous discretionary power. A whole new vocabulary sought to differentiate juvenile court activities from adult criminal court activities. Juveniles were not arrested, they were "taken into custody;" instead of indicting a juvenile, prosecutors "petitioned the juvenile into court;" juveniles were not convicted, they were "adjudicated delinquent;" juvenile court sanctions were not referred to as sentences, but as "dispositions;" juveniles were not sent to prisons, they were sent to "training schools" (Fritsch and Hemmens 1996; Rothman 1980). Under the guise of *parens patriae*, the juvenile court, with its emphasis on treatment, supervision, and control instead of punishment, allowed the state to intervene in the lives of wayward youth (Feld 1987).

Despite the "child saving" agenda of the progressive juvenile court, some juveniles were still deemed beyond its scope. Even the initial juvenile court acts contained mechanisms for transferring a juvenile to criminal court (Mack 1909). The newly created juvenile courts struggled to maintain their legitimacy. Consequently, the potential inability to appropriately handle serious or chronic young offenders threatened their existence, so some youths were still handled in criminal court despite the exclusive jurisdiction the early juvenile courts were supposed to enjoy. Some states allowed for concurrent jurisdiction of offenders charged with certain offenses, others statutorily defined offenses that were excluded from juvenile court jurisdiction, and most states did not set 18 as the upper age limit of juvenile jurisdiction. Additionally, almost every state's juvenile code permitted the juvenile court to transfer juveniles to adult criminal court (Tanenhaus 2000). By transferring certain young offenders into the adult criminal justice system, juvenile court judges could avoid political pressure and excess attention on the newly established court.

Although waivers occurred in the early juvenile courts, the practice was infrequent and varied considerably by jurisdiction (Feld 1987). Moreover, and ultimately more important, there was little consistency in which juveniles were transferred. Under judicial waiver statutes, juvenile court judges enjoyed wide and relatively unmonitored discretion in making waiver decisions. Although there were several challenges in state courts throughout the 1930s, 1940s, and 1950s, the discretionary judicial decisions to waive were typically upheld (Tanenhaus 2000). In the decades to follow, unbridled judicial discretion would be curtailed and the practice of juvenile waiver began to change.

Due Process and a Formalized Juvenile Court

The rehabilitative ideal on which the progressives founded the individualized and informal juvenile court began to be questioned during the 1960s. Conservatives began condemning the individualized scheme that was used in both the adult and juvenile justice systems, arguing that it was the cause of societal discord and rising crime rates (Cullen and Gilbert 1982; Feld 2003; Rothman 1980; Ruth and Reitz 2003). Conservatives argued that the rehabilitation-driven juvenile justice system was soft on crime and instead advocated a retributive approach to juvenile crime (Feld 2003). While the conservatives were condemning the criminal and juvenile justice systems for their perceived failure to reduce crime and for being too lenient in their treatment of offenders, liberals were also becoming disenchanted with the individualized justice approach, albeit for different reasons. Liberals were concerned that the discretion that pervaded the offender-focused criminal justice system under the guise of rehabilitation was linked to discrimination (Feld 2003). They criticized the fact that offenders suffered unfair treatment at the hands of the judiciary and corrections officials and argued for procedural protections for criminal defendants and offenders. The denigration also filtered down to the juvenile justice system. The combined criticism of the left and the right changed the focus of the system from the offender to the offense (Feld 1987), which in turn placed greater emphasis on fairness and due process. It was during this period, following several cases that dealt with criminal procedural issues in the adult criminal justice system, that the U.S. Supreme Court decided for the first time to address procedural conduct in the juvenile court.

In *Kent v. United States* (1966), the Court extended several due process rights to juveniles involved in waiver hearings. The Court held that the decision to transfer a juvenile to adult criminal court requires a full and adversarial hearing. The Court also established the juvenile's right to have counsel present at the waiver hearing. One year after *Kent*, the Court decided *In re Gault* (1967). In *Gault*, the Court held that whenever a juvenile is charged with an act that could result in his or her being sent to a state institution, be it a prison or a reform school, the juvenile must be accorded due process. Rights guaranteed the juvenile under the rubric of due process include the right to counsel, the right to confront one's accusers and cross-examine witnesses, and the right not to incriminate one-self. The Supreme Court's decisions in *Gault* and *Kent* and several subsequent cases formalized the juvenile court. Some have argued that these decisions "criminalized" it (see, e.g., Champion 1989; Feld 1993; Feld 2003; Jensen and Metsger 1994).

One of the changes that occurred along with the formalization of the juvenile court was the modification of the process by which juveniles can be waived to adult criminal court. In response to the Supreme Court's decisions, states began adding formal criteria to their waiver statutes. Between 1970 and 1985, 26 states amended their judicial waiver statutes. Most added offense or prior record criteria in an effort to curb judicial discretion (Feld 1987). Several states mandated certain offenses for which juveniles are automatically transferred without a hearing. This method of waiver is identified as *statutory exclusion* or *legislative waiver*. Other states specified offenses for which the discretionary decision to waive rests in the hands of prosecutors. Known as *direct file* or *prosecutorial discretion*, this waiver scheme authorizes prosecutors to file certain cases in either juvenile or criminal court under a concurrent jurisdiction statute. Although some argue that statutory exclusion is another form of direct file since the prosecutor ultimately makes the decision about how a juvenile is charged (e.g., Sanborn 1994), it is important to distinguish these two methods because the state legislatures have done so. In fact, several states, such as Georgia and Vermont, have now statutorily excluded some offenses while allowing prosecutors the discretion to charge other offenses (without altering the offense that was charged) in either juvenile or criminal court.

The 'Get Tough' Era

The practice of juvenile waiver continued to evolve in the 1980s and 1990s, although for other reasons besides restricting judicial discretion. In the 1970s, juvenile violence began to rise, and it escalated substantially in the 1980s (Feld 1999; 2003; Snyder 1997). The arrest rate for violent juvenile crime rose 58 percent between 1980 and 1994 (Feld 1999; Snyder and Sickmund 1999). Addi-

tionally, the juvenile homicide rate doubled between 1987 and 1993, and although it declined in the late 1990s, it remained notably above the rate of the early 1980s (Ruth and Reitz 2003; Snyder and Sickmund 1999). Across most states, the response to the rise in juvenile crime was to "get tough" on juvenile offenders. Perhaps the most predominant way that states accomplished this was by enacting or amending legislation to make it easier to transfer juvenile offenders to criminal court.

By 1979, every state allowed some form of transfer option. Most had judicial waiver; only 13 states and the District of Columbia had some form of legislative waiver (Fritsch and Hemmens 1996; Steiner and Hemmens 2003). However, during the 1980s and 1990s, virtually every state modified or amended its juvenile court jurisdiction in some fashion. Most states added offenses that were judicial waiver-eligible and lowered the age at which a juvenile could be transferred to criminal court. Many states also added or expanded the scope of legislative waiver statutes (Steiner and Hemmens 2003). Currently, 48 states and the District of Columbia have judicial waiver laws (Steiner and Hemmens 2003); 14 states and the District of Columbia have direct file statutes (Griffin 2003), while 31 states and the District of Columbia now have a legislative waiver provision in place (Steiner and Hemmens 2003).

The added legislation had an immediate effect. In the 1980s, juvenile waivers increased nationally by 400 percent (Krisberg and Austin 1993). The number of juveniles transferred via judicial waiver reached an all-time high in 1994, and although the number has declined, the rate remains above the level from the 1980s (Puzzanchera 2001). In addition, juveniles can get to criminal court much easier through other waiver procedures (e.g., statutory exclusion) than by way of judicial waiver (Steiner and Hemmens 2003). In one study, Bishop, Frazier, and Henretta (1989) found that judicial waivers declined as the number of direct file waivers increased. Jurisdictional studies from Florida (Bishop et al. 1989; Bishop and Frazier 1991), Tennessee, Virginia, Mississippi, Georgia (Champion 1989), Texas

(Dawson 1992), and Canada (Ruddell, Mays, and Giever 1998) have also found an increase in the use of waiver laws.

Without a doubt, the state legislatures' goal in expanding their existing waiver statutes and enacting additional statutes is to have an effect on juvenile offending, whether through retribution, rehabilitation, or deterrence. Much empirical research has evaluated whether waiver laws have achieved any of these goals. Organized by the various decision points in the justice system process, the findings from the research are discussed in the following section. The evidence regarding general deterrent effects of waiver laws is also reviewed. Finally, the last section summarizes findings from surveys of the public and justice system personnel regarding their opinions of juvenile waiver laws.

Evaluating the Effects of Juvenile Waiver Laws

Before discussing the empirical studies of the effects of juvenile waiver laws, a brief comment on methodology is in order. The research on the effects of juvenile waiver laws is relatively recent in terms of criminal justice scholarship; thus, the majority of the studies are descriptive or are not as scientifically rigorous as one might hope. Most notably, few have examined all stages of the process in order to allow decisions made at the prior stage(s) to be controlled for so as to avoid sample selection bias (Smith and Paternoster 1990). For example, if the police decisions to arrest juveniles for waiveable offenses are influenced by a variable (X), and X is also thought to be related to the prosecutor's decision to charge the juvenile for a waived offense (Y), failing to control for what happened at the prior stage in the system (the police decision to arrest juveniles for waiveable offenses) could potentially bias findings from a study of prosecutors' decisions. A researcher could observe a relationship between X and Y, which suggests that prosecutors are more likely to charge juveniles for a waiveable offense because of the variable X, when the finding is actually the result of the cases that are presented to them, or the police's decisions.

An additional problem is that few studies have used multivariate designs to control for possible confounding influences from other unmeasured variables. If you recall from your research methods class, a *confounding influence* is a variable (Z) that is related to both the independent (X) and dependent variable (Y). Failing to hold Z constant (to control for it) could reveal a relationship between X and Y that is actually caused by Z, or what is known as a spurious relationship. While these are all important considerations to bear in mind when drawing overall conclusions that may guide future research or policy, the intent here is to convey general findings that can be useful for generating informed discussion and critical interest in this complex topic confronting today's juvenile justice system. As such, criticism of the existing studies will not be provided and therefore left for the reader to do on his or her own (although, for a recent critique, see Mears 2003a). Instead, some of the more scientifically rigorous studies will simply be highlighted within each section.

Finally, it is also worth mentioning that many states now have different waiver mechanisms (e.g., judicial and direct file) as well as unique age limits and different offense criteria for which they permit a transfer to occur (see, e.g., Feld 1987; Fritsch and Hemmens 1996; Steiner and Hemmens 2003). The findings of studies are, of course, influenced by these statutory differences across jurisdictions, as the administration of juvenile justice may be influenced by geography (Feld 1991). For example, several states statutorily exclude all offenders who are charged with violent index offenses (murder/ manslaughter, rape, robbery, and aggravated assault). Some of those same states also allow for judicial waiver of other lesser offenses. It may very well be that the majority of juveniles who were waived within such a state were transferred via statutory exclusion (see, e.g, Bishop et al. 1989; Steiner 2005). Pooling those juveniles with those who were waived judicially without controlling for the mechanisms by which a juvenile arrived in criminal court would likely lead to biased conclusions regarding juvenile court practices in that state (e.g., the juvenile

courts tend to waive primarily violent offenders). While this is a topic that will have
to be attended to in future studies, it has
rarely been addressed thus far; therefore, it
will only be discussed here when the authors
of the various studies provided the information and it is relevant to the decision being
evaluated. With these caveats in mind, we
begin by examining who is waived.

The Decision to Waive

While the extant literature has generally
assessed judicial waiver decisions, a few
studies have evaluated prosecutors' decisions to waive in direct file jurisdictions or
their decisions to motion in judicial waiver
cases. These few studies have revealed that
prosecutors file motions to waive or charge
juveniles as adults more often if the juvenile
has a prior record (Bishop et al. 1989; Bishop
and Frazier 1991; Podkopacz and Feld 1995;
1996; Sridharan, Greenfield, and Blakely
2004), is a minority (Podkopacz and Feld
1995; 1996), is from a broken home (Singer
1993), has dropped out of school (Sridharan
et al. 2004), or is older (Podkopacz and Feld
1995; 1996). Study findings are mixed as to
whether prosecutors motion or waive property offenders (Bishop et al. 1989; Bishop
and Frazier 1991) or violent offenders
(Dawson 1992; Podkopacz and Feld 1995;
1996; Singer 1993; Sridharan et al. 2004)
more often and whether prosecutors motion
or waive juveniles who have been previously
placed in a juvenile facility more frequently
(Podkopacz and Feld 1995; 1996) than those
youths who have not been afforded an opportunity in a juvenile residential placement
(Bishop et al. 1989; Bishop and Frazier
1991). Interestingly, differences between
studies also exist as to whether prosecutors'
motions are granted. Study findings from
some jurisdictions have revealed that most
of the motions to waive were granted
(Bortner 1986; Gillespie and Norman 1984;
Snyder, Sickmund, and Poe-Yamagata
2000), while others have observed that a significant amount of prosecutors' motion were
denied (Dawson 1992; Fagan, Forst, and
Vivona 1987; Podkopacz and Feld 1995;
1996).

As noted previously, the waiver studies
have been primarily descriptive and thus
merely provided a profile of who was waived
in a particular jurisdiction for a cross-sec-
tion of time. Findings from those studies
have revealed that juveniles who were
waived to criminal court were primarily
male, were from a minority group, were
older, were represented by the public defender (indicating they were indigent), and
had more extensive juvenile records (see,
e.g., Clarke 1996; Clement 1997; Dawson
1992; Fagan et al. 1987; Gragg 1986;
Hamparian, Davis, and Jacobson 1983;
Houghtalin and Mays 1991; Kinder,
Veneziano, Fichter, and Azuma 1995; Lee
1994; Lemmon, Sontheimer, and Saylor
1991; Nimick, Szymanski, and Snyder 1986;
Snyder, Sickmund, and Poe-Yamagata
2000). Findings from studies have been
mixed regarding the types of offenses for
which juveniles were waived. Several studies
have discovered that juveniles were waived
more often for property offenses (Gillespie
and Norman 1984; Hamparian et al. 1982;
Lemmon et al. 1991; Nimick et al. 1986),
while others have found that youths were
typically transferred for violent offenses
(Clarke 1996; Dawson 1992; Gragg 1986;
Kinder et al. 1995; Rudman et al. 1986).
Some studies have found that waiver decisions were not influenced by the types of offenses juveniles were charged with (Clement
1997; Lee 1994).

More-rigorous studies have revealed that
juveniles who were older (Fagan et al. 1987;
Fagan and Deschenes 1990; Mears 2003a;
Podkopacz and Feld 1995; 1996; Poulos and
Orchowsky 1994), were less educated
(Mears 2003a; Poulos and Orchowsky 1994),
had been previously committed to a juvenile
facility (Barnes and Franz 1989; Poulos and
Orchowsky 1994), had been charged with a
serious person offense (Barnes and Franz
1989; Fagan et al. 1987; Fagan and
Deschenes 1990; Podkopacz and Feld 1995;
1996; Poulos and Orchowsky 1994), were
recommended by court personnel
(Podkopacz and Feld 1995; 1996), had begun
their delinquent careers earlier or had more
prior referrals to the juvenile court (Barnes
and Franz 1989; Fagan et al. 1987; Fagan and

Deschenes 1990; Mears 2003a; Podkopacz and Feld 1995; 1996; Poulos and Orchowsky 1994), or had their case disposed of in a rural jurisdiction (Myers 2003a; Poulos and Orchowsky 1994) were more likely to be judicially waived to criminal court.

These more-rigorous studies demonstrate that legal factors such as the seriousness of the offense, prior record, and prior placements are the most consistent influences on the judicial decision to waive. Age was also consistently found to be an important determinate of waiver decisions in both the descriptive and multivariate studies, reflecting that judges consider a juvenile's maturity when granting motions to waive. Although many descriptive studies suggested that race plays a role in the transfer decision, none of the more rigorous evaluations revealed such a finding. Thus, race may not directly influence judicial decisions to waive. However, after controlling for legal factors, several extralegal factors were still important factors that judges in several jurisdictions apparently consider. These jurisdictional differences also suggest that justice by geography may be operating (Feld 1991).

Case Processing

In this section three areas are grouped under case processing: the pretrial detention decision, the time it takes to dispose of a cases, and conviction rates. In *Schall v. Martin* (1984) the Supreme Court upheld pretrial detention for juvenile offenders. As such, the study of pretrial detention decisions is a relatively new area of study for waiver research. Most of the scholars who have explored these issues have done so with archival data (for an exception, see Kupchik 2003) so we know very little about how cases are typically disposed (plea bargain or trial) or when plea decisions are made (before or after waiver). Indeed, future empirical endeavors should seek to explore these topics in order to better inform our understanding of how this process may work.

Studies in this area have usually examined a cohort of juveniles who were eligible for waiver. After waiver decisions were made, evaluations of subsequent decisions have compared those juveniles transferred with those retained in the juvenile court. Findings regarding the pretrial detention decision have generally indicated that those juveniles waived to criminal court are more likely to be detained than released (Kupchik, Fagan, and Liberman 2003; Mears 2003a). The few studies that have examined the time from arrest to disposition have uncovered that cases usually take much longer to dispose of in criminal court (Kinder et al. 1995; Mears 2003a; Rudman et al. 1986). Conviction outcomes have varied. Some studies have revealed high conviction rates in criminal court (Bishop et al. 1989; Bishop and Frazier 1991; Dawson 1992; McNulty 1996; Rudman et al. 1986), while others have observed that at least a fourth of waived cases resulted in acquittal or dismissal (Clarke 1996; Clement 1997; Kinder et al. 1995; Lemmon et al. 2005). Of those studies that have compared juvenile and criminal court outcomes, some have observed higher conviction rates in criminal court (Fagan 1996; Kupchik et al. 2003; Mears 2003a; Podkopacz and Feld 1995; 1996; Snyder et al. 2000), whereas others have observed higher conviction rates in juvenile courts (Kinder et al. 1995).

Overall, it seems juveniles who are transferred to adult criminal court are more likely to be detained prior to having their case decided, are more likely to have their case take longer to process, and are more likely to be convicted. On the other hand, the fact that conviction is not certain, and that cases take longer to process in criminal court, suggests that the harsher punishment that would be theoretically doled out in criminal court is not done so in either a swift or certain manner. Whether the punishment is, in fact, more severe in criminal court than it would have been had the youth remained in juvenile court is the subject of the next section.

Sentence Outcomes

The sentencing outcomes of juveniles waived to criminal court can be broken down into two decision points: the in/out or incarceration decision, and the determination of the sentence length. We examine the incarceration decision first.

Some descriptive studies have found that waived juveniles were sentenced to probation more often than prison (Bishop et al. 1989; Bishop and Frazier 1991; Bortner 1986; Champion 1989; Clarke 1996; Hamparian et al. 1982; McNulty 1996), while others have found that prison was the most common disposition for juveniles waived to criminal court (Clement 1997; Dawson 1992; Gillespie and Norman 1984; Gragg 1986; Houghtalin and Mays 1991; Snyder et al. 2000; Thomas and Bilchik 1985). It should be noted that several of the former studies found that waived juveniles were typically incarcerated (e.g., Bishop et al. 1989; Bishop and Frazier 1991; Bortner 1986), but the focus here is on prison sentences, because when examining archival data it is often difficult to disentangle when jail was imposed (before or after conviction) or how long individuals served.

A few studies, which have compared the sentence outcomes of waived youth with a similarly situated group of juveniles who were disposed of in juvenile court, have discovered that waived juveniles are handled more leniently in criminal court when compared to juveniles retained in juvenile court (Greenwood, Petersilia, and Zimring 1980; Kinder et al. 1995; Lemmon et al. 1991); however, other studies have revealed that waived juveniles are incarcerated more frequently (Eigen 1981; Greenwood, Abrahamse, and Zimring 1984; Podkopacz and Feld 1995; 1996; Rudman et al. 1986; Snyder et al. 2000).

More-rigorous studies have found that the decision to incarcerate waived juveniles is influenced by such factors as the seriousness of the offense (Barnes and Franz 1989; Kupchik et al. 2003; Lemmon et al. 2005; McNulty 1996), the number of prior referrals to juvenile court (Barnes and Franz 1989; Kupchik et al. 2003; Lemmon et al. 2005; McNulty 1996), whether the juvenile had a previous commitment to a juvenile facility (Steiner 2005), whether a weapon was used in the crime (Lemmon et al. 2005), whether the juvenile was detained prior to disposition (Kupchik et al. 2003; Mears 2003a), whether the juvenile was older (McNulty 1996), younger (Steiner 2005), or a minority

(McNulty 1996), and whether there was a plea bargain in the case (Barnes and Franz 1989). When compared to similarly situated juvenile offenders, juveniles sentenced for more serious offenses are sentenced to prison more often in criminal court (Barnes and Franz 1989, Fagan 1995; 1996; Lemmon et al. 2005; Mears 2003a; Podkopacz and Feld 1995; 1996), while juveniles sentenced for less serious offenses (e.g., property and drug offenses) are incarcerated more often in juvenile court (Barnes and Franz 1989; Podkopacz and Feld 1995; 1996).

Sentence Length and Time Served

Many of the same studies assessing whether waived juveniles were incarcerated also examined the length of sentences imposed in criminal court. Some scholars have observed that juveniles were sentenced to long prison terms in the criminal court (Thomas and Bilchik 1985), while others have found that they were sentenced to relatively short terms (Bishop et al. 1989; Bishop and Frazier 1991; Bortner 1986). A few of the comparison studies have revealed that juveniles transferred to criminal court have been sentenced to longer terms of confinement than similarly situated juvenile offenders (Hamparian et al. 1982; Kupchik et al. 2003; Rudman et al. 1986). Others have found that juveniles sentenced for more serious offenses are sentenced longer in criminal court (Clement 1997; Dawson 1992; Heide et al. 2001; Lemmon et al. 2005; Mears 2003a; Podkopacz and Feld 1995; 1996), while juveniles sentenced for less serious offenses (e.g., property offenses) receive more time in juvenile court (Clement 1997; Podkopacz and Feld 1995; 1996).

Expanding on these findings, Kurlychek and Johnson (2004) found that when offense type was controlled for, juveniles waived to adult criminal court were sentenced more stringently than young adults between the ages of 18 and 24. They also found that legal factors outperformed extralegal factors in predicting the sentence length of the transferred juvenile sample (Kurlychek and Johnson 2004).

Although the majority of the studies have examined the sentence imposed by the court, others have evaluated the amount of time that waived juveniles serve. For all those juveniles released from adult facilities nationally in 1997, the average length of stay was 231 days (Austin, Johnson, and Gregoriou 2000). Some researchers have uncovered that some courts imposed substantial sentences but that parole authorities typically released youthful offenders after serving less time than they would have had they remained in the juvenile system (Clement 1997; Fritsch, Hemmens, and Caeti 1996; Fritsch, Caeti, and Hemmens 1996; Heide et al. 2001). Within these studies, offense type was still the strongest predictor of total time served (Clement 1997; Fritsch, Hemmens, and Caeti 1996; Fritsch, Caeti, and Hemmens 1996; Heide et al. 2001). In the only multivariate analyses of time served, Steiner (2005) revealed that violent offenders, those juveniles who had previously been committed to a juvenile facility, and those youths who had been waived legislatively (as opposed to judicially) served more time in adult correctional facilities.

Taken together, the literature on sentencing outcomes suggests that juveniles waived to criminal court for violent offenses and those who have more extensive juvenile histories typically are incarcerated more often, are sentenced longer, and serve more time than they would have had they remained in the juvenile system. Similar to the waiver decision, some extralegal factors appear to influence judicial sentencing decisions in a few jurisdictions but play little role in others. However, these studies of decision points in the juvenile and criminal justice system do not tell us the effects of waiver laws on the individual juveniles who are transferred to criminal court or the effect of these laws on criminal behavior in general. These effects are assessed now, beginning with what happens in adult facilities.

The Confinement Experience

Along with the increase in juveniles waived to criminal court, discussed earlier, the number of juveniles in adult correctional facilities increased 366 percent between 1983 and 1998. Yet, the representation of offenders under 18 remained at about 2 percent of all those incarcerated. The average juvenile confined in adult facilities is male, 17, and nonwhite. Most offenders were convicted of a crime against a person (Austin et al. 2000).

Only 17 states and the District of Columbia maintain separate housing for waived or young adult offenders, and most of those facilities are overcrowded (Austin et al. 2000). As such, juveniles are typically housed with adult offenders. Interviews with waived juvenile offenders have revealed more positive feedback regarding the staff and climate of structured juvenile facilities when compared to adult facilities (Forst, Fagan, and Vivona 1989; Lane et al. 2002). Violent victimization rates for juveniles are also higher in typical adult facilities when compared to training schools (Forst et al. 1989). Interviews with some waived juveniles have revealed that these youths said that they were deterred by adult confinement and did not plan to return to criminal behavior upon release (Lane et al. 2002). However, post-release data would be needed to support these juveniles' claims. We focus on studies that have evaluated such data here.

Recidivism Outcomes

Much like the other areas of the juvenile waiver research, recidivism studies have generally compared juveniles waived to criminal court to those retained in the juvenile court. Despite claims as to the similarity of the two groups, no study has compared waived and retained groups that were exactly matched (see Fagan 1995, 1996 for groups matched on all characteristics but jurisdiction). Nonetheless, the scholars who have assessed recidivism outcomes have provided us with some of the more rigorous studies within the extant waiver research.

Findings have generally revealed that recidivism rates have been lower for youth retained in juvenile court when compared to those transferred to criminal court (Fagan 1995; 1996; Mears 2003b; Pokopacz and Feld 1995; 1996; Bishop et al. 1996). Transferred juveniles have also been found to reoffend quicker and more often than those youths sentenced in the juvenile system (Fagan 1995; 1996; Bishop et al. 1996; Winner et al.

1997). Heide and her colleagues (2001) revealed that among juveniles who were waived for murder, 60 percent were reincarcerated, and over 50 percent were reincarcerated two different times.

More-rigorous studies have revealed that youths who were transferred (Mears 2003b; Winner et al. 1997), convicted of a violent offense (Winner et al. 1997), younger, in school, younger when first referred to juvenile court, and incarcerated for less time were more likely to be rearrested (Mears 2003b). Interestingly, Fagan (1996) found that the sentence (prison or probation) did not influence recidivism rates.

All told, these findings are rather conclusive and suggest that waiving juveniles to criminal court may not be effective in achieving either rehabilitative or specific deterrent effects. On the other hand, the legislative intent in enacting these laws may have been to affect rates of general offending. However, these results would not have been detected by examining decision points in the justice system process. Instead, the aggregate juvenile crime rates before and after the various waiver laws were enacted would have to be examined.

General Deterrence

Singer and McDowall (1988) assessed the general deterrent effects of the New York Juvenile Offender Law. After examining monthly arrest data for juveniles who were eligible for legislative waiver, they found significantly lower rates of arrest for rape and arson in New York City after the law went into effect. However, they also found similar results for arson and significantly lower arrest rates for homicide and aggravated assault in Philadelphia, despite Pennsylvania not having a waiver law. Additionally, they observed significantly higher arrest rates for aggravated assault and robbery in upstate New York after the waiver law went into effect. Thus, Singer and McDowall concluded that New York's version of a juvenile waiver law had no appreciable effect on deterring violent juvenile crime. Evaluations of legislative waiver laws in Idaho (Jensen and Metsger 1994) and Georgia (Risler,

Sweatman, and Nackerud 1998) have reached similar conclusions.

In the most recent study, Steiner, Hemmens, and Bell (2006) evaluated the relative effects of legislative waiver laws on juvenile arrest rates for homicide and violent index crime in 22 states that have enacted such legislation since 1979 or modified their existing statutes substantially. No effects on homicide arrest rates were observed; however, effects on arrest rates for violent crime were observed in four of the states. Indiana and Missouri both experienced an increase in juvenile arrest rate for violent crime after their legislative waiver law went into effect. Maine and Wisconsin experienced a decrease in their level of juvenile arrests for violent crime; however, the change in Wisconsin was abrupt and soon returned to its previous level, indicating a publicity effect. Accordingly, Steiner and his colleagues (2006) concluded that the recent waiver legislation had little effect on violent juvenile crime.

Taken together, the findings from these studies are not very supportive of juvenile waiver laws' ability to deter violent juvenile crime, which is arguably what these "get tough" policies were designed to do. On the other hand, these laws persist and states continue to enact and modify such legislation (Steiner and Hemmens 2003). Is it possible that these laws serve some other function? Perhaps they are simply what people want?

Public Support

The decision to transfer juveniles to criminal court is one that seems to be generally supported by the public. When Wu (2000) and Mears (2001) both examined data from the 1995 National Opinion Survey of Crime and Justice they found that the majority of the public supported transferring juveniles to criminal court. More than two-thirds of the public supported the transfer of juveniles who commit violent, property, and drug-related offenses. However, the level of support declined when violent crime was separated from the other two categories as well as when the juvenile was younger (Wu 2000). Mears (2001) discovered that the respondents' level of education, marital status, and philosophy of punishment were consistently associated with support for sanctioning youth as adults (Mears 2001).

In an earlier survey of residents in Springfield, Illinois, Cullen, Golden, and Cullen (1983) revealed that slightly over half of the respondents supported transferring all juveniles who commit violent crimes to criminal court. Similarly, Feiler and Sheley (1999) found that the people in the Greater New Orleans Area support the waiver of juveniles who are older, are African American, and commit violent acts, especially those involving weapons. Bouley and Wells (2001) found that the majority of people in a Southern county believed juveniles should be tried as adults for serious property crimes, selling illegal drugs, and serious violent crime. Furthermore, support for the decision to try juveniles as adults was influenced by the respondents' income level and their opinion of the purpose of sentencing (rehabilitation or punishment). Interestingly, the majority of the individuals surveyed reported they felt the primary objective of sentencing in the juvenile justice system was to educate, train, and counsel offenders (Bouley and Wells 2001).

While the general public may support transferring juveniles to criminal court, those that work in the juvenile justice system have had slightly different views. Prosecutors (Bishop et al. 1989; Bishop and Frazier 1991), juvenile court personnel (Sanborn 1994), and prison guards (Cullen et al. 1983) were generally supportive of waiver policies, while judges, other lawyers, and many legislatures were not (Cullen et al. 1983). Among the prosecutors and juvenile court employees who were in favor of waiver laws, the reason most commonly given was that the youths were beyond the scope of the juvenile court. Societal protection, serious crimes, deterrence, and conservation of the juvenile system's resources were given as reasons by a substantial minority. Little agreement was reached about who should be transferred, although most thought only those charged with serious felonies were appropriate. When asked about the method of certification, the majority supported judicial waiver, followed by limited prosecutorial. Pure pros-

ecutorial waiver was seen as the least desirable (Sanborn 1994).

Accordingly, while the waiver of juvenile offenders may not have a deterrent effect on crime, the public and those working in the courts generally seem to be in favor of keeping it. Such knowledge places policymakers in a difficult predicament. They are forced to choose between what the data suggest and what the public, to whom they are accountable, may want.

Conclusion

Throughout the 1980s and 1990s, policy makers in most states responded to serious and violent juvenile offending punitively by increasing juvenile disposition options and adding or expanding juvenile waiver statutes allowing for easier transfer of certain youthful offenders to adult criminal court for prosecution (Bishop 2000; Feld 2003; Fritsch and Hemmens 1996; Steiner and Hemmens 2003). Most either lowered the age at which a juvenile could be transferred or added offenses eligible for judicial waiver to general jurisdiction court. Many states enacted legislative waiver statutes that automatically send a juvenile to adult criminal court for prosecution based on the offense alleged to have been committed. As a result, the number of juveniles waived to criminal court increased considerably during this period (Krisberg and Austin 1993; Snyder and Sickmund 1999).

Waived juveniles still represent only a small percentage of the convicted felons sentenced in adult criminal court (Bishop 2000; Snyder and Sickmund 1999). Criminal court judges have little experience dealing with this special population of offenders. Furthermore, they are rarely provided any information regarding the youth's juvenile court history or prospects for rehabilitation (Bishop 2000). The decision regarding whether a youth is dangerous or amenable to rehabilitative treatment is one of the most difficult issues confronting both juvenile courts and juvenile justice policymakers (Podkopacz and Feld 1996). Findings from the studies presented here suggest that some jurisdictions may be waiving the serious or violent offenders who may be responsible for a disproportionate amount of all crime, but other jurisdictions clearly are not. The extant research also suggests that some juveniles may be receiving harsher punishment in terms of incarceration or longer periods of confinement in criminal court; however, other juveniles are not. The scientific evidence also indicates that few states are equipped to deal with this youthful offender population in their prison and jails. Finally, juvenile waiver laws do not seem to have a deterrent effect on those youths who are waived to criminal court or on violent juvenile crime in general, which was arguably the justification for the enactment of these laws in most states.

On the other hand, the public is in favor of transferring juveniles to criminal court, as are most court workers. This dilemma has led some states to experiment with waiver reforms such as guidelines for who can be waived (see Osbun and Rode 1984) or blended sentencing strategies (see Podkopacz and Feld 2001; Torbet et al. 2000). Yet, early evaluations suggest that guidelines are ineffective (Osbun and Rode 1984) and that blended sentencing only serves to widen the net of juveniles who eventually receive adult sanctions (Podkopacz and Feld 2001; Torbet et al. 2000). As a result, the questions of who, when, why, how, or whether juvenile waiver is appropriate remains to be definitely answered.

References

Austin, J., K. Johnson, and M. Gregoriou. 2000. *Juveniles in Adult Prisons and Jails: A National Assessment*. Washington DC: Institute on Crime, Justice, and Corrections at the George Washington University and National Council on Crime and Delinquency.

Barnes, C., and R. Franz. 1989. "Questionably Adult: Determinants and Effects of the Juvenile Waiver Decision." *Justice Quarterly* 6(1):117–135.

Bilchik, S. 1998. "A Juvenile Justice System for the 21st Century." *Crime & Delinquency* 44(1):89–101.

Binder, A., G. Geis, and B. Dickson. 2001. *Juvenile Delinquency: Historical, Cultural and Legal Perspectives*, 3rd ed. Cincinnati: Anderson.

Bishop, D. 2000. "Juvenile Offenders in the Adult Criminal Justice System." In M. Tonry (ed.), *Crime and Justice: A Review of the Research*. Chicago: University of Chicago, Vol. 27 (pp. 81–167).

———. 2004. "Injustice and Irrationality in Contemporary Youth Policy." *Criminology and Public Policy* 3(4):633–644.

Bishop, D., and C. Frazier. 1991. "Transfer of Juveniles to Criminal Court: A Case Study and Analysis of Prosecutorial Waiver." *Notre Dame Journal of Legal Ethics and Public Policy* 5(2):281–302.

Bishop, D., C. Frazier, and J. Henretta. 1989. "Prosecutorial Waiver: Case Study of a Questionable Reform." *Crime & Delinquency* 35(2):179–201.

Bishop, D., C. Frazier, L. Lanza-Kaduce, and L. Winner. 1996. "The Transfer of Juveniles to Criminal Court: Does It Make a Difference?" *Crime & Delinquency* 42(2):171–191.

Bortner, M. A. 1986. "Traditional Rhetoric, Organizational Realities: Remand of Juveniles to Adult Court." *Crime & Delinquency* 32(1):53–73.

Bouley, E., and T. Wells. 2001. "Attitudes of Citizens in a Southern Rural County Toward Juvenile Crime and Justice Issues." *Journal of Contemporary Criminal Justice* 17(1):60–70.

Champion, D. 1989. "Teenage Felons and Waiver Hearings: Some Recent Trends, 1980–1988." *Crime & Delinquency* 35(4):577–585.

Clarke, E. 1996. "A Case for Reinventing Juvenile Transfer: The Record of Transfer of Juvenile Offenders to the Criminal Court in Cook County, Illinois." *Juvenile & Family Court Journal* 47(4):3–22.

Clement, M. 1997. "A Five-Year Study of Juvenile Waiver and Adult Sentences: Implications for Policy." *Criminal Justice Policy Review* 8(2–3):201–219.

Cullen, F., K. Golden, and J. Cullen. 1983. "Is Child Saving Dead? Attitudes Toward Juvenile Rehabilitation in Illinois." *Journal of Criminal Justice* 11(1):1–13.

Cullen, F., and K. Gilbert. 1982. *Reaffirming Rehabilitation*. Cincinnati: Anderson.

Dawson, R. 1992. "An Empirical Study of *Kent* Style Juvenile Transfers to Criminal Court." *St. Mary's Law Journal* 23:854–975.

Eigen, J. 1981. "The Determinants and Impact of Jurisdictional Transfer in Philadelphia." In J. Hall, D. Hamparian, J. Pettibone, and J. White (eds.), *Major Issues in Juvenile Justice Information and Training: Readings in Public Policy*. Columbus: Academy for Contemporary Problems, 333–350.

Fagan, J. 1995. "Separating the Men From the Boys: The Comparative Advantage of Juvenile Versus Criminal Court Sanctions on Recidivism Among Adolescent Felony Offenders." In J. Howell, B. Krisberg, J. D. Hawkins, and J. Wilson (eds.), *A Sourcebook: Serious, Violent, and Chronic Juvenile Offenders*. Thousand Oaks: Sage, 238–260.

———. 1996. "The Comparative Advantage of Juvenile Versus Criminal Court Sanctions on Recidivism Among Adolescent Felony Offenders." *Law & Policy* 18(1–2):77–113.

Fagan, J., and E. Deschenes. 1990. "Determinants of Judicial Waiver Decisions for Violent Juvenile Offenders." *Journal of Criminal Law & Criminology* 81(2):314–347.

Fagan, J., M. Forst, and T. S. Vivona. 1987. "Racial Determinants of the Judicial Transfer Decision: Prosecuting Violent Youth in Criminal Court." *Crime & Delinquency* 33(2):259–286.

Fagan, J., and F. Zimring. 2000. "Editor's Introduction." In J. Fagan and F. Zimring (eds.), *The Changing Borders of Juvenile Justice: Transfer of Adolescents to the Criminal Court*. Chicago: University of Chicago, 1–10.

Feiler, S., and J. Sheley. 1999. "Legal and Racial Elements of Public Willingness to Transfer Juvenile Offender to Adult Court." *Journal of Criminal Justice* 27(1):53–64.

Feld, B. 1987. "The Juvenile Court Meets the Principle of the Offense: Legislative Changes in Juvenile Waiver Statutes." *Journal of Criminal Law & Criminology* 78(3):471–533.

———. 1991. "Justice by Geography: Urban, Suburban, and Rural Variations in Juvenile Justice Administration." *Journal of Criminal Law & Criminology* 82(1):156–210.

———. 1993. "Juvenile (In)justice and the Criminal Court Alternative." *Crime & Delinquency* 39(4):403–424.

———. 1999. *Bad Kids: Race and the Transformation of the Juvenile Court*. New York: Oxford.

———. 2000. "Legislative Exclusion of Offenses From Juvenile Court Jurisdiction: A History and Critique." In J. Fagan and F. Zimring (eds.), *The Changing Borders of Juvenile Justice: Transfer of Adolescents to the Criminal Court*. Chicago: University of Chicago, 83–144.

———. 2003. "The Politics of Race and Juvenile Justice: The 'Due Process Revolution' and the Conservative Reaction." *Justice Quarterly* 20(4):765–800.

Forst, M., J. Fagan, and T. Vivona. 1989. "Youth in Prisons and Training Schools: Perceptions and Consequences of the Treatment Custody Dichotomy." *Juvenile & Family Court Journal* 40(1):1–14.

Fritsch, E., and C. Hemmens. 1996. "Juvenile Waiver in the United States 1977-1993: A Comparison and Analysis of Waiver Statutes." *Juvenile and Family Court Journal* 46(3):17-35.

Fritsch, E., T. Caeti, and C. Hemmens 1996. "Spare the Needle but Not the Punishment: The Incarceration of Waived Youth in Texas Prisons." *Crime & Delinquency* 42(4):593–609.

Fritsch, E., C. Hemmens, and T. Caeti. 1996. "Violent Youth in Juvenile and Adult Court: An Assessment of Sentencing Strategies in Texas." *Law & Policy* 18(1&2):115–135.

Gillespie, L. K., and M. Norman. 1984. "Does Certification Mean Prison?: Some Preliminary Findings From Utah." *Juvenile & Family Court Journal* 35(3):23–34.

Gragg, F. 1986. *Juveniles in Adult Court: A Review of Transfers at the Habitual Serious and Violent Juvenile Offender Sites* (Working Paper). Washington DC: Office of Juvenile Justice and Delinquency Prevention.

Greenwood, P., A. Abrahamse, and F. Zimring. 1984. *Factors Affecting Sentence Severity for Young Adult Offenders*. Santa Monica: Rand.

Greenwood, P., J. Petersilia, and F. Zimring. 1980. *Age, Crime, and Sanctions: The Transition From Juvenile to Adult Court*. Santa Monica: Rand.

Griffin, P. 2003. *Trying and Sentencing Juveniles as Adults: An Analysis of State Transfer and Blended Sentencing Laws*. (Special Project Bulletin). Washington DC: Office of Juvenile Justice and Delinquency Prevention.

Hamparian, D., J. Davis, and J. Jacobson. 1983. *Juvenile Transferred to Adult Court: Recent Ohio Experience*. Columbus: Federation for Community Planning.

Hamparian, D., L. Estep, S. Muntean, R. Priestino, R. Swisher, and P. Wallace. 1982. *Major Issues in Juvenile Justice Information and Training: Youth in Adult Courts: Between Two Worlds*. Columbus: Academy for Contemporary Problems.

Heide, K., E. Spencer, A. Thompson, and E. Solomon. 2001. "Who's in, Who's out, and Who's Back: Follow-up Data on 59 Juveniles Incarcerated in Adult Prison for Murder or Attempted Murder in the 1980s." *Behavioral Sciences and the Law* 19(1):97–108.

Houghtalin, M., and G. Mays. 1991. "Criminal Dispositions of New Mexico Juveniles Transferred to Adult Court." *Crime & Delinquency* 37(3):393–407.

Jensen, E., and L. Metsger. 1994. "A Test of the Deterrent Effect of Legislative Waiver on Violent Juvenile Crime." *Crime & Delinquency* 40(1):96–104.

Kinder, K., C. Veneziano, M. Fichter, and H. Azuma. 1995. "A Comparison of the Dispositions of Juvenile Offenders Certified as Adults With Juvenile Offenders Not Certified." *Juvenile & Family Court Journal* 46(3):37–42.

Krisberg, B., and J. Austin. 1993. *Reinventing Juvenile Justice*. Thousand Oaks: Sage.

Kupchik, A. 2003. "Prosecuting Juveniles in Criminal Court: Criminal or Juvenile Justice?" *Social Problems* 50(3):439–460.

Kupchik, A., J. Fagan, and A. Liberman. 2003. "Punishment, Proportionality, and Jurisdictional Transfer of Adolescent Offenders: A Test of the Leniency Gap Hypothesis." *Stanford Law & Policy Review* 14(1):57–83.

Kurlycheck, M., and B. Johnson. 2004. "The Juvenile Penalty: A Comparison of Juvenile and Young Adult Sentencing Outcomes in Criminal Court." *Criminology* 42(2):485–517.

Lane, J., L. Lanza-Kaduce, C. Frazier, and D. Bishop. 2002. "Adult Versus Juvenile Sanctions: Voices of Incarcerated Youths." *Crime & Delinquency* 48(3):431–455.

Lee, L. 1994. "Factors Determining Waiver in Juvenile Court." *Journal of Criminal Justice* 22(4):329–339.

Lemmon, J., T. Austin, P. F. Verrecchia, and M. Fetzer. 2005. "The Effect of Legal and Extralegal Factors on Statutory Exclusion of Juvenile Offenders." *Youth Violence and Juvenile Justice* 3(3):214–234.

Lemmon, J., H. Sontheimer, and K. Saylor. 1991. *A Study of Pennsylvania Juveniles Transferred to Criminal Court in 1986*. Harrisburg: The Pennsylvania Juvenile Court Judges' Commission.

Mack, J. 1909. "The Juvenile Court." *Harvard Law Review* 23(2):104–122.

McNulty, E. 1996. "The Transfer of Juvenile Offenders to Adult Court: Panacea or Problem?" *Law & Policy* 18 (1 & 2):61–75.

Mears, D. 2001. "Getting Tough With Juvenile Offenders: Explaining Support for Sanctioning Youths as Adults." *Criminal Justice and Behavior* 28(2):206–226.

———. 2003a. "Adult Crime, Adult Time: Punishing Violent Youth in the Adult Criminal Justice System." *Youth Violence and Juvenile Justice* 1(2):173–197.

———. 2003b. "The Recidivism of Violent Youths in Juvenile and Adult Court: A Consideration of Selection Bias." *Youth Violence and Juvenile Justice* 1(1):79–101.

Nimick, E., L. Szymanski, and H. Snyder. 1986. *Juvenile Court Waivers: A Study of Juvenile Court Cases Transferred to Criminal Court*.

Pittsburgh: National Center for Juvenile Justice.

Osbun, L. A., and P. Rode. 1984. "Prosecuting Juveniles as Adults: The Quest for Objective Decisions." *Criminology* 22(2):187–202.

Podkopacz, M., and B. Feld. 1995. "Judicial Waiver Policy and Practice: Persistence, Seriousness and Race." *Law and Inequality* 14(1):73–178.

———. 1996. "The End of the Line: An Empirical Study of Judicial Waiver." *Journal of Criminal Law & Criminology* 86(2):449–492.

———. 2001. "The Back-Door to Prison: Waiver Reform, 'Blended Sentencing,' and the Law of Unintended Consequences." *Journal of Criminal Law & Criminology* 91(4):997–1071.

Poulos, T., and S. Orchowsky. 1994. "Serious Juvenile Offenders: Predicting the Probability of Transfer to Criminal Court." *Crime & Delinquency* 40(1):3–17.

Puzzanchera, C. 2001. *Delinquency Cases Waived to Criminal Court*. (OJJDP Fact Sheet No. 35). Washington DC: Office of Juvenile Justice and Delinquency Prevention.

Risler, E., T. Sweatman, and L. Nackerud. 1998. "Evaluating the Georgia Legislative Waiver's Effectiveness in Deterring Juvenile Crime." *Research on Social Work Practice* 8(6):657–667.

Rothman, D. 1980. *Conscience and Convenience: The Asylum and Its Alternatives in Progressive America*. Boston: Little, Brown.

Ruddell, R., G. L. Mays, and D. Giever. 1998. "Recent Trends and Issues in Canada and the United States." *Juvenile & Family Court Journal* 49(3):1–13.

Rudman, C., E. Hartstone, J. Fagan, and M. Moore. 1986. "Violent Youth in Adult Court: Process and Punishment." *Crime & Delinquency* 32(1):75–96.

Ruth, H., and K. Reitz. 2003. *The Challenge of Crime: Rethinking Our Response*. Cambridge: Harvard University.

Sanborn, J. 1994. "Certification to Criminal Court: The Important Policy Questions of How, When, and Why." *Crime & Delinquency* 40(2):262–281.

———. 2003. "Hard Choices or Obvious Ones: Developing Policy for Excluding Youth From Juvenile Court." *Youth Violence and Juvenile Justice* 1(2):198–214.

Singer, S. 1993. "The Automatic Waiver of Juveniles and Substantive Justice." *Crime & Delinquency* 32(2):253–261.

Singer, S., and D. McDowall. 1988. "Criminalizing Delinquency: The Deterrent

Effect of the New York Juvenile Offender Law." *Law & Society Review* 22(3):521–535.

Smith, D., and R. Paternoster. 1990. "Formal Processing and Future Delinquency: Deviance Amplification as Selection Artifact." *Law & Society Review* 24(5):1109–1132.

Snyder, H. 1997. *Juvenile Arrests, 1996* (Juvenile Justice Bulletin). Washington DC: Office of Juvenile Justice and Delinquency Prevention.

Snyder, H., and M. Sickmund. 1999. *Juvenile Offenders and Victims: 1999 National Report*. Washington DC: Office of Juvenile Justice and Delinquency Prevention.

Snyder, H., M. Sickmund, and E. Poe-Yamagata. 2000. *Juvenile Transfers to Criminal Court in the 1990's: Lessons Learned From Four Studies*. Washington DC: Office of Juvenile Justice and Delinquency Prevention.

Sridharan, S., L. Greenfield, and B. Blakely. 2004. "A Study of Prosecutorial Certification Practice in Virginia." *Criminology & Public Policy* 3(4):605–632.

Steinberg, L., and E. Cauffman. 2000. "A Developmental Perspective on Jurisdictional Boundary." In J. Fagan and F. Zimring (eds.), *The Changing Borders of Juvenile Justice: Transfer of Adolescents to the Criminal Court*. Chicago: University of Chicago, 379–406.

Steiner, B. 2005. "Predicting Sentencing Outcomes in a Rural Northwestern State." *Journal of Criminal Justice* 33(6):601–610.

Steiner, B., and C. Hemmens. 2003. "Juvenile Waiver 2003: Where Are We Now?" *Juvenile & Family Court Journal* 54(2):1–24.

Steiner, B., C. Hemmens, and V. Bell. 2006. "Legislative Waiver Reconsidered: General Deterrent Effects of Statutory Exclusion Laws Post-1979." *Justice Quarterly* 23(1):34–59.

Tanenhaus, D. 2000. "The Evolution of Transfer out of the Juvenile Court." In J. Fagan and F. Zimring (eds.), *The Changing Borders of Juvenile Justice: Transfer of Adolescents to the Criminal Court*. Chicago: University of Chicago, 13–44.

Thomas, C., and S. Bilchik. 1985. "Prosecuting Juveniles in Criminal Courts: A Legal and Empirical Analysis." *Journal of Criminal Law & Criminology* 76(2):439–479.

Torbet, P., P. Griffin, H. Hurst, and L. MacKenzie. 2000. *Juveniles Facing Criminal Sanctions: Three States That Changed the Rules*. (Report). Washington DC: Office of Juvenile Justice and Delinquency Prevention.

Winner, L., L. Lanza-Kaduce, D. Bishop, and C. Frazier. 1997. "The Transfer of Juveniles to Criminal Court: Reexamining Recidivism Over the Long Term." *Crime & Delinquency* 43 (4):548–563.

Wu, B. 2000. "Determinants of Public Opinion Toward Juvenile Waiver Decisions." *Juvenile & Family Court Journal* 51(1):9–20.

Cases Cited

Kent v. United States, 383 U.S. 541 (1966).

In re Gault, 387 U.S. 1 (1967).

Schall v. Martin, 104 U.S. 2403 (1984).

Related Websites

Easy Access to Juvenile Populations: 1990–2004

http://ojjdp.ncjrs.org/ojstatbb/ezapop/

Census of Juveniles in Residential Placement Databook

http://ojjdp.ncjrs.org/ojstatbb/cjrp/

State Juvenile Justice Profiles

http://www.ncjj.org/stateprofiles/

National Council of Juvenile and Family Court Judges

http://www.ncjfcj.org/

The Juvenile Law Center

http://www.jlc.org/index.php

Discussion Questions

1. Are juvenile waiver laws appropriate? If so, when and for whom?

2. What makes juvenile waiver laws such a controversial topic?

3. Would public attitudes be swayed in opposition to juvenile waiver laws if people were aware of the scientific evidence (assuming they are not)?

4. Why do you think there is evidence of leniency by the system toward juveniles waived to criminal court? Is this a system-wide effort or the actions of a few individuals?

5. Is child saving dead? ✦

Chapter 17
Juvenile Curfews

Janice Ahmad, Katherine Bennett, and Jim Ruiz

In this chapter, the authors chronicle the court decisions both in support of and in opposition to juvenile curfew laws. Arguments either for or against curfews are developed in consideration of constitutional provisions and first require a level-of-analysis determination. This determination centers on whether cases involving juvenile curfew should be subject to strict scrutiny or to rational basis review. In cases that raise questions of differential treatment based on subjective factors, the Supreme Court has developed standard measures for determining whether differential treatment is found to be unconstitutional.

These standards, along with the appropriate classification, are referred to as strict scrutiny (suspect/fundamental rights classification), middle-tier scrutiny (quasi-suspect classification), and the rational basis (nonsuspect classification). Those who support a strict scrutiny analysis argue that curfews involve rights of minors similar to those rights of adults that have been deemed fundamental rights. Those who support a rational basis review believe that the state has a heightened interest, that children have lesser rights than adults, and that age is not a suspect classification.

The subsequent analysis provides yet another resource for understanding the many applications and interpretations of the Constitution. For example, the First Amendment in regards to political, religious, and expressive purposes, the Fourteenth Amendment's Due Process Clause in relation to the lesser rights of juveniles and standard of review, and Equal Protection Clause in regards to age discrimination.

Introduction

Curfews—laws restricting access to public areas at certain times—have been used for centuries, as a means of both social control and promotion of public safety. Curfews were used in the United States before the Civil War to control when slaves and free blacks could be on the street. Short-term curfews have been used in times of local or national emergencies. Since 1880, the most common curfew laws in the United States have been targeted at juveniles. Most recently, curfew statutes have been expanded to include graduated driver's licensing programs for minors. These laws prohibit or limit, among other actions, night driving for juvenile drivers and the number of other minors that can be in a vehicle operated by a minor. Laws restricting the movement and freedom of juveniles and the enforcement of such laws became popular during the last several years based on the (statistically unsupported) perception that juvenile crime is out of control and that a get-tough crime control policy toward juveniles, including curfews, will reduce the amount of crime juveniles are involved in, both as victims and as perpetrators (Hemmens and Bennett 1999). While generally popular, juvenile curfews are not without their problems and censure. In this chapter, we begin with a brief review of the history and theoretical underpinnings of juvenile curfews. Next comes a discussion of the arguments for and against juvenile curfews, with a focus on the legal arguments, as well as research supporting both sides of this issue.

History

The first juvenile curfew ordinance in the United States was passed in Omaha, Nebraska in 1880, requiring juveniles under 15 to be in their homes by 8:00 P.M. (Schwartz 1985). By 1900, over 3,000 similar ordinances had been passed, primarily to protect children, control juvenile crime and delinquency, and to intervene in cases where parents could not or would not control their children. Juvenile curfews were used during World War II as a means to check increasing delinquency, attributed in part to the fact that many parents were away in the military or otherwise working long hours in the defense industry (OJJDP 1997).

Curfews reemerged in the 1970s as a means of combating increasing juvenile crime (Henry 1995). They have continued to proliferate in the "war on crime" era and are popular sanctions among both policymakers and lay citizens. Researchers estimate that around 75 percent of major cities have juvenile curfew laws. In a recent survey of municipal police departments serving jurisdictions of 15,000 or more citizens, 68 percent of the 446 responding agencies had a juvenile curfew (Bannister, Carter, and Schafer 2003). In the 1996 presidential campaign, both Bill Clinton and Bob Dole embraced juvenile curfew, and in the same year Oregon passed a statewide curfew (Kalvig 1996). In addition, private entities such as shopping malls have also passed curfews prohibiting juveniles from entering the malls after certain hours unless accompanied by adults.

Local municipalities pass most juvenile curfew ordinances. Terms vary from city to city, but most require juveniles to be off the street or out of public places late at night (usually from 11:00 P.M. to 6:00 A.M.). These hours are sometimes extended on Fridays and Saturdays and during the summer. A few jurisdictions have daytime restrictions as well, limiting a juvenile's access to public places during school hours (Bannister et al., 2003). Most ordinances provide exceptions to these restrictions for specific purposes such as traveling to and from school, religious events, public functions, or jobs; in cases of emergencies; when traveling with the permission of the parent, if accompanied by an adult; or if married. Some curfew restrictions are limited to particular areas, such as high-crime or commercial areas that make victimization of juveniles more likely or that increase their potential to be involved in crime (OJJDP 1997). Responses and sanctions for curfew violators also vary from city to city, ranging from police arrest to simply returning the youths to their homes. Parental liability may be imposed in some ordinances (Kalvig 1996). See Table 17.1 for a summary of these restrictions.

Table 17.1	
Juvenile Curfew Ordinance Restrictions *	
Restriction	**General Guidelines**
Hours	Usually 10 or 11 P.M. to 5:00 or 6:00 A.M. the next day Friday and Saturday evenings may be later Summer (when school is not in session) may be later During school hours as truancy prevention
Age	Generally 17 and under Some provide earlier curfew time for younger juveniles
Exceptions	Attending or traveling to and from school, religious events, public functions, supervised activity, or employment In cases of emergencies When traveling with the permission of the parent if accompanied by an adult If married If engaged in interstate commerce If engaged in First Amendment rights If on sidewalk bordering residence
Miscellaneous	Restricts juveniles from particular areas, such as high-crime or commercial areas
Parental Responsibility	Parent or guardian can be fined or otherwise held responsible
* Not all juvenile curfew ordinances include all of these restrictions. Some jurisdictions have enacted highly restrictive models, while others have adopted less restrictive statutes.	

Theoretical Underpinning of Juvenile Curfew Ordinances

Deterrence, incapacitation, and critical race theories are generally used to explain the adoption of curfew laws. In this section, we briefly discuss each theory and its relevance to the recent proliferation of juvenile curfew ordinances.

Perhaps the most obvious theory underlying juvenile curfews is *deterrence theory*. Ostensibly, punitive sanctions for being out and about after curfew will deter juveniles from engaging in criminal or delinquent activity. Such curfews may also act as deterrence against both juvenile and adult victimization (Lundman 1993; Ruefle, Reynolds, and Brantley 1997).

Incapacitation theory applies to juvenile curfews in that apprehending curfew violators incapacitates them before they are victimized or before they commit crimes or other delinquent acts. *Selective incapacitation theory* can also be applied to juvenile curfew ordinances. Based on this theory, curfew laws are applied to only those juveniles identified as recidivists or repeat offenders. For example, Boston's Operation Nightlight used curfews for juveniles on probation and was declared successful in preventing homicides (Lundman 1993).

Critical race theory can also be applied to juvenile curfew laws if such laws are motivated, either overtly or covertly, by racial bias or stereotypes. Critical race theory emphasizes the role of racism and inequality in how law is written and experienced (Russell 1992). As noted earlier, early curfew laws in the 1800s were placed specifically on slaves and free blacks. During World War II, an ethnicity-based curfew was in effect against all Japanese and Americans of Japanese ancestry, as well as German and Italian aliens (Norton 2000). Today, applying juvenile curfews selectively in inner-city neighborhoods results in minority populations being overwhelmingly the target of such curfews.

Arguments for and against juvenile curfews are presented in the remainder of this chapter. Much of this discussion is concentrated on the legal issues that surround these arguments.

Arguments Supporting Curfews

Many juvenile curfew ordinances have survived judicial scrutiny in both federal and state courts. Determining the level of analysis is generally at the threshold of any judicial inquiry into the constitutionality of juvenile curfews, although courts are in disagreement as to whether strict scrutiny analysis or rational basis review is required. Courts applying *strict scrutiny analysis* argue that curfews implicate rights of minors similar to those rights of adults that have been deemed fundamental rights. *Rational basis* or an intermediate level of review, however, is applied when courts believe that the state has a heightened interest in regulating children's behavior, that children possess lesser rights than adults, that a minor's right to travel is not a fundamental right, and that children may be treated differently because age is not a suspect classification (Norton 2000). The standard of review is not the determining factor, however, in finding an ordinance constitutional. Some curfew ordinances have survived strict scrutiny analysis, where the law must be narrowly tailored to promote a compelling governmental interest. Other courts have applied intermediate scrutiny, which requires the ordinance to be substantially related to important governmental interests. The courts have not been consistent in these rulings.

From 1912 to 1972, seven state courts held juvenile curfews to be constitutional. One such example was Ohio's review of Columbus' curfew in *In re Carpenter*. In this case, the court of appeals applied a "reasonable" test to Columbus' daytime curfew prohibiting persons under the age of 18 from being on or about public streets within the city during school hours. The curfew was challenged on grounds of vagueness and alleged violations of the First, Fourth, Fifth, and Fourteenth Amendments. The Ohio appellate court disagreed with the vagueness charge, affirming the judgment of the trial court. Further, since the plaintiff's actions caused his arrest, the Fifth Amendment could not protect him. The plaintiff also was not engaged in the exercise of free speech and gave no reason for not being in school, so the state court saw no constitutional violations. The court considered the daylight curfew to bear a real and substantial relationship to public health, safety, morals, and general welfare.

In 1975, a federal district court for Pennsylvania became the first federal court to decide the constitutionality of a juvenile curfew ordinance (*Bykofsky v. Borough of Middletown* 1975). Middletown's curfew prohibited minors under 18 from being on the streets between specific times, depending on the age of the minor, unless the minors were accompanied by a parent, there was an emergency, or the minor was returning home from a legitimate social activity.

The plaintiff contended that the ordinance was impermissibly vague, violated First Amendment rights of minors, violated their right to travel, violated parents' right to control the upbringing of their children, and denied equal protection. The district court agreed that some phrases were impermissibly vague, but with the deletion of those words and phrases the ordinance itself was not impermissibly vague. No constitutional violation was found. The following sections discuss the relevant constitutional amendments and subsequent legal rulings in these areas that support juvenile curfews.

Juvenile Curfews Do not Violate Fourteenth Amendment Substantive Due Process Rights.

The *Bykofsky* court first noted that the standard of review to be applied to curfews for minors differs because juveniles do not have the same rights as adults. The conduct of minors may be constitutionally regulated to a greater extent than that of adults. Further, freedom of movement is not a fundamental right. Since strict scrutiny was unnecessary, the question was whether the ordinance was reasonable and advanced the legitimate concerns of the government against minors' competing interests. Because the city's chief of police testified to the amount of juvenile vandalism and disorderly conduct occurring at night and stated that the curfew had contributed to decreasing juvenile crime, the court saw a rational relationship between the ordinance and governmental interests in advancing and protecting the general community's welfare and safety.

Such interests outweigh freedom of movement.

Juvenile Curfews Do not Violate First Amendment Rights.

In the Columbus, Ohio, curfew ordinance, a section of the ordinance provided specifically for curfew exemptions for exercising First Amendment rights for political, religious, or expressive purposes, as long as prior notice was given to city officials. Thus, alleged First Amendment violations in the *Bykofsky* case were judged meritless. Plaintiffs also claimed that minors' First Amendment right to freedom of association for social purposes was also violated, but the *Bykofsky* Court said that governmental interests outweighed this right. Additionally, any First Amendment right to free speech was not violated because the curfew ordinance only regulated noncommunicative conduct.

Similarly, the Fifth Circuit overturned a district court's holding that a Dallas curfew violated minors' First Amendment freedom of association. Because exceptions were included in the Dallas curfew for associating for religious or political activities or for participating in activities when accompanied by a parent or guardian, the Fifth Circuit saw no freedom of association implications (*Qutb v. Strauss* 1993).

Juvenile Curfews Do not Violate a Parent's Right to Raise His or Her Own Children.

The court in the *Bykofsky* case agreed that governmental interference in the upbringing of children violates the Due Process and Equal Protection Clauses of the Fourteenth Amendment and the Ninth Amendment. However, this right is not absolute. According to the court, when the health or safety of a child is implicated or when there is a threat to public safety, peace, order, or welfare, legitimate state interests override the parental right to control the upbringing of children. The juvenile curfew was seen as only "minimal interference" with a parent's role in childrearing. The curfew was seen also as strengthening the family unit.

The Colorado Supreme Court applied a similar line of reasoning in 1989 in *People in Interest of J. M.* The state court saw the Pueblo, Colorado curfew ordinance as a legitimate way of reinforcing parental authority, encouraging parents to "take an active role in supervising their children" (*People in Interest of J.M.* 1989).

Juvenile Curfews Do not Violate the Equal Protection Clause of the Fourteenth Amendment. The *Bykofsky* Court applied the rational basis standard of review to the Columbus, Ohio juvenile curfew, finding that age discrimination is fairly and reasonably related to objectives of state action. However, strict scrutiny analysis of alleged equal protection violations has also been applied with favorable results for juvenile curfews.

The first time that a juvenile curfew ordinance successfully held up under strict scrutiny analysis occurred in 1993 in the Fifth Circuit case of *Qutb v. Strauss.* The Fifth Circuit noted that because the Dallas curfew ordinance differentiated classes of individuals based on age, the curfew must be analyzed under the Equal Protection Clause. The court was also willing to assume that the right to move about freely is a fundamental right. Thus, the question under strict scrutiny analysis was whether the ordinance was sufficiently narrowly drawn to accomplish the state's compelling interest in reducing juvenile crime and promoting the safety and well-being of children. The statistical data provided by Dallas regarding juvenile crime were adequate enough to show the court that the age classification of the curfew established the state's compelling interest. Because the ordinance also included numerous exceptions, the court held that it was narrowly drawn and was the least restrictive way to accomplish the state's goals of reducing juvenile crime and protecting children. The remainder of this section discusses the goal of reducing juvenile crime and victimization by implementing curfews.

Juvenile Curfews Reduce Juvenile Crime. Certainly the prime objective of curfews is to reduce juvenile crime. Some law enforcement officials see curfews as an effective tool for crime prevention, and a 1996 report by the Office of Juvenile Justice and Delinquency Prevention (OJJDP) on seven communities with curfew programs noted that all jurisdictions, except Jacksonville, reported decreases in juvenile crime. Jackson-

ville's program had been in existence for less than a year and was seen as too new to have made a measurable impact. The report concluded that "[t]he initial evidence offered by the seven communities profiled in this Bulletin is that community-based curfew programs that offer a range of services are more easily and effectively enforced, enjoy community support, and provide a greater benefit in preventing juvenile delinquency and victimization" (OJJDP 1996, 9).

Research has also been conducted relating to curfew enforcement and gang activity. In an evaluation of the Dallas Police Department's antigang initiative, Fritsch, Caeti, and Taylor (2003) found that using saturation patrol to enforce juvenile curfew and truancy laws could result in decreases in gang-related crime. However, while arrests for weapons violations and criminal mischief decreased, reported robbery and auto theft incidents increased. Quite possibly, citizens are more willing to report crimes when they see more police and gang members or, knowing there are more police in the neighborhood, do not engage publicly in illegal activities. Fritsch et al. (2003) concluded that while saturation patrol and enforcement of curfew violations may not lead to less gang membership, it can "affect the nefarious effects of gangs—crime and violence" (p. 279).

Anecdotal evidence regarding aggressive enforcement of curfews in Corpus Christi, Texas as part of a gang suppression initiative suggests that the number of curfew violations dropped substantially after the first few weeks of enforcement, indicating that such enforcement has an immediate effect (Bannister et al. 2003). Similarly, an evaluation of Detroit's curfew ordinance, intended to deter gang activity, concluded that criminal activity decreased during the hours covered by the curfew (Ruefle and Reynolds 1995).

Curfew ordinances targeting specific juveniles have also been shown to be successful. The Florida Department of Juvenile Justice conducted a pilot program that allowed police officers, instead of probation officers, to enforce court-ordered curfews of juveniles sentenced to probation. Research indicated a decrease in juvenile criminal activity, and both police and parents reported support for this program (Jones and Sigler 2002). Public support for juvenile curfews may be one of the strongest arguments for having such ordinances.

Juvenile Curfews Make Citizens Feel Safer. Surveys of residents in cities with juvenile curfews show that citizens support curfews because they make the citizens feel safer. It has also been found that support for juvenile curfews is high among both black and white citizens. A 1994 survey of African-American residents in Mobile, Alabama showed that 75 percent of them supported a proposed curfew (Crowell 1996). Further, city councils with a majority of black members have proposed curfews. For example, New Orleans' juvenile curfew was proposed by an African-American mayor and backed by a city council with a majority of black members (Ruefle and Reynolds 1996).

Juvenile Curfew Laws Identify At-risk Children. Enforcement of curfew laws may help identify at-risk children who are away from their homes because of abuse, neglect, or criminal behavior by the parent or other siblings, and once this identification is made, resources can be provided to the child and family (O'Brien 1999; Ruefle and Reynolds 1995). Recall that the *Bykofsky* Court saw the possibility for juvenile curfews to support and strengthen the family unit.

Despite the above arguments supporting juvenile curfews, courts have also found many to be unconstitutional, and the research supporting curfews is far from conclusive. In fact, much empirical research shows curfews to be far from effective. The remainder of this chapter focuses on those arguments opposing juvenile curfews.

Arguments Against Curfews

Arguments against curfews have existed since their early inception. In 1896, one critic noted that juvenile crime occurs mainly during the day rather than at night and that there are many legitimate reasons for juveniles to be out at odd hours (Buck 1896). These very same criticisms are still voiced today. Other critics contend that cur-

fews damage relationships between parents and children by inserting governmental authority and control, thus usurping the role of the parent (Chen 1997). Still other critics suggest that police agencies do not always enforce the curfew equitably, instead targeting minority youth (Ruefle and Reynolds 1995). In addition, juvenile curfew laws have been challenged on a number of legal grounds and have been struck down by both state and federal courts, beginning with *Ex parte McCarver* in 1898, when a Texas curfew was found to invade citizens' personal liberties and assume parental roles. Contemporary curfew laws that have been found to be unconstitutional are discussed in the following section.

Juvenile Curfews Are Unconstitutional. In 1973, the Supreme Court for the State of Washington reversed a lower court's conviction of a high school senior who violated Seattle's juvenile curfew (*City of Seattle v. Pullman* 1973). The ordinance made it unlawful for anyone who was not the parent or guardian of a minor or anyone not having the parent or guardian's consent to be in the company of the minor during curfew hours. Additionally, it was "unlawful for any minor child under the age of 18 years to loiter, idle, wander or play on or in the streets, sidewalks, highways, alleys, parks or other public places or in an automobile or other conveyance" (at 1061). The court found the ordinance to be unconstitutionally vague, as well as an unreasonable exercise of police power.

The court noted that "mere 'loitering-type' conduct ordinances" had been struck down by other jurisdictions and that the Supreme Court had ruled that "unwritten amenities" such as wandering and loitering "have been in part responsible for giving our people the feeling of independence and self-confidence" (in *Papachristou v. Jacksonville* 1972). The *Pullman* court did observe that a juvenile curfew ordinance with more specific prohibitions and that was "necessary in curing a demonstrable social evil" (at 1065) would be allowable.

In 1976, the Second Circuit Court of Appeals became the second federal court to address the constitutionality of juvenile curfew in *Naprstek v. City of Norwich* (1976). The Second Circuit invalidated a Norwich, New York curfew affecting minors under 17 that had been in existence for 56 years. The circuit court ruled that because the ordinance did not provide a termination time, it was void for vagueness and thus unconstitutional. The lack of a termination time was a violation of both the First and Fourteenth Amendments.

Ordinances with termination times, however, have not survived judicial review. In 1978, a Van Wert County, Ohio curfew prohibiting minors under 18 from "remaining in or upon any public place or establishment" between 10:30 P.M and 6:00 A.M. on school nights was declared unconstitutional (*In re Mosier* 1978). High school graduates were exempt from the ordinance, and exceptions were made for minors accompanying parents, minors who were lawfully employed, and minors on legitimate business at the direction of their parents. The *Mosier* court characterized this ordinance as the "remaining" type of curfew and thus "a minor may during the prescribed hours go anywhere he pleases as long as he stays in motion" (at 371), and the court noted several ridiculous results presented by such a reading of the curfew's meaning. According to this court, the curfew infringed on First Amendment rights and thus required strict scrutiny analysis. In applying this test, the court examined previous curfew cases, observing that decisions prior to *In re Gault* concluded that minors possessed much fewer constitutional rights than adults. After *Gault*, however, children, according to this court, are entitled to the same Fourteenth Amendment due process rights that are applied to adults. Accordingly, the *Mosier* court held that the Van Wert ordinance deprived minors of both First Amendment freedoms and fundamental Fourteenth Amendment due process rights without a compelling state interest. Additionally, the ordinance was unconstitutionally vague, and by exempting high school graduates it violated equal protection rights.

In 1981, the Fifth Circuit invalidated an Opelousas, Louisiana ordinance, finding it unconstitutionally vague and facially overbroad, in violation of First and Fourteenth Amendments, and in violation of the minor's right of interstate and intrastate travel guaranteed by the "Commerce Clause" of Article 1, Section 8 of the Constitution, and the Privileges and Immunities Clauses of the Fourteenth Amendment and Article 4, Section 2 (*Johnson et al. v. City of Opelousas* 1981).

The curfew in Opelousas prohibited "unemancipated minors under 17 years of age from being on the public streets or in a public place between 11 P.M. and 4 A.M.. on Sunday through Thursday, and 1 A.M. and 4 A.M., Friday and Saturday" unless accompanied by an adult or in response to an emergency (at 1071). The Fifth Circuit Court of Appeals noted that restrictions on minors that would be unconstitutional if applied to adults are justified only if they serve a significant state interest not present in the case of an adult. The Opelousas curfew was found to be unconstitutionally overbroad because it unnecessarily prohibited minors from engaging in First Amendment activities such as association and interstate travel. Some nighttime activities prohibited by the curfew, such as religious or school meetings, burdened minors' fundamental rights. The court stated that it was not expressing any opinion on "narrowly drawn" ordinances but that this curfew prevented juveniles from engaging in legitimate employment, being on the sidewalk in front of their own houses, and traveling through Opelousas even on an interstate trip.

Similarly, a district court in New Hampshire invalidated the fourth version of Keene, New Hampshire's curfew (*McCollester v. City of Keene* 1981). Keene's curfew applied to juveniles under 16 years of age and was in effect from 10 P.M until 5 A.M. The ordinance contained four exceptions, including where the minors were "passengers in a moving motor vehicle or if they are traveling before midnight to or from participation in a public assembly of 'persons seeking to publicize their position, which assembly has been authorized by a City permit' " (at 1383). Despite these exceptions, the district court found the ordinance to be overbroad and to impermissibly infringe on personal liberty interests in freedom of movement and privacy rights of both juveniles and their parents.

The district court looked at Justice Marshall's dissent to the denial of certiorari in the *Bykofsky* case discussed earlier in this chapter. Justice Marshall emphasized that freedom of movement was a protected Fourteenth Amendment liberty interest, subject only to narrowly drawn restrictions that further state interests. While states have legitimate interests in controlling crime and promoting public welfare, the *Keene* curfew was too broad because it provided no exemption for emergencies, and the exceptions it did include were limited to employment travel or being with a chaperone approved by the ordinance. Thus, the ordinance was overbroad, in violation of the Due Process Clause of the Fourteenth Amendment.

In 1987, the Superior Court of New Jersey found Bordentown, New Jersey's curfew to be unconstitutionally vague and overbroad, and, applying strict scrutiny, to deny equal protection to minors (*Allen v. City of Bordentown* 1987). This curfew prohibited minors under 18, with three limited exceptions, from being in public places between the hours of 9 P.M. and 6 A.M. Parents could be held responsible for their children's behavior, and, in the case at hand, faced a possible $300 fine and/or imprisonment of up to 30 days.

The court found several words and phrases in the ordinance to be unconstitutionally vague, such as "reasonable judgment" (referring to police officer discretion), "disturbance or annoyance," "free passage," and "emergency errand." With only three exceptions, the curfew was overbroad, and the court concluded that First Amendment rights to free speech, assembly, religion, and travel were implicated, thus requiring the strict scrutiny test. Since there was no compelling governmental interest in the curfew restrictions, the ordinance was a denial of equal protection.

Two years later, the district court for Washington, D.C. ruled unconstitutional the Temporary Curfew Emergency Act of 1989 in *Waters v. Barry* (1989), thus continuing this judicial trend of invalidating municipal curfew ordinances. A modified ordinance prohibited all juveniles from being on the street or in public places between the hours of 11 P.M. and 6 A.M. The curfew contained numerous exceptions, including minors traveling with their parents in a car, returning from a job, and/or on an emergency errand.

Following the 1984 ruling in *McCollester*, the District of Columbia court noted that "the right to walk the streets or to meet publicly with one's friends whenever one pleases is an integral component of life in a free and ordered society" (at 1134) and is protected by both the First Amendment freedoms of association and expression and the Fifth Amendment guarantee of substantive due process. Whenever the government restricts these rights, "it must do so in a manner that is narrowly focused on the harm at hand, as well as sensitive to needless intrusions upon the constitutional interests of the innocent" (at 1135). Such restrictions are subject to strict scrutiny analysis.

Applying this strict scrutiny analysis, the court determined that protecting juveniles from harm is a legitimate and compelling interest, but the curfew ordinance was not narrow enough to accomplish that purpose. No credible evidence showed that minors committed more crimes or were more likely to be crime victims during the hours the curfew was in effect. In fact, none of the juvenile victims of homicide in the District of Columbia had been killed at a time or place that could have been prevented had the curfew been in effect. While violence in the area was widespread, no evidence was presented showing that juveniles were more involved than adults.

In 1995, Washington, D.C. enacted another curfew ordinance, and a year later, the district court addressed its constitutionality in *Hutchins v. District of Columbia* (1996). The curfew in this case took effect on September 20, 1995, and targeted persons under 17 years of age. In addition, persons under 18 who possessed valid District of Columbia driver's licenses were prohibited from operating motor vehicles after midnight. The curfew ordinance contained eight exceptions, copied verbatim from the Dallas juvenile curfew upheld in *Qutb*. However, the plaintiffs offered numerous activities that would be prevented or burdened by the curfew, such as modeling assignments, study group sessions, ballet performances, swim practices that began at 6 A.M., debate team rounds, and dog walking during the curfew hours.

The *Waters* court (1989) noted that crimes of violence in the District of Columbia affected all its citizens, not just minors, so different treatment of minors could not be supported. This idea was continued by the *Hutchins* court in their comment that there was no evidence that most parents in D.C. were unable to control or protect their children and that there were no legitimate grounds for treating the minors' fundamental rights differently from adults.

The District of Columbia offered statistical information to substantiate a compelling state interest in reducing juvenile crime and victimization. The District also maintained that the eight exceptions in the ordinance showed the ordinance to be narrowly drawn and the least intrusive means necessary to achieve its stated goals. The court, however, was not convinced, describing the statistical information as a "hodge-podge of national, as opposed to local, statistics, other cities' statistics, unverifiable charts, and statistics for people over the age of 17" (at 678). Crime statistics were not broken down by time when the crime occurred or by the age of perpetrators and victims. Also, other statistics showed that more than 90 percent of all juveniles do not commit crimes and are not arrested at any time. The *Hutchins* court further found many of the exceptions to be vague and undefined. Thus, the court ruled that the ordinance was not narrowly drawn and was unconstitutional.

In 1992, the Iowa state court invalidated a Maquoketa curfew that had been modeled after a Panora city ordinance that had been upheld three years earlier (*City of Maquoketa v. Russell* 1992). This time, the court ruled that juvenile curfew laws required strict scrutiny because they implicated fundamental rights of juveniles, including the First Amendment freedoms of religion, speech, and association. The juvenile curfew was in-validated because it was not sufficiently narrowly tailored to achieve the state's interests.

San Diego had enacted a curfew ordinance in 1947, and in 1994 the city begun to aggressively enforce the ordinance. Three years later, in *Nunez v. City of San Diego* (1997), the Ninth Circuit Court of Appeals found the ordinance to be unconstitutional when the strict scrutiny analysis was applied.

The ordinance was invalidated for four reasons. First, the ordinance was found to be too vague. Second, the court held that the curfew was a violation of equal protection rights. Under strict scrutiny analysis, ordinance restrictions were not narrowly tailored to accomplish the city's compelling interest in reducing juvenile crime and juvenile victimization. Third, the ordinance provided no exceptions for "expressive association" and was thus a violation of First Amendment rights. Finally, the ordinance unconstitutionally usurped parents' fundamental right to rear their children without undue interference from the state. After this decision, the San Diego City Council quickly approved a new ordinance with nine exceptions, modeled after the Dallas ordinance upheld in *Qutb*.

This section of the chapter began with a 1973 curfew struck down by the state of Washington and closes with another Washington state case decided 30 years later (*City of Sumner v. Walsh* 2003). In 2003, the State of Washington Supreme Court ruled that the Sumner, Washington juvenile curfew ordinance was unconstitutionally vague. In addition to restricting times that juveniles could be in public places, Sumner's ordinance held parents liable for permitting or knowingly allowing their children to remain in any public place during curfew hours. The ordinance provided exemptions for traveling to or from work, from an adult-supervised or school-sponsored event, on an errand for a parent, and for interstate travel.

The court first noted that the 1973 Seattle curfew had been invalidated because the terms "loiter, idle, wander or play" during curfew hours were not sufficiently precise and violated the Due Process Clause of the state and federal constitutions. The *Sumner* ordinance was similarly deficient and was thus found void for vagueness.

The state court referred to the *Nunez* ruling that in order to avoid unconstitutional vagueness, an ordinance must "(1) define the offense with sufficient definiteness that ordinary people can understand what conduct is prohibited; and (2) establish standards to permit police to enforce the law in a non-arbitrary, non-discriminatory manner" (*Nunez* at 940). The Sumner ordinance was deemed to afford police too much discretion and did not include any standards that would distinguish between innocent and unlawful behavior.

The court acknowledged the difficulty that cities have in trying to draft curfews that do not fall to the charge of vagueness. The difficulty arises when cities try to include exceptions to their curfews. However, a blanket curfew with no exceptions is going to face constitutional challenges, at the very least, on grounds of being overly broad and restrictive. As the previous discussion illustrates, curfews have been seen to violate minors' freedom to travel and associate, freedom of expression, and rights to equal protection and due process. Curfews, ordinances without a compelling state interest or not being narrowly drawn to achieve that interest, will usually result in invalidation. Beyond the legal challenges to curfews, opposition also can be found in research regarding the effectiveness of curfews.

Curfews Are not Supported by Research. Ruefle and Reynolds (1995) and Lait (1998) conducted research relating to juvenile curfews and gang activity. Evaluation of the Detroit curfew ordinance targeting gang activity discussed earlier in this chapter found the curfew to be effective during curfew hours covered, but crime *increased* in the early afternoon hours prior to curfew, suggesting time displacement (Ruefle and Reynolds 1995). Analysis of a six-month period of stringent enforcement of a Los Angeles curfew revealed no effect on violent crime by juveniles or on crime in general (Lait 1998).

The Center on Juvenile and Criminal Justice (2002) examined juvenile arrest data from the California Department of Justice's Law Enforcement Information Center cov-ering 1980 to 1996. While expecting to find that communities with rigid curfew enforcement would have lower arrests for curfew violations and serious juvenile crime compared to communities with lax curfew restrictions, the study instead showed that in "many jurisdictions serious juvenile crime increased at the very time officials were touting the crime reduction effects of strict curfew enforcement" (CJCJ 2002, 9). They concluded that curfews had no measurable effect on juvenile crime.

In another study on the effectiveness of juvenile curfew laws, Reynolds, Seydlitz, and Jenkins (2000) used time-series analysis to compare victimizations and arrests before and after juvenile curfew enforcement in New Orleans. The researchers found no significant decrease in overall criminal victimizations, juvenile victimizations, and juvenile arrests. In fact, victimizations during noncurfew hours increased after the curfew was implemented. Reynolds et al. (2000) noted that juvenile curfew laws are ineffective because they do not affect older adolescents and young adults who are a large group of crime perpetrators, and they do not include the hours that juveniles most commonly commit crimes.

The conclusions of Reynolds et al. (2000) are similar to those of Cole (2003). Cole compared total juvenile arrests before and after each implementation of the curfew ordinances in Washington, D.C. that were discussed previously. No differences existed in the arrest rate of juveniles after the implementation of the curfew laws, leading Cole to speculate that enforcement of curfew violations was not uniform and to note that juvenile crime occurred during noncurfew times, especially the hours immediately after school. Further, the D.C. curfew law excluded 17-year-olds who accounted for almost one-third of all juvenile arrests.

The suggestion of nonuniform enforcement practices is borne out by a study by Bannister et al. (2003). In a survey of 797 municipal police departments, these researchers found that 58 percent of responding jurisdictions with curfews reported enforcement of curfew laws to be "aggressive" or "fairly aggressive," while almost 42 percent reported that enforcement was sporadic, left to the discretion of individual officers or only during special circumstances. Bannister et al. (2003) state that "[t]his variance in enforcement practices also raises a legal question: If curfew enforcement is sporadic and intentionally targeted to specific groups (i.e. gangs), does this equate to a denial of equal protection or fundamental fairness (due process)?" (p. 237).

Two research projects undertook more comprehensive analyses regarding curfew enforcement and effectiveness. In 2002, the Center on Juvenile and Criminal Justice published a review of 25 studies of the effects of curfew laws nationwide since 1990. They determined that there was no evidence that stricter curfew enforcement reduces juvenile crime. In fact, "[I]n those few instances in which a significant effect was found, it was more likely to be positive (that is, greater curfew enforcement was associated with higher rates of juvenile crime) than negative" (CJCJ 2002, 5).

In 2003, Adams published an examination of results of ten research projects relating to curfew enforcement. He concluded, "[B]y and large, . . . the research fails to demonstrate that curfews produced a decrease in juvenile crime" (Adams 2003, 144).

Practical Reasons for Opposing Curfews. Opponents of curfews also offer more pragmatic arguments. The National Council on Crime and Delinquency (NCCD) claims curfews are unproductive, resulting in net-widening by channeling nondelinquent youth into an already overburdened criminal justice system. Joseph (1999) argues that curfews criminalize status behavior and take childrearing responsibility from the parent. Further, he argues that limited governmental resources would be better used in the detection and prevention of criminal behavior instead of status offenses. Using police resources to enforce curfews is expensive, and the efficacy in preventing crime may be questionable.

The study by Bannister et al. (2003) found that many jurisdictions lacking juvenile curfew ordinances had no plans to adopt ones. Reasons given by the respondents included comments such as "Police do not have the re-sources to enforce it;" "There is no need for it;" "It is too difficult to enforce;" "Political leaders do not want a curfew;" and "Citizens do not want a curfew."

Conclusion

Shoemaker (1990) noted that "the concern over youthful deviance stems from the thought (however accurate) that today's delinquent is tomorrow's criminal, if nothing is done to change the antisocial behavior of the youth" (p. 4). The widespread support for juvenile curfew ordinances certainly reflects this concern. A majority of police agencies with curfew laws (whether or not they aggressively enforced the law) see enforcement of such curfews as wise use of resources and believe that curfews reduce crimes such as vandalism, graffiti, burglary, and gang-related offenses, even though many agencies do not collect crime statistics to determine curfews' actual effectiveness (Bannister et al. 2003). The empirical evidence does not tend to support any proposition that curfews reduce juvenile crime and juvenile victimization.

Curfews clearly threaten the exercise of a number of rights. Historically, juveniles have been treated as second-class citizens, under the rationale that they needed more protection (legal custody) than adults. But courts are split over the constitutionality of curfew laws. The U.S. Supreme Court has denied certiorari in three cases concerning the constitutionality of curfew laws (*Bykofsky v. Borough of Middletown* 1976; *Qutb v. Bartlett* 1994; *Schleifer v. City of Charlottesville* 1999). Mixtures of rulings currently exist, and as Hemmens and Bennett (1999, 118) concluded, this "confusion among the lower courts" regarding the constitutionality of curfew laws will continue without a definitive pronouncement by the Court. Without Supreme Court guidance, courts currently wrestle with balancing: (1) the government's interest in protecting children and the community from crime and victimization, (2) the least interference with juveniles' freedom of movement and practice of First Amendment rights, and (3) limited interference with parental responsibility of raising their children. Juvenile curfews remain a debatable issue.

References

Adams, K. 2003. "The Effectiveness of Juvenile Curfews at Crime Prevention." *The Annals of the American Academy of Political and Social Sciences* 587:136–159.

Bannister, A. J., D. L. Carter, and J. Schafer. 2003. "A National Police Survey on the Use of Juvenile Curfews." *Journal of Criminal Justice* 29:233–240.

Buck, W. 1896. "Objections to a Children's Curfew." *North American Review* 164:381, 382.

Center on Juvenile and Criminal Justice (CJCJ). 2002. *The Impact of Juvenile Curfew Laws in California*. http://www.cjcj.org/pubs/curfew/curfew.html.

Chen, G. Z. 1997. "Youth Curfews and the Trilogy of Parent, Child, and State Relations." *New York University Law Review* 72:131–174.

Cole, D. 2003. "The Effect of a Curfew Law on Juvenile Crime in Washington, DC" *American Journal of Criminal Justice* 27:217–232.

Crowell, A. 1996. "Minor Restrictions: The Challenge of Juvenile Curfews." *Public Management* 79:4–9.

Fritsch, E. J., T. J. Caeti, and R. W. Taylor. 2003. "Gang Suppression Through Saturation Patrol and Aggressive Curfew and Truancy Enforcement: A Quasi-Experimental Test of the Dallas Anti-Gang Initiative." In S. H. Decker (ed.), *Policing Gangs and Youth Violence* (pp. 267–284.) Belmont, CA: Thomson Wadsworth.

Hemmens, C., and K. Bennett. 1999. "Juvenile Curfews and the Courts: Judicial Response to a Not-So-New Crime Control Strategy." *Crime and Delinquency* 45:99–121.

Henry, T. 1995. "Curfews Attempt to Curb Teen Crime." *USA Today*, April 5:1.

Jones, M. A., and R. T. Sigler. 2002. "Law Enforcement Partnership in Community Corrections: An Evaluation of Juvenile Offender Curfew Checks." *Journal of Criminal Justice* 30:245–256.

Joseph, P. 1999. "Are Juvenile Curfews a Legal and Effective Way to Reduce Juvenile Crime? No." In J. D. Sewell (ed.), *Controversial Issues in Policing*, (pp. 62–66.) Boston: Allyn and Bacon.

Kalvig, K. A. 1996. "Oregon's New Parental Responsibility Acts: Should Other States Follow Oregon's Trail?" *Oregon Law Review* 75:829–901.

Lait, M. 1998. "Report Questions Teen Curfews." *Los Angeles Times*, February 10: A15.

Lundman, R. 1993. *Prevention and Control of Juvenile Delinquency*. New York: Oxford Press.

Norton, D. E. 2000. "Why Criminalize Children? Looking Beyond the Express Policies Driving Juvenile Curfew Legislation." *Legislation and Public Policy* 4:175–203.

O'Brien, L. F. 1999. "Are Juvenile Curfews a Legal and Effective Way to Reduce Juvenile Crime? Yes." In J. D. Sewell (ed.), *Controversial Issues in Policing*, (pp. 59–62) Boston: Allyn and Bacon.

Office of Juvenile Justice and Delinquency Prevention (OJJDP). 1996. *Curfew: An Answer to Juvenile Delinquency and Victimization*. Rockville, MD: U.S. Department of Justice.

———. 1997. "Juvenile Justice Reform Initiatives in the States: 1994-1996". http://ojjdp.ncjrs.org/pubs/reform/contents.html.

Reynolds, K., R. Seydlitz, and P. Jenkins. 2000. "Do Juvenile Curfew Laws Work? A Time-Series Analysis of the New Orleans Law." *Justice Quarterly* 17:205–230.

Ruefle, W., and K. M. Reynolds. 1995. "Curfews and Delinquency in Major American Cities." *Crime and Delinquency* 4:355–358.

———. 1996. "Keep Them at Home: Juvenile Curfew Ordinances in 200 American Cities." *American Journal of Police* 15:63–84.

Ruefle, W., K. M. Reynolds, and A. Brantley. 1997. "Curfews Can Be Effective and Constitutional." In D. Bender and B. Leone (eds.), *Juvenile Crime: Opposing Viewpoints* (pp. 187–192) San Diego: Greenhaven.

Russell, M. 1992. "Entering Great America: Reflections on Race and the Convergence of Progressive Legal Theory and Practice." *Hastings Law Journal* 43:749–767.

Schwartz, R. 1985. "Rights Issue, Teen-Age Curfews: A Revival." *Los Angeles Times* August 10: D1.

Shoemaker, D. 1990. *Theories of Delinquency: An Examination of Explanations of Delinquent Behavior*. New York: Oxford University Press.

Cases Cited

Allen v. City of Bordentown, 524A.2d 478 (N.J. 1987).

Bykofsky v. Borough of Middletown, 401 F. Supp. 1242 (M.D. Penn. 1975), *aff'd without opinion*, 535 F.2d 1245 (3d Cir. 1976), cert. denied 429 U.S. 964 (1976).

City of Maquoketa v. Russell, 484 N.W.2d 179 (Iowa 1992).

City of Seattle v. Pullman, 514 P.2d 1059 (Wash. 1973).

City of Sumner v. Walsh, 148 Wn.2d 490 (2003).

Ex parte McCarver, 46 S.W.936 (1898).

Hutchins v. District of Columbia, 942 F. Supp. 665 (D.D.C. 1996), 188 F. 3d 531 (D.C. Cir. 1999).

In re Carpenter, 287 N.E.2d 399 (Ohio Ct. App. 1972).

In re Mosier, 394 N. E. 2d 368, 369 (1978).

Johnson et al. v. City of Opelousas, 658 F.2d 1065 (5th Cir. 1981).

McCollester v. City of Keene, 514 F. Supp. 1046 (D.N.H. 1981).

Naprstek v. City of Norwich, 545 F.2d 815 (2d Cir. 1976).

Nunez v. City of San Diego, 114 F.3d 935, 939 (9th Cir. 1997).

Papachristou v. Jacksonville, 405 U.S. 156, 164 (1972).

People in Interest of J.M., 768 P.2d 219 (Colo. 1989).

Qutb v. Strauss, 11 F.3d 488 (5th Cir. 1993).

Schleifer v. City of Charlottesville, 159 F.3d 843 (4th Cir. 1998), cert. denied 526 U.S. 1018 (1999).

Waters v. Barry, 711 F. Supp. 1125 (D.D.C. 1989).

Related Websites

American Bar Association Section of Individual Rights and Responsibilities

http://www.abanet.org/irr/home.html

American Bar Association: Juvenile Curfews: The Rights of Minors vs. the Rhetoric of Public Safety

http://www.abanet.org/irr/hr/fall99humanrights/budd.html

American Bar Association: Juvenile Justice Committee

http://www.abanet.org/crimjust/juvjus/

Crimes Against Children Research Center (CCRC)

http://www.unh.edu/ccrc/about-ccrc.html

National Center for Missing & Exploited Children (NCMEC)

http://www.missingkids.com

Office of Juvenile Justice and Delinquency Prevention

http://ojjdp.ncjrs.org/

Curfew: An Answer to Juvenile Delinquency and Victimization?

http://www.ncjrs.gov/pdffiles/curfew.pdf

The U.S. Conference of Mayors

http://www.usmayors.org

Best practices highlighting Phoenix, Arizona juvenilecurfew enforcement

http://www.usmayors.org/uscm/best_practices/bp_volume_2/phoenix.htm

A Status Report on Youth Curfews in America's Cities

http://www.usmayors.org/uscm/news/publications/curfew.htm

Discussion Questions

1. Of the three theoretical underpinnings discussed in the chapter, which theory do you think best explains the adoption of juvenile curfew laws by municipalities? Explain why you chose that theory rather than one of the other theories.

2. Choose three of the arguments that were given for supporting juvenile curfews that you feel are the most compelling. Explain why you chose these reasons and not the others given for supporting juvenile curfew laws. Now, choose three of the arguments against juvenile curfews that you feel are the most compelling. (You may break the legal arguments into separate issues.) Again, explain why you chose these reasons for not supporting the adoption of juvenile curfew laws.

3. Assume you are a parent of a 14-year-old. You have read in the local newspaper that the city council where you live will be holding a public forum to explore the possibility of adopting a juvenile curfew in the city. You decide that you want to appear at this meeting and discuss your feelings, as a parent of a teenager, toward such an ordinance. What will your position be, and how will you convince the city council members to vote for or against the ordinance based on your position? Your answer should be in the form of a three-minute presentation that you will give at the public hearing.

4. Assume you are 15 years old. You have read in the local newspaper that the city council where you live will be holding a public forum to explore the possibility of adopting a juvenile curfew. Up to this

time, there has not been a curfew in the city. You decide you want to appear at this meeting and speak to the city council members concerning your stand on the adoption of a juvenile curfew ordinance. What will your position be and how will you convince the city council members to vote for or against the ordinance based on your position? Your answer should be in the form of a three-minute presentation that you will give at the public hearing.

5. You are a member of a task force that has been given the responsibility of writing a draft city ordinance that will establish a juvenile curfew for your community. What elements should be included in this ordinance? The ordinance that you are proposing must remain within constitutional guidelines.

6. Determine whether your jurisdiction has passed a juvenile curfew law. If it has, what restrictions are placed on juveniles in your municipality? If no law exists, why do you think this is so? Should a juvenile curfew ordinance be adopted? Explain your answer using the information from this chapter. ✦

Section V

Miscellaneous Legal Issues

Chapter 18
The Criminal Justice System's Treatment of Assisted Suicide

David C. Brody

This chapter examines several key issues surrounding euthanasia and physician-assisted suicide. First, the author presents the arguments for and against the legalization of those practices. Those in favor argue that assisted suicide is a fundamental human right not to be interfered with by the government, that doctors have a duty to relieve pain and suffering, and that it is similar to other acts of passive euthanasia. Those who are opposed argue that doctors who provide life-ending (instead of life-supporting) treatment violate the Hippocratic Oath, that assisted suicide violates moral standards, and that legalizing assisted suicide may open the door to possible future arbitrary actions.

Second, the author presents some research findings on the criminal justice system's treatment of people who engage in acts of euthanasia or physician-assisted suicide. In all, 33 states view physician-assisted suicide as a criminal action. However, most of these states do not prosecute individuals for violations under these statutes. Additional studies have explored this issue by highlighting the discretionary power of state prosecutors, along with other influential factors such as unclear guidelines and outcomes, questionable evidence quality, and increased possibility of jury nullification.

Finally, the author examines the constitutionality of laws against physician-assisted suicide, along with an analysis of related U.S. Supreme Court rulings, Oregon's Death with Dignity Act, and subsequent federal actions. Two cases, *Washington v. Glucksburg* (1997) and *Vacco v. Quill* (1997), shed light on the constitutional issues present within this analysis. In *Glucksburg* (1997), the Supreme Court addressed whether a Washington State code violated the Due Process Clause of the Fourteenth Amendment, particularly if criminalizing assisted suicide deprived an individual of a fundamental right. In a 9–0 decision, the Court ruled that there is no fundamental right to assist a person in committing suicide. In *Vacco*, the Supreme Court addressed whether a New York statute violated the Equal Protection Clause of the Fourteenth Amendment because the statute permits a competent person to refuse medical treatment, even if doing so will result in death, even though a competent, terminally ill person is not allowed to take medication that will hasten his or her death. The Court ruled in favor of the statute. A Federal Controlled Substances Act directive, which set a standard for criminalizing assisted suicide in light of Oregon's Death with Dignity Act, also came under the scrutiny of the Court, which affirmed a lower court's ruling in favor of the Oregon Act.

This chapter addresses key concepts within the realm of physician-assisted suicide. Particularly, the author explores both sides of the issue, provides a general background regarding criminalization and prosecutorial discretion, and reveals the constitutional arguments related to euthanasia and inherent within the Fourteenth Amendment. This chapter is important because it gives rise to questions that further our understanding of constitutional rights while addressing the difficult and sensitive topic of death.

Introduction

The criminalization of assisted suicide, often referred to as "mercy killing," began to attract much thoughtful attention by Americans in the 1990s. For the first half of the decade, Dr. Jack Kevorkian, a Michigan pathologist, participated in well over 100 acts of euthanasia and physician-assisted suicide. Although he was prosecuted several times for these deeds, for most of the decade he avoided being convicted. The event that brought the issue to a head occurred in November 1998 when the television program *60 Minutes* broadcast a tape of Dr. Kevorkian giving a lethal dose of barbiturates to a man suffering from Lou Gehrig's disease. The video outraged many citizens and policymakers alike. Shortly after the tape aired, Dr. Kevorkian was charged with first-degree murder. He was later found guilty of second-degree murder and sentenced to a term of 10–25 years in prison.

Since Dr. Kevorkian's activities first became widely known, the treatment of people who participate in acts of euthanasia and physician-assisted suicide has been a controversial and contentious area of criminal law. The issue has produced mixed feelings among the public, mixed policy responses from politicians, mixed messages from the Supreme Court, and mixed ethics opinions from the medical profession. This chapter will examine what precisely is meant by the terms *euthanasia* and *physician-assisted suicide*, the arguments for and against their legalization, the criminal justice system's treatment of people who commit euthanasia and physician-assisted suicide, and rulings of the U.S. Supreme Court on the constitutionality of laws against physician-assisted suicide.

Before looking at the criminal justice system's treatment of cases of euthanasia and physician-assisted suicide, it is important to understand what these terms mean. *Euthanasia* comes from the Greek word *euthanatos* and literally means "good death." It occurs when a person actually performs the act that ends another person's life. *Physician-assisted suicide*, on the other hand, occurs when a doctor provides the means and information necessary for a patient to end his or her own life. The typical case of physician-assisted suicide involves a doctor, upon the request of the patient, prescribing a lethal dose of a medication and telling the patient how to use the drug to bring about death.

Euthanasia can be active or passive. In *active euthanasia* a person directly and intentionally causes another's death. A doctor physically injecting a patient with a lethal dose of a medication is an example of active euthanasia. Acts of active euthanasia are punishable as homicide under the criminal law. In *passive euthanasia* a person does not directly take another's life, but permits him or her to die. Removing a feeding tube from a comatose patient, knowing that eventually

the person will starve to death, is an example of passive euthanasia. Acts of passive euthanasia are generally not considered criminal. Given that the law surrounding euthanasia is well settled, the remainder of this chapter will discuss the criminal justice system's actions regarding assisted suicide.

Assisted suicide involves aiding another to die, usually by providing the drugs or some other means that a person will use to end his or her life. *Physician-assisted* suicide occurs when the helping party is a medical doctor. Physician-assisted suicide has been a lightning rod for controversy for the general public and the justice system.

Arguments for and Against Legalizing Assisted Suicide

Supporters of the legalization of assisted suicide make three major arguments. The most prominent one deals with individuals' liberty and self-determination (Dworkin 1998; Quill 1991). Advocates of assisted suicide say that competent, rational, and informed adults have the right to decide that their life is no longer worth living and should be able to plan the time and manner of their death. As this right does not affect other individuals, it is believed that it should not be interfered with by the government.

Another argument involves the duty of doctors to relieve pain and suffering. When dealing with a terminally ill patient who is in extreme pain and who will suffer greatly for the rest of his or her life, it is asserted that upon request, a doctor should be permitted to show mercy and help end the patient's suffering.

A further argument for legalizing assisted suicide equates it with acts of passive euthanasia. The U.S. Supreme Court has found that a competent adult has the right to request (in writing or to a third person) that life-sustaining treatment be removed should he or she enter a vegetative state (*Cruzan v. Director*, Missouri Department of Health 1990). Supporters of legalizing assisted suicide say that it is illogical and unfair to permit the withdrawal of life-sustaining treatment yet to prohibit physician-assisted suicide (Dworkin et al. 1998). They assert that the two acts are morally equivalent and should be treated similarly by the law.

Arguments against legalizing assisted suicide fall into three general categories: philosophical/ethical, paternal, and the "slippery slope." From a philosophical perspective, it is considered a violation of the Hippocratic Oath for a physician to provide a patient with treatment that is not intended to extend life or ease symptoms. It is argued that appropriate pain-relieving medications can be prescribed to make a patient more comfortable. Once these treatments are provided, the patient may reconsider suicide and no longer seek death.

Many opponents of legalizing physician-assisted suicide do so on moral grounds (see *Washington v. Glucksberg* 1997). They believe that life is precious and that it is simply wrong to take active steps to hasten death. Under this viewpoint, killing is always unacceptable (with the possible exception of capital punishment) and should not be legally permitted.

Another category of arguments against legalizing assisted suicide involves the protection of individuals. Terminally ill people are likely to be depressed and in pain from time to time. These conditions, however, can be treated. While a person may feel like ending his or her life at one particular moment, that feeling may be fleeting. If physician-assisted suicide is permitted, a situation could arise in which a person who has been given a supply of medicines and instructed on how to use them to cause death may take his or her own life in an otherwise temporary moment of desperation.

Perhaps the most frequent argument against legalizing physician-assisted suicide is the fear that it will lead down a "slippery slope." Opponents repeatedly warn that regulated physician-assisted suicide may be but a first step toward active euthanasia of individuals who are not terminally ill. Chronically depressed people or individuals with a chronic though not terminal illness may seek to end their suffering. Relatedly, there is concern that disabled and vulnerable individuals could be led down the path of suicide by ill-willed doctors, family members, or health care administrators. De-

pending on consent requirements and the delegation of health care decision-making authority, unwilling patients could be signed up for assisted suicide.

Physician-Assisted Suicide and the Criminal Law

While suicide and attempted suicide are generally not considered criminal offenses in the United States, the act of assisting a person in committing suicide is entirely different. As seen in Table 18.1, the vast majority of states explicitly criminalize physician-assisted suicide. Nine states treat aiding a person in committing suicide as homicide either by statute or as part of their common law ("case law" issued by a court). Many other states have statutes that describe assisted suicide as a crime in its own right. These statutes generally follow the language of Section 210.5 of the Model Penal Code: "Aiding or Soliciting Suicide as an Independent Offense. A person who purposely aids or solicits another to commit suicide is guilty of a felony of the second degree if his conduct causes such suicide or an attempted suicide. . . ."

Although assisted suicide is forbidden in a vast majority of states, it is rarely prosecuted. To determine how often doctors are prosecuted for assisting a patient in ending his or her life, Alpers (1998) searched national databases within the Lexis Nexis system. The search was designed to find any mention of a prosecution in media outlets or court records between 1990 and 1997. In all, Alpers found that 13 doctors and 2 nurses were criminally investigated but not formally charged. Five other doctors and two nurses were charged with murder. There is no indication that the level of prosecutions for physician-assisted suicide has increased in the years since the Alpers study.

Several studies have examined the likelihood that a criminal prosecution would happen if an act of physician-assisted suicide should come to a prosecutor's attention. In 1994 Alan Meisel and several associates conducted a mail survey of 2,844 district attorneys nationwide (Meisel, Jernigan, and Youngner 1999). The survey presented pros-

Table 18.1

State Criminalization of Assisted Suicide

Physician-Assisted Suicide Treated as Homicide

Homicide by Statute	Homicide Under Common Law
Arizona	Alabama
Arkansas	Massachusetts
Colorado	Nevada
Florida	South Carolina
Hawaii	

Statute Criminalizing Assisted Suicide

California	Michigan	Oklahoma
Georgia	Minnesota	Pennsylvania
Illinois	Mississippi	South Carolina
Iowa	Montana	South Dakota
Kansas	Nebraska	Tennessee
Kentucky	New Jersey	Texas
Louisiana	New Mexico	Washington
Maryland	New York	Wisconsin

Source: Oregon Department of Human Services 2005, p.12.

ecutors with several scenarios involving terminally ill patients. Of particular interest was a vignette involving a terminally ill woman with only several months to live. Although mentally competent, the woman was bedridden and in extreme, ever-increasing pain. The patient and her husband made repeated requests to her doctor to provide medication that she could take to end her life. The survey asked prosecutors whether they would take any action against the doctor if it came to their attention that the doctor prescribed a lethal dose of medication and the patient died. Of the 761 prosecutors who returned completed surveys, only 39.1 percent stated they would take some kind of action against the doctor.

In a study involving the same vignette, Ziegler (2005) asked 110 prosecutors in four states (Connecticut, Maryland, Oregon, and Washington) what they would do if the doctor's actions came to their attention. Of the 84 prosecutors who responded to the survey, roughly 50 percent said they would recommend a police investigation of the doctor. Since a recommendation that police investigate is far short of filing formal charges, we can assume that the number of prosecutors that would prosecute such a case is appreciably lower than 50 percent. More interesting is the fact that of the prosecutors surveyed, only 29.8 percent believed that no crime had been committed. Thus, of the approximately 70 percent who believed a crime had been committed (42.9 percent) or might have been committed (23.8 percent), a full 20 percent would not even have requested further investigation.

There are several explanations for why physician-assisted suicide is rarely prosecuted. First and foremost is the fact that it seldom comes to the attention of prosecutors or police. Unless a family member or friend of the victim reports the incident as a crime, it is unlikely that an act of assisted suicide (as opposed to euthanasia) will receive any scrutiny. However, the underground nature of assisted suicide does not completely explain the scarcity of prosecutions.

The reluctance of prosecutors to pursue cases of assisted suicide is a product of a prosecutor's nearly unlimited discretion in deciding what will or will not be prosecuted in a jurisdiction. Because there are no legislative or judicial guidelines on charging, and a decision not to file charges ordinarily is immune from review, a prosecutor can use his or her individual criteria in deciding what cases to pursue.

A number of reasons might explain the lack of prosecutions in cases of physician-assisted suicide. The most prominent is the desire to avoid uncertainty (Albonetti 1987). Given the limited resources available in the criminal justice system, prosecutors are leery to file charges in cases where the outcome is unclear. This uncertainty may stem from the amount and quality of the evidence, the likely guilt of the defendant, and the nature of the crime (Albonetti 1987; Schmidt and Steury 1989; Spohn and Holleran 2001). According to these criteria, physician-assisted suicide is a crime for which it will be hard to obtain a conviction. Under most statutes, the prosecutor would have to prove that the defendant provided a prescription to a patient intending or knowing that the patient would use the medication to commit suicide. Without an admission by the defendant, this is a mental state that is extremely hard to prove. Furthermore, it is unlikely the defendant has a criminal history, and he or she may appear sympathetic to a jury. Finally, even if a juror believed that a crime was committed, he or she may still refuse to vote for conviction through the power of jury nullification: the juror may believe that the defendant did not do anything morally wrong and should therefore not be held criminally liable. Each of these factors make the outcome a prosecution for physician-assisted suicide uncertain.

A Constitutional Right to Assisted Suicide?

In 1997 the Supreme Court decided two cases involving the constitutionality of statutes making assisted suicide unlawful. In *Washington v. Glucksberg* (1997) and *Vacco v. Quill* (1997), the Court answered one question, in stating, "Statutes prohibiting assisted suicide are generally constitutional"—yet raised another: "Might there be a right under some circumstances to suicide and assisted suicide?"

Washington v. Glucksberg

Section 9A.36.060(1) of the Washington Revised Code states, "A person is guilty of promoting a suicide attempt when he knowingly causes or aids another person to attempt suicide." In 1994, a group of physicians and patients in Washington State filed suit in federal district court seeking a declaratory judgment that the statute was unconstitutional. The court found that the Washington statute deprived the plaintiffs of a liberty interest and therefore violated the Due Process Clause of the Fourteenth Amendment: "Like the abortion decision, the decision of a terminally ill person to end his or her life involves the most intimate and personal choices a person may make in a lifetime and constitutes a choice central to personal dignity and autonomy." Finding such an interest to be compelling, the court held the statute unconstitutional.

This decision was appealed to the Ninth Circuit Court of Appeals, which at first reversed the District Court ruling (*Compassion in Dying v. Washington* 1995). This ruling was vacated by an *en banc* panel of the Ninth Circuit (*Compassion in Dying v. Washington* 1996). By an 8–3 vote, the court held that the statute violated a person's right to self-determination. Like the district court, the *en banc* panel considered the right to terminate one's life to be a basic life decision and therefore a fundamental right subject to limitation only by a compelling state interest.

The Supreme Court granted certiorari, and by a 9–0 vote reversed (*Washington v. Glucksberg* 1997). Although the result was unanimous, Chief Justice Rehnquist's majority opinion was joined in by only four other justices. The majority framed the issue presented as a question of whether the Due Process Clause of the Fourteenth Amendment protects one's right to commit suicide or to be assisted in so doing. As the issue involved a "fundamental right," the Court then conducted traditional substantive due process analysis.

The first step in this analysis is determining if the purported right is "fundamental." This step is a crucial—in fact often *the* crucial—factor affecting cases involving substantive due process. If a right is found to be fundamental, state action infringing on it must further a compelling state interest, use the least restrictive means available to further the state interest, and be closely tailored to directly further the goals of the state action. This standard, often referred to as the *compelling state interest test*, is very difficult to meet. On the other hand, if a right is not considered to be fundamental, state action affecting its exercise need only be rationally related to any state interest to pass constitutional muster.

A right is considered fundamental if it is "implicit in the concept of ordered liberty." This criterion is determined by examining the nation's history and traditions. In doing this analysis, Chief Justice Rehnquist noted that assisting suicide has been outlawed since the nation was founded. He also observed that assisting suicide was a crime in all but one state, and that states that had considered proposals legalizing assisted suicide in recent years had overwhelmingly rejected the proposals. "That many of the rights and liberties protected by the Due Process Clause sound in personal autonomy does not warrant the sweeping conclusion that any and all important, intimate, and personal decisions are so protected. . ." (*Washington v. Glucksberg* 1997, 727). Justice Rehnquist concluded that there is no fundamental right to assist a person in committing suicide.

Having found that any potential right to assisted suicide is not fundamental, the majority opinion considered whether there is any rational basis for the state laws prohibiting its exercise. The Supreme Court noted and accepted six state interests identified by the Ninth Circuit: (1) preserving life; (2) preventing suicide; (3) avoiding the involvement of third parties and use of arbitrary, unfair, or undue influence; (4) protecting family members and loved ones; (5) protecting the integrity of the medical profession; and (6) avoiding future movement toward euthanasia and other abuses. (*Washington v. Glucksberg* 1997, 728).

Chief Justice Rehnquist found that these items were clearly related to the state ban on assisted suicide. Accordingly, he found that the ban was constitutional.

Vacco v. Quill

In 1994, Timothy Quill, a noted doctor, scholar, and defender of the right to assisted suicide, filed suit in district court challenging New York's law banning the intentional assistance or promotion of suicide. The suit argued that the New York statute violated the Equal Protection Clause of the Fourteenth Amendment because the statute permitted a competent person to refuse medical treatment, even if doing so would result in death, but did not allow a competent, terminally ill person to take medication that will hasten his or her death. The district court rejected this argument, holding that New York State needed to present only a "reasonable and rational" basis for the distinction in its law. Noting that a patient who refuses treatment is merely allowing nature to take its course whereas suicide involves intentionally using an artificial death-producing device, the court found such a distinction to exist.

The Second Circuit Court of Appeals reversed (*Quill v. Vacco* 1996). It held that ending the life of a terminally ill patient by withdrawing life-sustaining treatment is indistinguishable from physician-assisted suicide. It went on to find that different legal treatment of terminally ill patients is not rationally related to any legitimate state interest; thus, the New York statute violated the Equal Protection Clause of the Fourteenth Amendment.

The Supreme Court then reversed again (*Vacco v. Quill* 1997). Writing for the same majority as in *Glucksberg*, Chief Justice Rehnquist held that since the New York statute did not treat people differently based on a suspect classification, the statute was entitled to a strong presumption of validity. In considering the assisted suicide statute and the statute permitting the withdrawal of life-sustaining treatment, he wrote:

> On their faces, neither New York's ban on assisting suicide nor its statutes permitting patients to refuse medical treatment treat anyone differently from anyone else or draw any distinctions between persons. *Everyone*, regardless of physical condition, is entitled, if competent, to refuse unwanted lifesaving medical treat-

ment; *no one* is permitted to assist a suicide. Generally speaking, laws that apply evenhandedly to all "unquestionably comply" with the Equal Protection Clause.

The Concurring Opinions and Their Implications

While the Court's majority opinions strongly rejected the claim that states may not ban assisted suicide, they did not rule out future challenges to statutes similar to Washington's. It is likely that this situation was necessary in order obtain the fifth vote necessary to produce a majority opinion.

Justice O'Connor, who provided the fifth vote in support of the majority opinion in both cases, was clear in her belief that a statute banning assisted suicide could be unconstitutional under certain circumstances. In a concurring opinion covering both cases, which was joined by Justices Breyer and Ginsberg, she said the issue faced by the Court was whether the statute in question was facially valid, not whether there was a constitutional right to suicide. Justice O'Connor found that the Washington and New York laws against assisting suicide had at least some constitutional applications. She explicitly stated, however, as did Justice Stevens in a separate concurring opinion, that states are free to permit assisted suicide so long as such a statute is narrowly tailored to protect vulnerable individuals.

The opinions in *Glucksberg* and *Quill* present mixed messages. While the Court unanimously agreed that the statutes in question were constitutional as applied, it appears that five justices believevd that there is potentially a right to assisted suicide. Given Justice O'Connor's retirement and the death of Chief Justice Rehnquist, the Court appears now evenly divided on this issue.

Oregon's Death With Dignity Act

Prior to *Glucksberg* and *Quill*, Oregon enacted a statute that permitted physician-assisted suicide under certain, very controlled circumstances. The Oregon Death With Dignity Act was a citizen's initiative ("Measure 16") approved by Oregon voters (51–49 percent) on November 8, 1994. Its implementa-

tion was delayed for several years by a legal injunction issued by the U.S. District Court of Oregon. The Ninth Circuit vacated the order granting the injunction, and on October 27, 1997, after a petition for review was denied by the U.S. Supreme Court, the Ninth Circuit Court of Appeals lifted the injunction. One week later, a measure appeared on the ballot asking Oregon voters to repeal the Death With Dignity Act (Measure 51, authorized by Oregon House Bill 2954). The measure was rejected by a margin of 60 percent to 40 percent and the Death With Dignity Act went into effect shortly thereafter.

The Death With Dignity Act provides that a person is eligible to receive a prescription for a lethal substance with the intent of ending life only if he or she is:

- An adult (18 years of age or older)
- A resident of Oregon
- Able to make and communicate health care decisions
- Diagnosed with a terminal illness that will lead to death within six months

If a person meets these requirements, the following procedures must be taken:

- The patient must make two oral requests separated by at least 15 days to his or her physician to receive a prescription for lethal medication.
- The patient's request must be in writing and signed in the presence of two witnesses.
- The prescribing physician and a second doctor must confirm the diagnosis and prognosis.
- The prescribing physician and a consulting physician must determine whether the patient is mentally capable of making the request.
- If either physician believes the patient's judgment is impaired by a psychiatric or psychological disorder, the patient must be referred for a psychological examination.
- The prescribing physician must inform the patient of feasible alternatives to assisted suicide, including comfort care, hospice care, and pain control.

It is clear that the Death With Dignity Act addresses many of the concerns raised by opponents of physician-assisted suicide. To protect against a person who is only depressed or individuals who may be chronically but not terminally ill from obtaining medications for use in committing suicide, the law requires that a person must have less than six months to live, as determined by two physicians. To protect against a person committing suicide with the help of a doctor based on a rash decision made when in pain or in a negative mental state, the law requires that multiple requests be made to at least two doctors over a two-week period. To protect a person from being manipulated by family or others, the law states that a request must be made in writing and signed in the presence of two witnesses.

One area of the Death With Dignity Act that may draw criticism is its near silence regarding the mental state of a patient. There is no necessity that a patient be evaluated by a psychologist or psychiatrist. While the act requires a doctor to refer a patient to a mental health care provider if he or she believes the patient's judgment is impaired by a mental disorder, it leaves that determination solely to the primary or secondary doctor. Moreover, the act is silent on how the second examining physician should be chosen. As such, it is likely that the primary physician will select a doctor he or she is familiar with, and presumably one who will agree with his or her diagnosis.

The Death With Dignity Act calls for the Oregon Department of Human Services to collect information about actions taken in connection with the act and to prepare an annual report based on information collected. As shown in Figure 18.1, instances of assisted suicide under the act increased steadily until 2004, when there was a slight decline (Oregon Department of Human Services 2005). In 2004 Oregon physicians wrote 60 prescriptions in accordance with the act that led to the deaths of 35 terminally ill people (13 patients died from their illness). Of note, 12 of the patients who were provided with the prescribed medication were still living at the end of 2004, indicating

the importance of requiring multiple requests and appropriate waiting periods.

Perhaps the most troubling item presented in the data is lack of consideration of patients' mental state throughout the process. As shown in Figure 18.2, in 1998 29 percent of patients who requested to commit physician-assisted suicide were referred to a specialist for a psychological evaluation. In 2004, only 2 patients (5 percent) were referred (Oregon Department of Human Services 2005).

Figure 18.1
*Number of Prescriptions and Deaths
Under Death With Dignity Act*

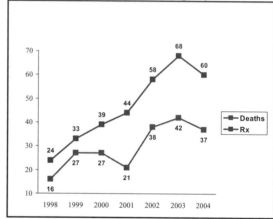

Source: Oregon Department of Human Services 2005, p.12.

Figure 18.2
*Death With Dignity Act Cases With Mental
Health Evaluations*

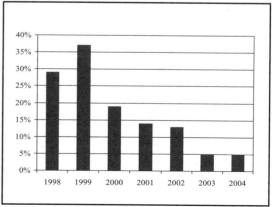

Source: Oregon Department of Human Services 2005, p.12.

The Ashcroft Directive and Subsequent Litigation

On November 6, 2001, Attorney General John Ashcroft issued a directive entitled "Dispensing of Controlled Substances to Assist Suicide" that "criminalizes conduct specifically authorized by Oregon's Death With Dignity Act." (*Oregon v. Ashcroft* 2004, 1120). Under the federal Controlled Substances Act, physicians may not prescribe or dispense a controlled substance except for a "legitimate medical purpose" and "in the usual course of professional treatment" *United States v. Moore* (1975).

The directive states that physician-assisted suicide serves no legitimate medical purpose. Under the federal Controlled Substances Act (CSA) physicians may not prescribe or dispense a controlled substance except for a "legitimate medical purpose" and "in the usual course of professional treatment" (*United States v. Moore* 1975, 124). It follows that a physician who prescribes medications in accordance with the Death With Dignity Act will be considered to have improperly prescribed medications and may have his or her DEA registration, which is necessary to prescribe controlled substances, revoked.

The State of Oregon brought an action in the District Court of Oregon seeking to prevent federal enforcement or application of the directive. On April 17, 2002, U.S. District Judge Robert Jones blocked its enforcement with a permanent injunction against enforcement of the directive. (*Oregon v. Ashcroft* 2002). The Ninth Circuit Court of Appeals accepted multiple petitions for review, and in a divided opinion ordered the injunction against enforcement of the directive continued.

The majority opinion framed the issue as whether "Congress authorized the attorney general to determine that physician-assisted suicide violates the Controlled Substances Act." (*Oregon v. Ashcroft* 2004, 1123.) The opinion concluded that physician-assisted suicide is a general medical practice subject to state regulation absent explicit, unmistakably clear Congressional authorization. The majority found that not only did the CSA fail to address assisted suicide, but the directive went well beyond the scope of the CSA's stated purpose of dealing with drug abuse.

The majority also closely examined a 1984 amendment to the CSA that authorized the attorney general to revoke a doctor's prescription-writing privileges if he determined that the physician committed acts that would render his or her registration "inconsistent with the public interest." Under the CSA, in determining what acts are inconsistent with the public interest, the attorney general must consider the following factors:

1. The recommendation of the appropriate state licensing board or professional disciplinary authority

2. The applicant's expertise in dispensing controlled substances

3. The applicant's conviction record under federal or state laws relating to the manufacture, distribution, or dispensing of controlled substances

4. Compliance with applicable state, federal, or local laws relating to controlled substances

5. Such other conduct that may threaten the public health and safety

The majority held that the directive did not consider the five factors, but stated only that physician-assisted suicide is against the public interest entirely because it threatens public health. The court found that the other four factors clearly indicate that the practice of assisted suicide as delineated in the Death With Dignity Act is not inconsistent with the public interest.

The U.S. Supreme Court affirmed the Ninth Circuit's decision. In a 6–3 decision, the Court wrote that the CSA explicitly provides for a leading role for states in regulating the medical profession. The Court went on to find that the attorney general lacks the training and expertise to define what is a legitimate medical purpose. The setting of medical standards of care authorized under state laws should be left to the states themselves rather than the federal government.

The Criminal Law and Physician-Assisted Suicide in the Future

The future treatment of assisted suicide by the criminal justice system is unclear. On the one hand, surveys show that a majority of American's have consistently favored the legalization of physician-assisted suicide over the last 20 years (Taylor 2005). In April 2005, this figure reached 70 percent of those surveyed (Taylor 2005). On the other hand, every state other than Oregon that has considered the legalization of physician-assisted suicide has soundly rejected it in the legislature or the ballot box. The debate is unlikely to end, and the efforts by both sides of the issue are not likely to subside. With ever-increasing medical treatments and technologies that have the capability of extending lives, it is likely that more terminally ill individuals will seek alternatives to their lives of pain and suffering. It will be left to policymakers and prosecuting attorneys to decide how society will treat these decisions.

References

Albonetti, C. 1987. "Prosecutorial Discretion: The Effects of Uncertainty." *Law and Society Review* 21:291–313.

Alpers, A. 1998. "Criminal Act or Palliative Care? Prosecutions Involving the Care of the Dying." *Journal of Law, Medicine, & Ethics* 26:308–331.

Dworkin, G., R. G. Frey, and S. Bok. 1998. *Euthanasia and Physician-Assisted Suicide*. Cambridge, MA: Cambridge University Press.

Dworkin, R. 1998. "Euthanasia, Morality and the Law." *Loyola Los Angeles Law Review* 31:1147.

Emanuel, E. J., E. R. Daniels, D. L. Fairclough, and B. R. Clarridge. 1998. "The Practice of Euthanasia and Physician-Assisted Suicide in the United States: Adherence to Proposed Safeguards and Effects on Physicians." *JAMA* 280:507–513.

Meisel, A., J. C. Jernigan, and S. J. Youngner. 1999. "Prosecutors and End-of-Life Decision Making." *Archives of Internal Medicine* 159:1089–1095.

Oregon Department of Human Services. 2005. *Seventh Annual Report on Oregon's Death with Dignity Act*.

Quill, T. A. 1991. "Case of Individualized Decision Making." *New England Journal of Medicine* 324:691.

Schmidt, J., and E. Steury. 1989. "Prosecutorial Discretion in Filing Charges in Domestic Violence Cases." *Criminology* 27:487–510.

Spohn, C., and D. Holleran. 2001. "Prosecuting Sexual Assault: A Comparison of Charging Decisions in Sexual Assault Cases Involving Strangers, Acquaintances, and Intimate Partners." *Justice Quarterly* 18:651–689.

Taylor, H. 2005. *The Harris Poll #32*.

Ziegler, S. P. 2005. "Physician-Assisted Suicide And Criminal Prosecution: Are Physicians at Risk?" *Journal of Law, Medicine, & Ethics* 33:349.

Cases Cited

Compassion in Dying v. Washington, 49 F.3d 586 (9th Cir. 1995).

Compassion in Dying v. Washington, 79 F.3d 790 (9th Cir. *en banc* 1996).

Cruzan v. Director, Missouri Department of Health, 497 U.S. 261 (1990).

Oregon v. Ashcroft, 192 F.Supp.2d 1077 (D.Or.2002).

Oregon v. Ashcroft, 368 F.3d 1118 (9th Cir. 2004).

Washington v. Glucksberg, 521 U.S. 702 (1997).

Quill v. Vacco, 80 F.3d 716 (2d Cir. 1996).

United States v. Moore, 423 U.S. 122 (1975).

Vacco v. Quill, 521 U.S. 793 (1997).

Related Websites

Oregon Department of Human Services
http://egov.oregon.gov/DHS/ph/pas/index.shtml

Euthanasia.com
http://www.euthanasia.com

Euthanasia Research & Guidance Organization (ERGO)
http://www.assistedsuicide.org/index.html

International Task Force on Euthanasia and Assisted Suicide
http://www.internationaltaskforce.org

Nightingale Alliance
http://www.nightingalealliance.org/index.php

Discussion Questions

1. In your opinion, does the Oregon Death With Dignity Act adequately address the concerns raised by opponents of legalizing physician-assisted suicide? What modifications would you make to the act?

2. What role should a judge's moral and philosophical beliefs have in his or her evaluating the constitutionality of issues such as physician-assisted suicide?

3. What interests does a state have in prohibiting assisted suicide? On a scale of 1 to 10, how would you rate their importance?

4. Do you believe that passive euthanasia is significantly different from active euthanasia and assisted suicide? Should they be treated differently by the law? If yes, how so?

5. It has been argued that both sides of the debate regarding the legalization of physician-assisted suicide were both pleased and angered by the Supreme Court's decisions in *Glucksberg* and *Vacco*. Do you agree with this sentiment? Explain why or why not. ✦

Chapter 19
Surfing for Porn
Obscenity and the Internet

Jeff Maahs and John Liederbach

This chapter provides a framework for understanding the evolving legal context surrounding pornography and its dissemination over the Internet. First, the chapter provides a general discussion concerning how pornography has been interpreted within the context of First Amendment free speech rights. Second, the chapter provides an overview of federal and state obscenity laws. Third, the chapter reviews more recently enacted regulations specifically designed to address new issues posed by the Internet. Fourth, the chapter concludes with a discussion regarding the primary legal and technological issues involved in regulating obscenity on the Internet.

In relation to First Amendment free speech rights, the key question revolves around defining what constitutes free speech and what (in this case pornographic material) can be considered obscene by community standards, as illustrated in *Miller v. California* (1973) and subsequent Supreme Court cases. The obscenity regulation is further explored in the context of several court cases.

Historically, radio and television were recognized as the major communication mediums or forms of media that fell under the scrutiny of state and federal obscenity laws. However, with the onset of the Internet, this media facet became a center of attention in the fight to regulate obscene content, as illustrated in the passing of the Communications Decency Act of 1996. Additionally, the Child Pornography Prevention Act of 1996, the Child Online Protection Act of 1998, and the Children's Internet Protection Act of 2001 are analyzed. Specific to the "borderless" Internet, it is important to note the many issues at hand in dealing with pornography and obscene content, such as the impact of the Constitutional Commerce Clause, that make the regulation and development of restrictive law difficult. As you shall see, the effective development and enforcement of obscenity laws, especially in regard to the Internet, proves to be difficult in finding a resolution.

Introduction

As a result of the explosive growth that has occurred in information technologies over the course of the last several decades, computers have quickly become common fixtures of everyday life for most Americans. In fact, our newly created information-based society would scarcely be recognized by those who helped create this information revolution with the advent of the first computer in 1945. Through the 1960s, growth in the use of computer technologies was slow and was limited primarily to military, academic, and corporate elites. However, the pace of the revolution quickened with the growing popularity of personal computers in the 1980s and the widespread availability of information on the World Wide Web (WWW), or the computer-based network of information resources that can be accessed through the Internet (Taylor et al. 2006).

The Internet has revolutionized information and communication by creating a global network of computer users who are linked by satellite and telephone connections (Encarta Encyclopedia 2005). Currently, there are roughly 171 million named hosts on the Internet, with each host representing a network of up to 254 million computers (Internet Software Consortium 2001). These connections have allowed for the instant exchange of information for many applications, including online commerce, financial transactions, and personal communications such as email and instant messaging.

Of course, the Internet has also been a boon to those who disseminate sexually explicit material. The pornography industry was well established in the United States prior to the current information revolution. For example, by the 1980s the industry included over 800 adult movie theatres and somewhere between 15,000 and 20,000 adult bookstores. These businesses employed over 100,000 people (Kirk et al. 1983). Nonetheless, growth in information technologies and the Internet has made what was once only available in back alleys and seedy live "peep shows" very easy to obtain through a simple click of the mouse.

The wide-scale availability of pornographic material over the Internet has helped create a $10 billion-a-year adult entertainment industry in the United States. This figure exceeds the annual revenue of the three major broadcasting networks combined (CBS News 2003). The Internet contains an estimated 4.2 million pornographic websites (12 percent of all websites) including 372 million online pages of pornography. Annual revenue generated specifically from Internet pornography sites exceeds $2.5 billion. Some 40 million U.S. adults regularly visit Internet pornography sites, and 10 percent of those admit to being addicted to Internet pornography (Internet Filter Review 2005).

Internet technologies have also made pornographic material more accessible to children and teens. Surveys sponsored by Internet Filter Review (2005) show that young males aged 12–17 may be the largest consumers of Internet pornography, and the average age at which they were first exposed to pornography on the Internet was 11. The emergence of "easy access" pornography over the Internet has also reinvigorated the child pornography trade (Durkin 1997). In the past, child pornography was often homemade and consisted of old pictures, magazines, or videotapes. Now, pedophiles may use the Internet to access child pornography or engage in inappropriate communication with children (Taylor et al. 2006). While there are few hard statistics concerning the prevalence of child pornography online, one researcher estimated that there may be up to 1 million sexually explicit pictures of children on the Internet (Henley 1996).

The proliferation of online pornography (especially the wide-scale availability of pornography to children) and the resurgence of child pornography have created increased public concern regarding the appropriate use of new information and communications technologies. Federal and state legislatures have enacted numerous statutes designed to curtail obscenity or pornography

on the Internet as a result of these trends. This chapter provides a framework for understanding the evolving legal context surrounding pornography and its dissemination over the Internet. First, the chapter provides a general discussion concerning how pornography has been interpreted within the context of First Amendment free speech rights. Second, the chapter provides an overview of federal and state obscenity laws. Third, the chapter reviews more recently enacted regulations specifically designed to address new issues posed by the Internet. Fourth, the chapter concludes with a discussion regarding the primary legal and technological issues involved in regulating obscenity on the Internet.

Pornography, Obscenity, and the First Amendment

The First Amendment to the Constitution provides the primary legal context for the debate concerning the regulation of sexually explicit material. The amendment specifically limits the Congress from enacting laws that abridge the "freedom of speech." The central issue concerning pornographic material is whether it can be considered a form of "free speech" that is protected from government restriction. If a particular piece of *pornographic material* (material that is sexually explicit and designed to cause sexual excitement) is determined to be *obscene* in a legal sense, the material will not be protected by First Amendment restrictions, and lawmakers are free to enact restrictions of that material.

The landmark case that defined obscenity is *Miller v. California* (1973). In *Miller,* the Supreme Court used a three-pronged test to determine whether a work will be considered obscene under the Constitution: (1) Would an average person applying contemporary community standards find that the work appeals to certain "prurient interests"? (2) Does the work depict or describe in an offensive way (as measured by community standards) sexual conduct that is specifically defined by the law? (3) Would a reasonable person find that the overall work lacks serious literary, artistic, political, and scientific value?

Most legal scholars agree that *Miller's* three-pronged test is somewhat "mushy" and difficult to define. First, what are the "prurient interests" described in the first prong of the test? The dictionary defines *prurient* as something that is "lustful or appealing to an inordinate and unhealthy sexual interest or desire," a definition that is clearly open to individual interpretation (Free Press Dictionary 2005). It is also difficult to define the "community standards" phrase contained in prongs one and two. Is a community a specific geographical area such as a town, county, or state? If so, how do we define the community for obscene material that is displayed over the Internet—a medium that does not conform to any geographical boundaries? Even in cases where "community" can be well defined, there may be substantial disagreement about what the "average person" may find offensive. In light of the problems associated with the *Miller* test, a student may raise the question of whether our definition has improved much beyond the one used by former Supreme Court Justice Potter Stewart, who stated, "I know it (obscenity) when I see it" (*Jacobellis v. Ohio* 1964, 197).

The Limits of Obscenity Regulation

Courts are generally suspicious of content-based restrictions on freedom of speech. These restrictions are only permitted in cases where (1) the regulation furthers a compelling state interest, and (2) the government has shown that the regulation is the least restrictive means of achieving its goal (Wheatland 2005). Over time, the Court has tried to work within these restrictions to determine whether certain pornographic material should be considered "obscene" and not protected by the First Amendment.

The Court justified the exclusion of obscenity from First Amendment protections in *Paris Adult Theater I v. Slaton* (1973). In the *Paris* case, the Court identified several valid government interests that could be used to prohibit obscene material, including the maintenance of a community's quality of life, commerce, and public safety. The Court reasoned that issues related to sexuality were central to family life and community welfare and that the wide-scale dissemination of obscene material would threaten important family and community values.

Despite the fact that obscenity is not a protected form of speech, the Court has also ruled that the government may not regulate

Table 19.1	
Federal Obscenity Statutes	
Federal Statute	**Type of Obscenity Provision**
18 U.S.C. 1461	Mailing obscene matter
18 U.S.C. 1462*	Importation or use of a common carrier to transport obscene matter
18 U.S.C. 1464	Broadcasting of obscene language
18 U.S.C. 1465*	Interstate transportation of obscene matter
18 U.S.C. 1466	Wholesale and retail sale of obscene matter that has been transported in interstate commerce (must be engaged in business of selling or transferring obscenity)
18 U.S.C. 1467	Obscene material, property traceable to profits, or property that facilitates the offense is subject to criminal forfeiture
18 U.S.C. 1468	Distribution of obscene matter by cable or satellite TV
47 U.S.C. 223	Making an obscene communication by means of telephone

*Statutory provisions amended to include distribution via the Internet.

obscenity in a manner that overly burdens nonobscene speech (Wheatland 2005). On the other hand, the Court *does* permit regulation of material that falls short of the *Miller* test within the context of minors. In *Ginsburg v. New York*, the Court upheld a statute prohibiting the sale of pornographic material to minors. The Court reasoned that in the particular case of minors, the right to read pornographic materials is limited by parental childrearing interests, as well as the state's interest in protecting the well-being of youths. Similarly, in *FCC v. Pacifica Foundation* (1978), the Court permitted regulation of sexually explicit but nonobscene broadcast material because television broadcasts are "uniquely accessible to children."

As the *Pacifica* case suggests, the type of regulation permitted depends greatly on the medium used to deliver the material. Radio and television broadcasts are subject to the highest level of scrutiny for at least three reasons. First, these types of broadcasts are distinctively accessible to children. Second, because space on the broadcast spectrum is limited, those allowed to use this resource should serve the public interest. Finally, greater restrictions can be justified on the grounds that radio and television broadcast are not amenable to the inclusion of "warnings" regarding the content of a particular program, since individuals are free to tune in at any time during the broadcast (Wheatland 2005).

In the *United States v. Playboy Entertainment Group* (2000), the Supreme Court distinguished cable television from broadcast television. At issue here was a federal regulation that required cable TV operators to either *completely* scramble the signals for pay-

---

Table 19.2

Overview of Federal Legislation Targeting Pornography and/or Obscenity on the Internet

Federal Legislation	Specific Provisions Related to the Internet and Sexual Content	Current Legal Status
Communications Decency Act of 1996, 47 U.S.C. 223	Prohibits the transmission of "indecent," "patently offensive," or "obscene" materials to minors over the Internet.	In *Reno v. ACLU*, the Supreme Court struck down the "indecent" and "patently offensive" portions of the statute. The provision banning transmission of obscene speech to minors remains in effect.
Child Pornography Prevention Act of 1996, 18 U.S.C. 225	Prohibits the production, distribution, and reception of computer-generated sexual images of children.	The Supreme Court struck down the provisions of the statute that involved *simulated (e.g., adults doctored to look like children) child pornography*.
Child Online Protection Act of 1998, 47 U.S.C. 231	Prohibits the commercial distribution of material that is "harmful to minors" via the World Wide Web. "Harmful" is defined as material that is obscene or that meets a minor-specific three-pronged test similar to *Miller*. An affirmative defense (requiring age verification through a credit card or other means) is offered to defendants.	An injunction granted by a district court remains in effect. In *Ashcroft v. ACLU* the Supreme Court held that the injunction was valid because the government had failed to rebut the plaintiff's contention that there were plausible, less restrictive means to serve the government's interests.
Children's Internet Protection Act of 2001, 20 U.S.C. 9134, 47 U.S.C. 254(h)	Requires public libraries and libraries within public schools to install Internet filters or forfeit federal subsidies designed to encourage library access to the Internet. The filter may be disabled for legitimate uses.	In *United States v. American Library Association*, the Court upheld the provisions in the statute. The Court reasoned that the Internet is not a "Public forum" and that libraries already engage in content-based judgments in selecting materials.

for-porn channels (so that the signals would-n't "bleed" into TV sets of nonsubscribers) or to air the imperfectly scrambled signals only from 10 P.M. to 6 A.M. Here, the Court pointed to technological differences between these forms of media. More specifically, cable television has the technology to allow users to block specific programs. The key is that a *less restrictive alternative* was available to the Court, one that was much less burdensome than requiring cable companies to completely scramble adult-content channels or to limit sexually explicit content to certain time periods.

Federal and State Obscenity Laws

The federal government and most states have enacted laws prohibiting the possession and/or distribution of obscene materials. The federal laws are summarized in Table 19.1. Federal laws offer no specific definition of obscenity. In the absence of a specific definition, the courts are most likely to apply the *Miller* test. Table 19.1 shows that federal laws cover the various forms of traditional media, including mail, telephone, radio, broadcast television, and cable television. Two sections of the obscenity statutes were amended in the 1990s to include the Internet. For example, Title 18, section 1462 prohibits the importation or transportation of obscene materials from an *"interactive computer service"* (emphasis added).

A 1984 amendment to the Federal Racketeer Influenced and Corrupt Organizations (RICO) statutes made "dealing in obscene matter" a predicate offense. Through RICO provisions, as well as other federal obscenity statutes, the government can confiscate property that has been "tainted" by illegal activity (Goldberg 1995). The government has used these provisions to confiscate a huge amount of property tied to the illegal production and distribution of obscene material. In fact, the former chief of the Department of Justice's Child Exploitation and Obscenity Section (CEOS) recently claimed that monies received from fines and forfeiture cases ($24 million) during his tenure were greater than the CEOS' *total* operating budget during those years (Senate Hearing on Obscenity Prosecution 2005).

Finally, child pornography is categorically illegal. There is no need to prove that child pornography is "obscene" and hence illegal, since one of the main goals of these statutes is the protection of minors from sexual exploitation and abuse. As we explain below, however, the advent of computer technology and the Internet has created a new grey area in terms of "virtual child pornography." This type of pornography involves the use of pictures altered or generated by computers to simulate child pornography.

Currently, 43 states have obscenity statutes (Alaska, Hawaii, Montana, New Mexico, Oregon, Vermont, and West Virginia have no such legislation). State laws by and large mirror federal legislation (Morality in Media 2005). Minnesota statutes, for example, define obscenity using the exact language of the *Miller* test. Specific provisions prohibit the distribution, mailing, or carrying of obscene material (Minnesota Code 617.241-.246). More recently, some states and the federal government have specifically targeted Internet obscenity, a growing area of concern that is discussed in more detail later in this chapter.

Internet-Specific Federal Regulation of Obscenity and Pornography

One way to gauge the legal status of sexually explicit material on the Internet is to assess the Court's response to attempts by the federal government to regulate Internet content. Since 1996, Congress has passed four acts dealing specifically with the Internet and obscene or pornographic content. Table 19.2 provides a summary of this legislation, including the provisions related to sexual content and their current legal status. An examination of this legislation and the subsequent response by the courts can be used to provide a context for understanding some of the crucial legal issues that have emerged since the creation of the Internet, including:

- What type of "medium" is the Internet?
- Whose "community standards" apply to content on the World Wide Web?
- Are less-restrictive alternatives a viable alternative to blanket legislation?

The Communications Decency Act of 1996

Within Title V of the Telecommunications Act of 1996, the Communications Decency Act (CDA) prohibited the transmission of "indecent," "patently offensive," or "obscene" material to minors over the Internet. The statute also offered an affirmative defense to those making "good faith efforts" (e.g., an age verification system) to restrict minors' access. Immediately after President Bill Clinton signed the bill, plaintiffs challenged the constitutionality of two provisions. The first challenge involved the provision that prohibited the "knowing transmission of obscene or indecent messages to any recipient under 18 years of age." The second challenged the prohibition regarding "knowing, sending, or displaying of patently offensive messages in a manner that is available to a person that is under 18 years of age."

A three-judge District Court issued a preliminary injunction against enforcement of these two CDA provisions. On appeal, the Supreme Court found that the "indecent transmission" and "patently offensive display" provisions violated freedom of speech under the First Amendment but preserved the portion of the act relating to "obscene" materials (*Reno v. ACLU* 1997). The Court held that the terms "indecent" and "patently offensive display" were unconstitutionally vague. In essence, they captured only one prong of the three-prong *Miller* test and did not tie this one prong to "applicable state law" as dictated by the *Miller* decision. The Court reasoned that the vague nature of the CDA provisions would create an unnecessarily "chilling" effect on free speech, since individuals would be hard-pressed to understand what types of speech would be defined as "indecent" or "patently offensive," and hence illegal. Finally, the Court found the affirmative defense unpersuasive as a factor that limits the scope of the legislation, because the provisions were not confined to commercial sites, and noncommercial sites would not likely be able to afford age verification.

In *Reno*, the Court explicitly considered the Internet as a medium of communication. The Court noted that (unlike broadcast media) the Internet had no history of extensive government regulation, was not subject to the "scarcity of available frequencies," and was not "invasive" in nature. Therefore, regulation of free speech on the Internet is subject to the "most stringent review" of the Court (*Reno*, 868–870). The Court affirmed that government has a legitimate interest in protecting children from harmful materials. However, the justices also cautioned that the CDA attempts to protect children by suppressing a large amount of speech that adults have a right to access. In particular, the Court suggested that Internet filters controlled by parents would be at least as effective as the restrictions contained in the CDA.

The Child Pornography Prevention Act of 1996

The Child Pornography Prevention Act (CPPA) amended federal statutes enacted to prohibit the production, distribution, and reception of computer-generated sexual images of children—in other words, images that were "doctored" to appeared to be sexually explicit images of children. In *Ashcroft v. The Free Speech Coalition* (2002) the Supreme Court resolved a split among the federal circuits by striking down the provisions related to "virtual" child pornography.

The central legal issue was the purpose of child pornography laws. The Court noted that such laws are intended to protect children from *actual* sexual exploitation. When actual children are not involved (i.e., adults are used, or the image is created by a computer), the government's interest is substantially reduced. While the government claimed that "virtual pornography" could incite pedophiles and ultimately harm children, the Court said that the government could not prohibit speech purely because it may increase the chances of criminal activity "at some indefinite future date" (*Ashcroft*, 253). In short, the Court was concerned that speech was being limited in accordance with vague and uncertain standards.

In 2003, Congress responded to this ruling by passing the Prosecutorial Remedies and Other Tools to End the Exploitation of Children Today (PROTECT) Act. The PROTECT Act used a revised definition of child pornography. Legislators moved quickly to pass this act because a growing number of defendants wanted previous convictions overturned on the grounds that the government had failed to prove that they knowingly possessed "actual" (as opposed to "virtual") child pornography (Rogers 2005). Congress was concerned that the government's burden of proof had become too large because they now would have to prove that (1) an actual child was used to create the pornography, and (2) the suspect knew that the image was an actual child.

The PROTECT Act alters the CPPA's definition of pornography by prohibiting images that are "indistinguishable from" that of a "minor engaging in sexually explicit conduct." In effect, this definition treats virtual and actual pornography as identical if an ordinary person viewing the depiction would conclude that the depiction is of an actual minor engaged in sexually explicit conduct. In deference to the *Free Speech Coalition* case, "Drawings, cartoons, sculptures, or paintings depicting minors or adults" are expressly excluded from the provision. Although this statute is narrower in scope, it does not appear to escape the constitutional problem (e.g., no children are actually harmed) that doomed the CDA (Rogers 2005, 97–98).

The Child Online Protection Act of 1998

The Child Online Protection Act (COPA) was a follow-up to the failed CDA. The act imposes up to $50,000 fine and 6 months in prison for the commercial distribution of material that is "harmful to minors" by means of the World Wide Web. Like the CDA, COPA provided an affirmative defense to those who require age verification through use of a credit card or any other feasible means. Unlike the CDA, COPA defined "harmful to minors" by inserting "with respect to minors" into the language of the *Miller* test for obscenity. COPA also further narrowed the scope by limiting regulation to the World Wide Web rather than the entire spectrum of the Internet (e.g., email, bulletin boards) and by regulating only commercial sites (Wheatland 2005).

COPA was intended to go in effect on November 29, 1998; however, an injunction currently remains in effect and the constitutional status of this legislation continues to remain unsettled. Plaintiffs including website authors and others concerned with freedom of speech issues filed suit in October 1998, and a district court granted an injunction after concluding that the plaintiffs were likely to win on the argument that there were less-restrictive alternatives (*ACLU v. Reno* 1999). The Third Circuit affirmed, but on different grounds. Specifically, the court argued that the "contemporary community standards" language contained in the statute (consistent with the *Miller* test) is troublesome within the context of the World Wide Web. This is because web publishers do not have the means (as a magazine publisher does) to limit distribution to specific geographic locations. "Community standards" for the Internet then defaults to the most stringent, puritan community standards. The Circuit Court believed that this would require web speakers to shield "vast amounts" of material, and therefore ruled that this aspect of COPA would likely render the statue unconstitutional.

The Supreme Court granted certiorari to review the court of appeals' determination that COPA's reliance on community standards would likely violate the First Amendment (*Ashcroft v. ACLU* 2002). Justice Thomas, authoring the plurality opinion, reviewed the Court's prior community standards jurisprudence in cases dealing with obscene material delivered through other technology. In cases involving the mail and phone ("dial-a-porn") service, the Court held that a speaker can be required to observe varying local community standards when the scope of an obscenity statute's coverage is sufficiently narrow (e.g., using the *Miller* test). The plurality acknowledged (and the government conceded) one important difference between these media and the web: access to mail and phone can be controlled based on geographic location, whereas web publishers have no control regarding access to their content.

Despite this acknowledgment, the plurality concluded that a different approach to the web was not required. In the plurality's view, "If a publisher chooses to send its material into a particular community, this Court's jurisprudence teaches that it is the publisher's responsibility to abide by that community's standards. The publisher's burden does not change simply because it decides to distribute its material to every community in the Nation" (*Ashcroft*, 583). In other words, publishers who wish to be judged by the standards of only select communities can utilize a medium designed for that purpose. The plurality opinion vacated the Court of Appeals and remanded the case for further proceedings, leaving the injunction intact.

It is noteworthy that in addition to Justice Stevens (who dissented and would have affirmed the Third Circuit ruling), five other justices (O'Connor, Breyer, Kennedy, Souter, and Ginsburg) had substantial reservations regarding the community-based standards approach. In her opinion (concurring in part and dissenting in part) Justice O'Connor argued for a national obscenity standard:

> I agree with Justice Kennedy that, given Internet speakers' inability to control the geographic location of their audience, expecting them to bear the burden of controlling the recipients of their speech, as we did in *Hamling* and *Sable*, may be entirely too much to ask, and would potentially suppress an inordinate amount of expression. For these reasons, adoption of a national standard is necessary in my view for any reasonable regulation of Internet obscenity. (*Ashcroft*, 587)

Justice O'Conner also noted that although the plaintiffs had failed to submit sufficient examples of material that would both violate COPA and lead to varying results among local communities, future challenges against a local community standard might succeed with more convincing evidence.

In his partial concurrence, Justice Breyer focused on COPA's legislative history and found that it clearly called for a standard that is "national and adult." He concluded that interpreting COPA to include a national standard would avoid the serious First Amendment problem created by a construction adopting the community standards of every locality in the country, which would

provide the communities most likely to object to sexually explicit material with a "heckler's Internet veto" (*Ashcroft*, 590).

The legal status of community standards with the medium of the Internet remains in question. Upon remand, the appeals court once again affirmed the district court, this time on the grounds that the statute was overbroad, was not narrowly tailored to serve a compelling government interest, and was not the least-restrictive means for serving the government interest. In *Ashcroft v. ACLU II* (2004) the Supreme Court agreed, upholding the preliminary injunction. The Court found that the provisions of COPA likely violated the First Amendment and remanded the case for trial. The central contention in Justice Kennedy's majority opinion was that the government had failed to demonstrate that the provisions in COPA were the least-restrictive alternative.

The Court paid special attention to the role of Internet "filters," which are content based and allow the user to screen out sexually explicit material. While noting that filters are imperfect (some pornography is not stopped, and some nonpornography is filtered), Justice Kennedy pointed out three ways in which filters may be more effective than COPA (*Ashcroft II*, 702):

- Filters can prevent pornography from all sources, including foreign sources, which are not subject to COPA. The Court went so far as to argue that COPA might drive adult websites to move their operations overseas.

- Filters work on all facets of Internet communication (such as email), unlike COPA, which restricts only content on the World Wide Web.

- Age verification systems may be circumvented or evaded.

Apart from filters, the Court noted that Congress has already passed legislation subsequent to COPA that has the same intent (to protect children from exposure to harmful material) but is more narrowly tailored to meet that intent. In particular, the Court pointed to a statute that prohibits website owners from disguising pornographic sites in a way that would likely cause uninterested persons to visit (18 U.S.C.A. § 2252B). Another statute created a "Dot Kids" Internet domain with content restricted to materials fit for minors. Finally, in response to the government's contention that filters are insufficient because they cannot be required by Congress, the Court noted that the government could encourage the use of filters through monetary incentives. To illustrate, the Court pointed to the provisions in the Children's Internet Protection Act (CIPA) of 2001 that tie federal funding for libraries and schools to their use of filters.

The Children's Internet Protection Act of 2001

Unlike earlier Congressional attempts to curb minors' exposure to obscene or pornographic material, the CIPA does not stipulate civil or criminal penalties based on content. Rather, it requires public schools and libraries that receive federal funds to install Internet filters. In particular, Congress was concerned about reports that minors and other library patrons regularly searched for online pornography (*American Library Association v. United States* 2002). CIPA requires that a "technology protection measure" block all users from accessing "visual depictions" that are obscene or a form of child pornography. For minors, the filters must also protect against access to visual depictions that are "harmful to minors." Obscenity is defined according to federal statue—which is to say it is undefined apart from the presumption that the Court will apply the *Miller* test. Child pornography is defined by reference to the PROTECT Act amended statues, which includes virtual child pornography that is "indistinguishable" from authentic child pornography.

With CIPA, it appears as though Congress has found at least one constitutional mechanism to protect minors from sexually explicit material. The Supreme Court upheld the provisions of CIPA by reversing a decision made by a district court. The three-judge district court panel had enjoined the government from withholding federal funding for noncompliance. The district court's finding was based on its view that the Internet constituted a "public forum" and its

interpretation of Congress's spending power (Sanchez 2005).

The Supreme Court explicitly addressed whether the Internet, within the context of library access, is a "public forum" (*United States v. American Library Association* 2003). In rejecting the possibility of stronger judicial scrutiny in this area, the Court portrayed the Internet access provided by libraries in much the same terms as the provision of readily accessible stacks of books to the public. In other words, public libraries do not acquire Internet access in order to allow web users to express themselves or to encourage a diversity of views among private speakers. Rather, Internet access is provided as a means for individuals to access information. Noting that libraries already exclude pornography from their collection, the Court reasoned that, "We do not subject these decisions to heightened scrutiny; it would make little sense to treat libraries' judgments to block online pornography any differently, when these judgments are made for the same reasons" (*United States v. American Library Association* 2003, 208). Because libraries constantly make content decisions, the Court rejected the argument that CIPA required libraries to violate the First Amendment. Therefore, Congress had not overstepped the limits of its spending power.

Internet-Specific State Level Regulation of Obscenity and Pornography

State legislators have also moved to regulate pornography (in the context of minors) and obscenity on the Internet. Similar to the efforts of the federal government, several states have amended their obscenity statutes to include material such as "electronic images" or "computer images." Moreover, at least six states have sought to regulate material "harmful to minors" (Walsh 2005). All of these statutes have been struck down as unconstitutional because they violated the First Amendment and/or the Commerce Clause of the Constitution. We have already discussed the breadth of First Amendment issues related to obscenity and the Internet within the context of federal legislation. Issues specifically related to the Commerce Clause, however, are worth some additional comment because the clause speaks once again to the unique nature of the Internet.

The Commerce Clause (Article I, Section 8, paragraph 3 of the Constitution) grants the federal government the authority to regulate trade with foreign nations and among the states. In using the Commerce Clause to strike down state-level regulation of Internet content, the courts have used three rationales (Shapiro et al. 2001, 9):

- State-level statutes regulate conduct that is wholly outside the states that enact them.

- State-level statutes impose burdens on interstate commerce that exceed any state benefits they confer.

- State-level statutes subject Internet users to inconsistent state regulations.

In *American Library Association v. Pataki* (1997), plaintiffs argued against a New York statute that prohibited any individual, "Knowing the character and content of the communication which, in whole or in part, depicts actual or simulated nudity, sexual conduct or sado-masochistic abuse, and which is harmful to minors, [to] intentionally use any computer communication system allowing the input, output, examination or transfer, of computer data or computer programs from one computer to another, to initiate or engage in such communication with a person who is a minor" (New York State Consolidated Laws, 235.21(3)). In finding in favor of the plaintiffs, the district court held that the unique nature of the Internet makes it increasingly likely that the New York statute would subject individuals to "haphazard, uncoordinated, and even outright inconsistent regulations" by a state that the individual never intended to reach (p. 168). That is, the court ruled that New York (or other states) could not limit communications that were never specifically intended for persons within that state's jurisdiction.

In addition to statutes that mimic federal legislation, some states have charted new ground. For example, Pennsylvania enacted the Internet Child Pornography Act (10 Pa. Cons. Stat §§ 7621-7630) in 2002. This act required Internet service providers (ISPs) to remove or disable access to child pornography "residing on or accessible through its service." This was the first attempt by a state to impose criminal liability on an ISP that provided only access (not the actual content) to child pornography through its network.

The Center for Democracy and Technology (along with the ACLU and other parties) filed suit, noting that the efforts of ISPs to disable access to child pornography led to the blocking of more than one and a half million innocent websites not targeted by the attorney general. The statute was struck down based on the Commerce Clause and because it excessively blocked free speech in violation of the First Amendment (*Center for Democracy and Technology v. Pappert* 2004).

Despite the limited impact of these types of statutes thus far, states have continued in their efforts to limit the availability of pornography over the Internet. For example, a Utah bill signed into law in 2005 requires (Walsh 2005):

- The Attorney General's Office to compile an Adult Content Registry of Internet sites that include content that is harmful to minors

- Internet service providers to block access to those sites

- Utah companies that operate websites that could be considered "harmful to minors" to rate their own sites and regulate children's access

The statute gives Internet subscribers the option to "opt out" of those sites that are in the Adult Content Registry. A group of bookstore owners, artists, and the ACLU have filed suit for a preliminary injunction.

Obscenity on the Internet: A Summary of Legal and Technology Issues

Some common themes emerge from our discussion concerning the continuing tug-of-war that has occurred between lawmakers and the judiciary in regard to defining and limiting access to sexually explicit material on the Internet. First, the "borderless" nature of the Internet has created significant problems for legislators at both the state and federal level who have tried to craft statutes that regulate pornography and obscenity. For their part, legislators at the state level run the risk of violating the Commerce Clause if they enact laws that are too restrictive. On the other hand, a central problem for federal legislators continues to be the *Miller* test's reliance on "community standards" language.

As a recent district court case illustrates, the Supreme Court has yet to definitively rule on the meaning of "community" within the context of the Internet. In *Nitke v. Ashcroft* (2003) an artist specializing in sexually explicit material sought to have the remaining obscenity provision from the CDA overturned. The primary basis of the plaintiff's argument was that the "community standards" language of the *Miller* test rendered Internet regulation of obscenity unconstitutional. Specifically, the "hecklers veto" of the most puritan community may suppress a substantial amount of speech that is constitutional in other locations. Indeed, there is evidence that federal prosecutors are capitalizing on this situation by "shopping" for the most conservative districts in which to bring obscenity charges (Walls 2004).

A three-Judge district court initially refused to dismiss the case, ruling that the Supreme Court's plurality opinion in *Ashcroft* did not settle the issue of community standards in the context of the Internet. Despite finding a "reasonable likelihood" that some communities may view Nitke's (and others') work as obscene, however, the Court upheld the obscenity provision of the CDA. The Court reasoned that the plaintiffs had not provided sufficient evidence regarding the amount of material that would be suppressed due to community differences in what constitutes obscenity. Nevertheless, the fact that the court was open to this legal theory signals the uncertain legal status of the "local community standards" language contained in the *Miller* test. This raises the question of alternatives.

Alexander (2002) reviews several new standards that might replace "local communities" and notes the arguments against each:

- The recipient's jurisdiction (where material is downloaded): This community standard doesn't resolve the problem—the least tolerant community will decide what is "obscene" for all Americans.

- The Internet (virtual community) standard: The "virtual community" is ill-defined—is anyone who has ever surfed the web part of this community?

- A national standard: In *Ashcroft*, several justices appeared to lean toward an adult national standard for obscenity on the web. Even with a "national" standard, the trial venue will likely determine the true standard applied by jurors.

- The provider's jurisdiction (where uploaded): This standard would ensure that the defendant is aware of the local community standards, and there would be no "chilling effect" due to concern about other communities' standards. Unfortunately, this process allows the *least-restrictive* communities to determine the content of the Internet.

Alexander concludes that there is no viable standard that will conform to the principles contained in the "top-down" broadly based *Miller* test. Given the rapidly developing technology that fuels the Internet, it is possible that new technologies might yet save the *Miller* test. "Geocoding," for example, might eventually allow web-posters to make their material available only to certain geographic locations.

A second factor that has frustrated federal regulation of Internet pornography is the continually evolving notion of "less-restrictive alternatives." In both *Reno* and *Ashcroft*, the Court suggested Internet filters as a means to protect children without violating the First Amendment. The Court also upheld CIPA provisions that tied federal funding to the use of filters. As currently constituted, however, filtering technology is far from perfect. A recent study by the Electronic Frontier Foundation (EFF) and the Online Policy Group (OPG) concluded that the blocking software used by libraries to comply with CIPA often block appropriate materials and fail to block inappropriate content. For example, content including comedy, short poems, personal care, and pogo-sticks was blocked by the software (Sinrod 2003).

Another "less-restrictive" alternative to blanket legislation is the creation of content-specific domains. The Dot Kids Implementation and Efficiency Act of 2002 launched a domain under ".us.kids." Legislators rejected a top tier ".kids" site because there would be no way to regulate content without raising constitutional issues (Sweet 2003). The domain is administered by a private company, to ensure that content is suitable for minors. A more controversial approach, supported by some in the adult entertainment industry, is the creation of an ".xxx" domain. Critics believe that such a domain would only encourage pornography and obscenity on the Internet.

A final legal issue involves the role of Internet service providers. ISPs are the "backbone" of the Internet—they carry the information that is uploaded and downloaded by Internet users. They can range in size from large conglomerates (e.g., America Online) to smaller "mom and pop" shops. Section 230 of the Communications Decency Act makes clear that no interactive computer service will be classified as a publisher or speaker as long as third parties had provided the content. In other words, ISPs are not legally liable for material found on their sites. Still, there has been some movement toward holding ISPs legally accountable.

The Protection of Children from Sexual Predators Act of 1998 (Sexual Predators Act) requires that an ISP notify a designated law enforcement agency after learning that a website containing child pornography exists on its server. If the ISP "willfully" fails to report the website, the ISP can be fined. This Act does not require ISPs to actively monitor websites for violations of federal child pornography laws. Both Pennsylvania and Utah crafted laws that focused on ISPs. Although the Pennsylvania law was ultimately struck

down (Utah's law is under litigation), this type of legislation hints at a future legal debate.

Conclusion

Enforcement of obscenity statutes waxes and wanes according to the prevailing political climate—Internet-specific statutes and enforcement are no different. Under President Clinton, enforcement of obscenity statutes was not a priority, and his administration generally took a "hands off" approach to Internet regulation. Under President Bush, Attorney General Alberto Gonzales and his predecessor, John Ashcroft, declared the prosecution of obscenity and child pornography cases to be a high priority (Lichtblau 2005). The Justice Department has committed more lawyers and resources to this area and has secured almost 40 obscenity convictions since 2001 (U. S. Department of Justice 2004).

The high priority recently placed on obscenity enforcement has dovetailed with the Internet in an interesting manner. In 2004, Congress approved an omnibus appropriations bill that included $150,000 to support the "obscenity crimes project." The funding goes to support "obscenitycrimes.org," a website run by Morality in Media (Hynes 2005). Among other things this site allows users to electronically report obscene material from websites, email, or other sources to the appropriate United States Attorney. Between June 2002 and March 31, 2003, almost 20,000 complaints have been sent to the Justice Department (LaRue 2005).

Despite stepped-up enforcement, attempts to police obscenity on the Internet continue to create legal issues that are difficult to resolve. There is little doubt that the Internet is a unique and exciting medium. The Internet allows people worldwide to communicate and share information; it provides a forum for discussion and a wide audience for speakers. The unique, borderless nature of the Internet, however, has largely "confounded the legislative attempts to draft constitutional regulations that screen 'unwanted' content" (Shapiro et al. 2001, 8). This difficulty also stems from the fact that the Supreme Court has characterized the Internet as a medium that is subject to strict scrutiny.

Legal scholars continue to debate the best manner to regulate obscenity on the Internet. Many argue that the most effective methods (e.g., geocoding, filters) are "bottom-up" technologies that will allow users and/or posters to limit their exposure to certain content. Others believe that legislators are in a better position (they make it a point to know citizens' concerns, they have sanctioning power) to protect children from obscene or harmful material (Wheatland 2005). Given the current political commitment to enforcement of obscenity laws, the rapidly evolving technology of the Internet, and recent Supreme Court decisions, this legal discourse will continue.

References

Alexander, Mark C. 2002. "The First Amendment and Problems of Political Viability: The Case of Internet Pornography" *Harvard Journal of Law and Public Policy* 25:977–1030.

CBS News. 2003. *60 Minutes* November 21. http://www.cbsnews.com/stories.

Durkin, K. F. 1997. "Misuse of the Internet by Pedophiles: Implications for Law Enforcement and Probation Practice." *Federal Probation* 61(3):14–18.

Encarta Encyclopedia. 2005. http://www.encarta.msn.com/encyclopedia.

Free Press Dictionary. 2005. "Prurient." http://www.thefreedictionary.com/prurient.

Goldberg, Ronald M. 1995. "RICO Forfeiture of Sexually Explicit Expressive Materials: Another Weapon in the War on Pornography, or an Impermissible Collateral Attack on Protected Expression?" *William Mitchell Law Review* 21:231-289.

Henley, J. 1996. "The *Observer* Campaign to Clean up the Internet: Hackers Called in as Cybercops to Drive Out Porn." *Observer,* September 1.

Hynes, Ed. 2005. "A View From Riverside Drive." Posted by *Morality in Media.* http://www.moralityinmedia.org/index.htm?reviewOfTheNews/0501.html.

Internet Filter Review. 2005. "Internet Pornography Statistics." http://www.internet-filter-review.topreviews.com.

Internet Software Consortium. 2001. *Internet Domain Survey, January 2001.* Redwood City, CA: Internet Software Consortium.

LaRue Jan. 2005. "Let's End Victims of Pornography Month." http://obscenitycrimes.org/news/EndVOPMonth.cfm.

Kirk, S., P. Mancust, T. Palmer, and M.E. Malone. 1983. "A Rift Within Organized Crime." *Boston Globe,* February 16.

Litchblau, Eric. 2005. "Justice Department Fights Ruling on Obscenity." *New York Times* February 16:25.

Morality in Media. 2005. "Federal and State Obscenity Statutes." http://www.moralityinmedia.org/nolc/index.htm?statutesIndex.htm.

Rogers, Audrey. 2005. "Playing Hide and Seek: How to Protect Virtual Pornographers and Actual Children on the Internet." *Villanova Law Review* 50:87–115.

Sanchez, Barbara A. 2005. "*United States v. American Library Association:* The Choice Between Cash and Constitutional Rights." *Akron Law Review* 38:463–502.

Senate Hearing on Obscenity Prosecution, Subcommittee on the Constitution, Civil Rights and Property Rights Committee on Judiciary: Statement of Patrick A. Trueman. 2005. http://www.obscenitycrimes.org/news/trueman.cfm.

Shapiro, Alexandria A. E., Christopher Harris, Michele Pyle, and Kate Bolger. 2001. "Internet Speech Still Resisting Regulation." *New York Law Journal* (January 16). http://web.lexis-nexis.com/universe.

Sinrod, E. J. 2003. "CIPA-Regulated Filters Fall Far Short." *USA Today.* http://www.usatoday.com/tech/columnist/ericjsinrod/2003-07-22-sinrod_x.htm.

Sweet, Lynn. 2003. "Children-Friendly Internet Zone Opens." *Chicago Sun-Times* September 5:2.

Taylor, R. W., Tory J. Caeti, D. Kall Loper, Eric J. Fritsch, and John Liederbach. 2006. *Digital Crime and Digital Terrorism.* Upper Saddle River, NJ: Pearson Prentice Hall.

U.S. Department of Justice. 2004. Statement of James B. Comey, Deputy Attorney General of the United States before the United States House of Representatives Committee on Appropriations Subcommittee on the Departments of Commerce, Justice, State, the Judiciary and Related Agencies, March 24, 2004. http://www.usdoj.gov/dag/testimony/2004/03232004dagstatementombbudgetcomfina l.htm.

Walls, Allyson. 2004. "Prosecutors Seek Conservative Venues for Porn Trials." *Pittsburgh Tribune Review,* May 18.

Walsh, Rebecca. 2005. "Suit: Utah's Web Porn Law Unconstitional, Too Broad. Free

Speech? The Diverse Collection of Plaintiffs Hopes the Law's Fate Will Mirror That of Similar Statutes That Courts Overturned in Other States." *The Salt Lake Tribune*, June 10:A1.

Wheatland, Tara. 2005. "*Ashcroft v. ACLU:* In Search of Plausible, Less Restrictive Alternatives." *Berkeley Technology Law Journal* 20:371–396.

Cases Cited

ACLU v. Reno, 31 F. Supp. 2d 473 (1999).

ACLU v. Reno, 217 F.3d 162 (2000).

American Library Association v. United States, 201 F. Supp. 2d 401 (2002).

American Library Association v. Pataki, 969 F. Supp. 160 (1997).

Ashcroft v. The Free Speech Coalition, 535 U.S. 234 (2002).

Ashcroft v. ACLU, 535 U.S. 564 (2002).

Ashcroft v. ACLU II, 542 U.S. 656 (2004).

Center for Democracy and Technology v. Pappert, 337 F. Supp. 2d 606 (2004).

FCC v. Pacifica Foundation, 438 U.S. 727 (1978).

Ginsburg v. New York, 390 U.S. 629 (1968).

Jacobellis v. Ohio, 378 U.S. 184 (1964).

Miller v. California, 413 U.S. 15 (1973).

Nitke v. Ashcroft, 253 F.Supp.2d 587 (2003).

Pope v. Illinois, 481 U.S. 479 (1978).

Paris Adult Theater I v. Slaton, 413 U.S. 49 (1973).

Reno v. ACLU, 521 U.S. 824 (1997).

United States v. American Library Association, 539 U.S. 194 (2003).

United States v. Playboy Entertainment Group, 529 U.S. 803 (2000).

Related Websites

Adult Website Legal Issues

http://www.adultweblaw.com/laws/index.html

Morality in Media

http://www.obscenitycrimes.org/helpfirst amend.cfm

American Civil Liberties Union

http://www.aclu.org/freespeech/internet/ index.html

Wired News (use search terms "obscenity" or "pornography")

http://wired-vig.wired.com/

LibraryLaw.com

http://www.llrx.com/features/updatecipa.htm

Cybertelecom: Free Speech and Internet Censorship

http://www.cybertelecom.org/cda/Firsta.htm

Discussion Questions

1. What is the current legal definition of "obscenity"?

2. To what extent may laws curtail pornographic but nonobscene material without violating the First Amendment?

3. Describe the Child Online Protection Act (COPA) of 1998. How did the Supreme Court respond to the Third Circuit's contention that the act was unconstitutional because of its reliance on "contemporary community standards"?

4. Are "bottom up" (typically private) alternatives a better avenue to control content on the Internet than state or federal legislation? Why or why not?

5. Is the "local community standards" language of the *Miller* test applicable to the Internet? Why or why not? ✦